Roger Sherman's Connecticut

ROGER SHERMAN (1721–1793). Portrait by Ralph Earl. Courtesy of Yale University Art Gallery, gift of Roger Sherman White.

Roger Sherman's Connecticut

*Yankee Politics and the
American Revolution*

By

CHRISTOPHER COLLIER

WESLEYAN UNIVERSITY PRESS

Middletown, Connecticut

Copyright © 1971 by Christopher Collier

ISBN: 0–8195–4035–8
Library of Congress Catalog Card Number: 78–153104
Manufactured in the United States of America
First edition

For Bonnie

Contents

Illustrations

Preface

I suppose that the dearth of Roger Sherman materials is what has kept historians away so long from this apparently very influential statesman. That I must still use the word "apparently" after over a decade of more or less continuous study of the old man indicates how little about him can be discovered. A more imaginative approach might have given him some flesh to cover the skeleton I present. But after all this time and study I have yet to discover a single verifiable instance of either humor or humanity.

It might be difficult in this period of the hail-fellow-well-met politician to understand Sherman's extraordinary success. But New Englanders of his day admired the old Puritan virtues of reserve, personal integrity, and an intellectual approach to problems. People felt safe in Sherman's hands. Merchants and farmers trusted him, and the sharper and speculator dared not attack him in public. It is proof enough of his influence that most of what we know of him is from the comments of his enemies. They found him the most frustrating of adversaries, for he had no failings to attack, no actions open to public opprobrium. Sherman's whole line of conduct, however, struck many insiders as a bit devious and even at times deceitful. He was, in the words of one Connecticut pusher, the most "twistical" politician there was. And from the superficial evidence available it would appear that at crucial moments the old Yankee was more concerned with position and power than particular policies. He was a shrewd politician certainly, and perhaps something of a trimmer, too.

Sherman, of course, never saw it that way. If his position shifted with the majoritarian winds, he would never admit a connection. His movement from one side of the center to the other—his customary pattern—was usually so subtle and so timely that it appeared to his constituents as natural as the tides and as normal as the seasons. Indeed, his reputation was one of personal integrity so profound that not the severest storm could snap it. But a more accurate portrayal might see him as withstanding the strong winds of change because of suppleness rather than rigidity.

Whatever Sherman's inner character—and I am convinced we shall never know it—an understanding of his political character can best be attained when portrayed against the political currents in which he functioned. I have paid much more attention to the political movements dominating Connecticut during Sherman's career than I might have, had adequate personal materials been available. The focus is Sherman, but colony, state, and national politics are developed as he and they act and react on each other. That is why the study moves in and out of New Milford and New Haven, Connecticut, and the Congress. A fairly continuous—though suggestive rather than definitive—political narrative of Connecticut during the Revolution and Confederation unfolds in these pages, but much that is significant in the colony and state is omitted as not sufficiently relevant to an understanding of Sherman's place in it. No effort has been made to tell anything like a complete or continuous national story.

Besides a picture of Sherman the politician what is shown that is new? Young scholars have given up the old depiction of Connecticut as the land of steady habits. Virtually everyone working in the field in the past decade and a half has made a point of discarding that view. In an earlier work I contributed to that school myself. However, some restraint needs to be advised. Connecticut in the eighteenth and early nineteenth centuries, at least, when compared to neighboring areas, was indeed one of at least *relatively* steady habits.

This is, then, old-fashioned history. Though harboring no prejudices against psychological, quantitative, or cross-disciplinary approaches, my materials allowed me no adventures into these interesting jungles. Nevertheless my findings are well inside the current historiographic playing field. Though I hope it is honest coincidence, I cannot pretend to absolute insulation from the heat of the new history. My Confederation Connecticut is one of class: of economic divisions, of psychological antagonisms, aristocratic controls, and deferential politics. It is also one of provincials and nationalists, agrarians and merchants, puritans and Yankees, conservatives and progressives, democrats and aristocrats. It is, in short, no consensus interpretation. Rather it is a qualified and I hope sophisticated study suggesting without thoroughly describing those antagonisms of class and character that one would normally expect to find in any society at any time.

Acknowledgment

THE research for this study, carried on sporadically over more than ten years, has brought me into contact with many archivists and librarians who without exception have graciously and generously given the time and attention so necessary to the completion of this book. I wish to thank Doris Cook and our friends at the Connecticut Historical Society; the staff of the New Haven Colony Historical Society; Judith Schiff at the Sterling Library and the cheerful staff at Beinecke; Marion Tinling at the National Archives; and the wonderful ladies at the library of the University of Bridgeport. Miss Schiff, Kamela King of the State Library, and Francis Hoxie of the CHS generously helped me find pictures to illustrate the book. A special debt of gratitude is extended to Howard Peck, Town Clerk at New Milford.

The writing of certain chapters has been influenced greatly by discussions with Philip Jordan, Charles Loucks, Gaspare Saladino, and Chester Destler. Messrs. Saladino and Destler, in particular, directed me to materials essential to my development of Connecticut politics during the Confederation. Sylvie Turner, formerly Archivist at the Connecticut State Library, has been of inestimable assistance over a period of years. Her extraordinary knowledge of the Archives and understanding of history and historians cannot be surpassed. Courtesies have been extended also by Leonard Rapport of the National Historical Publications Commission, Robert J. Taylor, editor of the *Susquehannah Papers*, and Albert E. Van Dusen of the "Trumbull Papers Project." I thank them for their gracious assistance.

I am grateful to Richard Bushman, who read the entire manuscript in its last stages, saving me from several errors and helping to sharpen the focus in a number of vital spots. Jackson Turner Main and George A. Billias read sections where their knowledge is extraordinary. The study is very much their beneficiary, and to them I wish to express a great personal debt of gratitude.

Louis L. Tucker was kind enough to read sections dealing with Thomas Clap, for which I extend many thanks.

To Lawrence Cremin, Robert Cross, Richard Whittemore, Frederick Kershner, and William Miller who, years ago, read portions of this study as a doctoral dissertation, I extend my very tardy thanks. Erling Hunt, my exacting and hard-bitten mentor for many years, carried me through my professional infancy and sent me off with just the right measure of carrot and stick.

Mary Balgach and Patricia Murphy each typed the hundreds of pages of manuscript once, and never complained of my slovenly drafts or my badgering nature. My mother, who typed no less than three times the unbelievably tedious dissertation on which sections of this work are based, cannot be thanked enough here. That is an effort I shall have to make in other ways. James Collier, my brother the writer, read the final draft and made some indecipherable pencil marks for which I would thank him if I knew what they were. I do thank him, however, for the encouragement and good cheer that are his constant gift to me.

The part of this section that goes "Thanks to——without whom this book could not have been written" is filled in with the name of Bonnie, my researcher, proof-reader, copy-editor, index-maker, colleague, friend, inspiration, and wife. It is really *our* book.

I thank my children, Ned the proof-reader and Sally, who put things in alphabetical order, for their always friendly interest. They can recall no time when Roger Sherman was not their father's shadow. They have been kind to share me with such a dull old man.

CHRISTOPHER COLLIER

Roger Sherman's Connecticut

CHAPTER I

The Making of a Solid Citizen

ROGER SHERMAN, it is reported, claimed to have gained control of his emotions at the age of twenty-one. Every statement made about him while he lived and since bears witness to the truth of his claim. But fortunately it isn't true. The key to Sherman's career, the element that informs his character throughout, is ambition: perhaps the one emotion most potent in the course of human history. Every ounce of effort and every minute of time of his first fifty years was expended in attempting to satisfy what is of its very nature an insatiable passion. And even as he aged, using up his threescore years and ten, he continued always responsive to flattering opportunities for public favor.

The most significant act in Sherman's life was his move to Connecticut when he was twenty-two years old. Motivated by cheaper land prices in the western part of the colony and an opportunity to prepare for the county surveyorship, he no doubt also sensed the greater dynamism of that corner of New England as opposed to the mature and relatively static society of eastern Massachusetts. Though a land of apparent stability throughout the seventeenth century, Connecticut was becoming increasingly less so as material temptations gradually won the hearts of men away from what they had been taught was the way of God. Always politically contentious and socially and economically mobile, the pace of change was accelerating in the eighteenth century, as it has ever since. Pressures generated by war, rapidly increasing population, the maturing economy, and the diminished impact of the Puritan revolution all contributed to this increased rate of change. It was clear to young Sherman that a person of energy, intelligence, and moderate capital would find it less difficult to satisfy a churning drive to pre-eminence in Connecticut than in Massachusetts.

Sherman's ambition was not unqualified, however. A powerful brake was the rational Calvinism that encased his spirit and chastened his ego. He was always concerned that his way would be God's way, and frequently drew up others with biblical admonitions. Fortunately for him, he had come of age while Calvinism was still dominated by rationalists rather than by the enthusiasts of the second half of the century. He believed that self-interest was best served by cooperating with an ordered society; or as one preacher he listened to put it, "the principle of self-love alone, will engage men to that obedience to good rulers, by which their own happiness may be promoted and secured."[1]

Sherman was not going to spend his life as a "plough-jogger" or a cobbler or settled in at any calling with a low ceiling of aspiration. He might be called bookish, though it is doubtful that he ever read for pleasure. Books for him were instruments, tools, if you will, for building a better fortune. For a man of his temperament with capital but without connections or college, there were a number of ways into the establishment. There was surveying, for instance, a trade of more than moderate respectability and a natural entrée into land speculation. This was the road taken by Sherman's contemporary George Washington, and though the Virginian had more to start with, he was one of the continent's leading speculators on the eve of the Revolution. Or like Patrick Henry, Sherman could have taken to the law. Though the lack of a college degree might slow him down a bit at first, many men rose to the highest colonial courts without a liberal education. A third line of promotion lay in commerce. With Sherman's canny wit and the availability of an inheritance at twenty, his career could have paralleled the Liverpool immigrant to Philadelphia, Robert Morris, "the Financier of the Revolution." Perhaps it requires too much of a stretch of the imagination to see Roger Sherman making his way into colonial and even intercolonial prominence through almanac-making in the manner of another emigrant from Massachusetts, Benjamin Franklin. But it was a possibility.

As a matter of fact, Sherman tried all of these things, and not unsuccessfully. Even his almanacking, the least auspicious of his undertakings, added to his fame and provided the first introduction of his name outside of Connecticut. His land speculations and mercantile enterprises made it possible for him to retire respectably, if modestly, in his early fifties. And at law he excelled, reaching the pinnacle of the profession in Connecticut in his mid-forties. Nevertheless, it was none of these vehicles that ultimately carried Sherman to the positions of honor and influence that he wanted so badly and that were ultimately his.

Sherman's way to fame, if not fortune—though there was some of that, too—would never have occurred to him in 1740, or to Washington or Henry, Morris or Franklin, either. He became a politician; for the last two decades of his life a regular full-time professional politician. Indeed, during a good part of that period his principal source of income was from public service. He is one of the earliest of this genre in America; men who actually made their livings by seeking elective office and serving that way. His is, then, the story of a puritan politician.

Beginnings

By 1758 when Roger Sherman was thinking of leaving his western Connecticut village of New Milford, he was one of the wealthiest men in town and perhaps the largest landowner in Litchfield County.[2] In view of the fact that he had arrived in town just fifteen years earlier, a twenty-two-year-old heavily burdened with family and personal debt, it might be a cause of wonder that he now sought to leave so kind a place. In 1741 when his father had died, New Milford looked like a place of unlimited opportunity for an ambitious boy just out of his teens. Stoughton, Massachusetts, where William Sherman had taken his family when Roger was two, was a well-settled town, and the farm there had prospered moderately. Indeed, the older Sherman was one of thirteen taxpayers ranked fourth in value of real estate out of 109 in his precinct, though his personal property assessment was below the middle mark. The year before his death he was eleventh out of 119 in total taxes paid.[3]

Stoughton, in Roger Sherman's youth, was a busy little town of mills and farms. On its streams, especially the Neponsit, there were six or seven sawmills, and four ironworks for both smelting and shaping. In 1724 over 770 tons of iron were made into implements, a profitable business in a day when local ore sold for three shillings a ton. Small as the industrial faction may have been, it was influential enough to fight off the objections of farmers and Indians who protested that the dams prevented the little herring called alewives from traveling the streams, thus making them unavailable for fertilizer. There were about 120 families in town, and the farm faction was neither the most influential nor the most prosperous.[4]

William Sherman, who had moved to Stoughton in 1723 when it was Dorchester's South Precinct, came from Newton, where Roger had been born in 1721, the third of William and Mehetabel Wellington Sherman's seven children.* William had paid £180 to some local Indians for half of a 270-acre

---

*The part of Stoughton Sherman grew up in was set off in 1797, and is now the town of Canton.

piece of land in Stoughton, but by the time of his death the farm had been reduced to seventy-three acres. It was a modest, typically sparse environment that surrounded the Shermans. There were but three beds for the family of nine, most of whom must have slept in a loft, and a few chests, tables, and chairs. But an expensive looking-glass and a considerable number of books raised the home life well above the level of squalor. The livestock consisted of three cows, two steers, a heifer, and two sheep, just about the average for the town.[5]

Apparently William Sr. had some shadowy but supportable claim to a few acres of land in New Milford, and Roger's older brother William Jr. had moved there in 1740, buying another seven acres some time after he arrived.[6] Less than a year later, in March, 1741, the boys' father died. With his older brother gone and his older sister married and away, Roger took over the responsibilities of settling his father's estate. This was a complicated business, for there was no will. The estate was assessed and shares were allocated: a third to the widow, a double portion to the eldest son, and equal parts of the remainder to the other six children. A bond was posted by family friends to cover the amount of assessed valuation, and the administrator took it upon himself to dispose of the estate and pay off the shares. Unfortunately, the property was greatly overappraised, and the income from its sale was not nearly sufficient to cover the amounts due the heirs.* Young Roger apparently asked his family to wait for their money, for it appears that he used the estate as collateral to borrow an amount just about equal to the sum put up for the bond. With this in hand he followed his brother to Connecticut, where he bought 250 acres of land, a house, and two barns for £1300.[7]**

---

*The estate was assessed at £558, but brought in only £157. Under Connecticut intestacy law, the administrator of the estate was responsible to the heirs for the full assessed amount, whether realized in actual income or not. Thus Sherman's financial responsibilities far outweighed the cash available to him. Sherman finally finished paying off the last shares in 1777, thirty-six years later. Sherman. *Genealogy*, pp. 135–38; receipt from James Buck in Yale, Hist. Ms. Room, "Sherman Collection," (Papers Relating to the Estate of Roger Sherman); Huntoon, *Canton*, p. 236.

**Considerable mystery still clouds the detail of this purchase, principally because of the destruction by fire in 1867 of the New Fairfield records. Apparently Adoniram Treadwell, the owner, received a grant in 1738 from the colony government, part of a recent Indian purchase. Sherman gave Treadwell £1300 o.t. on April 5, 1743, for 250 acres, "a certain Tract or parcel of Land Called New Dilloway," including a dwelling house and two barns. CSL, "Towns and Lands," Ser. 1. VIII:1–25, 32, 33ab; CSL. "Ecclesiastical Affairs." IX:292–99. See *The Sherman Sentinel* for November 13, 1968, where I tell the whole story.

This was an auspicious start for a young man in a new town. Two hundred and fifty acres was an extraordinarily large holding in Connecticut, even in a frontier town. But for Roger Sherman it was only a start. The twenty-two-year-old had brought his mother with him and his teen-age brothers and sisters, two of each. He had large ambitions to fulfill, but large responsibilities, too. He settled down as a cobbler for perhaps a year or so, and studied surveying as he worked. Certainly he did little or no farming. And indeed, he was to stay only a short time on his new estate. Sherman thought, when he came to Connecticut, that he was moving to New Milford. Adoniram Treadwell, from whom he bought the land, believed it to be in New Milford, too. But in 1742 the neighboring town of New Fairfield divided into two parishes and the north society began assessing the Sherman land. This gave rise to a call for a survey which, when finally completed in 1744, showed that the estate in question was indeed in New Fairfield. With the location in doubt, and presumably because of his brother's residence in New Milford, Sherman chose to move again.[8]

The First Rung: County Surveyor

Even at twenty-two, however, Roger Sherman was too careful a calculator to move from settled Stoughton to the dynamic but uncertain frontier on the mere promise of a cobbler's income. He had been to school as a boy, and apparently had learned some arithmetic either there or in the library of Samuel Dunbar, the town's Congregational minister, who took an interest in the alert, intelligent lad. When brother William had arrived in Connecticut he found the most plaguey municipal problem to be boundary disputes. The "west line," a short border apparently between New York state and New Milford* just south of Kent, was unclear, and the town meeting was unable to get accurate information from the General Assembly.[9] Frequent actions to lay out roads and to distribute town lands were delayed because of the lack of a local surveyor.

William knew of his younger brother's mathematical talent, and furthermore knew of the text on surveying, *Norwood's Epitome*, that had been passed along by their great-grandfather and was now among the books in Roger's possession. The opportunity was golden. Assiduous study made it possible for the young man to secure an appointment in 1745 as the county

---

*The present boundaries of New York and New Milford are not contiguous at any point.

surveyor from the General Assembly.[10] Surveying in those days of rapid and ragged settlement was a job of great importance. A surveyor performed a public service of the first magnitude, was given great responsibilities, high respect, and large fees. Sherman now held the key to economic and social advancement.

When Litchfield was set off from New Haven County in 1752, Sherman was appointed surveyor for the new unit. The next year, after a scorching fight among various applicants, a second man was appointed for the northern area of Litchfield. But the half-county surveyorship was fast outrun by the ambitious young man, and in 1758 he asked to be relieved of the job because "my present avocations are such that I cannot Conveniently attend the Business of Surveying."[11]

In his surveying handbook, which is called in full *Norwood's Epitome being the Application of the Doctrine of triangles*, there are 197 pages, the first 108 a "how to do it" of surveying. The remaining 89 pages had been blank, and Sherman composed, or copied from some English text, in a full round handwriting that was to become crabbed as he matured, a comprehensive treatise on the art of surveying. The style is simple and direct; "How to layout land in various shapes and areas," he heads one section. "How to divide a triangle and various other figures," says another; one more reads, "How to use table of functions."[12] Sherman's notes on surveying are dated 1756 to 1760. It is not without significance that Samuel Moore, author of America's first surveying text in 1796; the Reverend Mr. Abel Flint, who wrote *Surveying* in 1804; and Roger's son-in-law Jeremiah Day, who wrote *Principles of Navigation and Surveying* in 1817, were all young men living in Litchfield County when Sherman was in his prime. Sherman certainly was the father of Litchfield surveying, for what that might be worth, but it also appears that he can claim to have inspired its formal teaching in America.[13]

The Way to Riches

Though developing his craft as a surveyor was an important outlet for Sherman's early ambitions, perhaps more to the point for his later history is the opportunity it gave him for economic progress, the basis for both social and political pre-eminence. It is, of course, impossible to determine just how much money the young mathematician collected in the course of his surveyorship. The per diem rate for surveyors was prescribed in 1747 as eight shillings, but his fees were considerable. One commission alone, from the

Colony government, was for over £83. Although he had given up cobbling by 1745, a year after he received his surveyor's commission he was able to buy a £60 piece of real estate from his brother. Of course, he may not have had to pay cash to William. The brothers were engaged in various joint mercantile schemes, and the land may have been deeded over to Roger as part of some other bargain. But between 1746 and 1761, when he left New Milford, Sherman bought well over a thousand acres of land in that town, only small bits of which were resold while he still lived there. In addition he acquired from various original proprietors many shares of town land yet to be laid out. He also bought land in neighboring Kent, and undoubtedly in other county towns as well. Indeed, the records appear to show that Roger Sherman was at one time the largest individual landowner in Litchfield County.[14]

Obviously Sherman had other sources of income beyond cobbling and surveying fees. Indeed, it is hard to escape the conclusion that the real plum in the surveyorship was the opportunity it gave to engage in real-estate trading. Though he was not to unload the major part of his landholdings until the eve of his removal from New Milford, Sherman did sell land before 1761. In 1748, just five years after the unfavorable settlement of his father's estate, he was able to buy a house and lot in the Park Lane section near the center of town, at a price of £1500 old tenor (about £187 sterling at the time). Roger moved his brothers and sisters there and also his mother, to whom he deeded one-third of the house, her share of her husband's estate.[15]

Economics was not the only motivation for the move to New Milford's center. In days of foot and horse transportation town politics was dominated by men who lived near the Town House. As a matter of fact, there is a close correlation between proximity to the center of town and political participation and influence in eighteenth-century western Connecticut towns. No man could be at the center of power if it took a day or two for information to drift seven or eight miles out to a remote farm. It would take a major controversy to persuade most men to put aside their scythes or plows and make the trip in.[16] But Roger Sherman was not most men, and made the effort to get to all town meetings almost as soon as he moved to town—an effort not made by his older brother, nor, for that matter, by the greater number of out-living New Milford inhabitants. Thus his move close to his adopted town's center has great significance. It represents an economic milestone on the way to greater wealth; and it represents a political move growing out of the young man's interests and drives that would give him the leverage to lift a career.

More might be said about Sherman's ability to buy this handsome house, but the records don't show the shadows behind the deals. It may have been a trade, for the seller moved up to New Dilloway—perhaps the New Fairfield estate. The major source of cash for Roger and William before 1749, when Roger began to sell land, was the younger brother's surveying practice, for farming was largely a subsistence affair with barter transactions taking any surplus. It is safe to conclude that a lot of shrewd real-estate trading was involved in these various moves, moves which finally brought Sherman to high economic station.[17]

Roger Sherman was only twenty-seven when he bought one of the most substantial houses in his adopted town. And now, his financial and professional standing secure, he journeyed to his old home town to acquire another piece of social equipment essential to a young man in a puritan town. Sherman could not be called handsome, really, but he was manly and rugged. He stood about six feet tall, raw-boned and craggy, awkward of movement, but powerful. His eyes were flint blue and his hair, which stayed with him through old age, was brown and always close-cropped. In later years this vulgar head of hair was to stand out among the powdered wigs of Philadelphia and New York.[18]

Unfortunately there is no evidence that this stern and massive exterior concealed any softness either of intellect or of heart. In later life Sherman's unsympathetic character would be frequently remarked. The man that John Adams thirty years later was to call an "old Puritan" was just that in his late twenties. But though he learned to "control and govern his passions" as a teenager, the intense young man had attractions that might appeal to a sensible, not too lively girl. And in Stoughton, where he returned as often as he could to talk with his old mentor, Mr. Dunbar, or to visit friends he had grown up with, Roger met Elizabeth, twenty-four, the eldest daughter of Deacon Joseph and Mary Tolman Hartwell. Intentions of marriage were announced on November 1, 1749, and the couple were married by Mr. Dunbar on the 17th.[19]

Very little is known about Elizabeth. If one can judge from her offspring, she was neither strong-willed nor strong-minded. But she saw her husband through eleven years of marriage and bore him seven children, three of whom died in infancy. The four who survived were John, William, Isaac, and Chloe. Though the three boys served in the Revolutionary War, only Isaac had moments of glory, and all met failure in civilian life. In 1794 Chloe, by then in her mid-thirties, married Dr. John Skinner of New Haven.[13]

Sherman's Almanacs

Whatever it was—ardent industry or ambition or both—that stimulated the young Roger Sherman to his incessant activity drove him in 1749 to begin publication of an annual almanac. Whether a desire for renown or economic enterprise gave birth to the project would be hard to say, but it is not likely that the almanacs fattened Sherman's pocketbook. They did, however, serve to get his name about—at least as far as Philadelphia, where the competition was strongest. Benjamin Rush of that city remarked in 1776 that Sherman, "A plain man of slender education . . . taught himself mathematics, and afterwards acquired some property and a good deal of reputation by making almanacks."[20]

Almanacs were of considerable importance to eighteenth-century New England farmers. The core of each was a calendar with celestial information, probable weather conditions, and distances between towns. A knowledge of mathematics was useful to a would-be compiler, and literary taste was very much less of a requirement. Poems of the great English writers, accounts of historic events of provincial interest, aphorisms about the seasons, advice to the farmer and housewife on how to improve their products were staple material. Blank pages were expected, too, since the little volumes served also as notebooks and diaries.

Sherman's almanacs, which were published annually or biannually every year from 1750 to 1761, were modeled after those of Nathaniel Ames, who started his in 1725, the first in the Colonies. Sherman had provided Ames with mathematical calculations during the forties and continued to do this even after Sherman began to publish a competing product, indeed as late as 1753. The almanacs seem dull beyond the point of toleration today, but evidently they both informed and amused the contemporary reader. Aside from the astronomical data, they included quotations from the poems of Pope, Addison, Dryden, Milton, and other Englishmen. Some of the work may have come from the pen of Sherman himself.[21]

In his first edition, published in Boston in 1750, Sherman, in a Franklinesque manner, excused his efforts:

> I have for several Years past for my own Amusement spent some of my leisure Hours in the Study of *Mathematicks*; not with any Intent to appear in publick: But at the Desire of many of my Friends and Acquaintance, I have been induced to calculate and publish the following ALMANACK for the Year 1750—I have put into it every Thing that I thought would be useful that could be contained in such contracted Limits.

Things which Sherman thought useful were such advices as the avoidance of raw fruit (it will make you sickly) and of letting your mind range on "fickle objects and earthly things (it will lead you to ungodly ways)." A sample of his useful weather forecast is "The weather now is freezing cold / uncomfortable for young or old / but I can't tell how long 'twill hold." If this prediction for December, 1750, is of little use, then perhaps one for the same month four years later might help, "freezing cold weather, after which comes storm of snow, but how long after I don't say." Some of his forecasts were a good deal less equivocal; "Cloudy, and a Snow Storm without a Perhaps," for mid-January, 1753, and "The Winds are high as well as dry," in August, 1751.

Poetry and proverbs filled the gaps between calendars and weather. If the almanacs of Sherman can be said to have a point of view, it is here that it shows. Reflecting mid-eighteenth-century American society which was transferring its interest from theology to politics, Sherman moved with his audience, if, indeed, he did not lead it. Morality occupied the author's thoughts during his early literary period, and politics during his latter, though in the puritan mind the two were but different aspects of life. "Reason and passion," he wrote in 1753, "answer one great Aim, And true self love and social are the same." "An easy credulity argues want of wisdom," and "Improve your Season While you may / to gather in your Grain & Hay: / for soon there'll be a rainy Day," give way to, later, "The Health and Welfare of the People is the Chiefest Law," and "Liberty & Property are Dear to Englishmen." When Sherman wrote of true self-love, he meant that self-love which saw the individual's interests so tied into the well-being of society that selfishness would be willfully subordinated to the needs of society. Indeed, sin and selfishness become almost synonymous, as did virtue and a social consciousness. Republics, Sherman's Whiggery declared, were nourished on virtue and could not exist without it.* Thus "The light of nature and revelation"—protestant political science and protestant theology—were elements of the same blend rather than different interests.[22]

---

*It was impossible, Sherman thought, that an irreligious man be one of public virtue. To the end of his life he continued to promote this view. When Gouveneur Morris was nominated by President Washington to be minister to France in 1790, Sherman disapproved. He had never "heard that [Morris] has betrayed a Trust, or that he lacks integrity." But:

　　With regard to his moral character, I consider him an irreligious and a profane man—he is no hypocrite and never pretended to have any religion. He makes religion the subject of ridicule and is profane in his conversation. I do not think the public have as much security from such men as from godly and honest men—It is a bad example to promote such characters; and although they may never have betrayed a trust, or

In addition to the moralism and Whiggishness of the almanacs, they also evince a sense of sound economics. An advertisement in the *Connecticut Gazette* for November 6, 1755, says,

> As this ALMANACK is calculated in, adapted to, and printed for this Colony, it is hoped all Shop-Keepers will give it preference; which if they are Friends to the Country, they will do, when they consider, that if they purchase Almanacs from other Governments, so much Money must necessarily be carried out of it . . . .

He added that "they may be also assured, there is Nothing useful in any other, that is not in this." A few "Shop-Keepers" took his advice but lived to rue it, however. In one of Sherman's notebooks he wrote, "Rec'd back of Mr. Burr 118 Almanacks."[23]

Competition was stiff, and by 1760 Sherman was selling his almanacs for a lower price than those of Ames, but by then he had begun to get out of the business, having trained another to do the work. An advertisement for Joseph Prindle's Almanac in the *Gazette* of December 1, 1759, runs, "This Almanack is in the Method used by Mr. Sherman, and the Author is by him well recommended."[24]

Politics and the Law

Roger Sherman was an energetic young man who came to Connecticut with plans. He did not intend to tie himself down on a farm; he needed to get out and around the country. One of the first things he did was apply to the town meeting for free access to the new toll bridge that spanned the Housatonic River just west of town. The permission was voted in February 1743/4, less than a year after Sherman's move, and it is significant that it was the unmarried younger brother rather than William who "shall have the Liberty to pas and Repas over the tole Bridg and his famaley he paying ten Shilling money old tenor he not having any Benefit of the tole money."[25]

As a matter of fact, William seems to have been more typical of the yeoman farmer of the day than was Roger. The older man never held public office, and apparently never applied for admission to freeman status. Such

---

exhibited proofs of a want of integrity, and although they may be called men of honor—yet I would not put my trust in them—I am unwilling that the country should put their Trust in them, and because they have not already done wrong, I feel no security that they will not do wrong in the future.
King, *King*, p. 420. Morris' appointment was confirmed by the Senate 16 to 11 with Sherman's colleague Oliver Ellsworth voting against Sherman in favor of Morris.

status was easy to come by, for it was open to all white males over twenty-one who held an estate worth forty pounds or which gave an annual income of forty shillings—about the price of two bushels of rye in 1751, or a tax assessment on only four acres of meadowland.[26] Roger was admitted a freeman shortly after his New Milford purchase of 1746, and by 1749 he received his first appointment to local civil office as a grand juryman. For the twenty-eight-year-old newcomer this was recognition indeed, and he quickly dropped the title "cordwainer" he had used in public documents up to this time. But it was only the start; in 1750 he became list-taker with the largely clerical job of calculating individual taxes by setting the local rate against each property holder's assessed valuation. He was elected leather-sealer the next year, by this time a position without much application, to make sure that weights and measures were fairly taken. In 1752 he served as clerk and treasurer to receive the levy for the new meeting house, and was also appointed fence-viewer.[27] This list of positions demonstrates the leverage that could be obtained from a knowledge of mathematics and a reputation for honesty.

By 1753, just ten years after settling in town, Sherman was chosen one of the five selectmen and appointed town agent to the Fairfield County Court. Two years later he reached the apogee of local office when he was elected one of the two deputies to represent New Milford in the General Assembly. This position customarily carried with it the office of justice of the peace, and Sherman was appointed to the office for Litchfield County, which had been set off from New Haven County three years earlier. Sherman held these two jobs until 1761, a year after he had left New Milford.[28] This is a startling rise to political prominence for a youthful immigrant from Massachusetts. It is best explained, of course, by his large landholdings, but the interaction of the young surveyor's energy and intelligence with the economic and political dynamic of frontier Connecticut cannot be overlooked.

Large demands were made on deputies to the General Assembly, and they were as likely to be administrative as legislative. Sherman, for instance, was authorized to buy land for the running of a highway, to sell the lands of the idiot Thomas Welch to pay for his upkeep, to eject one MacIntire from colony lands, and to investigate the claims of Joshua and other Scatacook Indians that they were being deprived of a certain pass in the hills of Kent.[29] Such chores were considered the normal responsibilities of what passed for an aristocracy in the relatively level society of eighteenth-century Connecticut. But expenses were paid and fees remitted, so that service in the colony government, though onerous, had distinct advantages. Besides, a deputy would be on the inside when plums were passed around, plums like commissaryships to the militia, or the right to build a toll bridge over the Housatonic River.

For six years Roger Sherman served his adopted village well. He would not have been able to do the job if he hadn't had the mobility that his surveyorship and a growing mercantile business gave him. He seems to have deliberately chosen to stay away from the cramping life of a provincial farmer, the life of ninety-five out of a hundred of the rocky colony's yeomen. And in politics, as in surveying, Sherman wasn't satisfied just to do the job; he had to excel. So, in the early 1750's the almanacking surveyor turned to the law. Sherman had been acting as the town agent at the county court and came in contact with legal problems as a matter of course. At the Fairfield court sessions he met William Samuel Johnson, fast becoming one of the major figures of the Connecticut bar, and despite his membership in the deeply distrusted Anglican Church, an influential Stratford politician. Johnson, six years Sherman's junior, had all the things that Roger did not: ancient family respectability, a college training, and a finished, urbane demeanor. Sherman hired Johnson, who was only twenty-six when they first met, to act as attorney in his own and the town's cases, and it was probably Johnson who suggested that Sherman's own concisely drawn instructions showed a real bent for the law. The younger man became the elder's legal mentor, and remained so for the first decade of a forty-year professional and political comradeship.

The eighteenth-century bar of Connecticut was a largely amateur institution. Most lawyers were also merchants, farmers, or even soldiers. Roger Sherman points up both the amateurishness of the bar and the excellence that it could produce. It was a compact group, and though not as well educated on the average as the Connecticut clergy, it was gaining in prestige and drawing the best minds away from the godly profession. In 1754 Sherman had read enough and established sufficient connections to get admitted to practice before the new Litchfield County Court. During his maiden term he served in twenty cases with fees averaging about £2½. The next year he took to the circuit and pleaded before the county court in Fairfield as well, the total number of cases there and in Litchfield coming to 125 at fees of up to £12. Ezra Stiles, president of Yale College at the time of Sherman's death, hit the mark when he said that "Law & Politics were peculiarly adapted to his genius." The two complemented each other, though Sherman's concept seems to have been that the law was largely a tool of politics, his major interest. Because of pressing public and mercantile business, Sherman began to withdraw from the law practice in the mid-sixties, writing to one unpleasant client, "I forbear taking notice of your more severe reflections hoping that you will retract them in your next, for I think them but a poor reward for the many services I have done for you in this affair." And besides, he added, "I don't practice as an Attorney now and would desire you to committ the Business to some other hand."[30]

This sharp letter may have been an injudicious disregard of the truth in order to get rid of a harassing client, for two years later he wrote to William Johnson, about to sail for London, asking for some new law books. *"Hawkins Pleas of the Crown,"* reads Sherman's list, *"Hawkins Abridgment of Coke on Lit[tleto]n; Jacobs Law Dictionary; Jacobs Attorney's Practice; Ld. Raymond's Reports; Law of Evidence; Hale's History of the Common Law; Attorney's pocket Companion; Prussian Laws 2 vol; Conductor Generals.* Sir, The Above is a list of the Law Books I now have, Please to get for me Bacon's Abridgment if compleat and Such others on Law & Politics as you Shall think most beneficial to the amount of about £20." Books he read, but the bent was more political than legal, and years later Sherman was to say that riding the circuit was a much better way to learn the rights of the people "than by staying at home and reading British and other foreign Laws."[31]

A Mind for Business

In New Milford today the Town Hall squats where in 1750 William Sherman moved his dwelling place and operated next door the only detached store in town. The Sherman house was moved one block east in the late eighteenth century, where it now stands, with porches and asphalt shingles, unrecognizable as architecture of two centuries ago. Roger owned a half share in William's store; probably he put up the bulk of the £350 needed to buy it. He was busy with too many other things to actually tend shop, though he seems to have kept all the records. And, when William died in 1756 at the age of thirty-nine, Roger immediately took on a new partner, Anthony Carpenter, though he, too, died three years later.

The little provincial store that was run by Roger and his brother was typical of its time. Business, local in scope, was largely a barter-and-credit proposition. An exchange of ribbon and cloth might be made for cordwood or the hauling of some lumber, kettles or mirrors for wheat or corn, tin goods for cider, pottery for labor, etc. Of course, some cash was used and was often marked down as "three shillings, New Hampshire" or "1 pound N. Y.," "four shillings, o. t." to designate either the place or time of issue.[32]

The variety of items kept in the store is indicated by the inventory probated at the time of William's death. A "Tin Lanthorn and a pair of shears" are listed along with barrels of saltpork and corn, as well as empty barrels, boxes, tubs, and bottles. "Musquask" skins, linen and woolen sheets, tablecloths and towels were stocked alongside looking glasses, iron shovels, pincers, and a wig box. Tables, chairs, tongs, gridirons, toast irons, hand irons—small and large—snuffers, heaters, warming pans, and candlesticks all passed over the counter of the busy store. Pepper boxes, tea chests, pans, platters, tin and pewter plates, pails, baskets, trunks, drinking glasses, earthenware, kettles, knives, forks, trenchers, and razors were exchanged for local produce. Cows, oak boards, money scales, trays, books, brooms, and every other item designed to please milady of New Milford or ease the work of milord could be obtained at Sherman's store.[33]

In 1751 the imperial government had forbidden any further issuance of paper money by the New England governments. Parliament tried to soften the blow by reimbursing the colonies for their outlays in behalf of the imperial cause during King George's War, which ended in 1748. But business could not be carried on entirely by barter, and the old, rapidly depreciating colony emissions that drove specie into hiding continued to circulate. Connecticut and Massachusetts were diligent about taxing to support their paper money, but still in Connecticut it depreciated to one-eighth of its value between 1709 and 1744, and another 50 percent in the next fifteen years.* New Hampshire and Rhode Island were almost promiscuous in their fiscal policy, and no one as far away as western Connecticut ever knew how much the bills of those colonies were worth. A calculating New Milford shopkeeper, used to the precision of surveyor's drawings, was more than a little frustrated by the disorder and guesswork and risk that necessarily characterized colonial commerce.[34]

Sherman was a rationalist and an individualist. He saw neither the justice nor the necessity of accepting depreciated currency from other colonies. It was his practice to insist upon Connecticut paper, even to the extent of suing for it. In 1752 he entered over £200 worth of suits demanding such manner of payment, and the suits, largely unsuccessful, continued throughout the decade.[35] In turn, he was sued by his Massachusetts importers for payment in currency of their choice. He made, then, an irritated entrance into the debate

---

* In Stoughton, Massachusetts, for instance, a committee established to adjust the salary of Sherman's mentor, the Reverend Mr. Dunbar, concluded that £100 worth of necessaries in 1727 would cost almost £190 o.t. in 1740. Stoughton Town Records, "Earliest Town Records," pp. 67–69 (May 19, 1740).

on public economics in 1752 with the publication of a little pamphlet, "A Caveat against Injustice, or an Inquiry into the evil consequences of a fluctuating medium of exchange." The title-page continues, "wherein is considered whether the Bills of Credit on the Neighboring Governments are a legal tender in payments of money in the Colony of Connecticut for debts due by Book and otherwise, where the contract mentions only Old Tenor Money. By Phileunomos."[36] It was printed by Henry Deforest, who also made up Sherman's almanacs. The point of the pamphlet was that Rhode Island and New Hampshire paper money should be outlawed in Connecticut. The argument proceeds in four logical steps.

Sherman first pointed out what everyone knew, namely that Rhode Island and New Hampshire made no effort to back their paper with any kind of specie or even admitted the possibility of exchanging colonial currency for specie. Thus it circulated, losing value with each exchange. And so also did it cheapen any other currency with which it came into contact, driving out honest specie altogether and despoiling the comparatively high-value paper of Massachusetts and Connecticut as well. Sherman's second point was that only usage and custom required the acceptance of foreign paper; there was no such requirement in ancient law. To be forced to accept a depreciated paper in fulfillment of last year's contract was no more fair than to compel the acceptance of clipped coins.

Then Sherman answered those who claimed that commerce would stop for want of a medium if paper from other colonies was not used. This was nonsense, declared the outraged merchant. All that was necessary was to give up the luxuries imported from other places—especially liquor—work hard, and the fruitful soil of Connecticut would yield up sufficient commodities for all to fatten on, and an ample base for a sound currency. Then he took the final step: there was no legal requirement to accept foreign paper ("a cheat, vexation and snare") nor was it fair or even necessary to do so; thus only a *stable* medium of exchange should be legal tender in contracts. Since Connecticut and Massachusetts followed prudent economic policies, taxing higher and more often than the wayward sisters, and since the fruits of the soil were ample if hardly worked to produce riches enough for all, their notes would be sound. All others should be legally excluded.

In many ways typical of "new traders" moving from agriculture to commerce, as the colonial wars stimulated a cash economy, Sherman was in some important respects different. For one thing, he was better capitalized than most, having behind him years of very active and highly profitable land speculation. For another, he was unwilling to stock his store through credit—a striking conservatism among the easy-risk commerce of late colonial Connecticut. These two factors put him in the forefront of the New York-oriented inland traders of western Connecticut. East of the Connecticut River, trade had been overheated by an extraordinary increase of population, largely through immigration from Massachusetts and Rhode Island. Tremendous dynamism was generated by the entry into commerce by well-capitalized and highly esteemed figures from old families. Trumbulls, Huntingtons, and Saltonstalls all entered trade, building or buying ships and sailing to the West Indies from Norwich and New London. The colony's cash supply was strained by this sudden burst of business activity, and in imitation of their competitors in the bordering colonies the easterners began to press for more paper money and, while it was short and expensive, used Rhode Island and New Hampshire bills, which were constantly depreciating. New York's paper, more commonly circulating in the west, had greater stability, and western Connecticut traders preferred that currency. One contemporary commented that the "eastern townships have been tainted by the adjacent paper-money-making colonies of Massachusetts-Bay and Rhode-Island, and followed that fraud instead of going into the better currency of their western adjoining province of New-York."[37]

Sherman's fiscal conservatism is more representative of his position as a large landowner and established small merchant than of the "new trade" class that he might most logically identify with. But the publication of his views ingratiated him with old-line families and did his political fortunes no harm. It is difficult to assess the impact of this pamphlet, for like views were already circulating throughout the colony. A legislative committee had suggested such a program as early as 1747, and, indeed, a bill to outlaw Rhode Island and New Hampshire currency emitted before 1750 was passed by the Council in 1751, but dissented to by the lower house till the next year. But petitions arose in various parts of the land-short province which paralleled Sherman's argument very closely. One from Hartford, for instance, read, "As the medium of trade is that whereby our dealings are valued and weighed, we cannot but think it ought to be esteemed of as sacred a nature as any weights and measures whatsoever, and in order to maintain justice must be kept as stable." This petition was dated May, 1752, the year of Sherman's pamphlet, and in that same year the General Assembly passed remedial legislation, outlawing Rhode Island bills issued since December, 1750. Even this was tightened up in 1755 by making illegal the use of such bills in future contracts.[38] It is difficult, in view of Sherman's later career, to believe that his writings were without influence.

Establishing a New Base

Roger Sherman never got to be first selectman of New Milford. As a matter of fact, only once in the course of an active and successful political life that spanned half a century did he gain an executive position, Mayor of New Haven. But other than this, Sherman had won over his adopted town by the late fifties. The question then of why, just when he was at the top of the heap, did he leave New Milford answers itself. Roger Sherman wanted bigger worlds to conquer. His move to a larger town, as his move to New Milford, was no mere act of restless discontent. It was a purposeful, calculated step, affected, but not dictated, by circumstance.

If Sherman's driving ambition was the prime mover in his march to bigger worlds, certainly conditions forced the decision in 1760. There was a general restlessness that pervaded the heavily populated colony in the years after the Canadian campaigns that closed in 1759. Large numbers of Sherman's neighbors from Litchfield County, as well as from the rest of the colony, moved to Nova Scotia in 1761 and 1762, and during the generation after 1750 even larger numbers went west to the rich Wyoming Valley of Pennsylvania. Many of these pioneers had been unable to find lands in Connecticut after fighting in the king's wars against the French. Connecticut had more troops in the field, some five thousand of them, than any other colony during the campaigns at Crown Point and Ticonderoga. When the battles were won in 1759 and the militia was disbanded, colony disbursements for their support ceased, and these had amounted to over a quarter of a million pounds sterling. The depression that followed the end of the fighting in 1760 and became intense after 1763 was foreshadowed in 1759.

Then, too, Sherman had a number of major disappointments in 1759 and 1760. One of the most lucrative plums to be picked from the General Assembly was commissary to the militia. This officer bought goods authorized by the colony government and distributed them to the troops in the field. The commissary had to act as purchasing agent and supply officer without salary, but was permitted a 50 percent profit on luxury goods, and 25 percent on necessities to be shared with four regimental assistants. Sherman sought this spot from his fellow deputies in 1759, and managed to get the appointment. But John Law, better connected and already on the spot in Albany, where the commissary was to be located, persuaded the upper house to pass the bill "with the alteration viz. that Mr. John Law of Milford be inserted instead of Mr. Roger Sherman of N. Milford." But that his esteem in the Assembly was growing is attested by a grant to Sherman for £50 for some other unspecified service.[39]

Sherman was not a bitter man, and his disappointment at the economic prize snatched away from him was probably buried under more profound troubles. In 1759 Anthony Carpenter, his partner of three years, died. The partnership was dissolved that year, though payments were continued to Carpenter's widow until 1772, when Sherman, intending to retire, attempted to turn the business over to his son William, who proved incompetent for the work. And then in 1760 Elizabeth died after only eleven years as wife to the aspiring merchant. Elizabeth had given birth seven times, and three of the babies, including the last two, died in infancy. Especially the last, to have been named Elizabeth, must have hastened her mother's death at thirty-five. So Sherman began to sell his real estate in New Milford, close out his business there and make plans for a removal to a more expansive location.

Sherman and Carpenter had always been run conservatively. The proprietors had not let debts accumulate, collecting payment in cash or more often country produce, and seldom letting debts to their Boston and New York suppliers become large. Indeed, the little inland store was run much more carefully than was customary among Connecticut coastal and river dealers who imported from the West Indies, Boston, New York, and Newport. So when hard times began, Sherman was not pressed. The western part of the colony was now growing much faster than any other part, and his business benefited from the influx. As a result he and Carpenter had been making more and more frequent trips to Boston, New York, and New Haven in order to expand their inventory and accelerate the business. A coastal town would have considerable appeal for Sherman for mercantile reasons alone. New Haven was also a much better political base. Not only did Sherman have business connections there, but it alternated with Hartford as the seat of the General Assembly. So in June 1760, Roger Sherman sold his store for £300 (and a small boat for twenty shillings), rented a house in New Haven, and moved down. In December he bought the house at the south end of the Yale campus where he was to spend the rest of his life.[40]

Sherman had frequently used the *Connecticut Gazette*, a New Haven paper, to advertise his almanacs, and on July 12 he burst forth in it with the announcement of the opening of his store at the house of Abigail Carpenter with "a great variety of Goods, suitable for the season." Additional information was volunteered that "They likewise intend to have goods to sell at Wallingford at the house of Widow Sarah Johnson by the 24th inst. July." On the 21st of March, 1761, he reported to the public that

I have removed my Store to the House, which lately belonged to Mr. Jabez Mix, opposite to the South West End of Yale college; where I shall attend said Business. I have in my stores at New-Haven and Wallingford, an Assortment of goods, suitable for the Season, to the Amount of about £.2000 Currency, which I would sell by wholesale, at Nine Month's Credit, as cheap as they could be purchased in Boston or New-York. If I can dispose of the Whole, or the greater Part of said Goods, speedily, I purpose to cease Trading in both the Places aforesaid. But till then, continue to sell cheap by Retail at both said Places for Cash, or Country Produce, at what it will clear.

He did not cease trading for over a decade.

Judging from later advertisements, from the inventory left at his death, and his surviving account books, Sherman's stock was more elegant than had been his New Milford offerings. More ribbons, satin and silk, looking glasses, snuff, and spices were handled at the New Haven store than had been usual at the earlier enterprise. Another significant difference was the large number of books and pamphlets that went through Sherman's hands at his new store. Reinforcing the usual almanacs were Watt's Psalms, texts in Latin, Greek, mathematics, and astronomy, Milton's works, maps, histories, and philosophical, religious, scientific, and especially political treatises. This reflects both propinquity to Yale College and the rapidly maturing political mind of the prospering merchant, for it is very likely that a good deal of the political writing was read by Sherman before it crossed his counter.[41]

In other respects the store was managed very much as had been its predecessor at New Milford. Goods were exchanged for cash, for "Country Produce," and for service such as tutoring the children, dressmaking, hauling, laboring, and the pasturing and care of horses. Apparently it was well run, for the debit-credit columns were brought into balance fairly often. Sherman, unlike many of his Connecticut mercantile colleagues, made prompt payment to the Massachusetts and New York importers from whom "English and India" goods were received. In 1772 Sherman retired and turned the store over to his eldest son, William. The latter quickly demonstrated the incompetence characteristic of all three older boys by running the business into the ground.[42]

It was all very neat, really. Sherman's mind was nothing if not orderly, and he ran his life according to schedule. He must have been pleased indeed, to look back over his first forty years, for in that time he had laid a solid, secure foundation on which to build a major career far greater than that of a country merchant-lawyer. As his successes mounted from minor objectives fulfilled to major goals achieved, his aspirations grew. In terms of these goals, Sherman scarcely knew failure at all. He was now a mature man with not only the economic and intellectual but also the psychological resources necessary to launch himself into the rushing streams of colonial, perhaps even intercolonial, politics.

The Connecticut Scene

LOOMING large in Sherman's pre-Revolutionary career were local political and economic factors. Connecticut was undergoing political changes brought about by population pressures and western colonization schemes. The little colony was rent by church disputes of the most intense kind, which split congregation after congregation and finally hit Yale itself. In the rural villages and along the coast the strictly agrarian economy was being challenged by the increasing importance of small industrial enterprise and the dynamism of a new trading class. All of these changes affected Sherman's political life, and all had the ultimate effect of driving him toward the radical view which he held by 1776.

A Self-Governing Colony

Connecticut's colonial political structure resembled a pyramid with its apex, the Governor and Council, consisting of a few old families with fairly frequent intrusions of new ones. The average length of service as governor during the eighteenth century was about nine and a half years, and two pairs of father and son are represented—the brace of Jonathan Trumbulls holding the job between them for over twenty-five years. And between 1682 and 1776 members of the Governor's Council were re-elected on the average of fourteen times. The Revolution made little immediate change in this situation.[1]

The largest part of the pyramid, however, consisted of the House of Representatives, which rested on the great broad base of the local governments. On these levels there was widespread participation and considerable dynamism, with frequent changes, contested elections, and often sharp infighting. Deeply concerned as they were with local business, most Connecticut yeomen were willing to leave colonial affairs in the hands of a few whose interests were broader.[2]

The well-born men of property had the leisure and means to carry on the affairs of the colony, and they were almost invariably given the power to do it. The idea that human election was mere evidence of divine election was still strong, and rulers were looked upon as God's lieutenants as late as the early years of the eighteenth century.[3] There was good rule, no graft, no demagoguery; the main job of the voters was to return to high colonial office year after year

> those who were most worthy in the sight of God and man to govern by virtue of their orthodoxy, family, wealth, talents, education, and political experience. . . . The effort to keep men in power was less for party purposes than to preserve intact the principles and standards of a Puritan ideal and preserve unaltered an attitude of conservatism and steady habits.[4]

The conservatism represented adherence to the Crown, but before that to the ideals and modes of the traditional government of the nearly independent colony. Only three eighteenth-century governors were turned out of office by the popular will, and this was because they had failed in the voters' ideas of devotion to duty and loyalty to the commonwealth. Roger Wolcott had seemed insufficiently partisan in the celebrated case of the Spanish ship in 1754; Thomas Fitch had stood by the Crown instead of the colony in swearing to administer that hated Stamp Act;[5] and Roger Griswold was thought to be too old.

It is possible, however, that the conservatism evinced by colonial voting habits represented nothing more than a lack of concern for matters of less than local import. Connecticut's conservatism is frequently laid to the preachings of the colony's established Congregational ministers, but it was in the ecclesiastical societies themselves that the earliest real political battles took place. The seldom rejected Governor and Council, after all, were only the peak of the iceberg showing above the vast sea of local government and politics. The claims of the colony to political stability and calls to the voters to maintain it became more strident as the 1700's wore on. Finally, by the close of the century, the panicky appeals for steady habits from the established old guard sound more like shrill whistling in the dark than like any picture of the Connecticut political scene as it actually existed. What stability remained by the end of the century resulted more from apathy and inconvenience than from respect for the traditional aristocracy. The great yeomanry, living at inconvenient distances from the locus of town and colonial government, would act when it thought it had cause. But except on the parish and town level, grievances were seldom sufficiently sharp to bring out the vote during most of the eighteenth century.

In hotly contested elections only about one in twelve of the males over twenty actually voted.[6] How many of the 40,797 adult men who lived in the colony in 1774 were admitted freemen is not known, but certainly far more than went to the polls. As late as 1790 the *American Mercury* boldly advised voters to "avoid too much veneration for family names," but a writer three years later complained that chief magistrates were still chosen by one-twentieth of the legal voters. A partial explanation of this is that colony and state officers were voted on at the end of town meetings, and large numbers left earlier after local business had been transacted.[7] Experience with twentieth-century New England town meetings would lead one to accept the accuracy of this statement. Another factor important in keeping conditions in Connecticut settled was the propensity of the "Wandering Yankees" to do just that. Westward migration was a major factor in both the internal affairs of the colony and in her intercolonial relations. Whether immigration removed the degenerate as some claimed, or carried off the more enterprising and energetic, it acted as a safety valve for the dissatisfied. "To the Standing Order, it was a Godsend"; remarks an historian of Connecticut's revolutions, "for otherwise this discontented mass must have broken down restraints and forced . . . reform, if not a thorough upheaval." At any event, the development of broad-scale participation in state-wide elections had to wait until the development of a two-party system after 1798.[8]

In view of this state of affairs, it is remarkable that Roger Sherman, cordwainer, should rise to high public place above the local level. He was not a native of the colony, his family had no special esteem either in Massachusetts or Connecticut, and his education was self-given—hardly the Yale standard.

This lack of collegiate training and family background was always a distinct handicap. On several occasions when his experience obviously made him the most qualified choice for high public office he was passed over. In 1774, for instance, he was picked to go to the Philadelphia Congress only after three others had refused to attend. In 1787 he was included among the delegates to the Constitutional Convention as a substitute for Erastus Wolcott. And he was not made a senator in the Federal Congress until after the resignation of William S. Johnson, having served first as a representative, when surely more deserving of the higher appointment than the quasi-Tory Johnson or the well-connected but young Oliver Ellsworth.[9] His crude accent and manner of speaking were often remarked by both fellow Connecticuters and more urbane citizens from other colonies.[10] But Sherman was not typical of the politicians of the time and place. If deficient in family and proper education, certainly he had proven his talents, gained wealth and political experience, and acquired a very sharp and useful education, however unrefined. It is true, of course, that immense land holdings are the key to his prominence, but it was his political craftmanship that turned the key and opened the door. He had more drive than most, and a combination of shrewdness and intelligence perhaps unequaled in the Connecticut of his day. Clearly he took advantage of the relative social mobility of eighteenth-century Connecticut.

Connecticut was not unique among the Eastern seaboard colonies. Democracy was hardly rampant anywhere before the Revolution, and if it developed more slowly in Connecticut after the war than in some places, it developed faster than in others. Connecticut's class structure was more fluid than others, and the differences between the wealthy and the poor less extreme. Self-government was older there than elsewhere, and suffrage restrictions were more traditional than legal or formal.[11] Connecticut, whether typical or not, did occupy a privileged position within the empire. She was practically autonomous and paid more lip service than respect to the laws of Parliament that were supposed to bind her. The king had no legal power to appoint officials in Connecticut or to proscribe her legislation unless clearly contrary to the laws of England. Indeed, with Rhode Island, Connecticut was the most independent and autonomous colony in America, possessing and exercising complete local self-government.

Connecticut was governed in a republican rather than democratic manner. At the top was the governor, elected by the eligible adult males, and his lieutenant, who usually succeeded to the higher office almost as a matter of right. The governor's influence was lodged principally in esteem for his person, for the office was given very little real power under the Charter. He served as the administrator of the will of the Assembly, on the approval of the Council of Assistants, which had veto power over both the lower house and the governor.

At one time this Council, consisting of twelve elected officials, constituted the magistracy of the colony, but at a later date a division was created and, in theory, the judiciary was set off from the legislative branch. However, the Assembly continued to appoint as Judges of the Superior Court the same people who had been elected to the Council, so in fact the upper house and the judiciary continued one and the same. In addition, all judges of the Superior Court were the judges of the county courts, and until 1784, the court of highest appeal was the Assembly itself. The administration of justice was a part of the general administrative operation of the government. Judicial business, then, as well as executive and legislative affairs, was dominated in large measure by a single important board, the Assistants to the Governor.

The lower house, the House of Representatives,* was the primary deliberative body of the colony. It consisted of two members elected from each town, representing the popular aspect of the government. The number of freeholders voting for deputies was a larger proportion than for statewide office. The lower house provided the personnel to carry out most of the legwork involved in running the colony, as there was no administrative staff under the governor other than the treasurer—an elected official. Members of the Assembly were called on to make on-the-spot investigations of claims against the government, to arbitrate disputes between towns, to eject squatters from colonial lands, to determine the fitness of applicants for various colonial offices such as surveyor or customs collector, and so on. But the actual work of the deputy was not too onerous because most responsibilities still rested with the local governments. His basic function was the obvious one of passing laws for the governing of the colony. These laws had to secure the approval of a majority of the Council as well, but could not be vetoed by the governor.

The Population Explosion

The population of Connecticut was a mobile one with large migrations both in and out. On the eve of the Revolution, Yale's versatile President and man of many facts, Ezra Stiles, reported, "In A.D. 1762 the Numeration of the Colony of Connecticut was 141 Thousand Souls; now A.D. 1774 it amounts to 197 Thousand Souls; there are about 6,000 Negroes and Indians in the Colony. So that the Colony had increased above 50 Thousand in the 12 years besides about 30 Thousand Emigrants from the Colony in that space."[12] Among the six counties the average increase in population for the colony between 1756 and 1774 was 51.5 percent. An analysis of the movement shows that, besides the large emigrations to other colonies, a pronounced urban trend was under way. New Haven County grew only 45 percent in the same period that the town of New Haven increased about 63 percent, and the town of New London almost 88 percent, while the county

---

*Sometimes called the General Assembly, this body is more properly referred to as the House of Representatives in the late colonial period. Its members were called deputies. The term General Assembly should be used to identify the whole government: governor, assistants, and deputies together.

was increasing a mere 43 percent. Along with the emigration to areas further west, there was also a westward trend within the colony. Litchfield, Connecticut's wild northwestern corner, for instance, grew 130.7 percent in the eighteen-year period.[13]

In the twenty-four years prior to 1756 the population of the rocky colony was said to have doubled. The growth is thought to have been largely due to natural increase and the intestacy law, which encouraged the breaking up of farms into smaller and smaller units with the death of each landholder. There were also large migrations from Massachusetts and Rhode Island into the eastern counties. However, it should be noted that Connecticut had a smaller growth proportionately than Pennsylvania, New York, New Hampshire, and Vermont. But much of the growth of these areas resulted from emigrations from Connecticut. Indeed, in 1774 Jared Ingersoll reported from Philadelphia that "The people begin to Consider the Northern New England men as a Set of Goths and Vandals who may one day overrun these Southern Climes unless thoroughly opposed, ..." The colony's increase could not go on forever, however. The emigrants were mostly men, leaving a large number of surplus women, probably dry-eyed but forlorn. And indeed, the population growth dropped to 5.5 percent in the decade 1790–1800, a period when the nation as a whole continued to mushroom with an increase of over 35 percent.[14]

Economic Factors

Roger Sherman's rise to prominence, mercantile and political, coincided with an economic revolution in Connecticut that was to shift the balance of power from the more or less stable agricultural interests to the rising mercantile minority. Basically self-sufficient in 1750, the colony was transformed into a commercially oriented economy by the end of the century. The dynamism of the movement was provided by the merchants, principally those of the inland towns after the French and Indian War, when the important West Indian trade was sharply restricted.[15]

Since the 1750's Connecticut's farmers had been producing ever-increasing surpluses that they exchanged for the products of the West Indies, Europe, and the other American colonies. A postwar economic collapse in the sixties was exacerbated by the old problems of indebtedness to neighboring merchants; the population explosion; a lack of good seaports and an undeveloped internal transportation system; and the capital-exhausting lust for land speculation, mostly external. In addition, the lack of large urban centers with a dynamic business-oriented core retarded both the growth of large-scale trade and government involvement in the economy. About 1750 and clearly by the sixties, business influence in government began to show, however. Tax and public service exemptions for manufacturers became more numerous, bounties for certain goods were offered, and incorporations for bridges and toll roads were established in great number. Especially, the nature of the colony's agriculture changed to favor export commodities such as livestock, lumber, and flaxseed.[16]

Between 1756 and 1768 the value of export-import trade tripled.* But the only favorable balance was with the West Indies, and British and French restrictions drastically reduced the rate of increase after 1763, so that Connecticut never had an over-all favorable balance of trade at any time between 1750 and 1775. Boston had dominated Connecticut's intercolonial trade up to the mid-century, but New York gradually took over a larger share of the business after that time. This was brought on primarily by a 1749 Massachusetts law prohibiting the circulation of other colonies' bills of credit, and after the occupation of New York City, trade swung back to Boston. But by that time New Haven merchants owed over £20,000 sterling to New York importers.[17]

New Haven and Norwich were the fastest growing towns in the colony after 1750, and the former was generally considered the most flourishing. Roads were built in and out of New Haven and at mid-century it dominated

---

*The most remarkable increase occurred between 1768 and 1770, reflecting the abnormally low importations during the non-importation agreements at the time of the Townshend Acts. The tonnage figures for the coasting trade with New York and Boston are:

	1768	1770	1772
To New York	318	4230	2727
To Boston	509	3240	2922
From New York	70	4471	2222
From Boston	618	3181	2833

Connecticut's trade was almost entirely coastal and West Indian. The percentages of tonnage for 1769 are:

	From	To
American Continent	55.3	44.4
West Indies	43.2	51.2
Southern Europe	.6	1.1
Great Britain & Ireland	.8	3.2

Adapted from Van Dusen, "Trade of Revolutionary Connecticut," ps. 141, 147. See also Sutherland, *Population Distribution*, pp. 277–295.

the trade of all western Connecticut. In 1761, the year of Sherman's removal, a cart road was built along the Housatonic from Canaan through New Milford down to Derby Landing, less than ten miles from New Haven. Of the 150 vessels averaging about ten tons that sailed from Connecticut's harbors, eighty considered New Haven their home in 1762. Most of these were coasters, of course, but nearly half went to the West Indies and other foreign ports. By 1750 port facilities and the development of inland transportation gave New Haven a dominant position over the trade of the entire western half of the colony.[18]

The Lure of New Haven

The village of New Haven, the largest in the colony, had a rapidly growing population of about 6000 with 1500 living in the "compact part of the Town." Indeed, it had increased by about 3600 in the eight years preceding 1756, and the average annual increment, which had been about twenty persons between 1724 and 1748, was nearly 225 in the period 1748-74. But the augmentation of wealth during the thirty years preceding the Revolutionary collapse of trade far outstripped even the considerable population growth. Tonnage increased fortyfold, and value of exports (with inflation) multiplied by 470. On or near the green, about which the most influential people lived, stood three churches, the old Statehouse, and four buildings of Yale College. The colony's only newspaper was published in New Haven, and there was a regular post office and a customs house.[19] It held real attractions for an ambitious merchant.*

Religious Divisions

The political situation that Roger Sherman encountered in New Haven was a complex of religion, economics, and tradition. It had a pattern, however, which can be discerned. Sherman's own church affiliation was Congregational, of course, but there were in Connecticut three major factions among the Congregationalists.

The Great Awakening of the 1740's made a notable impact on Connecticut society and politics.[20] The long dormant opposition to the

---

*New Haven was not quite perfect for the rigid Sherman, however. When David Wooster, deputy from that town, tried to block the seating of a Norwalk delegate on grounds of "his having been very frequently Drunk . . . ," another colleague retorted that such behavior was also common in New Haven. CHS, "William Williams Papers," Journal of 1757 Assembly session, typescript of Mrs. Sylvie Turner.

Saybrook Platform, which institutionalized the Half-Way Covenant and created a presbyterian church organization, was reactivated. Large numbers of Connecticut people were thrown back on their Calvinist breeding by the enthusiastic preaching of various revivalists who attempted to follow the example of the great evangelist, George Whitefield. Ezra Stiles reported that the Awakening peaked in 1743, with about 130 out of 400 New England ministers enthusiastic, but, he noted, "of these only 30 violent."[21] The call to return to a primitive puritanism was felt by many whose headlong dash for material enlargement had exacerbated the usual guilt bred into every son of a Calvinist society. But the New Light showed them the way to salvation: a return to experiential rather than rational religion. Study of scripture would perhaps open the mind to Christ, but this was worthless without a change of heart. Each man must experience the entrance of the divine spirit into his bosom. Only this brought Christ's saving grace. Church membership, then, should be open only to the truly saved.

This was in part a return to the old seventeenth-century form. But the emphasis on emotional approaches would have shocked a Cotton or a Davenport who looked to rational study and intellectual exercise as the proper preparation for acknowledging grace. The New Lights, however, were a determined lot. In parish after parish they fought to control the selection of ministers and the choice of doctrine. Where they failed, they attempted to break off into separate societies as the Anglicans and Baptists had been permitted to do.[22] The county consociations fought these moves through their own organizations and through the legislature, where relief from society taxes would have to be approved. But gradually the old order lost ground. Laws against itinerancy were repealed in 1750, and starting as early as 1730 groups of separates were excused from paying church taxes, though not actually qualifying as ecclesiastical societies.[23] Other separations took place; by 1750 Litchfield County and the eastern part of the colony, which Stiles said was "of a very mixt & uncertain character as to religion," were dominated by New Lights. It wasn't long before the General Assembly and then the county consociations were also under heavy New Light influence.[24] To understand Sherman's varied posture throughout these controversies, a return to New Milford is required.

Roger Sherman had joined the conservative church in Stoughton upon the death of his father in 1742. As a matter of course he presented his letter of membership to the Reverend Mr. Daniel Boardman in New Milford and settled into the ecclesiastical niche of the establishment. But almost immediately there was a fight, for Boardman, failing for years, died in 1744.

Boardman was the only minister New Milford had ever had, having been ordained there in 1716. The question of supply was one never faced before, and it could not have come at a worse time. The effects of the Awakening were still very strong, and a significant number of society members wanted to give up the Half-Way Covenant and return to the old Cambridge Platform.[25]

The congregation could not agree on a new minister. In anticipation of this contingency it had been resolved by the town meeting in 1743 that the church lands should go to the first minister to be settled on condition that he abide by the Saybrook Platform. This Old Light victory was won by explicitly providing that Anglicans and Quakers in town should retain their proportional share of church lands. The Quakers, the first such congregation in Connecticut, had broken off in 1731, and built their own meeting house in 1741. The Anglicans, as late as 1760, one of only two Church congregations in Litchfield County, broke off in 1735. Despite the 1743 resolution, the New Lights kept battling and successfully prevented the settling of a minister until 1747 when apparently they stopped attending altogether. In December of that year, Nathaniel Taylor was unanimously chosen by the Old Light remainder with the proviso that his salary would be cut off if he deviated from the Saybrook Platform.[26]

By 1750, however, the majority faction sought to bring back the wayfarers, eleven of whom they listed in the church records. A committee was set up to deal with the miscreants, but one of the committeemen, a deacon at that, joined them, giving the New Light faction new strength and resolve. They were told merely to report in six months with their reasons, in writing, for absenting themselves from meeting. When, in March, 1751, the minority appeared at the Reverend Mr. Taylor's house with nothing in writing, a new committee of five was established and this one included Roger Sherman. Early in May, according to Taylor, the dissenters appeared and "signed some reasons offered in writing, which ye Church judged to be no reasons at all; and returned ym an answer in writeing to gether with an admonition to return unto us." But they did not return, and in 1753 formally separated, building their own church eight years later.

The theological grounds upon which this battle raged, and it was being fought all across the colony, becomes clearer when viewed in terms of individuals. The majority held that anyone who had "acknowledged ye Covenant, and been received under ye Watch and Care" of the church was under the discipline of the church until dismissed or recommended to another congregation. Specifically, it was the belief of the New Lights that the Saybrook Platform endorsing the Half-Way Covenant was not strict enough in delimiting the grounds of church membership. That is why the minority faction refused to accept Taylor, who had been put forward by the New Haven County Association, dominated until the mid-fifties by Old Lights. One of Taylor's flock, Joseph Ruggles, moved to New Haven in 1752 and according to church rule needed a letter of dismissal or of recommendation in order to associate with a congregation there. He chose Samuel Bird's New Light church, and was denied the letter he sought by Taylor. Ruggles traveled back to New Milford to protest "In as much as I have absented myself from your Communion Supposing you to be upon an anti-christian [position] with respect to government, and Discipline, and further I apprehend yt the Doctrines of Grace which I hold to, (viz) ye Calvinist Doctrines you are not Strict enough in; and therefore I desire you would dismiss me from your Watch and Care." He was refused his letter, and even after conceding that "ye difference of government in ye Cambridge and Saybrook platforms should not break Communion," was denied a legal transfer.

Though some separators drifted back into the conservative church, by 1755 the Old Lights were on the defensive and in many towns were behaving like a minority party. In New Milford, Sherman, who acted as clerk of the Church Meeting, began to refer to his Old Light congregation in 1754 as "Presbyterian—Congregational" and a year later as the "Presbyterian order."* When a new church was built he handled the church funds that were divided among the three Presbyterian societies in what had been the original limits of New Milford, the First in New Milford, and Newbury and Preston. By this time the New Milford Separates felt strong enough to petition to be relieved from paying church taxes because they "Soberly Dissent from the way of Worship and Method of Supporting the Ministry Established by the Laws of this Colony and they do maintain and attend the Public Worship of God among themselves in a way agreeable to ther Consciences." This was agreed to "by a great majority without Computing any of the Persons making sd Request," wrote Sherman as clerk.

The separation required an alteration in the method of supporting the public school, which had been within church jurisdiction. In 1756 it was voted by the Old Light church that parents would pay for schools and masters in proportion to the number of children attending, except that all

---

*The term "Presbyterian" was used to differentiate the Old Lights, who still abided the discipline of the County Consociations, from the renegade New Lights. After about 1760, when the New Lights came to control the Consociations, the term Presbyterian had little relevance. Heimert, *Religion*, p. 361n.

Connecticut in 1766; map by Moses Park. From the original map in the Map Collection of the Yale University Library.

children between five and ten years old living within one and a half miles of a school would be counted whether they attended or not. Thus the Consociation church still laid down the rules binding all New Milford inhabitants. Discrimination against the New Lights did not cease entirely, for when the old meetinghouse was torn down in 1756, the seats, pulpit, and other physical remains were divided among the three Presbyterian societies, the Quakers, and the Anglicans, with no share for the New Lights.

The Litchfield County Consociation was dominated by the powerful Joseph Bellamy, a nonseparating New Light, and most societies there gave up the Half-Way Covenant in the forties. In 1760 Ezra Stiles reported that a Cornwall minister told him "that not one Chh. in Litchfield County are on Saybrook Platform by explicit Vote with their present Pastors." But New Milford, with its left and right radicals long gone into Quakers and Anglicans, put the lie to that statement. It was not until 1769 that the Old Light congregation: "1. Voted that this Church looks upon it that there is no halfway Covt—but those who [revere?] the Covt, have a right to privileges in full." This ambiguous latitudinarianism was expanded by resolutions: "2. Voted that we look upon it the duty of the Church to use their influence and endeavors to convince Persons of their duty and obligations to attend ye ordinances of the gospel understandingly. 3. Voted. If any in Covt remain unconvinced of their Duty to come to the Table, we out of tenderness to their Tender consciences will allow them Baptism for their Children."[27] This kind of liberality and rationalism resulting in what amounts to a political solution would have been unthinkable twenty years earlier. It demonstrates the marked movement away from the dominance of theology and ecclesiastical affairs that characterized the colony during the mid-eighteenth century.

Sherman was influential in the Old Light parish. Once he was appointed to confer with the pastor, youthful Nathaniel Taylor, "on account of encumbering himself with other affairs, whereby he is too much diverted from his studies and ministerial work." Later he was named treasurer of the church building fund and clerk of the ecclesiastical society (services for which he was paid thirty pounds). He was a deacon for the regular two-year term starting in 1755, and on the school committee, an arm of the church society. He continued on that committee and as clerk of the meeting right up until he moved to New Haven. In 1751 and 1752 his brothers acknowledged the covenant, and his children were baptized in the Old Light meetinghouse. Indeed, as late as October 1761, three months after his removal to New Haven, his daughter Elizabeth was baptized in the New Milford Congregation.[28]

The division between New Lights and Old Lights was only one of a series of controversies reaching back to the infamous Spanish Ship case of 1752, and further. The line begins at least as early as argument over establishment of a land bank in New London in the first part of the century, on up through to the divisions between Patriots and Tories. Benjamin Gale, a Killingworth physician with a penchant for political polemic, wrote in 1766 that the divisions in Connecticut originated with "the New London Society—thence metamorphosed into the Faction for paper Emissions on Loan, thence into N. Light, into ye Susquehannah & Delaware Factions—into Orthodoxy—now into Stamp Duty—the Actors the same each change drawing in some New Members."[29] One of the "New Members" picked up in 1761 was to prove most valuable in the coming years of heated controversy. If the matter were merely theological we might wonder at Sherman's apparent about-face. But, as Gale pointed out, church membership had become very political, and the real question was one of polity—ecclesiastical *and* civil.

Of course it was Gale himself who had been most prominently employed in making ecclesiastical association an important political matter. Motivated by family loyalties, a rationalist anticlericalism, and a just plain ornery temperament, Gale had been attempting since the early fifties to re-establish Assembly control over Yale. He published pamphlet after pamphlet on the subject, attacking Clap, calling for investigations and demanding the cessation of public support of the College. He was aided by Clap's equally cantankerous and uncompromising nature, which had impelled the President to a tyrannical administration involving religious dogmatism, and an arbitrary and harsh student discipline. By 1755 Clap had hardly a friend among his natural supporters, the Old Lights. He took the only course that appeared likely of success; he became a New Light. In his search to find legislative support his eye lit upon Roger Sherman, and so the recent comer to New Haven, almost naturally drifting into the New Light church, easily obtained the backing of Clap and his followers, by now a majority in New Haven.

The New Haven Consociation had always been a loosely organized affair, really more congregational than presbyterian. But by 1760, all the consociations as well as the lower house of the Assembly were guided by New Light majorities. Not only would Sherman find the members of the new, but already quite respectable, church in New Haven more his kind—aggressive, mercantile, and liberal; but he would also be joining the fastest growing congregation in town, perhaps already the largest. It is true that Sherman had helped prevent Joseph Ruggles from transferring to this church eight years earlier. But now, with the New Divinity dominant, he chose to cast in his lot

with the faction in power. And in time Sherman was to become the hub of
the New Haven interlopers, as the new traders were called, aided by Benedict
Arnold, David Wooster, and James Hillhouse, David Austin, and others.
Indeed, Sherman became the leader "above all" and the "foremost man in
New Haven, if not the State," and "the central figure around which the
progressive elements in society clustered."[30]

During the early years of the Great Awakening, officeholders had found it
to their disadvantage to be associated with the New Lights, and often lost
position because of it. But in the 1750's "with increasing frequency election
hinged upon the changing strength of the Old and New Light factions."
President Clap had made the switch, and was working hard to replace New
Haven's Old Light deputies with New Lights. The opportunity was just right
for Sherman. William Samuel Johnson attributed New Light success to "the
superior attention that its followers gave 'to civil affairs and close union
among themselves in politics.' " The remarkable Benjamin Gale, brain trust
and leading pamphleteer for the conservative faction, implied in 1755 that
some people became New Lights for no other reason than to advance their
political fortunes. And in 1761 Roger Wolcott warned against party
ambitions disguised "under the Paint of Religion." By 1763 a majority of the
lower house was New Light and William Samuel Johnson sadly wrote, "The
N.L. within my short memory were a small Party merely a religious one . . . in
this short period by their continual struggles they have acquired such an
Influence as to be nearly the ruling part of the Government. . . ."[31]

In the economic and political dynamic of Connecticut in the second half
of the eighteenth century, there was a kind of ambivalence pulling ambitious
men out of their inborn conservatism and sense of place, order, and
hierarchy, and toward mobility, change, and material progress. The philosophical justification for this course of action is stated in Sherman's almanac
of 1753: "Reason and Passion answer one great Aim, / And true self love and
social are the same." Here the Lockean replaces the Calvinist view. The chief
use of reason is no longer to glorify God for His sake, but rather to find
self-expression or personal advantage within sensible, moral bounds.[32]

The Susquehannah Company

In salty Benjamin Gale's six steps to revolution, the fourth mentioned was
"ye Susquehannah & Delaware Factions," and on this enterprise attention
must be continually focused. The Susquehannah disturbance was an
outgrowth of the overcrowding of the infertile eastern part of rocky

Connecticut.[33] Eastern radicalism seems to have been founded on the area's too rapid and disorderly settlement from Massachusetts just after 1700, with its concomitant speculation and uncertainty of titles. Associated with this speculation was the presence of numerous petty traders and an interest in paper currency, all of which created a social dynamism and turbulence laying the people open to a ready acceptance of Great Awakening ideas. The Susquehannah movement grew "from a half-dozen petitioners for a western grant in 1750 . . . in three years to over a thousand advocates . . ." and finally to where, in 1770, it had a controlling influence in the government. Clearly, it is not to be slighted.[34]

The rapid increase in the population of the colony became too great a problem to bear when coupled with certain economic facts: agriculture, the mainstay of the economy, was inefficient, ignorantly pursued, hampered by lack of water transportation, and based on the premise of an ever-available supply of cheap land. When the land gave out both qualitatively and quantitatively, the Connecticut farmer was in real trouble. He had to move elsewhere.

The most important "elsewhere" in this instance was the northern tier of Pennsylvania counties. Connecticut's original charter from Charles II granted her all the land lying between the forty-first and forty-second parallels from the "Narrogancett Bay on the East to the South Sea on the West," but Connecticut had not objected to a number of conflicting grants of subsequent date, most significantly one to William Penn in 1681. And no attempt was made by Connecticut settlers to move to the western lands until 1750, when petitions began to be sent up to the General Assembly asking for the right to inhabit the land west of the Delaware River.

Ultimately three companies were formed to survey, sell, and settle the Pennsylvania lands. These were the First and Second Delaware Companies, located bewteen the Delaware and Susquehannah Rivers, and the Susque-hannah Company, whose claims covered the entire northern third of Pennsylvania west of the Susquehannah. Land was purchased for the companies by dubious contract with the Iroquois through a disreputable Dutch trader of Albany, and shares were sold throughout Connecticut. The idea of a settlement in western lands, detached from Connecticut but part of it, quickly took fire in the most heavily populated eastern part of the colony. Overpopulation on enervated soil made for incipient poverty, a condition the virile and energetic Yankees of east Connecticut would not allow to develop. Thus the locus of both paper money sentiment and New Light strength became the center also of the Susquehannah scheme, and the smoldering radical faction began to kindle.

The leadership of the Susquehannah group was not institutionalized in any particular form, but through control of standing committees that were part of any town government a few men like Eliphalet Dyer of Windham and John Franklin of Canaan were able to dominate the group. The company was not chartered (indeed there was doubt that a chartered colony could legally grant charters), but it had a secretary and a treasurer, and ran itself as though it were a town. Slowly opposition grew up in Connecticut, and by the early sixties conservatives in the colony had begun to have serious misgivings about the adventure. The dubious legality of the claim; the expense involved in bringing the claim to the crown courts and in protecting it once Connecticut jurisdiction was extended; and the control of the movement by the radical elements all tended to alienate such men as Jared Ingersoll and other important figures. However, the power of the left-wing faction was on the rise, and influential members of the government and clergy were among those pushing the western lands scheme. Among the clergy, New Light ministers were particularly involved in land speculation.

In addition, the Susquehannah Company controlled the newspapers. Its leaders and pamphleteers made constant use of the printing press in spreading its propaganda throughout the unusually literate colony. By 1763 Ezra Stiles would write that opponents

> would bring upon them 'the Curse of the Company who with their connexions are large eno' to influence one Third of the Voters in the Government, & might possibly shake some out of the Council and Assembly.' Stiles was also of the opinion that the company was 'headed by Men of the first Sense and Character in Connecticut.'[35]

Such a baldly factual sketch hardly does justice to one of the most dramatic escapades in the history of western settlement. The Indian massacres, the bitterness and bloodshed between Pennsylvania proprietors and the Connecticut settlers and their frontier Pennsylvania allies, the wild Paxton Boys, have been well described elsewhere. Of particular interest here is the part played by the Susquehannah group in shaping Connecticut politics and Roger Sherman's role therein.

Earlier writings on Sherman and the western land movement claim that Sherman was a leader in the Susquehannah scheme.[36] This was ultimately true, but not at first. His part in the business was one of no participation in the early period, rather cautious association in the middle period, and heated

partisanship only from the climactic moment and after. This analysis follows
the logic of the crafty politician's career. There would be little likelihood that
he would be part of an eastern, New Light movement during the fifties when
living in one of the western outposts of the colony and fighting off the New
Light drive in his own congregation. After 1760, when he moved to New
Haven, Sherman's slide to the theological and political left was just about
even with that of the dominant movement in the colony, and by the
mid-seventies he was among the most radical of the middle-of-the-road forces
in the colony.

In 1769 at both the January and October sessions of the Assembly Roger
Sherman was appointed a representative of the Council on a joint committee
to investigate the Susquehannah land claims. On both occasions the other
member from the upper house was a proponent of, indeed a participant in,
the Susquehannah claims; there was Matthew Griswold, who had signed a plea
for lands in 1752, and Robert Walker, who owned a share of the company
and had signed the deed from the Six Nations in 1754. Whether Sherman had
been put on the committee as a counter to Griswold and Walker or because
the Council had wanted to stack the committee is open to conjecture.[37]

The Susquehannah faction was thoroughly in control of both Council and
Assembly by 1769, so it is unlikely that Sherman was hostile to the western
claims. An important factor is that New Haven, Sherman's constituency, was
deeply rent by the controversy, and the anti-Susquehannah faction was still in
the majority there as late as March 1774, by which time Sherman had
committed himself to support the claim. So for necessary political reasons, he
may have been publicly more circumspect than he was privately and in the
sessions of the Council. The relationship between these radical movements—
paper money through New Light to western lands—and the independence
drive will be demonstrated in a later chapter. But there were opposing forces
in mid-eighteenth-century Connecticut, and the radicals did not have
everything their way.[38]

The Conservative Faction

The leadership of the conservative movement in Connecticut, like most
such movements, was not cohesive; indeed, it was individualistic in the
extreme. The prime spokesman of the Old Light faction was Dr. Benjamin
Gale of Killingworth.[39] One of the most fascinating characters of eighteenth-
century Connecticut, Gale deserves a biography of his own. For some reason
Gale never joined the Church and seems to have been more of a deist than

anything else. But, of course, open profession of such convictions in the old Puritan colony would have been unthinkable even for the most outspoken and courageous of men. At any rate, Gale was dead set against returning to the old orthodoxy as represented by the reactionary New Lights and had an especial hatred for President Clap of Yale, who had moved into the New Light camp in the fifties. Gale's antipathy to the New Lights, and especially Clap, caused his successful attempt to stop a hundred-pound appropriation to the college when he was a member of the Assembly.

Gale, a prolific writer of steamy pamphlets and newspaper notices, was skilled in playing upon popular feeling. But he was too conservative even for central Connecticut, and in 1766 was temporarily removed from his seat in the Assembly when he supported the Stamp Act. Though he owned stock in the Susquehannah Company, Gale came back to the Assembly in 1768 as an anti-Susquehannah man, primarily in order to defeat the New Light faction. He was probably secretly a Loyalist, and he was against the adoption of the Constitution in 1788, charging that it would enslave three-quarters of the people of the country. Gale finally died in 1790, but he had led the Old Light faction from 1754 to 1764, the last year of its dominance, and continued to be the most outspoken though increasingly ineffective of the conservative leaders.

Another right-wing spokesman was Jared Ingersoll, naturally a conservative, but not naturally inclined to martyrdom. Ingersoll's position as Stamp Agent for the colony of Connecticut forced him to the right and ultimately made his residence in the colony impossible. He was driven out by mob action, a victim of the rapidly shifting winds of the stormy politics of the late 1700's. A third leader, and by far the most effective, was William Samuel Johnson of Stratford, son of Connecticut's first Church of England minister. Both father and son served as president of Kings, later Columbia, College.

Johnson, overcoming the political disadvantage of his religion, played an important part in the affairs of Connecticut. He was a moderate conservative, in the same way and with the same effectiveness that Sherman was a moderate radical. Johnson was able to win the support of the Susquehannah group through a deal which tied the radical eastern part of the colony to the ultra-conservative Anglican minority in the western part. But these strange political bedfellows managed to carry the day, and the moderate Johnson was elevated to the Council in 1767. Except for the actual war years when Johnson remained in political hibernation, he was always in the forefront of the political scene, and ultimately served as one of Connecticut's first senators to the Federal Congress. Johnson was typical of the Anglican membership, except that he kept his Loyalist sympathies to himself. The core of conservative, though anti-establishment, sentiment throughout the fifteen years following 1760 was the Episcopal congregations, most of which were located in the western part of the state. Indeed, Connecticut, with eighteen S. P. G. missionaries, one a schoolteacher, had more than any other colony.*[40]

The political structure of Connecticut, then, was basically the same throughout the whole period of Sherman's participation in it. The membership of the various factions, religious and political, remained fairly constant though with an accelerating left movement, and a deepening of the separating fissure as the colonial policy of the mother country began to exert pressure. This colonial policy that finally brought these sharpening divisions to a complete falling away of one part from the other must be the subject of the next chapter. It was in the heat of Connecticut's internal conflict over the economic policies of England that the temper of Sherman's political mettle was to be tested.

---

*New York and Massachusetts had sixteen and twelve respectively. Actually, Anglicanism was not the kiss of death in Connecticut politics that it has usually been described as. Research in progress by Bruce Steiner at Ohio University shows that about fifty Anglicans served in the Connecticut lower house between 1740 and 1775, while many more were justices of the peace. See also Steiner, "New England Anglicanism."

CHAPTER III

The Politician Comes of Age

Conditions at Yale College in New Haven were greatly unsettled in the late 1740's as its rector Thomas Clap waged unremitting war on the factious New Lights and their student supporters. Sherman was still strongly Old Light, but apparently something about the frenzy at New Haven, "the eye of the religious hurricane sweeping through the colony," disturbed him. Most of the Connecticut boys who went to the College of New Jersey rather than Yale were sons of New Lights, and in the 1740's and 1750's as many as a quarter of the matriculants at Princeton were Connecticuters. The relative economy of the New Jersey college, however, was probably the more important determining factor.[1] The College of New Jersey was, though New Light, still Presbyterian and, with the lowest tuition in the colonies, looked sound, so Roger's brothers, Nathaniel and Josiah, were packed off there to graduate in '53 and '54. Both boys became ministers, and Roger visited Josiah, his junior by eight years, at his parish in Woburn, Massachusetts, on his frequent business trips to Boston.

Tradition has it that on one such visit Sherman, a widower now for nearly three years, left accompanied by his brother. By chance they happened to meet Rebecca Prescott, the twenty-year-old niece of Josiah's wife. Evidently her attractions were abundant and immediately observed by the older Sherman, over twice her age, for he wheeled about and trotted back to his brother's house to take care of new business. Roger and Rebecca were married by the girl's grandfather, Benjamin Prescott of Salem, on May 12, 1763. Rebecca was several cuts above Sherman's first wife, Elizabeth Hartwell. Both her father and grandfather were Harvard graduates, and her father was a prosperous merchant and magistrate in Salem. The young Roger Sherman who left Stoughton in 1743 would never have had the temerity to seek so fine a bride. She was better educated than Elizabeth, and in other respects better bred.[2]

Rebecca was a fine horsewoman and charming and witty as well, characteristics, her family would claim, inherited from Geoffrey Chaucer. Chaucer's blood or not, the wit was quick, and the bride was beautiful. At a state dinner in later years George Washington picked Rebecca as his dinner partner, much to the chagrin of John Hancock's etiquette-conscious Dorothy and various other ladies present. When Washington was told of Mrs. Hancock's annoyance, he remarked "that it was his privilege to give his arm to the handsomest woman in the room." The youthful bride was no doubt of considerable help to dour old Roger, when in his capacity as mayor of New Haven he had to entertain such notables as Washington and John Adams. Rebecca bore six daughters, one of whom died in infancy, and two sons, Roger and Oliver. Certainly the seven children who lived to adulthood were far more successful in life than those of Elizabeth. All the girls married well, and seem to have been possessed of a spirit not found in the earlier family. Throughout his life Roger addressed his letters to Rebecca "Dear Wife," even on such solemn occasions as the death of a son.

Taxes and Stamps

Sherman, then, was developing his career in an orderly and constantly forward direction. He had a new house in a new town, and a new business. Now he could start on a new family with a new wife. The life to which Sherman brought Rebecca in New Haven could not have been very different from the busy commerce of her home town Salem. Even politics were at about the same temperature in both places and getting warmer rapidly. The ascension to the throne of the weak-minded but stubborn George III coincided with the beginning of the postwar economic troubles that ultimately were to drive the colonies out of the Empire. George III was determined to do away with party administration of his government, and in addition he supported the myopic and unpolitic plan of the Chancellor of the Exchequer to force the colonies, prime beneficiaries of the ousting of the French, to help pay for the late wars. The heat thus applied to the provincial political pots caused the simmering contents to bubble furiously for a while and at last boil over completely. And Connecticut had already demonstrated its own sources of heat.

During the last colonial war with France, the French and Indian War of 1754–63, Connecticut contributed some 5000 men, more than any other colony, and spent £259,000 sterling. Her spirit was fine and her men willing to fight; from 1757 onward one out of five of her men between the ages of sixteen and forty-five were under arms.[3] The women were no less spirited. The *Connecticut Gazette* for October 11, 1755, reported:

A Report prevails here, that many of our Men are coming back from the Camp, and that it is now doubtful, whether our Expedition will proceed against Crown-point this Fall or not; on this Report we are told, many of the good Women of this Colony are so enraged, that they declare if their Husbands come back without attacking the French in their Intrench-ments, they shall not come near them; but that instead of receiving them with Joy, they will fling their P-s-pots at their Heads, as unworthy the Name of New-England men.

Taxes as well as spirits were high during the late fifties, in some years twenty-six times as high as in the pre-war days, but the wartime prosperity seemed to still complaints for the time being. When Parliament reimbursed Connecticut for expenses incurred during the war, the people were relieved of paying any colony taxes at all from 1765 to 1770. But Governor Trumbull was to claim later that the colony was still out some £400,000 for the costs of the war. Though Englishmen in England were heavily taxed, the freemen of Connecticut were reluctant to pay anything to the colony; their town taxes they deemed high enough.[4]

At a time of economic slackening and declining spirit of sacrifice—for the French menace to the north had been removed—King George chose to levy new kinds of taxes and heavier ones than ever before. And what is worse, he managed to antagonize and strengthen the Susquehannah forces at the same time. In 1763 the King's Board of Trade obtained an order commanding the Connecticut settlers in the Wyoming Valley to move home again. At the same time the Pennsylvania government rebuffed the wild Paxton Boys, who had asked for help in their battles with the Indians of western Pennsylvania, thus driving the rambunctious Allegheny settlers into alliance with the Connecti-cuters. In the fall of the same year the Crown formalized its opposition to western settlement by the Proclamation of 1763, which forbade migration beyond the Alleghenies, including a large part of the Susquehannah claims. Indeed, there is good support for the view that local left-wing forces began to direct their activities against the British home government only after this hostility to the Susquehannah claims became evident.[5] The passage of the Sugar Act and the Currency Act in 1764, along with new and serious attempts to enforce the various existing trade measures, appeared designed to ruin the colonial economy. And when added to the already boiling pot of local politics, these imperial policies nearly caused the stew to spill.

In the fall of 1759 the Superior Court rendered decisions unfavorable to the New Light factions in both New Haven and Wallingford. By this time the

New Lights were near to domination of the New Haven Consociation, so a struggle took place between the two elements of the establishment—the Assembly and the Consociation. An effort was made to purge the Council of Old Lights Newton, Silliman, Burr, Chester, Wolcott, Edwards, and Hamlin, and Governor Fitch himself.[6] The Old Lights were reaping the rewards of an unsteadiness they had instituted back in 1754, when something of a revolution had seen Fitch replace Roger Wolcott by votes rather than retirement or death—an unprecedented event in Connecticut.

New Haven in the late fifties was erratically moving from Old Light dominance to New Light. Pairs of Old Light deputies were elected regularly until 1759. In that year Daniel Lyman, a deacon of the Old Light First Church till the year before, when he switched allegiance to the White Haven congregation, was elected along with his brother-in-law, John Whiting, still a First Church deacon. In October Clap and the others of the Yale-New Light faction supported Samuel Sherman* and Daniel Lyman for the lower house, but Chauncey Whittelsey wrote triumphantly that "we beat them, and chose Coll. Hubbard & Mr. Whiting."[7] Through the six elections between 1759 and 1761 the New Haven delegation jumped back and forth from New Light to Old Light, but from May '61 on it was completely New Light with Lyman and Samuel Bishop elected eight times in a row. In May 1764, the grip was broken, and Whiting and a prominent Old Light merchant, Enos Alling, were chosen for a single term. October 1764 saw the return of the New Lights in the persons of Bishop and one Roger Sherman. They continued to represent the town till Sherman was elected to the Council in the October upset of '66, when Lyman filled his place in the lower house, Lyman and Bishop remaining in office for many sessions after.[8] Sherman had given up his New Milford seat in the Assembly after May 1761, and also the office of justice of the peace when the term was up in June 1762. However, he soon found his way into New Haven politics; indeed he had most probably laid plans before moving there. His new larger political base was immediately manifest in his nomination for assistant in the fall of 1761, when he ranked seventeenth. Twenty men were nominated every September, and twelve were chosen in April, normally the twelve receiving the largest vote.[9]

It was the infamous Stamp Act of 1765 that really turned the heat on under the still simmering pot. This was the first direct tax ever laid on the colonies; that is, it was the first internal levy designed solely for the purpose

*No relation to Roger.

of raising revenue for the Empire. While the right of Parliament to regulate trade within the Empire was recognized, her right to impose local internal taxes on the colonists was deemed unconstitutional. The colonists held that Parliament did not have the authority to legislate for their internal governments because they were not, and, in view of the distance, could not be represented there. In addition to this theoretical consideration, the Stamp Act seemed intentionally designed to antagonize the most influential members of colonial society. It laid taxes on newspapers, legal documents, and ships' papers, thus incurring the wrath of journalists, lawyers, and the commercial class. The uproar that resulted throughout the seaboard colonies was enormous, and in Connecticut it was the flame that brought the political pot to a boil.

Sherman was prominent in neither the theological nor the Susquehannah fight at this time, but entered the colonial squabbles with the impending passage of the Stamp Act. The first official action of the Assembly in this regard was to elect a committee, of which Sherman was chairman, to consider what measures ought to be taken to prevent the imposition of "Stamp Duties and other Internal Taxes." The committee was balanced with conservatives such as David Rowland of Ridgefield and Ebenezer Silliman of Fairfield, and the strongest measure it could recommend was an instruction to the colony's agents at Westminster to take every step they could to prevent passage of the Act. These instructions to Jared Ingersoll and Richard Jackson explicitly stated the Assembly's confidence in Ingersoll, already suspected by some of insufficient patriotism.*[10] Despite the best efforts of Ingersoll and other agents such as Benjamin Franklin, the odious act became law in 1765.

Ingersoll, on the advice of Franklin, accepted the position of Stamp Agent for Connecticut, a mortal blunder, but the vehemence of the opposition to the Act in America had not been anticipated by anyone on the English side of the Atlantic. Opposition to the Act, however, was overwhelming. Throughout the summer and early fall of 1765 the radicals, especially in the eastern part of the colony, had been organizing furiously. Fiery letters had been sent off to the papers and Jared Ingersoll, the now

---

*Ingersoll was in England not only on his colony's behalf. He was also attempting to get a vice-admiralty court established in Connecticut as a lever to control the lucrative business of supplying masts to the Royal Navy. He failed at the project, but the stampmastership was a worthy consolation prize. It paid £8 for every £100 of stamps sold. In 1768 Parliament established vice-admiralty courts for Boston, Charleston, and Philadelphia. Ingersoll was appointed judge of the last. Jensen, *Foundation*, ps. 61, 65, 228.

despised Stamp Agent, was burned in effigy in the eastern towns of New London, Norwich, Lebanon, and Windham. But the leadership of the radical movement was not monopolized by rabble-rousers. It consisted in part of some of the most respectable men in the colony. William Williams, Jonathan Trumbull, Eliphalet Dyer,* the various Huntingtons, Hugh Ledlie, Colonel Israel Putnam, and Major John Durkee led the mobs in the east. This mob pressure paid off in two specific actions. First, the resignation of Ingersoll was forced by a crowd of over a thousand men on horse and foot. Then a special session of the General Assembly was called by conservative Governor Fitch of Norwalk, a session forced by mobs led by the very respectable Jonathan Trumbull, later to be governor himself.[11]

The situation in New Haven was politically tense. The hotheads like Benedict Arnold and the conservatives like Ingersoll and Thomas Darling were at each other's throats. The moderates, Sherman, David Wooster, and others had but a tightrope to walk. Professor Napthali Daggett wrote to the *Gazette* calling for noncooperation with the Agent and in anticipation of Ingersoll's return one anonymous writer declared "A little Time will bring Matters to a Crisis and oblidge every Man to take his Side. We shall then see Who is Who." Even Ingersoll said in the *Gazette* that he wished the people would think more about getting rid of the Act and less about getting rid of the Agent.[12]

Meanwhile, plans were made to use the bumper crop of currants to make wine "as good as Lisbon," and enough extra to sell to the college men so they would not have to import.** Married couples, carried beyond reason by the patriotic hysteria, swore absolute abstention from sex until the Act was no more.

It was said in town the meetinghouse bell tolled "Nov-em-ber." Canny Roger Sherman, who missed nothing, took note of the anti-importation talk and put in an order in October for goods from New York valued at over £2082, very much larger than his usual purchase. Though this was not paid off until 1771, he did better than most New Haven merchants, who were

---

*It is tempting to speculate on the importance of family connections here: Trumbull was father-in-law to Williams, who was brother-in-law to Dyer, who was father-in-law to Trumbull's son, Joseph. Neither Dyer nor Joseph Trumbull liked Williams personally, so one can continue to speculate whether political association was stronger than marital.

**"To make currant wine: 1 part strained current juice; 1 part water; 3 lbs. brown sugar per gallon of mixture. Stand in a cask for eight to ten months."

indebted to Yorkers to the extent of £20,000 sterling by 1774.* Sherman advertised his New York order in August 1766 when he offered 5 percent off for every purchase over twenty shillings at both the Wallingford and New Haven branches—and all sales cash.[13]

A special session of the Assembly was finally called for September 19. Sherman was elected deputy at a New Haven freemen's meeting on the 17th at which particular instructions were voted. The New Haven meeting was a hot one, but the townsfolk were unanimous in their view that the Stamp Act must be repealed. Sparks flew, however, when Ingersoll, who was present, was called upon to resign immediately. One freeman protested that this was unnecessary in view of the colony's efforts to bring about repeal, and Ingersoll himself rose to say he would do nothing until he had been to Hartford to get the view of the Assembly. This was clearly a delaying action, for there was no doubt of the Assembly's mind on the matter.[14]

Many deputies had been specifically instructed by their town meetings, and in New Haven Sherman had drawn up instructions that were adopted by the meeting, binding him and his fellow delegate, Samuel Bishop. "As the Parliament of Great Britain," he wrote,

> have lately passed an Act for imposing and collecting certain Stamp Duties in this and the other American Colonies which if carried into Execution will be very Grievous to his majestyes Loyal subjects in Said Colonies,
>
> 1. In that it will impose a Tax upon them without their consent by themselves or Representatives
>
> 2. That it will occasion much trouble and Embarrasment in transacting their affairs
>
> 3. That is not so equitable a way of raising money as their ordinary way of taxing
>
> 4. That it extends the Jurisdiction of the Court of Admiralty in the Colonies in that it subjects them to prosecutions in that Court for any supposed breaches of the Stamp Act or any other Revenue Act and so deprives them of the priviledge of Tryal by a Jury, and that herein the Colonists are distinguished from their fellow subjects in great Brittain
>
> And what necessity can there be for these extraordinary measures?
>
> Are not the Americans as Loyal as any of the Kings Subjects?

---

*Sherman's New York importer was James Jauncy, later arrested as a Tory. NHCHS, "Sherman Papers," (Daybook, February 1771); Becker, *Political Parties in New York*, p. 264, 264n.

Did not this Colony and the other Northern Colonies whose Forces Acted in conjection in the late war readily and chearfully exert themselves in raising men & money for his majesties service persuant to his Majesty's Requisitions?

And will not a principle of Self Preservation, and a sense of Duty and Allegiance to their King who is the safe guardian of their Liberties always be sufficient Inducement to a Loyal and Free People chearfully to Tax themselves when ever it appears necessary for their own Defence or for the support of government?[15]

The Assembly chose Windham's radical Eliphalet Dyer, moderate William S. Johnson of Stratford and David Rowland of conservative Ridgefield—east, center and west—to represent Connecticut at a Stamp Act Congress in New York. But always suspicious and provincial, the deputies and councillors ordered their delegates "to form no such junction with the other Commissioners as will subject you to the major vote of the commissioners present," and report fully to the Assembly for "acceptance and approbation." Johnson especially was a happy choice, and he played a major role at New York as principal author of the remonstrance to the king. He was able to write James Otis at Boston shortly after that the Connecticut Assembly had approved the measures of the Congress: "Even *due Subordination* passed. They were not indeed in this respect as well as in some others, perfectly such as they would have wished, but a union of the Petitioning Colonies, even in language as well as sentiment, wás justly thought of more importance than mode of expression or elegance of diction." The Connecticut Assembly, he reported, considered sending him back to England with instructions "to insist upon the right of the Colonies to tax themselves and the privilege of trial by jury, as principles which we cannot depart from." But instead it limited itself to incorporating these views in new instructions to agent Richard Jackson. Ezra Stiles was able to record on October 24, 1765, "Connect Assembly Lower house passed Resolves agt. Stamp Act; full house, only five dissenting Votes, viz. Messrs. Seth Wetmore, Thos. Fitch, Junr., Mr. Platt, Mr. Glover & Dr. Gale. The house consists of about 130 members."[16]

At the regular October session the lower house consisted of 132 members, but three from Hartford County did not attend. Of these, fifty-five were new, New Haven, New London and Windham counties seeing half their deputies replaced. The aroused legislature made a last-ditch attempt to forestall the Act's operation. A petition was drawn up by a committee on which Sherman served, and at the same time a set of instructions was sent to Richard Jackson, Connecticut's agent in London.[17]

The petition was more moderate in tone than some of those offered by other distressed colonies, but it was firm enough. It began with a preamble claiming that the Stamp Act tended "to deprive us of the most interesting, important and essential . . . rights, which we hold most dear and cannot on any possible considerations be induced willingly to depart with . . . ," so it was deemed a duty to make known the legislative sentiments. In eleven numbered paragraphs the committee spelled out its case against the obnoxious act. The colonists were faithful to the king, and had enriched his domains by their diligence and hard work; they had the same rights of self-taxation as any Englishmen, and had not given their consent to the Act in question; they were governed by their own assembly as had always been recognized by the King and Parliament; the new act was different from previous ones because it disposed of their property without their consent; and placing the administration of the Stamp Act under the Admiralty Courts took away "one of the most darling rights," that of trial by jury; they would "cheerfully" at any time give their lives and treasures for the king; and finally the best basis for the well-being of the colony was union with Great Britain, and the best basis for union was respect for and practice of the ancient modes of government.[18]

The same committee drew up instructions for Jackson that paralleled the petition; the Stamp Act "is inconsistent with the principles and spirit of the British constitution, and an infringement of the essential liberties of the colonists . . . ." Jackson was ordered to "firmly insist upon the exclusive right of the Colonies to tax themselves, and the privilege of tryal by jury." He was to prefer and support the petition with his utmost ability and vigor. The instructions to Jackson were not dissimilar from some that had been drawn up by a New Haven town meeting in September calling on her deputies, among them Sherman, to exert themselves to obtain repeal of the Stamp Act. Since Sherman had drawn up these New Haven instructions, the similarity may not have been coincidental. However, instructions from all the towns were much the same, so that no especial innovation can be attributed to the New Haven delegate. Appointment to this committee, an important assignment, was a mark of Sherman's prominence in the Assembly.[19]

The opposition to the Stamp Act was furious; Ingersoll reported the colony "in a great ferment." In New London the port collector was forced by mob action to clear ships without stamped paper, and "throughout eastern Connecticut the people demanded that the courts and lawyers immediately resume their business and ignore the legal requirements about the use of stamps." Indeed, a "treaty" was signed by eastern Connecticut Sons of Liberty promising "military aid" to New York Sons in case of attack by British soldiers. The western part of the colony was much less vehement, but New Haven closed down all judicial actions that required stamps, and kept them closed until the third Tuesday in June of 1766, even after the Act had been repealed. The customs house, however, opened in January and cleared ships without stamps, though a Fairfield ship returned from Barbados in May with its manifest stamped, much to the disgust of the *Gazette* editors.[20]

The Sons of Liberty, grown up during the crisis under the leadership of Ledlie, Durkee, and Putnam, military leaders and idols of the people, took over the effective government in most of the eastern part of the colony.[21] In October, 1765, Stiles had reported that three-fourths of the men were "ready to take up Arms for their Liberties . . . very Boys as well as the hardy Rustic . . . full of fire and at half a Word ready to fight," and now they took over. A number of unofficial conventions of dubious legality were held protesting the stamps. The one in Lyme, termed by Benjamin Gale the "Babel Convention," was, he said, attended by "several Pimps, Smugglers to Gull the Rabble & sift out everything that passes from Head Quarters." A Wallingford body published a list of preferred names for the nomination to the Council. It was a moderate, perhaps even a conservative list, omitting for instance William Williams and Jonathan Trumbull while including Benjamin Hall and Jabez Hamlin. Sherman was included, eleventh on the list, and he ranked ninth in the number of votes received in that conservative and anti-Susquehannah town. And a convention in Hartford of Sons of Liberty set up a Committee of Correspondence consisting of Israel Putnam, John Durkee, Hugh Ledlie, Thaddeus Burr, Jonathan Sturges, Samuel Bradley, Jr., John Brooks, and LeGrand Cannon. Inevitably the influence of the Sons of Liberty soon began to sweep into the western counties. Effigies were burned, suspected stampmen were tarred and feathered, and Ingersoll's mail was broken into and published in edited and altered form.[22]

Sherman's attitude was in keeping with the political situation in his own constituency. On January 11, 1766, he wrote half a thousand words on the situation to Matthew Griswold, member of the Council from Lyme.[23] The passing and publishing of resolves by "great numbers of people Assembling and assuming a kind of legislative authority," he considered "a little extraordinary," and feared that they might be "prejudicial to the interests of the Colony."

> Will not the frequent assembling such large bodies of people, without any laws to regulate or govern their proceedings, tend to weaken the authority

of the government, and naturally possess the minds of the people with such lax notions of civil authority as may lead to such disorders and confusions as will not be easily suppressed or reformed?

After all, Connecticut's government is "one of the happiest and best in the world," so why jeopardize it? But Sherman was a politician, so he continued,

I have no doubt of the upright intentions of those gentlemen who have promoted the late meetings in several parts of the Colony, which I suppose were principally intended to concert measures to prevent the introduction of the Stamp Papers, and not in the least to oppose the laws of authority of the government.

But there was a danger in going too far and jeopardizing the Charter privileges. Perhaps with Ingersoll's resignation such meetings would be considered needless. Sherman's stand on the opening of the ex-Stamp Agent's mail to England faced two ways, too; he was distressed that the letters were opened, but glad that the erstwhile Stamp Agent had promised not to write anything more "but what should be inspected and approved by persons that the people of the government would confide in. . . ."

How to deal with the Stamp Act once it had become a *fait accompli* created the most vexatious situation for the New Haven moderates. The radicals wanted to go right ahead with all business and legal matters just as if the Act had never been passed. The *Gazette* reported:

We hear that a person in a neighboring government lately refusing to pay a debt for which he was attached, because the writ was not on stamped paper; the populace immediately passed the three following votes, and resolve, viz. Vote 1. That this man is not a Christian Vote 2. That he ought to be of some Religion Therefore, 3dly, Voted That he be a Jew Whereupon, Resolved, That he be circumcised.

This resolution so terrified the poor chreature, that he begged forgiveness for his improvidence. . . .

The sentence was remitted and the erstwhile Jew was dismissed, mercy being a tempering force even among the rabid, and in this case probably drunken, Sons of Liberty. After all, Benedict Arnold pointed out, the Stamp Act ran against the principles of Magna Carta and so could be ignored in good conscience. The conservatives were for closing the courts until the Act was repealed. What was a moderate to do?[24]

A New Haven town meeting was called on February 3, 1766 to deal with the question. The high point of radical strength had been reached the previous December, when conservative Thomas Howell was released from being a selectman. But by now the county court had not done business since October 22. It met regularly, but adjourned without day each time, the same docket continuing from November to June. The justices of the quorum were conservatives Thomas Darling and John Hubbard, an enemy of long standing to Clap and his cabal, and moderates Elihu Chauncy and Sherman, but Sherman did not attend the adjourned meetings from late October to April.[25]

In the meantime, things had gotten out of hand. Benedict Arnold was playing the radical rabble-rouser in New Haven. As a shopkeeper and merchant, Arnold had engaged in considerable illegal trade with the French West Indies, as was so common at the time. One Peter Bolles, a sailor in Arnold's employ, attempted to inform on Arnold as a matter of spite. He was found out and stripped, tied to a post, and given "near forty Lashes with a small cord" by a mob led by his master. This affair outraged the respectable element in town, and Sherman as justice of the peace issued a warrant for Arnold's arrest. The rowdies were tried and Bolles was given fifty shillings damages, though Sherman managed to avoid the trial, which was presided over by Enos Allen and David Wooster. Arnold had good fun with the matter and wrote the *Gazette*:

QUERY. Is it good policy; or would so great a Number of People, in any trading Town on the Continent (New-Haven excepted) vindicate, protect and caress an Informer—a Character, particularly at this alarming Time, so justly odious to the Public?

Every *such* Information tends to supress our Trade, so advantageous to the Colony, and to almost every Individual both here and in Great-Britain and which is nearly ruined by the late detestable Stamp and other oppressive Acts—Acts which we have so severly felt, so loudly complained of, and so earnestly remonstrated against, that one would imagine every sensible man would strive to encourage Trade and discountenance such useless, such infamous Informers.

The collectors answered, somewhat ingenuously, that no such illicit trade existed in any considerable degree. Besides, they protested—for the record at least—every Master swears to the accuracy of his manifest and posts a £1000 bond to back up his word.[26]

The February town meeting, moderated by Colonel John Hubbard, drew a crowd of 274; all but one, reported the *Gazette*, were clear on the unconstitutionality of the Stamp Act. But on the main question, whether the courts should proceed as usual, but without stamps, the vote was 226 to 48. This meeting seems to have been called by the Sons of Liberty, pretty much the same people who had been involved in the whipping of Bolles. A resolution drawn up and easily passed read:

. . . for several months past there has been a total suspension of the laws in Civil and Probate matters in this Colony . . . Officers . . . having (for some reason) wholly declined proceeding therein . . . which will involve the people in great difficulties . . . . the respective officers . . . are hereby requested to proceed in and transact the usual business of such Courts in the usual and accustomed manner agreeable to the laws of this Colony.

The affirmative vote—to go ahead with business as though the Stamp Act had never been passed—was the radical position. However, the report in the *Gazette* claimed that all judges and justices of the peace voted that way. Oddly enough, then, the radicals looked to the reopening of the courts to vindicate their position, and they urged full compliance with colonial law and order.[27]

On the other hand, the conservatives, afraid to act without stamps, but powerless to obtain them, justified their vote to keep the courts closed with agrarian-oriented argument. A petition was already on its way to the king from the Stamp Act Congress, they said, and a delay will give debtors—of which there are many industrious ones—more time to raise money; and real estate values will collapse because of the uncertainty of deeds without stamps. Besides, "If there be a number in this interval damnified, by the stagnation of their business, let them look at the general good, and live by hope as other Christians do." That the conservatives were aligned with the agrarian debtor group was recognized by a respondent who suggested that the writer above "does not here seem to have an equal Regard to the Interest and Good of the Creditor, as to that of the Debtor." And a year later John Devotion pointed out that the conservative defeat in the fall elections came about because "The Old Lights are not awake yet; Multitudes will not leave their Plow to have a Govr. to their Taste." The *Gazette* declared editorially that the colonial legislatures were competent in all cases, Parliament having no right to act over them at all, an advanced position, indeed.[28]

Three weeks after the meeting, however, the *de facto* compromise that had been operating continued as the court sat to hear criminal cases only. A report from radical New London told of ships clearing the customs house with unstamped certificates, and of justices and lawyers going about their business "in the usual way." W.S. Johnson wrote a Massachusetts friend: "The Stamp paper is not yet come into the Colony, but we are very generally agreed to submit to all the inconveniences of a total stagnation of business rather than admit the Act: indeed many are for proceeding in everything as usual, and taking no notice at all of it, but I fancy we shall lie still for the present."[29] The Stamp Act was repealed by Parliament in March, and on April 10 the news arrived in New Haven, but was skeptically received. Meanwhile, most Connecticut towns passed resolutions against the Act, and the view became widely disseminated and probably widely held, that Parliament had no power to legislate for Connecticut at all. When on May 19 official word of repeal came, New Haven burst out with bells, bonfires, dances, and militia exercises directed by Colonel David Wooster, all, the *Gazette* reported, "without any remarkable Indecency or Disorder."[30]

The Election of '66

It was under these explosive conditions that the April elections for the Council were held. The movement to dump the conservative, Old Light councillors had been launched over half a decade before, of course, when President Clap of Yale had been leading the internecine consociation battles of the late fifties. The New Lights had kept the pressure on, and finally in 1766, with the Stamp Act controversy, they had their winning issue. The Stamp Act required the governor and superior magistrates to take an oath to carry out its provisions. This was the crucial act in the drama of Connecticut's political tumult. Assenting to such an oath would be sure political death, yet the forces of conservatism still had strong leaders. Though opposition to the Act had been unanimous before its passage, many believed that once passed it must be obeyed. Governor Thomas Fitch in the eleventh year of his incumbency was one of these stalwarts, and so were four of the twelve assistants.

Though the Stamp Act was the cause around which Connecticut's dynamic political leadership rallied the people, the defeat of the Governor's party was engineered by the old New Light forces that had come to control the county consociations and the lower house. In 1765 Fitch had published a thirty-nine-page pamphlet attempting to show the limits of consociation authority, while at the same time supporting the Saybrook Platform, which established the presbyterian system in Connecticut. The Governor had to be the focus of the New Light drive, even if he had not laid himself open to attack on the Stamp issue. The authority, claimed Fitch, was not judicial, not binding. The consociation councils, charged the beleaguered Governor, "pretend to act judicially or to claim a judicial authority, out of character, and contrary [to] that plan upon which they are formed." This tyrannical approach, indeed, was the principal reason why associations were leaving the consociation.

> From the foregoing considerations, it also appears, that all attempts to support and vindicate the judicial authority of councils and to maintain, that their determinations are binding on the consciences of men, by virtue of the authority of such councils, are attempts to subvert the constitution

of the churches; to deprive them and their several members of their just rights, and to cause their faith to rest on human authority.[31]

Fitch's arguments were answered by Thomas Clap's loyal Yale Fellow, Noah Hobart, in a pamphlet published in New Haven later that year, 1765. John Hubbard wrote his son-in-law Ezra Stiles:

> The Stamp Act has drawn a gloom over every Face, and sowered the Temper of not a few, and all that don't run the extravagant Length of a giddy and distracted Mob are looked upon as Enemies to their Countrey and Betrayers of its Liberties. Among other fine Devices to set People together by the ears a Man's religious Principles are made the Test or shall I rather say badge of his political Creed. An Arminian, and a Favourer of the Stamp Act signify the same Man; think then what a Situation some of your Friends are [in].[32]

In March the Sons of Liberty held a colony-wide convention at Hartford, where explicit announcement was made that a change in government would be beneficial. Despite the opposition of delegates from Litchfield and New Haven counties, a list of Council nominees was drawn up "to give the Freemen a Lead in the ensuing Election . . . ." They agreed to support the moderates, a deal that Stiles believed to have been brought about by William S. Johnson.

> Dr. Johnson a Lawyer politically became a Son of Liby. was sent to the [Stamp Act] Congress. They struck a Bargain with the Sons of Liby. that they would as a Body vote for the Eastern Interest, if they would take Johnson into the Council. By this Stratagem he got 2000 Votes, which adds to 1000 of Episco. Votes & the Western Votes bro't him in. He was the first Episcopalian ever bro't into the Council in Connecticutt.

William Pitkin was set up to oppose Fitch and Benjamin Gale claimed that he counted up to twenty Pitkin votes put into the ballot box in rolls to look like one. Clearly, the defeat of Fitch's faction was brought about not only by the skillful use of the Stamp issue, but also by political techniques not wholly approved of at the time. Aside from outright intimidation and extralegal secret conventions, the New Lights also used "packet voting": ballots listing less than twelve names, thus giving favored candidates a relative numerical advantage. Indeed, the participants in the Hartford caucus had picked only eight names and limited their ballots to those. But either those methods or the stratagem outlined by Stiles, or a combination of both, worked. The rout was complete; not one conservative councillor was saved, and Pitkin replaced the Old Light favorite, Thomas Fitch. The *Gazette* and other papers are so full of controversy mixing the questions Stamps and consociation authority so thoroughly that it becomes clear that the overthrow of Fitch was not *fundamentally* a matter of the former.[33]

It was, rather, as a correspondent to the *Courant* put it, merely "a plausible Handle to raise a popular Outcry against [Fitch] and some others." Thus the objectives of the New Light-mercantile faction, stated as far back as 1759 by Chauncey Whittelsey as the removal of Fitch, Newton, Silliman, Burr, Chester, Wolcott, Edwards, and Hamlin were completed in 1766. The conservatives were crushed, and old John Devotion wrote to Newport, R.I., from Saybrook, deep in radical territory that he thought there would be no quiet in Connecticut "till we have a King in Person." The charter itself was endangered, Devotion quoted Richard Jackson from London, because of the tumults in the two self-governing colonies.[34]

Sherman was elevated to the Council in this election along with Johnson, Joseph Spencer, William Pitkin, Abraham Davenport, and Jabez Huntington. In addition, Jonathan Trumbull became lieutenant governor. Tradition directed that Sherman also be appointed a Judge of the Superior Court, an office he held concurrently with those of justice of the quorum for New Haven County, and justice of the peace for New Haven. He remained in the Council for nineteen years.

In most respects Sherman was typical of members of the Connecticut upper house. Normally election occurred before the age of fifty: he was forty-five. This election saw a great increase in men who were primarily merchants rather than lawyers: this was the case with Sherman. Assistants traditionally were men of considerable wealth: measured in terms of land holdings, Sherman was near the colony apex. A long apprenticeship in local and colony judicial, executive, and legislative office was a must: Sherman had been active since 1749, the year of his first appointment as grand juryman. Though most were Yale or Harvard graduates, many were not: Sherman was an honorary Yale M.A., treasurer of the college, and self-educated lawyer. In one important respect, however, he differed. The typical assistant was at least fourth-generation Connecticut, and to a man they were born among its rocky hills. Sherman, of course, was neither, nor did he possess the family connections normally found at this highest level of the political pyramid. Political leadership seems to be the prime explanation for his rise to power, though it could not have been accomplished without the accompanying accumulation of wealth.[35]

Sherman ran true to form. He was moderate and politic. His attitude was conservative without too strongly condemning the actions of the most extreme radicals. However, New Haven, his constituency, was neither radical nor conservative, but about evenly divided. It was a difficult situation for a popular representative, and Sherman tried to work out a position that would be both logical and politic. He was affected, of course, by a sort of colonial political insecurity that saw in every British action the threat of tyranny. John Dickinson was to write two years later that the question was "not, what evil *has actually attended* particular measures—but, what evil, in the nature of things *is likely* to attend them." Sherman was already on guard. Early in December of 1766 he wrote William Samuel Johnson, his old legal mentor:

> I have sent the Newspapers you spake of by the Post. Since that paper was published this Question hath been proposed to me viz, Does not the King hold his Dominions in Great Britain & America by the Same Title i e whether he is not King of America by virtue of his being King of Great Britain, and if so how are they distinct Dominions? There is no doubt but that the Colonies are bound by the present Establishment of the Crown, as they have consented to it Sworn Allegiance etc But Quare If the Succession according to the present Establishment Should cease for want of an Heir or if the Parliament should alter it and admit a Papist to the Crown would not the Colonies be at Liberty to joyn with Brittain or not
>
> These Questions may Serve for Speculation but it is not likely they will need to be Resolved in our Day, and I hope not till the time comes when the Nations Shall learn War no more.[36]

Almost a decade after this time Sherman told John Adams that he had believed in 1766 that Parliament had no right to legislate for the colonies at all. Such legislation as had been effectuated was merely acquiesced in on the basis of the implied consent of the colonists. Most colonists in 1766 would give Parliament legislative powers at least by consent, though always excluding taxation. Sherman in 1774 indicated that he had always disapproved Parliamentary legislative authority. There is no evidence, however, that he was clear in his mind about the distinctions between legislation by consent or by right; or taxation, internal and external, in 1766. Nevertheless he appears well ahead of most colonial opinion on the question of provincial self-government.[37]

The Aftermath

The Old Lights as "outs" were every bit as persistent as the radicals had been and tried hard for a comeback in the spring of 1767. Fitch, in 1764, had published a pamphlet against the Stamp Act, using the customary arguments of usage, charter, and the rights of British subjects as ardently and cogently as any. In 1766 he had again broken into print explaining the action of the four displaced councillors. "Every Governor or Councillor are bound," he wrote, "not only by their Allegiance, but by their office, and in the present Case also, by Agreement or Contract, by accepting their Offices to which the aforesaid Commission is annexed, to yield Obedience to the Requirements of the King and Parliament." Royal appointees failing to take the oath would merely be replaced by the king, but in Connecticut the people would be deprived of their right of electing officers, "and then the whole Charter would at once be struck up."[38] It is true that there was no statute law superior to the act requiring the oath of locally elected officials, but common law would have put the councillors at the king's mercy. Fitch seems clearly to have been mousetrapped by the Stamp Act. Certainly he opposed it and swore the oath only in what he saw as the long-term interest of the colony in maintaining its charter.

In February 1767 the *Gazette* published a series of very long letters on the consociation question; the geographical division of the colony east and west of the Connecticut River was once again emphasized. A satirical report showed that forty-four towns on the west side of the river contributed over one million pounds in colony taxes, while the twenty-eight towns to the east sent in less than £565 thousand. But at the same time the west had seven major magistries (governor, councillors, and superior court judges), while the east held twelve—a gross overrepresentation. "God knows," wrote Plain Truth to the *Gazette*, "we have had Distinctions enough already—Calvinism and Arminianism, have for several Years lost their theological Meaning, and have been used mostly in a political Sense. . . . But if in Addition to this, the Great River is to be the Boundary of two contending Parties, we shall be in a situation more deplorable." Further acrimony was published through March and April in which factions were deplored, eastern towns were accused of sending in more votes than they had freemen; easterners were accused of bullet voting, admitted it, and westerners were urged to use the same tactic.[39]

The main thrust of the argument was that the deposed councillors should be put back in office; no "Man of real Worth and Merit, will be willing to be made the *Tennis Ball* of a Faction." How will good men be persuaded to take public office if they can be put in and out at will by a "few designing politicians." Factious politics must be undone. The development of factions over the past thirty years had been brought about by a small group of schemers who first used the Spanish Ship case to change government, then, using "some new designing and crafty men," tried to throw off Fitch. This time they were aided by many other honest persons, "unwarily drawn in by the *Stamp Act*, to make a more vigerous Attempt, and at one *Push* to *thrust* out the late Governor Fitch and Four of our most respectable Counsellors." The only real question, wrote an anonymous correspondent on April 11, is

"Whether the old Ministry shall be brought in at the next Election, or the new continued?" John Devotion thought they would be: "Tis generally thot," he wrote from his eastern seat at Saybrook, "that Mess. Silliman & Hamlin at least will have a Resurrection; some have stronger Faith, and believe in John Chester & Benj. Hall." [40]

The election pulled about nine thousand of the colony's usually apathetic freemen to the polls—about two-thirds of the eligible voters. "We are so emerg'd in Politicks of the Rhode Island Kind of Parliamentering," wrote Gale, "that I fear the peace & happiness of the Gov't. is at an End unless we will submit to be rul'd by N. Lights, in whose Integrity we have not the least dependence, and who commonly judge Men, & not the Cause. . . ." If it was true that the agrarian yeomanry were largely in the conservative camp, then this election should show it. But Pitkin received 4777 votes to Fitch's 3481, and none of the Old Light councillors was returned, though one correspondent wrote that all had been sent by their towns to the lower house. Stiles' analysis showed a geographic division of radical east and conservative west with the western Anglicans supporting the eastern party.* The main beneficiaries of the vote were central moderates, Sherman, Johnson, and the other assistants elected the previous year. Sherman's vote was topped only by Pitkin and the future governor Griswold; he pulled almost a thousand more than the popular Jonathan Trumbull, Connecticut's Revolutionary governor. This was the best he ever did. New Haven sent Bishop and Lyman to the lower house, but it was a tight situation. "Col. Hubbard wanted but *two votes* of a choice; but," wrote Dr. Gale:

> After all our paper War, Squibs, Curses, Rhimes &c I am not yet satisfied Govr. Fitch will be chosen, however he has a large majority on ye West Side C——t River, even N. Haven have done it. Coll. Hubbard wanted but 2 votes of a Choice, but N. Light St——Act, & Satan hindered. Strange it is that such a Town as N.H. should be infatuated by such an Empty thing as Dr. Lyman when Coll Hubbard, Darling, Ingersol, & a Number of others, are among the living.

Hubbard, indeed, was elected moderator of town meetings in April and December 1767, and continued so throughout the next two years until replaced by the equally conservative Thomas Darling on Christmas Day, 1769. [41]

---

*The Reverend John Beach wrote from Newtown that the Anglicans there constituted a majority of the voters, "which is the first instance of this kind in this colony if not in all New England." Shepard, "Tories," p. 141.

Among the conservatives, of course, disgruntlement was intense. Under the name of Algernon Sidney* one conservative wrote, "When men of unblemished Reputation are turned out of Places of Trust and Profit, in which they have conducted themselves without Exception or Accusation; for no other Cause but to make Room for Others who are tools of those in Power . . . one main Support of Liberty is undermined . . . ." It is tyrannical, he continued, to displace such men with "Flatterers, Sycophants, and even a Fool . . . and we find it difficult to exculpate Some, whose Honesty has made the chief part of their Character in recommending them to their Constituents . . ." for putting friends, regardless of worth, in office, "judging themselves unsafe until all their rivals are out of office." The reference to honesty in all probability applies to Sherman, whose reputation for that quality was strong. And from the extreme right John Devotion wrote to Ezra Stiles, "Faction is encreasing in this Gov. and I never expect it will be laid among us or you . . . till we have a Kings Govr., ney till we have a King in Person, and are like other People."[42]

In Connecticut the American War for Independence brought with it no internal political revolution. The little republic was ahead of her sister colonies, her political upset taking place in 1766. There was always a certain amount of dynamism in Connecticut politics, and the Stamp Act crisis served as a catalyst to push to the top men who had been struggling just below the surface for positions of influence and esteem. In 1762 when Eliphalet Dyer was elected to the Council, he served as the "first harbinger of the ascendency in Connecticut politics which the Susquehannah Company was soon to enjoy." This marked the beginning of the moderate radical takeover. By 1766 the only Old Lights remaining on the Council were Chester, Silliman, Hamlin, and, of course, Governor Fitch. These men went out, and new blood came in, including Sherman, and at the same time there was a turnover of half the members of the lower house.[43]

This was as near as eighteenth-century Connecticut ever came to a political revolution, and Sherman, moderate as he was, stands as its archetype. He was the only member of the Council at that time—and probably for many decades before—not born in Connecticut, and one of the few who were not graduates of Yale. This was not a class revolution. Members of old families are found on both sides. It was a contest more of political temperament, though popular support for the radicals consisted largely of the

---

*A seventeenth-century British martyr to legal trial whose "Discourses Concerning Government" had been published four years earlier.

people from the overcrowded and poorer east, the area of the ancient land bank scheme and the emotional New Lights. Led by such men as Eliphalet Dyer and William Williams and feeding on the traditional resentments against the established, conservative Old Light powers, the rising group took control. But this new alignment managed to include most of the old established families. The earliest traces of an agrarian-mercantile division are visible, but it is only in retrospect that one would think to look for them.

A conservative by temperament, Sherman threw in his lot with the radicals, partly because his only chance for political success lay with them and partly because of his growing conviction that the colonial connection was too restricting for the natural development of the colonies, politically as well as economically. But the choice had not been entirely his. It might be more accurate to say that the radicals chose him, rather than the reverse. His own final political commitment did not come until six years later when the Susquehannah group forced his hand.

Like the alteration in political personnel in the colony as a whole, Sherman's prominence was no sudden occurrence. His election to the upper house was more or less predictable, for he had been creeping up in public esteem ever since he moved to New Haven. The method of election to the Council was to nominate twenty men by open ballot in October, with the highest twelve being officially ratified by a count in the lower house in May. As early as 1761, the first year of Sherman's residence in New Haven, he ranked seventeenth, just below the popular and well-established Eliphalet Dyer. In 1762 and 1763 he was again seventeenth, and in 1764 he stayed in that position. The next year he moved up to the fifteenth position again and upon his election to the lower house was made one of the four justices of the peace of the quorum for New Haven, giving him magisterial duties.[44] In May 1766, he was elected to the Council. His growing popularity is shown by the fact that he polled more votes than any member except Matthew Griswold in the May elections of 1767. His support came mostly from the conservative counties of the west, but with very strong eastern help, as Ezra Stiles reported.

How Sherman was able to maintain his position, let alone establish himself, among the chief politicians of the day in such heated circumstances is wondrous indeed. But the smelting process turned to very durable iron the raw material of his popularity in the colony. Working with a hard core of New Haven moderates and without antagonizing the conservatives, he somehow managed to collect support from both the eastern radicals and the western Old Lights. He was aided by the fact that the radical faction in New

Haven was kept in check by the force of the moderate and conservative element, and he did not have to stand up to them alone.[45] Moderation was the word in New Haven, and a man who could stand committed to neither the left nor the right was in an enviable position. Sherman was such a man, and, though he joined the New Light church, he shrewdly took pains not to become too openly committed to the cabals of either side. Though the Arnold case was originally brought to him, he bound it over to the next court, where it was handled by David Wooster and Enos Allen. These gentlemen levied a token fine of fifty shillings, the whole proceedings being approved by Arnold himself.[46]

The Customs House had been working as usual since the first of the year, so with commercial and criminal cases moving forward without stamps, a compromise seems to have been struck that satisfied both the radicals and the conservatives and put the moderates, though in a minority, in control. New Haven was unusual in this respect, for the radicals seemed to be dominant everywhere else outside Fairfield County.[47]

New Haven's politics were now highly favorable for Sherman. He could promote himself locally without being tagged as a member of either extreme faction; he could then use his New Haven County base as a keystone around which to build accretions of support from the east and west. How much of this was a matter of calculation, and how much the lucky consequence of being uncommitted at the right time and the right place, it is impossible to tell. There is no solid evidence that Sherman engineered his promotion to the Council. He was energetic, ambitious, and that he was among the best politicians operating in Connecticut at the same time seems obvious from his later career.

But all this is circumstantial. What is certain is that Sherman was going through a period of mental tumult, and it is quite possible that he had not made up his mind on the specific questions of Stamps and Courts by 1766. President Timothy Dwight of Yale, who came to know Sherman very well in later years, said of him after his death that "He had no fashionable opinions, and could never be persuaded to swim with the tide. Independent of everything but argument, he judged for himself: and rarely failed to convince others that he judged right."[48] Certainly he had a reputation for independent action, and his own philosophy was based on the autonomy of elected representatives. He may, then, have been genuinely afloat and able honestly to ride both tides. In any event, he emerged on his feet and well ahead of the rest of the crowd.

The Politics of Leadership

R OGER SHERMAN'S rapid rise to political prominence in New Haven was partly the result of his good relationship with Thomas Clap. The careful politician had kept clear of the religious strife that rent Yale College in the early fifties by sending his younger brothers to college in New Jersey. Clearly Clap felt no animosity, and in addition to lending political support, made the merchant treasurer of the college in 1765 and awarded him an honarary M.A. a few years later.

Clap, as usual, needed allies badly. His doctrinal battles over the previous decade, his unusually acrimonious temperament, and finally his arbitrary supervision of the social lives of his students had antagonized large segments of the Connecticut elite. By 1765 the students were determined to run him out of the college. In the opening foray of the final battle eight Yale men, led by Ralph Isaacs and accompanied by some town rowdies, joined at a neighboring tavern and attacked the President's house.* The attackers splintered windows and caused over two hundred pounds of damage to the college. But worse by far was their unintended wounding of Clap, who was cut by flying glass. The prosecution came before Sherman, his first judgment as a new justice of the peace in New Haven. The charge was "unseasonable nightwalking" and the court found the boys guilty of

> riotously assembling themselves together in the night season of the 30th day of July last, with evil intent to disturb the peace of our lord the King—and being so assembled, then and there by force and arms an

---

*Isaacs, an Anglican, was ultimately declared a "dangerous person," and removed to various inland towns during the Revolution. He was in the West Indian trade and was one of Connecticut's very few slavers. *Connecticut Gazette*, June 18, August 6, 1763; Dexter, *Sketches*, II: 699–701.

assault did make; and the mansion house of the President and Fellows of said College for the time being beset; and break the gate of the yard of said mansion house; and with furious violence did throw stones and cattle's horns into the windows thereof, thereby breaking the sashes and glass of said windows, whereby the life and limbs of the President, his family, and also the Fellows of said College then and there being, were greatly endangered, &c.[1]

This was not Sherman's first chore performed for Clap, however. The previous year in April the college had been hit by "violent Vomitings, great Thirst, Weakness in the Extremities and some with Spasims." Eighty-two of the ninety-two students, two tutors and a cook were attacked by these "Symptoms of Poison," and word spread that some recently arrived French Acadians had carried out a plot to wipe out the institution. But Clap was not so easily gulled. He appointed a committee that included Sherman to investigate, and then reported their findings that the disaster was a result of "either some accident, or some strong physic, and not any mortal poyson, put into the Victuals with a Design to bring a Slur upon the provisions made in the Hall."[2]

Sherman's Business Fortunes

During the early sixties Sherman's mercantile business took more and more of his time, and his frequent committee appointments in the Assembly, primarily dealing with finance and taxation, boundary and highway questions, and occasionally legal matters, occupied him too. It is not surprising then, that he should give up his law business in 1764. But he continued to dabble in real estate, though not as much as he had during his speculations on the rapidly falling land prices of the fifties. In 1761 he had opened two stores, one in Wallingford and one in New Haven, and these seemed to be worthwhile, though it is impossible to tell how much of a net profit he made. The New Haven store was located next to Yale, and almost naturally became a gathering place for professors, preachers, and especially politicians.

Sherman's Day Book opens on July 1, 1761, "Being the next day after I moved to New Haven," and continues intermittently to 1772, when he attempted to turn the business over to his eldest son. It indicates that he managed to capture the lucrative account for paper sold by the ream to the publishers of the *Gazette*, Thomas Green and Benjamin Mecom. A large part of his business was in books—not always of a college kind—paper, and sweets for Yale students, who ran up large bills. Sherman even had occasion to dun hapless fathers of a few of the colonial "Yalies." The store was not to be run solely for scholars, however, and the *Connecticut Gazette* for these years contains numerous advertisements of books, cloth, tea, indigo, coffee, and other India and English goods. Money was short and a 5 percent discount was allowed for cash, though Sherman was usually willing to accept country goods instead. He was still plagued by depreciating paper money, and a two-part anonymous essay on the subject appeared in the *Gazette* in June 1767 that echoes Sherman's views of 1756 and is written in the plain, exact style that is characteristic of his work.[3]

After 1760 the home government began to complain so loudly and so often about the illegal trade in provisions with the foreign West Indies that, in 1762, the Connecticut Assembly laid an embargo on grain, flour, beef, and pork in an effort to conform to the imperial system. Not content with these efforts, Parliament passed more stringent restrictions in 1763, and France shut off the important islands of Guadeloupe and Martinique. Though these restrictions slowed the rate of growth of the Connecticut economy, expansion continued. The number of merchants and traders increased, but the over-all mercantile debt of the colony grew also. The period of the sixties was not one of austerity, though cash was very scarce. It seems clear that Connecticut's trade was strongly influenced, if not indeed controlled, by British and French mercantile policy.[4]

Probably the most fundamental objection to British policy was the prohibition against paper money emissions laid on the New England colonies in 1751. Despite this, Ezra Stiles reported that the colony had struck thirteen emissions between 1755 and 1764, but had taxed enough to retire them all by the latter year.* Though colony taxes were paid, local taxes were not. The agrarian majority seems to have had no cash at all. Towns were indebted to the colony government to the extent of some £80,000 in 1765, and the statement by the conservatives at the time of the Stamp Act crisis that "We consider people are generally in debt, and money very scarce" was hardly questioned. The newspapers carried numerous pleas from merchants to their customers to come in and clear their accounts, and announcements that all business would be cash became more common as the decade progressed.[5] One merchant saw "little Business—Less Money," and in Hartford the *Courant* complained, "Our private debts are many and the cries of the needy continually increasing." The conservative Old Lights and agrarians could

---

*They were disguised as bills of credit signed by individual officers of the colony government.

sputter with John Devotion that though "Natural Wealth encreases in our Land greatly . . . Luxury & Pride eternally cry Poverty & bad Times . . . ," but most often heard throughout the colony, declared the *Gazette* editors, was the cry, "THERE IS NO MONEY." [6]

The shortage of circulating medium caused considerable suffering among the mercantile interests of the colony, especially in the principal seaports. In 1768 a London merchant was advised against doing any business with Connecticut. The whole colony was not worth eight hundred pounds, he was told, and her New Haven and New London merchants "were mortgaged to the full to the Bostonians and New Yorkers." The answer to the question raised by a seeming depression concomitant with an expanding economy obviously lies in the colony's unfavorable balance of trade. During the period 1756–74 exports increased from £130,000 to £200,000, but imports went from £75,000 to £250,000, a result apparently of a rise in levels of living during and just after the French and Indian War. Though New Haven was the most prosperous trading town in Connecticut in the decade or so before the war, her merchants owed some £20,000 sterling to the Yorkers. Gale, Trumbull, Arnold, and others were all deep in debt.[7] But Sherman apparently managed to maintain his payments to the wholesalers in these import towns. His account books show frequent clearing of debt by payment of cash and produce, principally the latter, to his suppliers in the larger cities. By 1771 he had even paid in full the account for his eleventh-hour Stamp Act order.

William, Roger's oldest son, took over management of the stores in 1772 and promptly ran them into the ground through bad judgment and worse luck. Coupled with a casualness concerning which pocket he reached into as a Revolutionary regimental paymaster, this spelled disaster for his father. Within a decade after taking over the store, William was bankrupt, and his father had to cover his losses. While the business had been run by its exacting founder, it had made money and paid its debts. Notices appear time and time again in the *Gazette* that "All Persons indebted to the said ROGER SHERMAN are desired to make speedy Payment." And though the income might be in the form of butchering, butter, making wine, or "teaching Betsy," the store was solvent at the close of the Day Book in 1772.[8]

Sherman, evidently with capital to spare, entered on some other speculative ventures. In 1766 and 1767 he financed a potash business that Jesse Leavenworth had started the year before. There is no indication that he made any profit from it, though potash became one of Connecticut's most important exports to New York. He also kept at farming between 1767 and 1771 as an absentee, hiring labor and selling the produce. Again there is no indication of profits or losses.[9]

The Merchants Challenge Parliament

It is during the early New Haven years that Sherman intensified his probing of the colonial connection. Perhaps he was stimulated by discussion at his store or by reading books and pamphlets before they went across his counter, and certainly he was moved by conversations with fellow legislators.* Such intellectual ferment was not taking place in a vacuum. Yeasts from the mother country, in the form of both land claims and taxation, kept the political vat frothing.

In March 1766, Parliament had repealed the Stamp Act, but it also passed the Declaratory Act, asserting its full authority to make laws binding the American colonists in all cases whatsoever. Determined still to make the colonies contribute a share of the cost of their protection in taxes and in provisions and quarters for the Crown's lobsterbacks, Parliament passed the Quartering Act later that year. New York refused full compliance, stalling until June 1767. By then riots and bloodshed had broken out, causing Parliament to suspend New York's legislative powers. Connecticut, not so heavily burdened, had responded less bitterly to the requirement. She permitted 136 troops to be billeted at New Haven, Branford, and Wallingford, but even arch-conservative John Devotion would write, "The Wedge has entered, and I expect Glut upon Glut."[10]

Quartering the lobsterbacks was but a pinprick, however, compared to the saber wound that was to follow in the form of the Townshend Acts. These acts placed import duties on glass, lead, paints, paper, and tea. The idea was to levy taxes disguised as duties. The acts also explicitly confirmed the power of superior court justices to issue writs of assistance, established new vice-admiralty courts, and set up a Board of Commissioners of the Customs directly responsible to the British Treasury Board. Townshend meant business.

The Townshend Acts received royal assent on June 29, 1767, and were to go into effect on November 20, but they had been under discussion since early in the year. The prospect of the new taxes stirred the wrath of Connecticut's yeomanry less than had the Stamp Act, but legislators and politicians all the way from the intellectual Benjamin Gale to the suspicious agrarian William Williams were immediately on guard. By June 10, the Assembly had issued a strong petition, this time to the king, bypassing

---

*Yale itself seems to have been a hotbed of American nationalist Whiggery. While perhaps 25 percent of Connecticut's citizenry held some degree of Loyalist sympathies, only 2.5 percent of Yale's living graduates sided with the Tories in 1776. Louis L. Tucker, "American Colleges as Sources of Pre-Revolutionary Whig Ideology." Columbia University Seminar Paper delivered December 9, 1969.

Parliament. It repeated the argument developed during the controversy over the dead Stamp Act, and emphasized the position of near slavery in which the new act placed the colonials.[11]

The petition, which Sherman helped frame, brought no redress, and the colonists began to organize. Governor Pitkin in a letter to Lord Hillsborough protested that any idea of separation was odious, but hinted at it just the same. Sherman took a similar tack, and in a letter to William Samuel Johnson at London protested the Act and questioned its legality and wisdom. "The Act of Parliament," he wrote on June 25,

> laying Duties on Paper, glass, etc. is esteemed here as unconstitutional as the Stamp Act, and the Application of the moneys to be raised as great a grievance as the Duties themselves—If these regulations are continued I fear they will be very Prejudicial to both countries—I wish the New Parliament may give a favourable turn to affairs—The Colony of Connecticut (as well as Several others) has thought proper to petition the King . . . [no] Colony Assembly on this continent will ever concede that the Parliament has authority to Tax the Colonies and that they will be unanimously agreed to use all legal methods to avoid the payment of such Taxes. Tis a great pity that the Tranquility and Commerce of both Countries should be Interrupted by measures which if executed afford the least prospect of being advantageous to either.

Nevertheless, he covered himself by asking for information concerning the form and method of issuance of the new writs of assistance, since the customshouse officers would probably seek to use them soon. His point of view was common throughout the colonies, Johnson pointed out in a September letter. But, agree as he did with Sherman's objections, the Connecticut agent had to report that the English were universally of the opinion that Parliament could tax the colonies at will, " . . . and many even go so far as to maintain [it] is even treason to deny it. . . ."[12]

At first the colonies, led by Massachusetts, tried nonconsumption as a counter to the new taxes. Eastern Connecticut towns were quick to follow, but New Haven held out. Finally in March 1768, the town meeting urged nonconsumption of such goods as hats, clocks, carriages, furniture, jewelry, and other imports. But it didn't work. Nutmeggers may have deprived themselves of some luxuries, but the merchants continued to fill up their shops with British goods. Something more was needed, and the next logical step was nonimportation.[13] If the strategy worked, it would serve the double purpose of pressuring the mother Parliament into removing the taxes and at the same time would encourage the domestic development of manufactures. Massachusetts and Rhode Island led off in December 1767, and by May of the next year the eastern Connecticut towns of New London, Norwich, and Windham followed. New Haven dragged her feet but finally acted after the May Assembly had encouraged nonimportation by levying a 5 percent duty on goods imported into the colony by nonresidents. And Roger Sherman put on homespun along with the other magistrates of the colony.[14]

The measures taken in New Haven were not strong enough to satisfy the embittered merchants of New York. Led by the intemperate Isaac Sears, who had felt redcoat steel in the riots of '66, the Yorkers petitioned their New Haven counterparts on April 26, 1769, to boycott certain British goods. The Connecticut importers agreed two months later. But still the Yorkers were not satisfied that New Haven was doing all it could in the case. More petitions arrived on July 12 and 27, protesting the landing of English goods at New York by New Haven ships. These two petitions were addressed to "Roger Sherman and other members of the Committee of Merchants of New Haven"; "other members" included such conservatives as John Hubbard and Thomas Howell.*[15]

Sherman was not the principal merchant in town. He neither owned ships nor traded directly with the West Indies, as did others such as Benedict Arnold, for instance. He must have been the man to deal with, then, on the basis of his political leadership in the colonial cause, as a person whose reputation for leadership in the anti-Parliament direction was known outside Connecticut. He was a member of the committee of merchants in New Haven that sought to enforce the nonimportation agreement there, and probably attended the colony-wide meeting of merchants held at Hartford in February 1770 to regularize nonimportation procedures. Enforcement was carried out efficiently by committees of inspection, by threats, by public exposure in the press, and by public embarrassment at town meetings. "I dare not receive" English goods, wrote one merchant, "for my house and them would certainly be Burnt Down;" and William Williams thought that importation, if discovered, would "prove fatal to [any merchant's] Station."[16]

---

*The New York signatories were Isaac Sears, Isaac Low, Samuel Verplanck, and Thomas Franklin, Jr. Sears had earlier negotiated the 1766 "treaty" with eastern Connecticuters. That earliest pressure for nonimportation came from inland eastern towns lends support to the interpretation of Merrill Jensen. Jensen argues that nonimportation was proposed by nonmercantile popular leaders and only reluctantly accepted by leading merchants. Connecticut's experience was not identical to that of other colonies, because she imported only indirectly through Boston, Newport, and New York. However, the picture developed in the account above would seem to support Jensen's view. Jensen, *Founding*, ps. 265, 265n, pf. 266.

But with the partial repeal of the Townshend Acts and finally the failure of the Yorkers to enforce the agreement there, Connecticut merchants began to get slack. Meetings were organized throughout the colony in an attempt to keep nonimportation alive. New Haven held one in July, and the Committee there wrote to the merchants at Wethersfield and Hartford. The document was signed first by Sherman and then by five other members.* It began, "The time is now come for us to determine whether we will be freemen or slaves, or in other words—whether we will tamely coalesce with the measures of our backsliding brethren of New York . . . ." who have decided on importation. "There is no time to lose"; we can buy from Boston without having to deal with "those degenerate impostors" of New York.[17] But it was all for naught, for nonimportation in Connecticut had collapsed by the fall of 1770. A last-ditch town meeting in New Haven on September 18 with the participation of even the most conservative merchants, such as Thomas Darling and Jared Ingersoll, could not keep importers and consumers in check. The situation was so out of hand by that time that the committee of thirty-eight, including Sherman, seems never to have been reported.[18] But the little colony had tried, and with only New Jersey and the Delaware counties, Connecticut had been true to her professions of nonimportation and nonconsumption. In the failure of the plan both her radicals and conservatives had seen that the only logical outcome of the differences between Parliament and the colonies was civil war. When mutual interest no longer bound the colonies and the mother country, "Each side must assuredly persue their own," wrote radical Governor Trumbull, and conservative Benjamin Gale agreed, that "The Stamp Act has laid the foundation for Americas being an independent state."[19]

Another question that plagued relations between England and Connecticut was the rise of Episcopacy in the colony. There was a real fear that a bishop might be dispatched to organize the Anglican Church. As early as 1752 a sermon preached before the General Assembly predicted "the unhappy day" when the Connecticut Anglicans, becoming a majority, would be able "to commit out invaluable Privileges to the Flames." Ezra Stiles, Newport's statistically minded Congregational minister, reported that Connecticut had more Anglican missionaries than any other colony, and he estimated the number of Anglicans at about one in thirty of the population.[20] Petitions had been sent to England asking for the establishment of an

---

*The other signatories were Thomas Howell, Jesse Leavenworth, Joseph Munson, David Austin, and Adam Babcock.

Episcopacy, and as early as 1750 Anglican Samuel Johnson of Stratford had urged a Bishop for the Americans because it would "reduce them to a better state of unity." But as Samuel Peters said later, Connecticut citizens were "fond to a madness" of popular forms and "would dislike a Bishop on any footing."[21] Sherman's beliefs about church association were reasonably liberal for the time. He had moved from Old Light to New Light doctrine easily, and later on, in 1776 and 1788, he acquiesced in changes in liturgy to simplify and shorten ceremony. But to institutionalize the Church of England in Connecticut would bring "the most grievous convulsion," he said in a letter to an Anglican friend in London in 1768.[22]

This letter on imperial relations to Johnson, one of Connecticut's agents at Westminster, stretches to over a thousand words. Sherman was especially concerned about the political consequences of an American Bishop. A moderate Episcopacy would be acceptable if its limits were fixed by Parliamentary authority, but it might be carried further. "Yea, from the restless spirit which some have discovered, we have reason to apprehend there is more in view." The possible tyranny of Bishop's Courts

> if now exercised in America, would drive us to seek new habitations among the heathen where England could never claim any jurisdiction, or excite riots, rebellions and wild disorders . . . . A covetous, tyrannical, and domineering prelate or his chancellor would always have it in their power to harass our country and make our lives bitter by fines, imprisonments, and lawless severity.

Sherman felt so strongly on this subject that he launched a minor propaganda campaign by publishing and circulating a pamphlet containing sermons by Charles Chauncey of Boston and Stamford's minister, Noah Welles.[23] These were both conservative but very American divines who took leading roles in the anti-bishop battles of the immediate post-Stamp Act years. Other Connecticut men of influence tried to forestall any such move on the part of Parliament, and this time successfully. But the fear remained as an additional ingredient in the boiling pottage of revolution.

The Colonial Connection Questioned

Sherman's mind was at work all through the late sixties and early years of the next decade on the problem of supporting colonial rights to self-government, for as the colonies marched toward the logical conclusion, the experience of Connecticut in particular in this matter was the most meaningful. Here was a province that from the time of its inception had nearly the same powers for which the Revolution was fought in other colonies. In July of 1775 John Adams wrote to Joseph Warren, "We ought immediately to dissolve all Ministerial Tyrannies, and custom houses, set up Governments of our own, like that of Connecticut . . . ."[24] One of Sherman's business connections in Boston, with whom he talked on his fairly frequent trips there, was the great merchant of that city, at this time Speaker of the House of Representatives of Massachusetts, Thomas Cushing. In the early months of 1772 Sherman's business correspondence with Cushing was expanded to include serious comment on the politics of intercolonial organization. In January Cushing replied to Sherman in a letter he asked to be kept secret. He agreed that union among the colonies was necessary and would be useful in coordinating action should another European war break out. For when England asked for money the colonies could jointly press their demands. "But Massachusetts," Cushing concluded, "by being foremost in such measures has brought the whole resentment of Great Britain upon them, we suffer at this day more than all ye collonies [sic] together—would it not therefore be reasonable that your Colony or some other should take the lead in this matter . . . ." Sherman answered in April, dealing first with business matters. Then, after agreeing with the measures suggested by Cushing, he declared,

> but in order to do anything effectual it will be needful for the people of the several Colonies to be agreed in sentiment as to the extent of their rights . . . . It is a fundamental principle in the British Constitution and I think must be in every free State, that no laws bind the people but such as they consent to be governed by, therefore so far as the people of the Colonies are bound by laws made without their consent, they must be in a state of slavery or absolute subjection to the will of others . . . .

Then Sherman showed his complete acceptance of the natural rights philosophy. He had read Vattel, and this would be enough. But he was also thoroughly familiar with other natural rights philosophers so popular in the colonies. If the right to be bound only by laws of their own making

> belongs to the people of the Colonies, why should they not claim it and enjoy it? If it does not belong to them as well as to their fellow subjects in Great Britain, how came they to be deprived of it? Are Great Britain and the Colonies at all connected in their legislative power? Have not each Colony distinct and complete powers of legislation for all the purposes of public government, and are they in any proper sense subordinate to the Legislature of Great Britain tho' subject to the same King? And tho' some general regulations of trade &cc. may be necessary for the general interest of the nation, is there any constitutional way to establish such regulations so as to be legally binding upon the people of the several distinct Dominions which compose the British Empire, but by consent of the Legislature of each Government?

These are points which appear to me important to be agreed in and settled right, and any concessions made by any of the assemblies, disclaiming any privileges essential to civil liberty which the Colonies are justly entitled to must greatly disserve the common cause. If they think it not prudent, at present to assert every right in the most explicit manner, yet all concessions which may be construed as a disclaimer, ought to be carefully avoided.[25]

This letter was written April 30, 1772, at a moment when "in both England and America the radicals' craft lay becalmed, their crews mutinous, and their rigging rotting from disuse," a time, indeed, when the colonies had not been so much as mentioned in Parliamentary debates for two years.[26]

The Sure Hand of Power

Sherman was more than anything else an ambitious man, but second only to that quality, his unemotional, concise rationality is most striking. Most of the colonial radicals, of which Benjamin Franklin is typical, passed through a whole series of ideological positions before arriving at a commitment to independence. These men started by acknowledging Parliament's right to legislate, then moved to a demand for representation there, went on to distinguish between internal and external levies, taxation and the regulation of trade, to the dominion concept of union only through the coincidence of a common sovereign and only then espousing independence. Of course, different men moved through these stages at different times and at different rates. It would be difficult if not impossible to find a strong colonial consensus on any one of these positions at any given time between 1766 and 1774. Federalism was not an articulated concept, and Sherman saw very early the illogic of any of the intermediate steps.[27] Only the concept of dominion satisfied the requirements of his orderly mind; the use of the words "distinct Dominions" in his letter to Cushing is significant. We cannot point with precision to the dates of Sherman's revelation. John Adams, writing in 1774, reported that Sherman

> said he read Mr. Otis's Rights &c. in 1764, and thought that he had conceded away the rights of America. He thought the reverse of the declaratory act was true, namely that the Parliament of Great Britain has authority to make laws for America in *no* case whatever. He would have been very willing that Massachusetts should have rescinded that part of their Circular Letter where they allow Parliament to be the supreme legislative over the Colonies in any case.[28]

James Otis had written in his *The Rights of the British Colonies Asserted and Proved* in 1764, that Parliament is limited by the common law, natural law, and the British constitution. Aside from these general and often vague limitations, "The power of parliament is uncontroulable, but by themselves...."[29] Clearly by 1772 Sherman believed that Parliament had no legislative authority over the colonies whatsoever; that he believed this in 1766 is only somewhat doubtful. In any event in the public debate of 1774 Sherman declared "The Colonies not bound to the King or Crown by the act of settlement, but by their consent to it. There is no other legislative over the Colonies but their respective assemblies. The Colonies adopt the common law, not as the common law, but as the highest reason." And eight years earlier Sherman had written that "There is no doubt that the Colonies are bound by the present Establishment of the Crown, *as they have consented to it Sworn Allegiance etc.* . . . [emphasis added]," though for tactical reasons he was playing at the same time the moderate politican in Connecticut.[30]

Roger Sherman, in his objections to Otis, was already denying that Parliament had any control over the colonies, and further claimed that the king's prerogatives existed only on the basis of prior colonial consent. In these contentions, he was ahead of much radical thinking of the time.[31] It was not just his lawyer's mind that prompted Sherman to warn against "all concessions which may be construed as a disclaimer." He saw the point to which logic would ultimately bring the thoughtful colonist. Where James Wilson was still admitting that the king's authority was "a dependence, which they have acknowledged hitherto; which they acknowledge now; and . . . will continue to acknowledge hereafter . . . ," Sherman had at least hinted years earlier that the situation could not always stand thus. In 1766 had he not asked, "But Quere If the Succession according to the present Establishment Should cease for want of an Heir or if the Parliament should alter it and admit a Papist to the Crown would not the Colonies be at Liberty to joyn with Britain or not?"

On paper Sherman was ahead of colonial political thought, but he cut a more moderate figure in the action politics of Connecticut's radical faction. Locally some of the bully boys had demanded an intercolonial congress to draw up a bill of rights. The wittier Sons of Liberty raised tankards to such slogans as "Every fool is not a Tory, but every Tory is a fool" and "The man who maintains the 'divine right of Kings to govern wrong' is a fool, and also a genuine Tory." Though Sherman was clear by the early seventies in his view of the constitutional relationship of England and the colonies, he still had to work out his position in the rapidly leftward sliding politics of Connecticut. A relative lull in both Connecticut politics and aggravations with the mother country permitted him to keep to himself even more than usual. But the forces driving Connecticut into a revolutionary position were not all intellectual; passion played its important part too. The economics of land for farming and speculation charged the emotions of many a Connecticut man unsuited to the more rational progress of a Roger Sherman.[32]

Susquehannah Again

The Susquehannah project had been stalled since 1763 because of the Royal Proclamation of that year, but its claims were revived in the last years of the decade. In 1768 the Treaty of Fort Stanwix fixed a new boundary that pushed the Indians farther west, and now that the earlier settlements of the Susquehannah Company were in legally available territory, the leaders struck for new migrations. The resulting embroilments with Pennsylvanian proprietors gave rise to fears among Connecticut conservatives that the colony's charter would be thrown into jeopardy, and that the costs of prosecuting the case would become more than they cared to pay. The framers of the western project had been attempting to make their cause a political question in Connecticut, and the period of 1769 to 1774 was marked by increased agitation on both sides. The hope that a victory of Susquehannah forces in the colony would bring about legislative support for the company was ultimately fulfilled. Large grants of land were given by the company to men of influence; even Governor Trumbull accepted a gift of five hundred acres.[33]

In 1774 the legislature chartered the western claims as the town of Westmoreland. Zebulon Butler, who had been acting head of the settlers' committee, was appointed justice of the peace and authorized to call meetings for organizational purposes. This action fanned the flames of faction and further fractured the colony along geographical lines, for the strength of the Susquehannah group lay in the east and that of its opponents in the west. Governor Trumbull, friend to the Wyoming forces, was re-elected in 1774, partly with the aid of votes from the new town of Westmoreland. The newspapers were filled during the first five months of that year with fiery, bitter, and colorful polemic on the blazing lands question. No real attempt by Pennsylvania authorities to eject settlers had been made since 1770, when the Board of Trade had refused to take a hand in the matter, so by 1775 there were almost two thousand Connecticut frontiersmen on the spot. In that year the Pennsylvania proprietors themselves determined to finance an expedition against the Connecticut men. Among these proprietors were James Wilson and Robert Morris, so the controversy, a matter of both policy and personality, boiled over into the Continental Congress, among whose members from Connecticut sat Eliphalet Dyer of Windham.

Though the Susquehannah group has been referred to as the "Sherman party," this scarcely seems accurate.[34] For a long time the chieftain of the Wyoming lands faction had been Eliphalet Dyer.* Though Dyer's partisanship eroded his influence in Congress, he continued to lead the company right down to the final settlement in 1786. Benjamin Gale, discussing the Susquehannah affair during the last days of '69, wrote Jared Ingersoll, "This has been Col. Dyer's Hobby Horse by which he has rose & as he has been unmerciful to Gov—Fitch & your self I never design to give him rest until I make his Hobby Horse throw him into the dirt." It was under Dyer's name that petitions were sent to the Assembly in January and October 1769.[35] On both occasions the upper house consented to the Susquehannah appeal for official sanction and aid in bringing the case to Westminster. Sherman sat in the Council at this time, and presumably voted for the company, for each time he was put on a committee to deal with the recalcitrant Assembly, which refused to adopt the western claims. Sherman's role on these committees probably was that of a moderating personality. Nothing came of the committee work, for the measure had to come up once again in the 1771 session of the Assembly. A committee was set up to aid the governor in preparing a case and, if necessary, to go to Philadelphia to negotiate with Governor Penn. Sherman was nominated by the Council, but along with three others was rejected by the lower house.** Ultimately however, though the others were kept off, Sherman was included.[36]

The conflict between the upper and lower houses on the Susquehannah issue would appear to grow out of their differing economic balance. It is even more evident in the Council's efforts at halting inflation with high taxes that mercantile preponderance there sometimes ran against the balance of farmers in the lower house. This Council support makes it quite clear that the principal impetus behind the Susquehannah scheme was speculation rather than homesteading.

---

*Once while declaiming on his "darling hobby" in the Assembly, Dyer inspired one of his wittier fellows to inscribe:
Cannan of old, as we are told,
  When it did rain down manna,
Wa'nt half so good, for heavenly food,
  As Dyer makes Susquehanna.
Quoted in Lossing, *Pictorial Field-Book,* p. 347n.

**The others objected to by the lower house were William Pitkin, Joseph Trumbull, and Samuel Huntington. Substituted were Silas Deane, William Williams, and Jedidiah Strong. The only suggestion put forth for these changes is that the House desired men who were not members of the Company to counterbalance the Governor's partisanship. Taylor, *Susquehannah Papers,* V:xxxii.

During the early years of Susquehannah's high controversy in Connect-icut, Sherman does not seem to have been a leader on either side. Susquehannah's chief historian claims that he among many others was "at one time or another . . . caught up by 'the Glory of this New World' which lay west of the Delaware River." But there is little evidence that this was true before 1772. In 1770, when he was on committees of the Assembly to decide the official stand to be taken by the government, Governor Trumbull sent him all the papers relating to the colony's claim to lands west of New York, but not those dealing specifically with the Susquehannah Company's claims against Pennsylvania. This may have been an attempt by the governor to involve Sherman, or it might have been a legitimate effort to get an unbiased view.[37] Sherman was at the March session of the Superior Court, which met in Windham, the Susquehannah Company headquarters, and was no doubt fully informed as to company affairs. The Court adjourned at the end of March, and on the 30th Trumbull forwarded the papers to Sherman. The governor instructed Sherman to discover "What Link in the Chain of our Title is wanting? what Injury is done [by subsequent patents] to our Title to the rest of the Lands contained in our Charter."[38]

In 1772 Sherman began to edge openly into the Susquehannah camp. He aided Benjamin Trumbull, a staunch Susquehannah man, who was then writing a history of Connecticut, with the work on the legal basis for the western claims. Evidently the study of the legal background of the case convinced Sherman of the correctness of the radical position. After serving on a committee to collect evidence attesting to the rightness of the western cause, Sherman and W. S. Johnson were appointed in October 1773 to press the colony's claims and even to go to Philadelphia if necessary to do the job. Opponents of the claims were notably missing from this and two other committees on which Sherman served in January 1774 for the purpose of collecting more relevant exhibits.[39] So by 1774 he became fully committed to the Susquehannah position.

The Susquehannah people, the dominant section of the radical party in Connecticut, had control of the upper house by 1770, as attested to by their acceptance of Dyer's petition. Four years later they were dominant in the lower house as well. A special session of the Assembly was called by Governor Trumbull in January of that year, and jurisdiction of the colonial government was extended to the new town of Westmoreland, an area about twice the size of the mother colony herself. The bill for granting town government was drafted by Sherman, and after early objections by the lower house he managed to persuade them to adopt the proposal, which was accomplished on January 29, 1774.[40]

At the January special session Sherman was again assigned to a committee to consider the claims of the land company. The legal brief that he prepared is the simplest, clearest, and fairest of any available. He began, "There is a real claim of title and jurisdiction by both parties over a tract of territory about seventy miles wide north and south, and about two hundred and fifty miles long east and west . . ." Then follow six paragraphs of lucidly written history of the rights and purchases of the two colonies. Sherman based the Connecticut claims largely on priority in charter rights to the land, priority in negotiating with the Indians there, and the fact of settlement before any Pennsylvanians were on the scene. The whole statement is not five hundred words long.[41]

The action of the January session was protested by an extralegal convention held by the conservatives in Middletown in March. Here a petition was drawn up asking reconsideration of the Assembly's endorsement of the Susquehannah Company. Of greater threat to the radicals was the organization by the convention of a list of candidates for governor, deputy governor, and members of the Council.[42]

Silas Deane, with his own western interests, wrote Governor Trumbull from Wethersfield that "The Towns to the westward are getting into a Flame and I confess It gives me the most uneasy apprehensions, as a popular Government however agreeable on many Accounts, is perhaps the very worst in the World, when the steadiness, and Virtue, or fairness of the People is lost, which though I fondly hope is not our case yet, there are shocking symptoms of it at this Day." Deane not only feared anti-western agitation, but also saw the threat to orderly government posed by extralegal conventions. He did everything in his power, he said, to defeat the Middletown Convention, thereby greatly offending some of his New Haven friends. He was able to report, though, that there had not been one town meeting in support of the Middletowners in all of Hartford County. Steady government was most important to many potential supporters of the Convention but, "Many Gentlemen who are open opposers of the Western Claim, to their horror, as openly oppose the present mad proceedings . . . ." But three weeks later he wrote officiously that he had detected "some Villainies in the Nomination . . . & am inquiring for others . . . ."[43]

Deane was incensed at publisher Watson of the *Connecticut Courant* for printing an anti-Susquehannah letter, and he started a movement to bring one Spooner to Hartford to begin a new paper. The Company was in trouble, he thought, and to his close friend Joseph Trumbull he wrote that though his father, the governor, might "live through The Storm . . . some of Us small folk are Ship Wreck'd." The dispute had upset politics so that one town "was exhausted by Nineteen Votings for one Deputy, so that no more than 12 or 13 Freemen were left to choose other Magistrates." Eliphalet Dyer, who was in on the effort to establish a new paper in Hartford, reported that he had difficulty in getting elected in Windham, where an ancient political enemy, Jabez Huntington, tried to "throw [him] by every mean & false artifice."[44]

The Susquehannans were not inactive in arranging their continued domination. On April 1, 1774 one member was able to report a Windham meeting of about three hundred members "Stil Spiriteed for the good of the Company," which raised £1600 for the cause. But, he warned, some of the southwestern towns are in "a mind By theire prosedings to thro out the Governer and Col. Dier and raise too of the Hive that Died in the Fire of the Stampt Act." "N.B.," he concluded, "we no our Friends and we no oure Foes and we Can Tell Who we shall Vote for in the uper House." His list of friends included Roger Sherman.[45]

Sherman's political behavior followed the pattern it took during the hectic Stamp Act crisis. He was moderate when the minds of the colony's freemen were not made up, but took a strong stand when the majority opinion seemed determinable. Yet even this policy took considerable courage, because his own town, a sensitive border area, lagged behind the tide of radicalism rising in the east. Sherman, then, was slower than the colony as a whole in taking his stand, but ahead of his home base. As Deane implied, the conservative faction was strong in the years preceding 1772–73, and still comprised a majority of New Haven's freemen. Over two hundred of the conservatives signed a petition for a special town meeting in March 1774, which the selectmen and justices Sherman, James Hillhouse, and Thomas Howell duly advertised in the *Connecticut Courant*. The selectmen were obligated to call the meeting, admitted a pro-Susquehannah writer in the *Connecticut Journal* later on, "altho' at the same time they all unanimously declared their opinion to this effect that there was no just reason for calling a town meeting, excepting the petition."[46]

The meeting, too large a crowd for the customary Old State House, was held at the Brick Meeting House. Over two hundred citizens voted by a "very great Majority" that the prosecution of the western claim would cause too great an expense, and sent delegates to Middletown to oppose it. The conservative majority notwithstanding, Sherman had made his decision by this time, and defended the Susquehannah group with firmness and some fire. The March meeting was adjourned to April 11, and Sherman in the meantime published an article of well over two thousand words putting forth the case for the claims. It is one of the careful politician's rare public pleas, so it bears a thorough examination.[47]

"There has been much altercation of late," he wrote in the *Journal* on April 8,

> concerning the doings of the honorable general assembly, relative to the western lands contained in our charter, and many false insinuations have been industriously circulated by some men, to prejudice the minds of the people against the assembly; from what motives I shall not undertake to determine. It is hard to suppose that the good of the colony has been the motive, when the measures taken have the most direct tendency to its destruction; for every *kingdom divided against itself is brought to desolation.*

Sherman thought that the people who met at Middletown were deceived and misled, and wondered why they would believe "an anonymous writer in a newspaper, whose character they knew nothing of, who, in an audacious, as well as false manner has undertaken to impeach the integrity of the general assembly of the colony." He then recited the facts of the controversy from a pro-Susquehannah view. He bolstered his position by presenting first-hand information on the debates and votes that took place in the Assembly when he was a member.

Sherman went on to take the Middletown Convention to task for holding that the title to the lands was contested. "In answer to which, I would say, that it is not contested, but acknowledged, by the proprietors of Pennsylvania. . . ." This might have been fairly said by Sherman at the time, but it was only a year later that the Pennsylvania legislature authorized an army of five hundred to move against the Connecticut settlers.[48]

He minimized the probability of mass migrations to Westmoreland and challenged the Middletown Convention's competence to judge the legality of the claim. He continued with a defense of the small expense involved in carrying the case to England, and went on to question Jared Ingersoll's statement.

> Mr. Ingersoll, in a piece lately published in the newspapers, says, "a defeat will be very detrimental; but a victory must be absolute ruin; at least I think so." But he gives no reason for his opinion; and can his bare assertion make the people of this colony, who are a company of farmers, believe that to be quieted in their claim to a large tract of valuable land would ruin them? I know some gentlemen, who love to monopolize wealth and power, think it best for lands to be in a few hands, and that the common people should be their tenants but it will not be easy to persuade the people of this colony. . . .

There was plenty of land for the people of Connecticut to acquire in fee-simple for fifty years to come, and the settlers there "will be connected with us, and by sharing in our civil and religious privileges, will be under the best advantages to be virtuous and happy"; and they will benefit those who stay in the old colony by the money that will be raised by the sale of the lands. Finally, if the new settlement eventually wants to separate from the old, "the crown doubtless would be ready . . . to constitute them a distinct colony."

The last part of what Sherman called a "short account" was given over to a plea for mature deliberation before any decision to relinquish the colony's claim. He pointed out that about four thousand freemen had already shown their desire that the claim be maintained, while the members of the company constituted another thousand. If this were true, then there should be nothing to worry about, for the active voters of the colony only numbered about eight thousand, but he did not mention that. Sherman was not one to use high pressure; he suggests only:

> I think no more need be done than to choose gentlemen of known virtue, integrity and prudence, to be members of the next general assembly, who have approved themselves firm friends to our civil and religious liberties, and not embarrass them with petitions and instructions: they will be under a solemn oath to act as, in their consciences, they shall judge most for the good of the colony, and that must be the only rule of their conduct.

Though Sherman was looking ahead to the Assembly elections, he was writing as much with an eye to the New Haven town meeting to be held later that week. But regardless of the reasons for the publication of the piece at the time, it is signficant in itself. For this was the first time Sherman took a public position on the Susquehannah question. Though he had enjoyed the support of the western lands faction since at least 1766, there is no evidence that he openly took their side before 1772. Indeed, one student of Connecticut radicalism says the "controversy of the spring of 1774 brought to light little that was new in regard to the membership of the Susquehannah Company, save perhaps the addition of the names of two active sympathizers, Benjamin Trumbull and Roger Sherman. . . ."[49]

When the adjourned town meeting finally reconvened at four o'clock on April 11, its major business was the election of deputies to the General Assembly. This took most of the afternoon and ultimately resulted in a compromise delegation of Samuel Bishop on the left and Thomas Darling on the right. By the time this was done it was nine o'clock and over three hundred freemen had drifted away. This left 201 to vote on the Remonstrance of the Middletown Convention. With conservative Thomas Darling as moderator, the vote was 102 to 98 in favor of the Middletown position.[50]

During this period Sherman also gave advice to Benjamin Trumbull, the New Light minister, who was at work on a pamphlet stating the case for the Susquehannah people. He sent it around for comment, and on the same day that Sherman's long article appeared in the *Connecticut Journal*, Trumbull wrote the Governor from New Haven, "Esqr Sherman and other friends to the Claims of the Colony, this way, give it as their opinion . . . that what I have written, ought to be republished in an Elegant Pamphlet before the Election."[51] There is no question, then, that by 1774 Roger Sherman had firmly committed himself to the western cause. There is much significance in this commitment. The connection between the leaders of the political upset of 1766 and those of the Susquehannah movement is clear.

In taking the stand that he did, and it was an inevitable choice, Roger Sherman passed the mark where he could turn back. He was in dead center no longer. The radicalism of Sherman was nothing like that of a Dyer or a Benjamin Trumbull, not to mention the Arnolds, Durkees, Zebulon Butlers, and others of the leaders of the country party, but it was headed in the same direction. The division between the east and the west, the conservative and radical, had reached that point of bitterness which allowed for no middle ground. No longer was there room in New Haven for the moderate, and when Sherman finally stood up to be counted he picked the winning side.

The First Continental Congress

ROGER SHERMAN was a thoroughgoing moderate. But his commitment to the Susquehannah faction in 1774 put him and most of his middle-of-the-road friends in alliance with the Connecticut radicals. This alliance was forged at a time when the whole continent was on the verge of the ultimate political decision. Connecticut radicals were in the forefront of the independence movement and the local moderates were willing accomplices. Indeed, organization had been proceeding for some years.

Organizing for Resistance

During the early years of the decade of the 1770's, the Connecticut radicals, as they increased in numbers, began to develop a degree of cohesion. As far back as the Stamp Act crisis in the mid-sixties, the Sons of Liberty had begun to evolve as a radical instrument. The name "Sons of Liberty" had been used in the forties and fifties by Benjamin Gale's conservative cabal. This earlier group was a rabid faction of no certain sect, but consisting of opponents of the New Lights, especially to President Clap of Yale, according to Gale "an Assuming, Arbitrary, Designing Man; who under a Cloak of Zeal for Orthodoxy, design'd to govern both Church & State, & Damn all who would not worship ye Beast." In addition to Gale, the probable New Haven members of this early group were Thomas Darling, John Hubbard, and of course Jared Ingersoll.[1] Jared Ingersoll, the leader of New Haven's bar since the forties, had been appointed King's Attorney for New Haven County in 1751 and later also represented Connecticut at London, where he, with Benjamin Franklin and others, led the opposition to the Stamp Act in 1764.

But this was in the early period of New Light ascendancy, and by 1765 "Sons of Liberty" had been stolen by the opposition. This included, even in the early period, men such as William Williams and Trumbull of Lebanon, the Huntingtons of Norwich and Windham, Griswold of Lyme, Dyer of Windham, and of course, Clap, in addition to Putnam, Durkee, and Ledlie. The eastern New Light complexion of the group is clear by the mid-sixties. The new Sons of Liberty throve on the popular rejection of the Stamp Act and "during the late months of 1765 and the first few months of the following year the regular governments in town and colony were practically superseded . . ." by this new authority. These town groups were of an extremely radical nature, threatening to level the governor's house to dust, or take the field if necessary to defeat the Stamp Act. Even in the border and western towns mobs were active, including, as we have seen, Benedict Arnold's riotous group in New Haven itself. Sherman, never one to condone unruly violence, had written Governor Pitkin a careful but cautionary letter warning against illegal assemblies and mob action, though agreeing with the anti-stamp aims of the Sons. The Sons of Liberty established contact with each other throughout the colony by use of committees of correspondence, and became influential, if not decisive, in the election of 1767. The term had not yet become identified exclusively with these loosely organized groups. Ezra Stiles thought that the Anglicans were trying to "besmirch" the name as being "antiamericans." Attempts continued to be made to identify the Sons of Liberty with the debtors and lower element in the colony, as when in the *Connecticut Gazette* they were accused of working for the nonresumption of court business merely to protect their members from being sued.[2]

The Sons of Liberty in Connecticut was not a secret organization as some historians have claimed.[3] The leadership was well known throughout the whole period of its existence. By 1774 it was an established organization of great influence; though it did not control the Assembly, its strength in that body steadily increased. The Sons were active in the battle against the importation of tea, now mobbing hapless peddlers and next year burning the obnoxious weed. But as meetings became more and more tumultuous and unruly, given to tarrings and featherings, and dominated by what Angilcan Samuel Peters called "drunken, barbarous people," the leadership of the Sons themselves recommended more orderly procedures.[4] There is no evidence to support an earlier chronicler's claim that Roger Sherman ever associated himself in any way with this extremist organization. His character makes it unlikely, and his explicit condemnation of their action in 1766, as a "little extraordinary" and "prejudicial to the interests of the colony," emphasized his aloofness. And though he claimed to have "no doubt of the upright intentions of those gentlemen," his conduct in the case of Benedict Arnold's mob action shows his distaste for their manners.[5]

When, in 1774, Parliament passed the series of measures known as the Coercive Acts designed to punish Massachusetts for her wild tea party, calls began to go out from Philadelphia and New York City for an intercolonial congress. Massachusetts was urging a general nonimportation instead, but had to act alone for the time being. Meanwhile Parliament continued to invite open insurrection by passing the Quebec Act on May 20 and the Quartering Act on June 2. In Connecticut the Assembly had already set up a Committee of Correspondence in May, 1773, during the heat of the passion stirred up by Royal Commission investigations of the burning of the British Customs schooner, *Gaspee*. The *Gaspee* incident was especially galling because the Ministry proposed to take the alleged offenders to England for trial. Immediately upon assembling, the Committee wished to join with Massachusetts and Rhode Island to thwart this possibility: "however seriously disposed the Ministry are to fix such a Court on the Colonies, it is the Wildest and most impracticable of all their schemes," fumed Silas Deane, "and at best will only Shew Us To what Lengths they would willingly go, had they the power to give force to their projects."[6]

The Committee was now busily spying out possible loyalty to the Crown. In a letter asking John Hancock to provide the names of any Connecticut men who had written letters to England "of an extraordinary Nature, tending to subvert the constitution of the Colonies in general, of this Province in particular," the officious little crew inquired what punishment Massachusetts had imposed on her miscreants. It concluded sententiously that "the Colonies are all Embarked in the same general Cause, A Union in Sentiment and Measures, are of the utmost importance effectually to oppose the wicked Designs of our Common Enemies."[7] In somewhat less restrained language, this hard-core group of radicals was merely echoing Sherman's letter to Cushing of a year earlier. In May 1774, the Committee of Correspondence reported in favor of joining with the colonies to the south in calling for an intercolonial congress rather than a colony-wide nonimportation, though the radical eastern towns would have preferred the more direct approach urged by Boston.[8]

Sherman, too, had to be cautious. The spring of 1774 was a bad one for the New Light-Sequehannah forces in New Haven. In March the town meeting sent delegates to the anti-Susquehannah Middletown Convention and in April voted against support for the western claims. The meeting returned Samuel

Bishop to the Assembly, but replaced arch-conservative Thomas Howell with arch-conservative Thomas Darling. The May meeting to discuss the Massachusetts call for nonimportation could agree only on the ambiguous resolution:

> that we will to the utmost of our abilities assert and defend the Liberties and immunities of British America and we will cooperate with our Sister Towns in this and other Colonies in any Constitutional measures that may be thought most conducive to the preservation of our inalienable rights and priviledges. . . .

A local Committee of Correspondence was organized, but again it had its sprinkling of conservatives. In June, however, the New Haven Committee called upon Samuel Bishop to inform the Colony Committee that "it would be very agreeable to this Town . . ." to have a general Congress "as soon as may be."[9]* For Connecticut, this was a moderate stand; even the usually cautious Sherman said he was enthusiastic for some kind of action. Later in that year, when Patrick Henry asked him "why the people of Connecticut were more zealous in the cause of liberty than the people of other States," he answered "because we have more to lose than any of them." "What is that?" said Mr. Henry. "Our beloved charter," the Massachusetts-raised Connecticut Yankee replied.[10]

The General Assembly granted to the Committee of Correspondence power to elect a slate of delegates to the Congress. This action was taken in June, and the Committee met in New London on July 13 to make its selection. Appointments went to Eliphalet Dyer, William S. Johnson, Erastus Wolcott, Silas Deane, and Richard Law.[11] Wolcott and Law declined, alleging

---

*Sherman was not a member of the New Haven Committee of Correspondence, nor of the original Committee for the Colony which had been set up on May 21, 1773 in response to a call sent out by the Virginia legislature in March. Though acting as early as June 1773, the first recorded meeting of the Connecticut Committee of Correspondence was not until July 13, 1774, and in August it changed its name to the Council of Safety. Sherman was appointed to it four times, the first in May 1777. The original members were Ebenezer Silliman, William Williams, Benjamin Payne, Samuel Holden Parsons, Nathaniel Wales, Silas Deane, Samuel Bishop, Joseph Trumbull, and Erastus Wolcott. It was re-established in May 1775, as merely a committee of no certain name provided to assist the governor in ordering and directing marches. It was almost exclusively military and at its earliest meetings referred to itself as "the Council or Committee of War." Those appointed in 1775 were, besides the Governor, Williams, Wales, Samuel, Benjamin, and Jabez Huntington, Matthew Griswold, Eliphalet Dyer, Jedidiah Elderkin, and Joshua West. With the exception of West, the same men were reappointed in May 1776. *CR*, XV:39; CHS, *Collections* "Deane Papers," II:235,239,243; *CR*, XII:156; CSL, "Revolutionary War," Ser. 1. I:53bc, 56, 54; *SR*, I:253; *CR*, XIV: 156, XV:39, 315, 84, 109. The members of the New Haven committee were Joshua Chandler, Samuel Bishop, Jr., Daniel Lyman, Stephen Ball, Pierpont Edwards, John Whiting, Isaac Doolittle, David Austin, Timothy Jones, Jr., Isaac Beers, Joseph Munson, Peter Call, Jere Atwater, Timothy Bradley, Silas Kimberly, Simeon Bristoll, John Woodward, and Joel Hotchkiss. New Haven Town Records, "Minutes," ps. 34, 41, 42.

ill health, and Johnson backed out on grounds of "previous engagements."
Johnson's excuse was a barefaced lie designed to cover his lack of sympathy
for the cause. He wrote Richard Jackson in England, "*inter nous*, I did not
think it advisable either on my own acct., or on account of the Colony to
make one of that Assembly, though it is very unpopular at present to doubt
in any measure either the legality or expediency of the measure." In
November Johnson resigned his militia commission as a lieutenant colonel.
The position, he pointed out, was accepted when it was merely honorary, but
now he was expected to act. This he could not do because he was too old and
tired; ignorant of military affairs; had insufficient time to take from his law
practice; and had no taste for glory. "My Ambition has long since been
extinguished," he wrote more than a little ingenuously, "I have Lost all
Fondness for Office or Employment of any kind—I seek no Preferment—I
desire no Glory—I wish no Honour, but that of being an honest man & an
upright Citizen."* When the war was over, he accepted appointments to the
congress under the Articles of Confederation; to the Philadelphia Convention
of 1787; as Senator from Connecticut in the First U.S. Congress; and as
president of Columbia College.[12]

Any three of the members were authorized to represent Connecticut in
the Congress, and it was thought necessary to fill out the delegation to at
least four, so on August 1 two more members were appointed. An effort was
made by the Deane-Joseph Trumbull-Parsons cabal to rally its strength, and a
compromise was struck where they got one new member and the older, more
steady faction got one, also. The new appointments caused some disagreement among the members of the Committee, and much cabal. Silas Deane
wrote to Johnson:

> The meeting of the Committee yesterday was very curious indeed, there
> were Eight of Us and schemers too you may well conclude, when you are
> informed that in order to lead off, from a Gentleman to the Eastward, it
> was insisted that a man at the Westward should be Nominated, the
> reasons urged were in sum this, That it would tend to quiet the Minds of
> the People by an equal location—Four of the Committee for Four against
> such a Measure Reasons, principally that the time was short, that to
> appoint any person We could not be positive would Accept & Attend
> would be very trifling, as We might probably be forced to meet again—A

---

*At the elections in Norwich the following spring, Jabez Huntington attacked Johnson
for hiding behind the excuse of an important law case in Albany which, he said,
everyone knew was not true. Johnson's Norwich vote fell from his usual seven-eighths of
the total to about a third. CHS, "Johnson Papers," B. Gale to WSJ (April 12, 1775).

vote was called and Mr. Sherman had Four for Four against, after repeated tryals they conferred and those against urged the great impropriety and real Danger of sending away Two of the Superior Court. The great dissatisfaction it would give the colony as more than one-half the Parties would beg and dispute and be dissatisfied with the Resolutions of the Court when thus weakened. . . . Finally as a compromise was made that We could nominate two One of which should attend, on this Mr. Sherman and Capt Trumbull were Nominated—Now it is very much left with Mr. Sherman, as he stands first in Nomination to determine the Matter and here I must ask you to say one word—You are on principle against such a weakening of the Court, the Consequences of which will most certainly be bad—Therefore wish if consistent with your delicacy that you would hint your Sentiments to this good Gentleman, on the Subject—I have most sincerely a high Opinion of that good Gentleman in the Capacity of a Judge, and a Magistrate . . . and I am of the opinion that Such a weakening of the Court will give great general umbrage, which I plainly see will turn in part on Us the Committee, and possibly in part on him, and I am sure he is not solicitous for the post.[13]

The day before this letter was penned, Deane, anxious that Johnson serve, had written that "We are really unfortunate in our nomination. . . . I'm sorry you can't attend." Deane was sure, he said, that the rumor of Johnson's lukewarmness toward the idea of an intercolonial congress was "as void of foundation as possible." But John Beach, Redding's high Tory Anglican saw it the other way. "I rejoice that you are not going to Philla," he wrote tersely.

Deane's underhandedness in the affair was known to the outside at least generally, for John Adams gives a garbled account of it in his diary. Deane, says Adams, "procured his first Appointment in 1774 to Congress by an Intrigue. Under the pretext of avoiding to commit the Legislature of the State in any Act of Rebellion, he got a Committee (of three) appointed with some discretionary Powers, under which they undertook to appoint the Members to Congress."[14]

At any rate, Sherman was elected finally, and with Dyer and Deane, left for Philadelphia on the 24th of August. "I wish they may be cool and wise," worried stay-at-home William Johnson. "There will be however, I know, many very warm spirits convened on this occasion and it will be happy if they are sufficiently tempered by others of a more cool and moderate make."[15] All three men were staunch Whigs, differing in temperament rather than ideology. Sherman, the coolest and most cerebral of the trio, was prone to less radical tactics perhaps, but not one bit less committed to the American cause.

The Curtain Rises

Deane, Dyer, and Sherman, Connecticut's delegates to the intercolonial meeting in Philadelphia, known now as the First Continental Congress, made an odd threesome. Eliphalet Dyer, who would turn fifty-three in three weeks, was just a few months younger than Sherman. He was born in Windham, his mother's town, and graduated from Yale in 1740. He studied law in his home town and ultimately rose to the top of the profession, becoming chief justice of the Superior Court in 1789. He moved through the usual political channels of the day and in 1762 was elected to the Governor's Council, an event that his biographer marks "a first harbinger of the ascendance in Connecticut politics which the Susquehannah Company was soon to enjoy."[16] Dyer had represented Connecticut in the Stamp Act Congress in 1765, and served on the first Committee of Safety. He had been to London as a lobbyist for the Susquehannah Company in 1764, but remained provincial in his politics. Dyer was a man of business as well as politics, owning a grist mill and a flour mill. He was wealthy enough to give his son a thousand pounds to start the first drugstore in the area, and to live in a very comfortable way with a household of three Negro slaves. His daughter was married to Governor Trumbull's son, Joseph.

Eliphalet Dyer's political interest probably sprouted about 1753, when he became one of the first organizers of the Susquehannah Company. He was a member of the commission sent to purchase land from the Indians of the Six Nations, as well as the Company's agent in England. His biographer reports him "clearly aligned with the left wing in [the First Continental] Congress." In the Second Continental Congress Dyer was not a leading member, "though punctilious in attendance [he] was on no important standing committee." Dyer seems to have favored independency by November 1775. Between 1779 and 1782, writes his biographer, "it is clear that the movement of his mind was toward a stronger Federal Government." But nationalist Madison thought otherwise. In 1783 he wrote that Dyer, "a man of gentlemanly manners, who had seen the world [was] not of very sound principle."

Dyer was more typical of the provincial politician than either Sherman or Deane. His public speaking was dull, clumsy, heavy, and worst of all, much too frequent. During the negotiations over the Susquehannah claims one Pennsylvanian reported that Dyer spoke "twenty times a day, and scarcely ever finishes one sentence completely," and from his testimony "we expect much amusement, though little information. . . ." John Adams had something to say about Dyer, too, evidently his public speaking showing no improvement. "Dyer is long-winded and round-about, obscure and cloudy, very talkative and very tedious, yet an honest, worthy man, means and judges well." "It is well known," Dyer admitted, "I am warm, impetuous and persevering."[17]

Silas Deane, Sherman's second partner, is much better known. His reputation is a mixture of famous and infamous, and its shaping was a matter of mysterious forces and events still not completely understood.[18] But whether the major supplier of stores for the Revolution or the major profiteer of the conflict, he was a good and ardent radical in the early Congress, though at first favored by the conservative delegates from the middle colonies who wanted to make him secretary.[19]

Deane and Sherman could not have been more different to start with. Deane, born sixteen years after Sherman, graduated from Yale in 1758 and by a pair of fortunate marriages turned a fair law practice into a very profitable mercantile business. He was well connected through these marriages with the best families of the colony, though himself the son of a blacksmith. He acquired all the necessary trappings of the ruling circles in the old Puritan Colony, and apparently always resented Sherman's prominence as the presumptious intrusion of a country bumpkin from Massachusetts. There was always a presumption of their superiority by college men, probably strongest among those reared in less refined circumstances. Sherman's coarse cant and rough demeanor benefited him by helping to hold the loyal support of most of Connecticut's yeomanry, who felt a class-conscious kinship with him. Resentment of Yale graduates in particular surfaced from time to time, and Sherman's future son-in-law told the college president "that the poor & those who don't educate their child. at Coll . . . ought not to be burdened with raisg. Revenues for the use of the rich. . . ." Deane's resentment of Sherman must have resulted also from the insecurity so common among the recently arrived in the face of economic or social competition from those just arriving. Whiggism had run mad, wrote William Goddard in Baltimore in 1777. "When a man, who is only fit 'to patch a shoe,' attempts 'to patch the State.' " If he "fancies himself a *Solon* or *Lycurgus*, . . . he cannot fail to meet with contempt." Most American leaders of the late eighteenth century expected wealth, education, experience, and connections to precede political aspiration. Sherman was perhaps pushing things too fast for the well-married Yale graduate Deane.[20] The wide differences in the backgrounds of Sherman and Deane were in a measure to shape the factional quarrels that immediately developed in Philadelphia.

ELIPHALET DYER (1721–1807). Portrait attributed to William Johnson. Courtesy of the Connecticut Historical Society (upper left). ISRAEL PUTNAM (1718–1790). Portrait by H. I. Thompson after a pencil sketch from life by John Trumbull. Courtesy of the Connecticut State Library (upper right). SILAS DEANE (1737–1789). Engraving by W. Angus after a portrait by Dusimetiere (opposite).

ROGER SHERMAN. Engraving after an original portrait by William P. Chappel.

Late in August, 1774, Roger Sherman set off with his two fellows for Philadelphia, the major city of the colonies. The weather was hot and the roads were dusty, but Deane's "Leathern Conveniency" made the ride as comfortable as possible. Along the way the delegates were entertained by the gentlemen of the towns, and in the major cities crowds were waiting to escort them to their lodgings. In New York, though still dusty from their ride, they were given a great ceremonial banquet. That was on August 25. By the 27th Sherman was beginning to wear a bit on finicky Silas Deane, from whose letters we get the account of this trip. Deane confided to his wife:

> Mr. Sherman is clever in private, but I only say he is as badly calculated to appear in such a Company as a Chestnut-burr is for an eyestone. He occasioned some shrewd countenances among the company, and not a few oaths, by the odd questions he asked, and the very odd and countrified cadence with which he speaks; but he was, and did, as well as I expected.

The next day, however, the store of Deane's patience was drawn on again by his Puritan colleague. "Mr. Sherman (would to Heaven he were well at New Haven,) is against our sending our carriages over the ferry this evening, because it is Sunday; so we shall have a scorching sun to drive forty miles in to-morrow. I wish I could send you his picture, and make it speak, and in the background paint the observations made on him here." If the picture were ever drawn there is no evidence of it, and by the time Trenton had been reached, Deane's distaste for Sherman could scarcely be concealed. A couple of weeks later Deane was still rehashing the miseries of the trip down. To his wife he wrote, "As I suspected our delay or rather superstitious neglect of getting over our Carriage the preceding evening, brought us under the mercy of the ferryman, who kept us until after ten that excessive hot day, and then part of us, not myself for one assisted in rowing over." Stopping to visit a friend in Trenton, Deane continued, "I never underwent more to keep up my part of the conversation," so sick was he with dysentery. "But so it was, I could not retire until past eleven, when, as fond as I am of sleep, the night and bed were worse to me than to have proceeded on my journey. I turn'd and turn'd, and groan'd while Judge Sherman who lodged in the same chamber snored in concert."[21]

The trio finally arrived in Philadelphia on the 1st of September and had some time to get settled and meet delegates from other colonies before Congress assembled on the 5th. Sherman stayed at Sarah Cheeseman's for the period of September 1 to October 26, at a charge of almost twenty pounds, which included his servant's board and his share of the wine, a bill he was able to pay despite the loss of his pocketbook containing over forty pounds. Actually, it wasn't a bad deal. The delegates were paid a pound a day wages and expenses, plus an allowance for their servants. Sherman was even reimbursed for the cash stolen, but later on he had second thoughts about the expense of taking along a "waiter."[22]

Sherman had met John Adams when the young Massachusetts lawyer had stopped at New Haven on his way to Philadelphia. At that time Adams wrote in his diary for August 17:

> This morning Roger Sherman, Esq. of the delegates from Conn. came to see us at the tavern Isaac Bears [Beers]. He is between fifty and sixty* a solid, sensible man. He said he read Mr. Otis's Rights &c. in 1764, and thought that he had conceded away the rights of America. He thought the reverse of the declaratory act was true, viz, that the Parliament of G.B. had authority to make laws for America in no case whatever. He would have been very willing that Massachusetts should have rescinded that part of their Circular Letter where they allow Parliament to be the supreme legislative over the Colonies in any case.

Adams' opinion of Sherman was not to change after twenty years of friendship, and a quarter of a century after Sherman's death, the ex-president wrote that Sherman "was one of the most cordial friends which I ever had in my life . . . one of the most sensible men in the world . . . one of the soundest and strongest pillars of the Revolution."[23]

The days in Philadelphia before the opening of Congress gave Sherman a chance to solidify this acquaintance and make himself part of the radical party forming around the Adamses and the delegates from Virginia. As a matter of fact, Benjamin Rush wrote of Sherman some time later that "He was so regular in business and so democratic in his principles that he was called by one of his friends 'a republican machine.' "[24]

Congress Gets Down to Business

The first business of the Congress was to settle the place of meeting. The conservative faction led by Joseph Galloway of Pennsylvania favored the State House, while the more radical members preferred Carpenters' Hall. There is no record of the vote, but every point of logic suggests that Sherman and Dyer voted with the radicals. Deane undoubtedly sided with the

---

*He was actually fifty-three.

conservatives, for he was their choice to be secretary. The man elected to this office was Charles Thomson, who was to outlast all the regular members of the Congress and was still at his job in 1789 when the new Federal Congress superseded the old one. Again, it can only be guessed how Sherman voted, but there is every likelihood that he voted against his highflown colleague from Wethersfield. Peyton Randolph was chosen president, the other organizational post filled at this time. One more procedural matter needed attention before Congress could move on to the main business awaiting it. This was the matter of determining relative votes of the colonies.

The issue of voting was perhaps the thorniest to be grasped by the various congresses of the colonies that assembled between the Stamp Act in 1765 and the Constitutional Convention of 1787. For over twenty-five years this indigestible bone of contention stuck in the throats of the assembled delegates time and time again. The method adopted at the Stamp Act Congress had been one vote per colony, but the three largest, Massachusetts, Pennsylvania, and Virginia, insisted that this arrangement was unjust. Patrick Henry in particular pleaded that the earlier practice not be used as a precedent. A colony's vote in Congress should be based on the number of inhabitants, he insisted. Another alternative was offered by Thomas Lynch of South Carolina, who would have the colonies given voting power according to the value of property combined with the number of residents. But the small colonies held out for the original plan of one vote each.[25]

Sherman, representing a middle-sized constituency, undoubtedly took the stand that he did later, that of the small colonies.* At any rate, the one-colony-one-vote forces had their way, partly because no one knew the relative values of property in the several colonies, or had accurate figures on population, but principally because of the evident intransigence on the part of the small colonies.[26] The Connecticut delegates reported to their Governor: "The mode of voting in this Congress was first resolved upon, which was, that each colony should have one voice; but as this was objected to as unequal, an entry was made on the journals to prevent its being drawn into precedent in the future."[27]

---

*Connecticut was thought at the time to have about the same population as New York, though the census of 1790 was to show that earlier estimates for New York had been low. In that year Connecticut was sixth and New York fifth in rank, still smaller than North Carolina. Roll, "Some of the People," p. 24. See below p. 238-39n Sherman's views on the question as they developed will be discussed at length in a later chapter, for it is on the method of voting in the national legislature that he made one of his major contributions to the American political system.

The main business of the Congress was handed over to two committees: one to draw up a statement of colonial rights along with a list of infringements and means of rectifying them, and the other to write a report on the various statutes dealing with the trade and manufacture of the colonies. The first of these committees consisted of two members from each of the colonies present, with a third one from each of the three large colonies. Sherman was appointed to this committee along with Dyer. John Adams recalled the discussions of this committee much later:

> The two points which labored most were: 1. Whether we should recur to the law of nature, as well as to the British constitution, and our American charters and grants. . . . 2. The other great question was, what authority we should concede to Parliament; whether we should deny the authority of Parliament in all cases; whether we should allow any authority to it in our internal affairs; or whether we should allow it to regulate the trade of the empire with or without any restriction.[28]

The factional lines that had begun to evolve out of the earlier differences over Carpenters' Hall and the selection of the secretary became more and more sharply drawn as the discussion on the statement of rights proceeded. The conservative leader, Joseph Galloway, put it this way; one party "intended candidly and clearly to define American rights, and explicitly and dutifully to petition for the remedy which would redress the grievances justly complained of—to form a more solid and constitutional union between the two countries," while the other was made up of

> persons, whose design, from the beginning of their opposition to the Stamp Act, was to throw off all subordination and connexion with Great Britain; who meant by every fiction, falsehood and fraud, to delude the people from their due allegiance, to throw the subsisting Governments into anarchy, to incite the ignorant and vulgar to arms, and with those arms to establish American independence.[29]

Discount as much as one wishes for Galloway's bias, there is still too much accuracy in the analysis to ignore it completely.

The position on matters of ideology of the Connecticut delegates was perfectly clear. The constitutional principles which they brought with them had been fully stated by their Governor and Assembly the previous spring. The resolution backing Sherman's views protested loyalty to the King, but decried Parliamentary acts laying taxes, closing Boston Harbor, extending the jurisdiction of vice-admiralty courts and numerous other infringements of customary rights. Americans were deserving of all rights and liberties of free-born Englishmen "by the laws of nature, by the royal grant and charter . . .,and by long and uninterrupted possession." Specifically, these rights included the holding of property free of taxation except by their own consent, trial by juries of peers, and in general complete control over local and internal affairs. Furthermore, declared the Connecticut Assembly, "it is an indispensible duty that we owe to our King, our country, ourselves, and our posterity, by all lawful ways and means in our power, to maintain, defend and preserve these our rights and liberties, and to transmit them entire and inviolate to the latest generation—and that it is our fixed determination and unalterable resolution faithfully to discharge this our duty."[30]

There is no question about Sherman's allegiance. He had made his position perfectly clear in letters to Thomas Cushing and others. When he wrote that "It is a fundamental principle in the British Constitution and I think must be in every free State, that no laws bind the people but such as they consent to be Governed by . . . ," he declared himself an advocate of imperial relations based on the law of nature. He further supported this view in the debates in Congress, for Adams reported in his diary:

> Mr. Sherman. The ministry contend that the Colonies are only like corporations in England, and therefore subordinate to the legislature of the Kingdom. The Colonies are not bound to the King or Crown by the act of settlement, but by their consent to it. There is no other legislative over the Colonies but their respective assemblies. The Colonies adopt the common law, not as the common law, but as the highest reason.

And Sherman's remark to Adams that he thought "that the Parliament of G.B. had authority to make laws for America in no case whatever," coupled with his support—which Silas Deane spitefully called confused—for the immediate organization and arming of a militia, placed him with the radicals. In addition, Sherman was for putting the opposition to Parliament on the broadest possible ground. He favored "taking up the Greivances at large" rather than merely objecting to specific acts. Sherman's logic was stronger than his politics in this instance. He saw clearly the ultimate outcome of the debate, and leaped over the intermediate stages now engaging his fellow congressmen. His was the most extreme position, and in the early days of October he appears to have been alone in promoting this course.[31]

When no full agreement could be reached, the statement of rights was postponed while the more practical problem of setting up a boycott was thrashed out. When Congress returned to the writing of a Declaration of Rights it turned out a document remarkably moderate in tone. It hedged on the question of the basis of colonials' authority by claiming only the right to participate in their own legislative councils. But since "from their local and other circumstances, they cannot properly be represented in the British parliament," legislative power in their own provincial assemblies was exclusive. Local legislative autonomy, then, was not only a question of right, but one of convenience and practicality. So in Roger Sherman's earlier terms, the Congress "conceded away the rights of America" as it adopted conservative James Duane's wording almost verbatim:

> But, from the necessity of the case, and a regard to the mutual interest of both countries, we cheerfully consent to the operation of such acts of the British parliament, as are bona fide restrained to the regulation of our external commerce, for the purpose of securing the commercial advantages of the whole empire to the mother country, and the commercial benefits of its respective members excluding every idea of taxation, internal or external, for raising a revenue on the subjects in America without their consent.[32]

Sherman's view of this can be easily guessed. The Connecticut delegates said only, "We have the pleasure of finding the whole Congress, and through them the whole continent, of the same sentiment and opinion of the late proceedings and acts of the British parliament. . . ." But Sherman could not have been happy, because for two years at least he had been convinced that "tho' some general Regulation of Trade &c. may be necessary for the General Interest of the nation . . . ," there was "no constitutional way to establish such regulations so as to be legally binding upon the people of the several distinct Dominions which compose the British Empire, but by the Consent of the Legislature of each Government. . . ." But whether he, with some of the others of the radical majority, acceded to the more moderate demands of the conservative faction, there is no way of knowing. Along with the rest of the delegates on October 26 he did, however, sign the Declaration of Rights in its final form.[33]

Although Sherman was not on the committee to deal with trade and manufactures, commercial policy deserves some consideration. It consumed more Congressional time than almost any other problem, and the Connecticut delegate was much involved with it a year later in the Second Congress. The findings of the committee on trade, reported on September 30, were mulled over during the first week of October, recommitted, reported out on the 12th and finally passed on the 20th. Earlier the principal points of debate had been whether the planned boycott should include nonexportation and nonconsumption as well as nonimportation, and whether it should go into effect immediately, on the first of November, or the first of December. Nonimportation and nonconsumption effective on December 1 had been agreed to unanimously on September 27. The real debate now revolved about the nature of nonexportation. Various colonies demanded exceptions to total nonexportation for goods vital to their economies. South Carolina in particular insisted on permission to export rice, at least. This finally being granted, the Articles of Association were signed by Sherman along with the rest, on October 20.[34]

How did Sherman stand on the twin questions of nonimportation and nonexportation? His theoretic radicalism was no veneer, and should have carried over into the practical matter of pressing the will of the colonies on Parliament. However, in early September, as the Congress had begun to gather in Philadelphia, Thomas Mumford, a connection of Silas Deane,* and significantly a wealthy Groton merchant, wrote to Deane:

> A universal non-importation and exportation will in my opinion be the most effectual and readiest plan we can adopt for relief but Mr. Adam Babcock of New Haven (lately here) says, Mr. Sherman, delegate with you, will be against either. But I hope better of him. If he has not goodness enough, I hope he has sense sufficient to keep him from declaring such sentiments.

Adam Babcock had been present at the August 17 meeting at Beer's tavern when Sherman had expressed his radical views to John Adams. He was thus in a position to know how Sherman felt generally, though the question of nonexportation may very well never have come up at that time. A year later Sherman took the view that some exportation should be permitted in order to provide specie for the purchase of powder and shot, and mentioned that this might mean "upon some men's principles we must have a general exportation." Whether he was hinting at his own position or not is unclear. Conditions were considerably altered by late 1775, and his views may have changed since the previous autumn, but there is also evidence to suggest that he favored a complete halt to exportation as well as a thorough nonimportation and nonconsumption in 1774.[35]

When the work of the Congress finally drew to a close, Sherman could view with satisfaction not only his public work, but also a number of personal accomplishments. He had met and come to know a good many of the influential men of the colonies, and had found his place among them. He was especially friendly, as was natural, with the other New England delegates, in particular the Adamses. He had established contact with radicals in the South as well as New England, and had become acquainted with the views of the small and large, commercial and agricultural, slave and non-slave colonies. On the negative side, Sherman's antagonism toward Deane, which had probably

---

*The men had married sisters.

begun earlier, certainly was strengthened in the autumn of 1774. This antagonism was to play a part in the politics of coming congresses.

In the First Continental Congress Roger Sherman put his name to the initial document of the four that were to make him the major signer in American history: the Articles of Association, the "memorable league of the continent in 1774," which, said John Adams, "First expressed the sovereign will of a free nation in America." Sherman was the only man who signed the 1774 document and the Declaration of Independence, the Articles of Confederation and the Federal Constitution. He also signed the Declaration of Rights and the ratification of the peace treaty with Great Britain in 1784. No one can gainsay his position as a major participant in the national politics that founded the American Nation.

Mending Fences

The unanimity of opinion claimed by Connecticut's colony-wide Committee of Correspondence was not so complete as alleged. Theophilus Morgan of Killingworth in New Haven County on the eastern edge, wrote on September 3, 1774 that most of the towns west of the Connecticut River had no such committees. Besides, it was well known, he continued, that the two sides of the Colony had long disagreed as to how best to protect liberty. Nonconsumption should wait until Congress had a chance to act, declared the moderate Morgan. As to Ingersoll—he should be left alone, for many good friends of liberty were also good friends to him. Many people had opposed the present government out of loyalty to former Governor Fitch, but now that he was dead the whole east-west dispute could be healed if differences were not agitated, Morgan concluded. Just five days later, as if to point up the geographical split, Gurdon Saltonstall wrote the Connecticut Congressmen that a meeting of delegates from the towns in the two eastern counties held that day had been very martial in its aspect.[36]

Sherman's first act on returning to New Haven was to arrange for a town meeting, at which he was moderator, to set up a Committee of Inspection chosen "in accordance with the eleventh article of association entered into by the late Continental Congress at Philadelphia." The Assembly had already endorsed this Congressional action and had ordered each town to establish committees. Church affiliation still structured local politics, so the committee consisted of five members each from the First, White Haven, and Fair Haven parishes, four from the Anglican church, and two each from the parishes of

West Haven, North Haven, Amity, Mt. Carmel, and Bethany, all still part of New Haven.* Though Sherman appears to have acted as chairman at times, Jonathan Fitch was more often so designated, perhaps because of Sherman's long attendance at Congress.[37]

Efforts of the New Haven Committee even went so far as to enjoin anyone from entertaining travelers from Ridgefield, where Jared Ingersoll's brother was minister, and from Newtown, Anglican John Beach's bailiwick, for those town meetings had explicitly attacked the Continental Congress and refused to enforce its measures. Several other western towns also were dominated by Tories—or at least "children of passive resistance" as William Williams termed them—and New Haven, close by, was rent with the opponents coalescing at the poles. But the Fair Haven ladies resolved to drink no more tea and at East Haven they bravely switched to coffee.[38]

Despite the compromise that put conservatives on the Committee, there was significant criticism of its personnel. A correspondent to the *Journal* appealed to the people to throw aside factional animosities and stop carping about the people who were chosen to enforce the Association in New Haven. In Stratford even William Samuel Johnson, shortly to retire from politics because he could not support anti-royalist measures, was placed on the Committee. Though well larded with conservatives, the Committees were vigilant and forceful, combining during 1775 into County Associations and at that level even going so far as to ban the shipment from New York of James Rivington's Tory *Press*. And in June the New Haven Committee declared that the Association could be violated by words alone because they tended to lessen the authority of Congress, disturb the peace of the town, and injure the common cause.[39]

Though Connecticut, relative to other states, seems to have been "exceedingly well organized to supervise the enforcement of the Association," considerable illicit trade with the enemy continued throughout the war. Even numerous patrol boats on Long Island Sound could not put a complete stop to the business, especially in Fairfield County, and as it increased after 1781 Washington had to call Trumbull's attention to it.[40] The

---

*The original members were, First Church: Jonathan Fitch, Samuel Bird, Michael Todd, David Atwater, Robert Browne; White Haven: David Austin, Timothy Jones, Joseph Munson, Peter Colt, Abraham Bradley; Fair Haven: Samuel Mansfield, Henry Dagget, John White, James Gilbert, Jonathan Osborn; Anglican: Thomas Bills, John Miles, Thomas Green, Daniel Bontocur; West Haven: Jonathan Smith, John Benham; North Haven: Jesse Todd, Giles Pierpont; Amity: Timothy Bradley, Enoch Newton; Mt. Carmel: Samuel Martin, Joel Bradley; Bethany: Joel Hotchkiss, Isaac Beecher, Sherman was not listed as elected.

chief problem, nevertheless, was not nonimportation, but nonconsumption, even though rising prices discouraged illicit purchases.

In addition to affording the biggest breach in the boycott, New York merchants irked Connecticuters in other ways, too. As the principal entrepot for European goods retailed in Connecticut, New York City creditors were pressing collections as intercolonial conditions became exacerbated. New Haven merchants alone were indebted to the Yorkers for £20,000 sterling, and among others Roger's son William was being severely pressed by his importers.[41] The reluctance of New York merchants to extend further credit added to shortages brought about by the nonimportation and began immediately to drive prices up. Another major difficulty, then, was that of enforcing regulated prices as prescribed by Article IX of the Association. Committees were set up to do this in the river and port towns, and the resulting extralegal trials seem for the most part to have been fair.

In an attempt to keep the British from getting foodstuffs, and, one suspects, to keep scarce commodities at home, Connecticut put the nonexportation provisions of the Association into effect in April instead of waiting for the date set at Philadelphia, September 10. Though Sherman's attitude on nonimportation was not entirely consistent, New Haven and other Connecticut towns tried to carry out the policy in both fact and spirit during the summer of 1775, though with difficulty. When products came into short supply in New York, merchants there sent agents into Connecticut to buy, among other things, flaxseed. This was against neither the letter nor spirit of the Association, but worried Connecticut townsfolk sternly warned the inhabitants against dealing with the engrossing Yorkers, and the New Haven Committee forbade the export of flaxseed to any place.[42]

In addition to assisting enforcement in New Haven, Sherman served on a committee of the colony to procure military stores. This job must have taken a great deal of time, for he wrote numerous letters to various New York and Rhode Island merchants ordering shot, powder, flints, etc. The stores were kept in his shop and at David Austin's.[43] He was, of course, elected to the Council of Assistants and appointed to the Superior Court in May 1775, and in September he stood eighth in the list of twenty men nominated for the twelve positions on the Council for the next April elections. Sherman was also chosen in November, along with Deane and Dyer, to represent the colony at the new Congress to be held in the spring of 1775. He had become good friends with some of his fellow delegates, such as John Adams, and would look forward to talking politics with them again. A visit to Adams two days before leaving Philadelphia in October 1774, was repaid during the lawyer's trip back to Massachusetts two weeks later. Adams recorded in his diary that when he again stayed at Beers', Sherman, Dyer and others had come to visit him. "Mr. Sherman," he wrote, "invited us to dine, but Mr. [Adam] Babcock claimed a promise, so we dined with him."[44]

By the time the doughty trio of Dyer, Deane, and Sherman left for Philadelphia in early May, blood had been spilled and both patriot and lobsterback lay dead on the road from Concord to Boston. Word of the battle of the 19th of April moved through an initially incredulous Connecticut during the next three days, reaching New Haven about noon on the 21st.[45] The Tory element here was still strong and did not melt away at the news of bloodshed, as was the case in most other Connecticut places. A town meeting was called immediately to meet in the Middle Brick Church, home of the conservative Old Lights, who, led by Jared Ingersoll, sought to control the meeting and elect a moderator from among their own ranks. This they failed to do; the radicals managed to put their own best man, one Roger Sherman, Esq., in the chair, though only by a one-vote margin. But it was no surprise to Ingersoll, who a month before had begun to doubt that New Haven would "be a proper asylum next summer for a Tory."[46]

Nevertheless, the close contest between Sherman and Ingersoll over the election of a moderator was symbolic of the pivotal point at which New Haven politics was poised at the moment of truth at Concord. Ingersoll had been appointed Vice-Admiralty Judge for the middle colonies in 1769 and had moved to Philadelphia in 1771. However, he made extended visits to New Haven during summer recesses, continued his law practice there through his nephew Jonathan, and kept a very strong hand in local politics. He had almost prevented the town meeting from endorsing the Continental Congress in 1774, and now he came within a single vote of dominating the meeting called to determine action in regard to the Lexington alarm.

But successful politicians must have temporizing personalities, and, though the pace of ideological polarization was hardly petty, Sherman and Ingersoll represented those favoring moderating tactics. Both were against tumults, opposed to hasty action and still hoping for a rational settlement of the colonial dispute. Thus when the Massachusetts contingent to the Continental Congress came through New Haven in August of 1774, Ingersoll organized a parade in their honor in order to divert the people from setting up a liberty pole. "Nothing shows to me the spirit of the town of New Haven in a stronger light," wrote John Adams, "than the politeness of Mr. Ingersoll who came over with his neighbors this evening and made his compliments very respectfully to Tom. Cushing, Sam. Adams, John Adams and Bob

Paine."[47] The delegation spent the night at Beers' tavern, and Sherman paid a call the next morning, more interested in discussing politics than in merely paying compliments.

Back in Philadelphia, away from the heat of local Connecticut partisanship, the Connecticut Whigs could consort with the villainous erstwhile Stamp Agent. "By the way Col. Dyer and Mr. Deane & I have smoakt the pipe together at my house," Ingersoll wrote his nephew at New Haven. And he gloated over being able to break to Sherman the news of Tory Joshua Chandler's election to the Assembly. But Ingersoll kept a wary eye on the local scene, for as soon as his back was turned the bully boys of New Haven erected their liberty pole. "Pray tell me where abouts on the Green Liberty Pole stands and who are the principal members of the Patriotic Club which meet at Steph. Munson's in order to take care of the N. Haven Tories?"

And take care they did, too. Though Chandler was elected again in 1775 and even made a selectman that year, the Patriotic Club was after him. A member of the Committee of Inspection challenged in the public prints, "What? Do you drink tea? Take care what you do, Mr. C____, for you are to know the committee commands the mob and can in an instance let them loose upon any man, who opposes their decree, and complete his destruction." Chandler was finally arrested in November and confined to his North Haven residence, ultimately to flee with the redcoats, after the 1779 raid on the town. Ingersoll, who had little business in the Admiralty Court after 1776, gave up his house in Philadelphia and lived for a while at Mrs. Cheeseman's with Sherman, Samuel Adams, and other congressmen. He returned under parole to New Haven in 1777 and died there four years later. At the end he was reconciled to independence and willing to cooperate with the new government.[48]

The issue of Toryism is one that exacerbated Connecticut politics from this time on until the matter was quieted a decade later. Anglicanism was a dissenting practice in the New England of Congregational establishment, and Connecticut Churchmen, unlike those in the other colonies, had no local crown appointees to look to for protection. Their chief lever for fair treatment was the tenuous position of the colony charter. It was generally believed by the Georges' ministries that the 1662 document had given far too much local autonomy to the distant little outpost. Anglicans in Connecticut knew that any real disruption of their church by the colony government would make an excellent reason for withdrawing the charter and establishing royal government, as had been done in Massachusetts and elsewhere. The Establishment knew this, too.

As a result, the Anglicans were tolerated, though they fell under suspicion and resentment until their help was needed by the rising New Lights. As has been shown, some political preferment came their way with the upset of 1766, when William S. Johnson was elected to the Council of Assistants. But now as relations with the mother country worsened and Anglican loyalty to the Crown became both more intense and more visible, Anglicans and Tories were virtually synonymous. Also working against further tolerance of Toryism was the fact of geographical concentration. There were about two thousand Tories in Connecticut on the eve of the Revolution, half of them in Fairfield County on New York's border. Most of the rest were in neighboring New Haven County. Tory strength in Fairfield County was strong enough to delay repression there. Indeed, one town, Redding, continued to send a Tory to the General Assembly until that body declared him *persona non grata* in 1776.

In New Haven, however, the division was close enough to cause grave concern among the Whigs, and threatening enough to create a degree of bitterness. And action followed soon. Meeting usually at the tavern of Stephen Munson, the activist New Haven Whigs formed a "Committee of the Friends of Constitutional Liberty." It was this group that Ingersoll identified as the Club at Munson's established to "take care of the N. Haven Whigs." It was one of their number who published the letter threatening Joshua Chandler, but by and large they had to act in secret. The election of Chandler as selectman and deputy in 1774 and 1775 points up the closeness of the division in New Haven. Anglican, anti-Susquehannah, and acquiescent in royal regulation, Tories temperamentally tended toward stability and order rather than dynamism and freedom. Elsewhere in the overheated colony, however, Tories were in a distinct minority. Physical intimidation, tar and feathers, insult and destruction of property either closed their mouths for the duration or forced them out of the colony altogether.[49]

Normal legal machinery seemed powerless to deal with the tumults. After being fitted with what his tormentors called a "new fashionable dress," but what felt to him like tar and feathers, an East Haddam Tory asked for redress in the courts. But Superior Court Judge Joseph Spencer insisted to the Governor that if action were ordered against the patriots "it will not be executed to any advantage without force from abroad to govern our people; for although the rough measures, lately taken place with us, are contrary to my mind, yet I am not able to prevent it at present." In general, Connecticut men of property were concerned for the colony's steadiness. Merchant Samuel Webb thought the Sons of Liberty ought to oppose mobs, for if they "are allowed to take hold of persons and private property, dissensions will follow, and we soon should be, instead of a United, a broken body. . . ." And Titus Hosmer wrote, "Is it not enough to make our family shudder? Consider how our matters are situated, should Mobism take place instead of good Government among ourselves." Sherman's old New Milford, always cautious, resolved that it would not be "bound by any unconstitutional assemblies of men whatever," out of fear of "the horrible prospects of anarchy and confusion."[50]

Ultimately about half of Connecticut's Loyalist element permanently expatriated itself to Nova Scotia, England, and other sanctuaries. They were not moving fast enough, however, and increasingly calls came to force "these parricides, to hide their heads in silence and darkness . . . or exterpate them from the face of the earth." Toryism was not clear-cut, of course. Men like Ingersoll and William Samuel Johnson were so ambivalent that they retired from politics during the war, but emerged approving the outcome in the early eighties. Benjamin Gale, who would ultimately give grudging approval to independence and stay alive long enough to polemicize against the Constitution of 1787, thought that he might now get his long awaited opportunity to see London. Even men considered good patriots would waver at times. Erastus Wolcott, son of a former and brother of a later governor, would accompany Johnson on a peace mission to General Gage after Lexington and Concord, and Governor Trumbull's own son-in-law, William Williams, attempted to halt actions of the Connecticut militia at the same time.*[51]

Although the Committee of Safety began to deal with the Tory problem as early as June, 1773, its efforts were limited to inquiring of Massachusetts what punishment she was imposing upon "our Common Enemies." But town committees began to take action. New Haven's committee held that Tory speeches were to be punished as contrary to the Continental Association, but seems to have settled for the social ostracism resulting from publishing the names of recalcitrants as enemies of the state. By 1776, in the western part of the state, the Tories were "Detected in Raising Men to Butcher their Country Men and [were] taken up & Imprisoned to the Number of 39 at Fairfield."[52] Meanwhile pressure had begun to mount for some official colony-wide legislation on the matter.

---

*Wolcott and Williams overcame their scruples, however, and became good patriots. It is perhaps significant that both men, large Connecticut landholders, were anti-federalists in 1787–88, but at the last minute changed their minds and voted to ratify the Constitution in the Connecticut convention.

Roger Sherman's activities in regard to factional Toryism evince the willingness of many Whigs to let sleeping dogs lie if only they will pretend at least to go to sleep first. When Sherman went to Philadelphia for the Second Congress, he left his legal affairs in the hands of Ingersoll's nephew Jonathan, despite his very close Tory ties. Less than two years earlier Sherman had sworn out warrants for the arrest of Jonathan and some college friends, including the high Tory Ralph Isaacs, when they had set off the town cannon one pleasant June midnight. Now Sherman, in November 1775, threatened economic retaliation against his own attorney. One John Simson of Boston had published comments complimentary to General Gage, and Sherman wrote Ingersoll, "If the aforesaid subscriber is your client, you will do well to consider, whether, consistent with Duty or safety, you can continue to do business for or correspond with such a Traitor to his native Country." Sherman went home later in the month, but even in his absence the town meeting had ordered its deputies to work for a colony-wide law regulating the Tories, and took steps to deal with their own locally. The *Connecticut Courant* reported that the election of ardent Whigs Samuel Bishop and Jonathan Fitch as deputies had been unanimous, which seems astounding in view of the sharp divisions of the previous spring.[53]

But by this time the east coast from New York to Portsmouth was in a ferment. Not only was Boston occupied and bottled up, but Captain James Wallace, with a fleet of about eight ships, was bombarding the coastal towns of Newport and Bristol in Rhode Island and Stonington at Connecticut's eastern edge. Tory activity was considerable, and there was a real fear of attack in New Haven.

In May one deputy wrote that "no Tories are allowed to Sustain any Office in the Colony five or Six Justices and Capt Hide for one are left out & Sundery Military Officers are Broken on Account of Toryism." Assembly members were sworn to secrecy, he said, and "it is a Terrible Time for the Enimies to their Country and I wish it might Never be better for them till they Repent." In December 1775, the legislature formally enacted a law for restraining persons found guilty of acts "inimical to the Liberties of this and the rest of the United Colonies." Penalties were limited, however, to three years in prison, disarmament, or disenfranchisement. In July 1776, the Council of Safety prohibited unknown persons to travel in the state without a certificate declaring that they were "friendly to the liberties of the American states." In June the Assembly passed an act for the confiscation of Tory estates and finally, immediately upon endorsing independence in December, passed a Treason Act providing for death to those convicted under its terms.

But by this time most of the active Tories had fled, and those remaining knew enough to lie still. Only one man was put to death for Toryism in Connecticut, a remarkably humane record.[54]

As late as October 1776, 107 inhabitants of New Haven felt it necessary to petition the Governor, so fearful were they of invasion and "a full persuasion & belief that there are Persons, now resident in this Town, who at least, would rejoice at the loss of our Liberties, & we fear, contribute their Mite to the obtaining that End . . ." They listed a half-dozen or so and asked that they be banished to the hinterlands; the Assembly sent some, at least, as far inland as Glastonbury just south of Hartford.[55] New Haven's conservatives not dangerous enough to be physically removed were driven into retirement. The effect of this was to knock off the right wing until after the war, and create instead a temporary division in the town between activists like Arnold and moderates like Sherman.

New Haven was, then, in Ezra Stiles' words, "unhappily divided on politics." Despite the victory in the election of Sherman over Ingersoll in the April 1775 town meeting, the conservatives were able to prevent the dispatch of armed aid to Massachusetts. The committee that was appointed to manage the town's interests was dominated by moderates. The plodding legality of the meeting was too much for the passionate young captain of the local militia, a druggist, book dealer, and West Indian trader named Benedict Arnold. He called out his company and with fifty men prepared to march to the Bay Colony. When the spoilsport town fathers refused to open the local armory to the impetuous firebrand, he threatened to blow down the doors of the powder house. Evidently local officialdom became convinced of Arnold's earnestness, for it quickly reversed itself and let him have the supplies. And off he marched to join Israel Putnam's force of several hundred already heading northward to battle.[56]

Governor Trumbull, reversing an earlier decision, called a special session of the Colonial Assembly for April 26.* The Whig governor urged a firm, deliberate, and unanimous course in "the most important Affair that ever came under Consideration within these walls." It was at this meeting that Connecticut decided to jump the gun on the September nonexportation provisions of the Association, and started running its economic boycott immediately. The Assembly also ordered a quarter of the militia out for

---

*Coincidentally, Governor Trumbull had declared April 19 a day of fasting to mark the curtailment of rights by the king. *Connecticut Journal*, April 5, 1775.

service and called for the purchase of various military stores including three thousand stands of arms, a job largely handled by Sherman. Two weeks later, on May 11, the regular spring session of the Assembly convened, but Roger Sherman was by this time riding the dusty road southward to Philadelphia.[57]

CHAPTER VI

The Second Continental Congress

IN the middle of April 1775, Eliphalet Dyer had written to Silas Deane proposing that they travel to Philadelphia together in Deane's "Leathern Conveniency" where "we can Chatt, we can sing, we can dispute everything, Scold and make friends again every half hour."[1] This doesn't sound like the kind of trip that would appeal to dour Roger Sherman, nor is it likely that Deane's enthusiasm about the Old Puritan's Company was very high. Nevertheless, travel together they did, and again the Wethersfield merchant provides us with an account of the trip.

The Connecticut delegates joined their Massachusetts counterparts as they passed through the colony, and the whole group went from town to town and entertainment to entertainment, greeted everywhere by joyous and noisy tumults. And where entertainments were not planned, they found their own. At Stamford, Connecticut, the group dined "with a company met at a wedding, which honest Mr. Cushing took for a company convened to wait upon us; and in he stumped, and led us to the head of the table, where, toward the close of our dinner, we found out our mistake, and were merry eno' on the occasion." They reached Philadelphia on May 10, and "were met," writes Deane to his wife,

> at about six miles on this side of the City by about two hundred of the principal gentlemen on horseback with their swords drawn; here we alighted and baited.* Thence began a most lengthy procession; half the gentlemen on horseback, in the van; next to them ten men on horseback with bayonets fixed; then Hancock and Adams, then Payne, next Mr. DeHart, next Col Floyd and Mr. Boerum in a phaeton with two most elegant white English horses; then your humble servant and Col Dyer; then Father Cushing and Jno Adams, Mr. Sherman next; then Mr. P. Livingstone. . . . [Mr. Alsop with Duane] . . . . Our rear closed with the

---

*Fed and watered the horses.

remainder of the gentlemen on horseback, with swords drawn, and then the carriages from the City. At about two miles distance we were met by a Company on foot, and then by a Company of Riflemen in their uniforms which is very curious. Thus rolling and gathering like a snowball, we approached the City, which was full of people and the crowd as great as at New York, the bells all ringing and the air rent with shouts and huzzas. My little bay horses were put in such a fright that I was in fear of killing several of the spectators; however no harm was done, and after much fatigue we were landed at the New City Tavern. Happily, a rain had laid the dust, and we were not so troubled as at New York.[2]

Generals and Politicians

The constitutional position of the Connecticut delegates had not changed from that expressed by the General Assembly in May 1774, for the statement passed then was ordered entered on the record in October, and in May 1775, Governor Trumbull went further in describing Connecticut's view to the King's ministry.[3] The Earl of Dartmouth, Secretary of State for the American Colonies, wrote Trumbull in the fall of 1774 urging that no new intercolonial assemblies be held. They would, he said, "be highly displeasing to the King." Trumbull responded during the spring session of the Assembly that

We consider the interests of the two countries as inseparable, and we are shocked at the idea of any disunion between them. We wish for nothing so much as a speedy and happy settlement upon constitutional grounds, and cannot apprehend why it might not be effected if proper steps were taken. . . . On the one hand, we do assure your Lordship that we do not wish to weaken or impair the authority of the British Parliament in any matter essential to the welfare and happiness of the whole Empire. On the other, it will be admitted that it is our duty, and that we should be even highly culpable, if we should not claim and maintain the constitutional rights and liberties denied to us as men and Englishmen; as the descendants of Britons, and members of an Empire whose fundamental principal is the liberty and security of the subject.

And he added "British supremacy and American liberty are not incompatible."[4]

The Second Continental Congress that convened in May 1775 was really an adjourned meeting of the earlier session. It re-elected the same officers and adopted the same rules as before, only adding a doorkeeper and a messenger and strengthening the obligation of secrecy. The membership was nearly the same too. Of the sixty-five members elected to the Second Congress, fifty-one had been members of the First. Only four of the First were not returned in 1775.[5]

The initial major business of the Congress was the very happy one of dealing with the accomplishment of Ethan Allen at Ticonderoga, which had put the American forces in possession of a large store of military supplies and also opened the way into Canada. Congress resolved itself into a committee of the whole to review the state of America, and kept at this for most of the time during the next six weeks or so. A number of resolutions were passed, among them one declaring that "these colonies be immediately put into a state of defence." Roger Sherman's maiden assignment arose out of this resolution. On June 24 he was placed on a committee of seven to "put Militia of America in a proper state for the defence of America."[6] This was the first of a long series of logistics assignments that Sherman was to be given, supply becoming one of his two principal areas of activity.

On June 15, when through John Adams' effort it was proposed that George Washington be sent to command the forces outside Boston, the choice was almost universally accepted. Sherman, however, along with his former business connection, Cushing, Pendleton of Virginia, and a few others, opposed the nomination. Sherman was very explicit in stating his feeling that New England troops then digging in on Breed's Hill north of Boston should have a New England commander. But all were persuaded to withdraw their opposition, evidently with some cajoling by Adams, and Washington was chosen unanimously. Dyer wrote his close friend Joseph Trumbull, "I don't believe as to his Military & for real service he knows more than some of ours . . . ," nevertheless he recommended the Virginian to Connecticut. He is, Dyer conceded, "Clever, and if anything too modest. He seems discreet and Virtuous, no harum starum ranting Swearing fellow but Sober, steady and Calm." Washington, he thought, would be "Very Agreeable to the Genius and Climate of New England." Three days later Dyer, with Deane and Sherman concurring, unsuccessfully recommended the ambitious Joseph Trumbull son of the governor, to Washington as secretary.[7]

Picking subordinate generals was a more difficult task than the election of Washington, however. Connecticut was to get one major general, and had recommended that the order of preference be David Wooster, Israel Putnam, and then Joseph Spencer. A report had recently reached Congress of a victory by Putnam in a small engagement at East Boston,* so he was chosen over the

---

*This was a patriot raid on Hog and Noddle's Islands in Boston Harbor. Putnam's men made off with large amounts of British livestock and provisions. They then waded out to the British relief ship, which had run aground, removed her cannon, and set her afire. Ward, *Revolution*, p. 58.

older Wooster, who outranked him. Sherman put up a fight in Congress to get the commission for his close friend Wooster. Dyer gave assistance on the New Haven general's behalf in hopes that Congress would follow the judgment of Connecticut. But Deane opposed Wooster, declaring him "totally unequal to the service"—a widely held view of the elderly general—and finally even Dyer voted for Putnam, so the battle was lost. Sherman had to write his proud friend, "Gen. Putnam's fame was spread abroad, and especially his successful enterprise at Noddle's Island, the account of which had just arrived, it gave him the preference in the opinion of the delegates in general, so his appointment was unanimous among the colonies."[8]

Francis L. Lee wrote during the winter Canadian campaign, "Old Wooster was ill suited to that long March, as I am: and . . . tho' brave enough to die in the bed of honor: he knew as little of a Soldier as I do." Wooster had had long experience, however, and was the only colonial militia major general not given equivalent rank in the Continental army. A recent biographer has written of this "general of the hayfield," that he was "dull and uninspired, garrulous about his thirty years of service, . . . tactless, hearty rather than firm with his undisciplined troops who adored him, at times brutal toward the civilian population of Montreal." He was married to the daughter of President Clap of Yale. The legislature remonstrated on behalf of Wooster and Spencer, and Governor Trumbull wrote to Sherman and the other delegates that he wished the Connecticut Assembly had been consulted again before the appointment was made official. Spencer resigned, and only after a lengthy conference with Trumbull at Lebanon was he persuaded to return to the Continental army in a command beneath that of his former subordinate. Dyer was disappointed at Spencer's retreat and wrote that he had "designed to have taken his birth my self, as I believed I might [have] had the offer."[9]

However, the matter continued to heat relations among the three Connecticut delegates. "Pray listen to these reports," about the generals, Deane wrote to his wife, "and inform me how far I am charged with being active in this arrangement. I have various reasons to expect their friends [Wooster's and Spencer's] will father it all on the old scape goat, as Sherman is known to favor Wooster, and Dyer and Spencer and brother Councilors." Later Deane told his wife that the attempts to prefer Wooster to Putnam were a "low, narrow, selfish, envious manoeuvre."[10] But if Putnam's promotion was not Deane's doing, then the crafty Wethersfield merchant was less than candid. He had recommended his stepson, Samuel Webb, to be Putnam's aide-de-camp and wrote Joseph Trumbull, "I have some little right to plead as I was the General's Friend in the Assembly, & have not been idle here of which I make no merit, & only wish I may not be censured by certain persons."[11] For his part, Wooster declined the brigadier's commission offered by Congress in favor of his commission in the Connecticut militia, despite Sherman's attempts to reconcile the disappointed old general to the lower rank.[12]

Wooster assured his fellow townsman in Congress that he would always remain his friend, and the matter was closed until March 1777, when another attempt to get a Continental commission for Wooster failed. This time it was because, as Sherman wrote Governor Trumbull, "Connecticut has more general officers than in proportion to the number of troops furnished by that State...."[13] But the effort would have been in vain in any event, for the brave David Wooster had been mortally wounded just the week before as he led a harassing action on the rear of retreating Redcoats near the pleasant little western Connecticut village of Ridgefield. And so he died in his "bed of honor."

Political Backing and Filling

Early in July two addresses by John Dickinson, leader of the advocates of conciliation, were before Congress for debate. One was the Petition to the King, known as the Olive Branch Petition, which begged for a cessation of hostilities until a reconciliation could be worked out. This reached the floor on July 5 and was signed on the 8th by Sherman and his fellow members. The second address was the Declaration of the Causes and Necessities of Taking Up Arms, which Dickinson had written jointly with Thomas Jefferson, a new member from Virginia. This, adopted on July 6, was a strong statement for liberty, though it rejected independence. Furthermore, it hinted at the possibility of seeking a foreign alliance, a particularly significant act.

Sherman went along with these addresses, but they were far too flaccid for his more radical predilections. While they were under consideration, he wrote to Joseph Trumbull:

> I have no expectation that administration will be reconciled Unless the Colonies Submit to their Arbitrary system, or convince them that it is not in their power to carry it into execution. the latter I hope will soon be done.... I want to know what measures the ministry will take after hearing of the Battle of Concord and Lexington; if they dont relax, but order reinforcements, I hope every Colony will take Government fully into their own hands until matters are settled.

It would be a year before the majority could be prevailed upon to declare similar sentiments; even strong Whigs were reported opposed to independence.*[14]

As Washington moved through New England to Boston, Congress moved on through questions of supply to the time-consuming problem of finance. On June 26, Dyer and Sherman could write Governor Trumbull that "the work is in such forwardness, that we hope soon to have it circulating and that several other important regulations now under consideration will be compleated and take place." A postscript adds, "Mr. Sherman has enjoyed his health well, his not signing personally the letters sent your Honor was owing to his having separate Lodgings." But in a private letter to his confidante, William Williams, Sherman wrote two days later:

> the reason I don't sign more of the Letters is not because our Lodgings are very far distant but because expresses are often sent off in haste and Colo Dyer and Mr. Dean [sic] being together have the Custody of the Papers. I sometimes sign with them, sometimes they sign my name others they sign only with their own names it not being very material and in Congress hours it is needful some should attend while others are writing. I have not been absent at any time while the Congress has been sitting. . . . It is very tedious sitting here this hot season:

Probably all the members were getting on one another's nerves by this time, for the emotional Dyer wrote the same day, "We are all exhausted sitting so long at this place and being so long confined together that we feel pretty much as a Number of passengers confined together on board ship in a long Voyage."[15] The much desired break came on August 2, as Washington's siege of Boston began its second month, when Congress adjourned until September.

The Connecticut delegates wasted no time in getting out of town. They picked up a Continental warrant for $50,000 to provision the Connecticut forces, and moved out immediately.[16] This trip was even more comfortable than previous ones, because Deane had had his carriage made over into a phaeton. The £50 alteration was made necessary by the apparent carelessness of Sherman, who had borrowed the chaise two weeks earlier and "had it broke intirely." Deane wrote his wife about this: "I lent my chaise to Mr.

---

*The ambivalence of most Americans is pointed up in the form for raising troops adopted in Rhode Island, where the soldiers were enlisted "in His Majesty's service, and in the pay of the Colony of Rhode Island, for the preservation of the Liberties of America." Peckham, *War for Independence*, p. 23.

Sherman yesterday and it is broke to pieces; but shall repair it, I believe, by a new one for the old one is totally broke and destroyed." And the more he thought about it, the more piqued he became. "I hope," he confided to his wife three days later, "to be home in three weeks if I get my carriage repaired in season; it must be made, in a manner, new. Mr. Sherman is, I think peculiarly unfortunate, at Philadelphia, tho' by no means faulty." But such is the ability of politicians to cover their personal animosities that the trio was able to travel together for the five-day ride home, sharing expenses as they went.[17]

Deane's phaeton was repaired in season, to the thanks of Dyer among others. Dyer made a trip back to Connecticut at the end of August with a horse and sulky borrowed from his soon-to-be brother-in-law, Joseph Trumbull, son of the governor. The horse, an old nag, "in passing a deep brook . . . finding a pleasure in ye coolness of the Water took a fancy to bath· him self, the water Near belly deep, he lay down in the middle of ye brook which brot the thrills over his back & there was poor I in a sad Situation with my game Leg. . . ." But a stranger chanced along, stripped and retrieved the stranded delegate, who "otherwise must have been soundly ducked. . . ." Dyer suggested that Trumbull get the old animal in "good Trimm" and sell him as fast as possible. And thanks, but no thanks, for the offer of the horse and sulky for the return to Philadelphia; "Mr. Deane Invites me to take passage with him in his leathern Conveniency. . . ."[18]

Military Supply and Foreign Trade

The first business to occupy Sherman's attention when Congress reconvened in September 1775 was that of export-import regulations. This question had been discussed in the earlier session, and a committee report of July developed some warm debate. "We have had in Contemplation," snapped John Adams, "a Resolution to invite all Nations to bring their Commodities to market here, and like Fools have lost it for the present."[19] And it was lost again later in the month. In September the question once more arose as part of the problem of supply. How would it be possible to buy powder without exporting some commodity? And where would be the best place to buy clothing?

The second question came up first. The discussion centered on a letter from Thomas Mifflin, at this time aide-de-camp to Washington, later Quartermaster General, member of the Conway Cabal against the commander-in-chief, and a good friend of Sherman. This letter had given rise on September 23, to a resolution, probably Sherman's, that a committee buy goods for the army and give them to the Quartermaster General to be sold to private soldiers at "prime cost and charges including a commission of five per centum, to the Quarter Masters General for their trouble." Sherman first suggested that clothing should be sent from the soldiers' homes to the encampments, as it was in the last French War, but added that suttlers might act as intermediaries to sell clothing to the soldiers, a system that was used in the Connecticut militia and worked well. Deane shot back that the suttlers had taken advantage of the soldiers in the last war, but Sherman suggested that £5000 be voted to the Quartermaster for the purchase of clothes. This suggestion was followed two days later when a committee was set up to buy the uniforms for the Quartermaster.[20]

The clothing should be bought locally, to keep specie at home, and to encourage manufactures as well. But Philadelphia had upset the Association already by raising prices 50 percent and it was charged in these debates that almost everyone in New York was still drinking tea. Still, the goods could be bought in these cities, Sherman thought, if a premium were paid. "I am not an importer," he declared, "but have bought of New York merchants, for twenty years, at a certain advance on the sterling cost." In the end Sherman's plan was followed, not so much because it was favored by the delegates, but because it seemed the only thing possible. It may be of some significance that Roger's oldest son, William, as a regimental Paymaster, became involved in some difficulties when he sold clothing to his soldiers and allegedly appropriated the funds to his own use.[21]

On the question of permitting exportation, Sherman believed that it was dangerous to permit ships to sail with provisions, for they were very likely to fall into enemy hands. In this prognostication he was correct, for just such a thing did happen to at least two cargoes of horses and wheat sent out in December. But the dilemma was hard to resolve, and Sherman ultimately came around to the view that some provisions must be exported for cash if powder was to be bought. He said, however, that it was not fair to permit the export of products from some colonies only; "upon some men's principles," he puzzled, this might mean "we must have a general exportation." Finally a modified nonexportation was enacted in November as the only expedient thing to do. But it included an amendment permitting exportation of provisions to foreign West Indies in order to allow importation of arms, ammunition, sulfur, and saltpeter.[22] Again Sherman seems to have figured the possibilities and become reconciled to them ahead of the majority.

Questions of supply became inextricably entangled with those of foreign trade, foreign alliances, and finally independence. The leading student of the Congress points to three intimately connected parallel developments in progress during the winter of 1775-76:

the growth of the spirit of independence, the increase of opinion in favor of opening the ports to world trade, the conviction that a foreign alliance, particularly with France, was essential. Foreign aid in any sufficiency seemed to point to independence as a prior requisite, a foreign alliance, necessarily so; and opening wide the ports was generally interpreted as leading straight to independence.[23]

How did these subtle ripples on the rising tide of independence affect Sherman's thinking?

Foreign aid Sherman considered a necessity, as evidenced in his part in the debates on supply. But that he favored it without an honorable alliance is doubtful. The idea of sending a secret committee to Europe for the purpose of buying or begging supplies did not appeal to him. Some time late in 1775 he entered in one of his notebooks:

The great principles of alliance the only solid effective one is a right resulting from a firm and dignified national courage to ask other powers to become sharers in our Strength, and not partners in our weakness. . . . The more attention we pay to our own resources and the less we rely upon others, the more Surely Shall we provide for our own honor and Success, and retrieve that balance between the contending European powers. . . .[24]

The impression given here is that the writer favored total implementation of the Association, both in its encouragement of domestic manufactures and its non-import-export provisions. His stand on procuring supplies had been the more expedient one of permitting some exportation, however, and ultimately importation, too.

Besides questions of honor there are other explanations that help to account for Sherman's reluctance to engage in under-the-counter deals with European supporters. He had the natural provincial suspicions of foreigners; he blamed the vicissitudes of European involvement for the tremendous debt of the colonies that grew up during the period of the French and Indian War and after;[25] and finally, in the last stages of the discussion, he may have suspected the operation because one of the committee to negotiate the supplies was to be his erstwhile traveling companion, Silas Deane. But more likely Sherman's ambivalence on the question grew out of his knowledge that alliances could not yet be negotiated, and supplies were needed immediately. Finally, his solution to the puzzle was to throw open the American ports to ships of all nations. But this smacked too much of independence for the majority, and therefore had to wait.

In the end Sherman was placed on the most important committee to deal with the problem, the one to consider the regulation of trade for the period beginning March 1, 1776. Trade regulation was of crucial importance because either an open-port policy or commercial agreements would imply independence. As John Adams was to write, "As to declaration of independency, read our privateering laws and our commercial laws. What signifies a word?" The radicals were eager to bring about a general European trade both in order to get material support and because it would bring the colonies nearer to independence. The conservatives were opposed to such a general trade for just that reason. Adams, who had grumbled the summer before over the failure of Congress to open the ports, tried continually to interest the members in foreign commercial treaties. And Sherman, who had long ago given up on reconciliation, went along with Adams in his minority view. Even the other Massachusetts delegates gave their brasher colleague little support, but Sherman, Richard Henry Lee, and Gadsden of South Carolina "were always on my side." "We cannot carry on a beneficial trade," said Sherman after his experience with the shiploads of horses and wheat, "as our enemies will take our ships. . . . a treaty with a foreign power is necessary before we open our trade to protect it." But it became clear that France would require a statement of intentions by the Congress before she would be willing to conclude such a treaty. And so debate on independence could not be avoided longer.[26]

Independence Like a Torrent

Sherman was reconciled to, even eager for, independence perhaps as early as 1772, and certainly by the time of the First Congress. In July, 1775, he wrote to Joseph Trumbull, "I want to know what measures the ministry will take after hearing of the Battle at Concord and Lexington; if they dont relax, but order reinforcements, I hope every Colony will take Government fully into their own hands until matters are settled." In late October of 1775 when New Hampshire asked Congress for advice about the administration of civil justice in the convulsed state, a committee of five including Sherman was set up to write the instructions. Adams "embraced with Joy the opportunity of haranguing on the Subject at large, and of urging Congress to resolve on a general recommendation to all the States to call Conventions and institute regular Governments."[27] Sherman among others, wrote Adams, "Spoke on the same side with me." Indeed, the committee was made up of ardent advocates of such a move. Adams pointed to its membership, John Rutledge, Samuel Ward, R.H. Lee, Sherman, and himself, as a measure of the growth of sentiment for independence; "These names, of themselves, show how much a little month had done to alter the temper of the majority."[28] But the fiery lawyer was still in advance of his fellows. The committee, though made up entirely of members as hot for the project as any in Congress, could not agree upon a report until Friday, November 3. The instructions finally advised a convention to establish a government for the province, but only for a time "limited to the present contest."

Ever since 1766 Sherman had been questioning the royal connection. At that early date he had implied his view as seeing the connection to the Crown as only by colonial consent. Surely now he was in full agreement with Governor Trumbull, who wrote him in November 1775, "The King's Proclamation [rejecting the Olive Branch Petition] is decisive We are now fully assured of the Inefficiency of Petitions. . . ."[29] Sherman was reading Rousseau at this time, copying long extracts into his notebooks, and here was more support for his opinions.[30] Clearly he was for independence along with the radical minority at least eight months before Congress could be brought to vote for it.

The majority of Congressmen seemed to be waiting for the people to push them to the declaration. The push began in May and by the 20th Adams was writing to James Warren, "Every Post and every Day rolls in upon Us, Independence like a Torrent."[31] The pressures in Congress and out increased steadily, but still a majority delayed, some demanding a confederation first, a few others still holding to the idea of a possible reconciliation. A resolution from Virginia calling for independence lay on the table until early June, when word came that the King had taken the desperate step of hiring German mercenaries to fight on American soil. And though efforts to capture Quebec had been abandoned, Washington moved triumphantly into Boston in March. Now the various states began to instruct their delegates to vote independence.

Connecticut fell in line on June 14, the Assembly now completely purged of Tories. In April Oliver Wolcott had written his wife that "A final Separation between the Contrys I consider as unavoidable." And this seemed to be the general sentiment among the Whigs, the dominant faction. Sherman had been trying to get away from Philadelphia for about a week but was unable to leave the debate until after the 19th of March, and had set out on the return trip on April 4, arriving back in Philadelphia on the 10th.[32] This time he brought his wife with him for a six-week visit to the great city. This, incidentally, was unusual among the delegates and indicates something of the attachment that Roger felt for Rebecca. He had hoped to rent Jared Ingersoll's furnished house for the summer, but that King's Judge of Vice-Admiralty had second thoughts about visiting home just then—"not being yet clear that New Haven will be a proper asylum next summer for a Tory. . . ."[33] Sherman had missed part of the debate on the independence question, but his sentiments were well known, and when Congress finally decided to do something about a declaration, he was picked for the committee.

On June 7 Richard Henry Lee offered a resolution "that these United Colonies are, and of right ought to be, free and independent States . . ." that it was time to form foreign alliances, and that a plan of confederation be drawn up for consideration by the colonies. John Adams seconded the resolution. On June 11 a committee of five was appointed to write the official declaration of independence. Lee was not put on the committee because, says Adams, he "was not beloved by the most of his colleagues from Virginia, and Mr. Jefferson was set up to rival and supplant him," or more likely because he wanted to be in Virginia while a government was being organized there.[34] The substitution of Jefferson was perhaps a fortunate one. Adams, Benjamin Franklin, and Roger Sherman seemed fairly logical choices, and Robert Livingston, who had opposed an immediate declaration on June 8, represented a more moderate point of view.

The committee's work is well known. Only Sherman's minor part in it need be dealt with here. The Declaration was written by Jefferson and shown to Adams, who made minor corrections. Recalling the event in 1822, Adams wrote, "We reported it to the committee of five. It was read, and I do not remember that Franklin or Sherman criticized anything. We were all in haste. Congress was impatient, the instrument was reported, as I believe, in Jefferson's handwriting, as he first drew it. Congress cut off about a quarter of it. . . ."[35] Franklin, Livingston, and Sherman, then, appear to have had no part in the writing of the document. Indeed, writing in 1779, only three years after the event, Adams didn't even remember that Sherman was on the committee and substituted the name of Benjamin Harrison instead.* It seems abundantly clear, however, that Sherman's sentiments coincided with those of the Declaration, and it is very probable that he supported it in the debates of late June and early July.

---

*Harrison served on another committee with Adams, appointed the same day.

Independence Comes to Connecticut

Independence came to Connecticut without a prolonged struggle. The fight had been fought and won a decade earlier, and efforts by the conservatives to re-establish their primacy in 1767, 1770, and even 1774, though sometimes close, fell shorter and shorter of the goal. Former Governor Fitch died in July 1774, and the government conspicuously ignored it; Ingersoll was in bad odor with the colony's voters. There was no longer a rallying point for what was left of the Old Light party. William S. Johnson, who had received 3840 votes and election to the Council in 1773, could claim only 991 in the following October and 137 the year after that. Sherman, incidentally, benefited by the quashing of his opposition and moved up to sixth position in the vote in 1775, and to fourth a year later, reaching his high point of third in 1778.[36]

Most Connecticut men with Tory sympathies were probably merely "perplexed, confused and distracted to know their duty in the great controversy," or, like Samuel Roberts, confessed that "entirely unacquainted with Politics, [he] did as almost every ignorant man generally does, swim with the Tide or current near him." But there were some who wanted to "Kill more Damnd Rebells than the best Brittain." Most of these either fled with the British or were shut up by patriot intimidation; a few crept into the legislature in 1775 and had to be denied seats there.[37] Indeed, one of the first jobs of the Assembly in October 1775, and again in May '76, was to purge not only itself of Tory sympathizers, but also the militia and other branches of the civil government as well, a job they had begun as early as the previous May.[38] Newtown's Tory delegates were purged completely, and her deputies didn't reappear until October 1777, when a pair of good Whigs were seated. Sherman's New Haven was still having its problems, too, for there militia captain Abraham Blaksley was dismissed by the legislature for "speaking contemptuously of measures taken by the General Assembly."[39]

The upshot of this was, of course, a totally Whig government by the end of 1775. In December the Assembly, the last to publish its ordinances under the imprint of the Royal Arms, passed a law making any kind of active or spoken aid to the British forces illegal. Since Connecticut was still a constituent of the Empire, this law marks the coming of civil war to the colony. When loyalty becomes treason, no wonder some men were perplexed and confused. In some towns the law was used to wipe out Tory politics altogether. The extreme was reached in Fairfield County's inland Newtown, where eighty-three local leaders were deprived of their privileges as freemen.

Detail from John Trumbull's *The Signing of the Declaration of Independence*. Courtesy of the Yale University Art Gallery. From left to right: John Adams, Roger Sherman, Robert R. Livingston, Thomas Jefferson and Benjamin Franklin.

JONATHAN TRUMBULL (1710–1785). Governor of Connecticut, 1769–1784. Portrait by George F. Wright after an original by John Trumbull. Courtesy of the Connecticut State Library.

And in New Haven they took Thomas Darling's three slaves away from him.*[40]

"A Revolution in Government . . . is about to take Effect," Oliver Wolcott wrote to Samuel Lyman in New Haven. "May God grant a happy Establishment of it, and secuerety to the Rights of the People." And to his wife he added, "to swear allegiance and act under an Authority which had not only cast us out of its Protection but for so long a Time has been carrying on the Most cruel War against us, was tho't not only absurd but impious."[41] Constitutionally, Whigs did not see themselves as rebels. Governor Trumbull voiced the views of his constituents when he pointed out that tyranny is the real crime and "the Rebellion is on the part of our Enemies." Thus the old treason law which provided the death penalty for acting against the King was repealed, and indeed all statutory references to royal government removed from the books.** This was followed up in October 1776, with the prescription of a new oath of fidelity to the state government and requiring agreement

> that you believe in your conscience the King of Great Britain has not, nor of right ought to have, any authority or dominion in and over this State; and that you do not hold yourself bound to yield any allegiance or obedience to him within the same; and that you will, to the utmost of your power, maintain and defend the freedom, independence, and privileges of this State against all open enemies or traiterous conspiracies whatsoever. . . .[42]

The Assembly spent a good many long hours of the month-long May session on military matters. The militia was reorganized, strengthened, and deployed; the governor was authorized to issue Letters of Marque; and other clearly rebellious business was promoted. A sort of excited foreboding overhung the last days of the session. The deputies and assistants were acutely aware of their role in history. Explicitly they intoned their anxieties in their closing resolution:

---

*The black population of Connecticut had been increasing rapidly—up from 3634 in 1756 to 6464 in 1774. *Connecticut Journal*, June 10, 1774.

**Connecticut citizens had always considered the Charter, the Fundamental Orders, and General Assembly statutes sufficient constitution to all purposes of local government. None of these were revoked by independence, so no new constitution was deemed necessary in 1776. Connecticut thus escaped the constitutional battles that saw the beginnings of ideological divisions that ultimately split the Whigs in other states. This is no doubt one reason why the articulation of party came much later in Connecticut than elsewhere in the Federal period. For a general discussion of constitution-making, 1776–77 see Wood, *Creation*, ch. IV, p. 133 n12.

The events of this year may prove most decisive to these Colonies and that all human care, efforts and exertions are but fruitless attempts for our security and defence, and will prove vain and abortive unless attended with the blessing of Heaven, which we have no reason to expect but on a sincere repentance and reformation:

Wherefore, in this day of darkness and threatening calamity, it is most earnestly recommended to and pressed upon all persons of every rank and denomination in this Colony, to promote and cultivate charity and benevolence one towards another, to abstain from every species of extortion and oppression, sincerely to repent and break off from every sin, folly and vice, to live together in peace, love and harmony among themselves, to look up with earnest importunity to Heaven for help, success, salvation and deliverance, and with careful attention to the use of means hope and trust in the Lord of Hosts, who presides over universal nature, guides and governs all, and we not fear or be dismayed at all the attempts or numerous hosts with which we are threatned.

But for the last time the Assembly styled itself "the English Colony of Connecticut."[43]

Little did the apprehensive patriots know how soon their forebodings would mature. They had adjourned on June 8, the day following Richard Henry Lee's famous resolution for independence. When word came from Philadelphia that the Connecticut delegates awaited instructions, the Governor called the weary legislators back to work. Reconvening on June 14, the delegates turned the next day to their principal task. The instructions to Sherman and his associates follow the general pattern established by states that had acted earlier. A preamble declares that;

Whereas the King and Parliament of Great Britain by many acts of said Parliament have claimed and attempted to exercise powers incompatible with and subversive of the antient just and constitutional rights of this and the rest of the English Colonies in America, and have refused to listen to their many and frequent humble, decent and dutiful petitions for redress of grievances and restoration of such their rights and liberties, and turning from them with neglect and contempt to support such claims after a series of accumulated wrong and injury have proceeded to invade said Colonies with fleets and armies, to destroy our towns, shed the blood of our countrymen, and involve us in the calamities incident to war, and are endeavouring to reduce us to an abject surrender of our natural and stipulated rights, and subject our property to the most precarious dependence on their arbitrary will and pleasure, and our persons to slavery; and at length have declared us out of the King's protection, have engaged foreign mercenaries against us, and are evidently and strenuously seeking our ruin and destruction. These and many other transactions, too well known to need enumeration, the painful experience and effects of which we have suffered and feel, make it evident beyond the possibility of doubt, that we have nothing to hope from the justice, humanity or temperate councils of the British King or his Parliament, and that all hopes of a reconciliation upon just and equal terms are delusory and vain. In this state of extreme danger, when no alternative is left us but absolute and indefinite submission to such claims as must terminate in the extreme of misery and wretchedness or a total separation from the King of Great Britain and renunciation of all connection with that nation, and a successful resistance to that force which is intended to effect our destruction: Appealing to that God who knows the secrets of all hearts for the sincerity of former declarations of our desire to preserve our antient and constitutional relation to that nation, and protesting solemnly against their oppression and injustice, which have driven us from them and compelled us to use such means as God in his providence hath put in our power for our necessary defence and preservation:

Resolved unanimously by this Assembly, That the Delegates of this Colony in General Congress be and they are hereby instructed to propose to that respectable body, to declare the United American Colonies Free and Independent States, absolved from all allegiance to the King of Great Britain, and to give the assent of this Colony to such declaration when they shall judge it expedient and best, and to whatever measures may be thought proper and necessary by the Congress for forming foreign alliances, or any plan of operation for necessary and mutual defence.[44]

These instructions differed in one respect from those passed by Virginia a month earlier upon which Connecticut's were based. The Virginians called for an end to allegiance to "the Crown or Parliament of Great Britain," while Connecticut omitted any mention of Parliament, demanding cessation of allegiance to "the King of Great Britain." Connecticut had seen itself as virtually self-governing for a long time. The Assembly urged Congress to start work on a "regular and permanent Plan of Union and Confederation of the Colonies" for the security of the liberties of the people, but always reserving the "forming governments for, and the regulation of the internal concerns of each Colony" to the colonial legislatures.

After the Declaration was published by Congress, the Connecticut General Assembly approved it as its first action at the October 1776 session.*

---

*Significantly, the secretary of the Assembly omitted the list of deputies present normally found at the opening of each session. Thus the list of members who instructed for independence has never been published. It is in CSL, "Revolutionary War," Ser. 1. IV:261ad.

The Assembly resolved "That they approve the Declaration of Independence published by said Congress, and that this Colony is and of right ought to be a free and independent State, and the inhabitants thereof are absolved from all allegiance to the British Crown, and all political connections between them and the King of Great Britain is, and ought to be, totally dissolved." The Declaration itself was recorded in August 1777.* [45]

Congressional Pick and Shovel Work

Roger Sherman, of course, missed this important session of the Assembly. Indeed he missed most of them in 1775 and 1776. But he was kept in touch, not only by post riders who came regularly from the Assembly and the Council of Safety, but also by more important emissaries. In March, for instance, Dyer and Williams had been sent down by the Committee of Safety to pick up £50,000 that Connecticut was trying to get from Congress to cover costs of current campaigns. They were also instructed to confer with the Philadelphia delegates. It seems odd that when they returned on April 26 they were unable to report sufficient independence sentiment to get action at the May Assembly. [46]

Not all, nor even most, of Roger Sherman's time was taken up with the basic issue of independence. During this second session of the Second Congress his main activity centered on the immediate problems of conducting the war. In this respect he was active in two areas: military supply and military planning. In the First Session, which had adjourned in August, he had served on the important committee to devise ways and means to put the militia in a proper state for the defense of America, which was equally interested in military arrangement and supply. In the Second Session he was again actively engaged in questions of war and supply. The work was largely routine performance of the most mundane kind of chores. He served on a committee to buy duffel, needles and thread for Schuyler's troops, to check

---

*The text of the document became available in Connecticut on July 11, when one could buy copies of it at the office of the *Connecticut Journal* in New Haven. *Journal*, July 10, 1776.

It is interesting to note that less than a year after the republican levelers of Connecticut cut themselves off from their king, they voted to style their governor "His Excellency." Trumbull's biographer claims that this was done without the Governor's knowledge, hard as that may be to believe. A year later Trumbull got around to protesting that "High sounding Titles intoxicate the mind, *ingenerate* envy, and breed disorders in a commonwealth, and ought therefore to be avoided." He requested repeal, but without success, and the Yankee state's governor is still "His Excellency." *SR*, I:229; Stuart, *Trumbull*, p. 363n.

into frauds in contracts, to supply the troops at New York, to buy 10,000 pairs of shoes and socks, and many other such essential but hardly glamorous needs of war.[47]

He was active also on a large number of committees that dealt with the conduct of the war itself. These duties, though of first importance, were the very pedestrian ones of answering letters from officers who wanted specific orders of march, dealing with resolutions on the raising of troops in the various states, and so forth. This was all good experience for what would come later when he joined the Board of War. As a member of various military committees, Sherman had met with Washington in Philadelphia and in the field; he had dealt numerous times with military correspondence; and he was active in the area of military supply. It was most appropriate to put him on the Board of War in June 1776, along with Adams, Benjamin Harrison, James Wilson, and Edward Rutledge. This Board, called a "new and great event in the History of America" by Hancock, never really worked well. It was one of many examples of attempts by committees to perform administrative duties that led finally to the establishment of executive departments. But it was the most active committee dealing exclusively with military matters at this time. Adams said that it

> kept me in continual Employment, not to say Drudgery from the 12 of June 1776 till the Eleventh of November 1777 when I left Congress forever. Not only my mornings and Evenings were filled up with Croud of Business before the Board, but a great Part of my time in Congress was engaged in making, explaining and justifying our Reports and Proceedings. . . . Other Gentlemen attended as they pleased, but as I was Chairman, or as they were pleased to call it President, I must never be absent.[48]

Sherman's reputation for diligence would indicate that he was absent seldom. There were those who wished he might be less active, however. In 1780 Alexander Hamilton wrote Philip Schuyler, to whose daughter he had just become engaged, regarding a committee of three to be sent out to confer with Washington, which had been given with him "a kind of dictatorial power." "Some good may result," he wrote, "if Gentlemen who love the General are not Jealous of the army, and of a Generous turn are sent, but should General Sherman be at the head of the Triumviri the General will be tormented with the thousand little theses which Roger has thrown together and which he Entitles a System."[49] Hamilton was bitter, though, because Sherman had been one of the wheels that had turned Schuyler out of his command in '77 in order to replace the New Yorker with the British-born Virginian Horatio Gates.

Another area of importance to Sherman was that of finance and currency. In this second session, for instance, he served on committees to ascertain the value of the several species of gold and silver, to investigate the circulation of counterfeit Continental bills, and to devise ways and means of raising ten million dollars. Still another phase of his activities involved Indian problems.

He had always taken an interest in Eleazar Wheelock's Indian school in the New Hampshire wilds, and Wheelock turned to him on several occasions for assistance. In March 1775, Wheelock had written that he was in terrible danger of attack from the north, for the Indians there were "determined to fight someone and will fight on which ever side gives them license first." But he had some of their children there at his school, Wheelock continued, whom he held hostage to their parents' good behavior. To get still more of these children, especially the son of a particularly important sachem, would be highly desirable. Then he suggested that more missionary work in the area might secure the northern boundary and thus make unnecessary the diversion of troops from the coastal areas. On June 26 the Connecticut delegates, writing to Governor Trumbull, took note of the situation. "By a Letter from Albany received Yesterday we are informed of the Defection [of the] Caughnawaga Indians, effected by the presents of Governor Carlton who is meditating Hostilities. Are not some of their children with Docr Wheelock? If so may not some Advantage be taken of that Circumstance?"[50]

On another and later occasion Sherman took the side of the Indians in a very modern way. In a debate over organizing the Confederation, the question of which government should have jurisdiction over the Indians, the usually strongly states'-rights Sherman moved that Congress be given this jurisdiction in order to prevent injustice to the Indians or to the colonies. And he agreed with Jefferson that only Congress should be permitted to purchase lands from the Indians. He was also placed on one committee to consider a letter from a group of sachems and to propose a treaty to them in November of 1775, and on another to discover why so many Indians had come to Philadelphia the following March. The information he brought back to a nervous Congress was that they were merely on hand for the traditional shake-down of the governor of the state.[51]

Congress adjourned on August 2, and when it reconvened in early September 1775 for the second session, members drifted in by ones and twos from the various colonies for several weeks, so that business was slow starting. John Adams used some of his idle hours to draw thumbnail sketches of his comrades in Philadelphia. He wrote on September 15,

Dyer is long-winded and round-about, obscure and cloudy, very talkative and very tedious, yet an honest, worthy man, means well and judges well. Sherman's air is the reverse of grace; there cannot be a more striking contrast to beautiful action, than the motions of his hands; generally he stands upright, with his hands before him, the fingers of his left hand clenched into a fist, and the wrist of it grasped with his right. But he has a clear head and sound judgment; but when he moves a hand in any thing like action, Hogarth's genius could not have invented a motion more opposite to grace;—it is stiffness and awkwardness itself, rigid as starched linen or buckram; awkward as a junior bachelor or sophomore.

Add to this picture the plain country dress, the short-cropped, unwigged head, the massive shoulders and tall frame, the sound of the nasal cant and back-country speech of the ex-cobbler, and Roger Sherman emerges as a striking, if peculiar, figure in a company of urbane and sophisticated men. It is clear that Sherman never accomplished anything on the basis of his looks or a honeyed tongue, though he was a capable and original debater once used as an example for Yale students of rhetoric.[52]

He was most effective backstage, behind the scenes, or in the term of the day, "out of doors." Thus it is understandable that he did not receive any important diplomatic positions from Congress, but was given inside jobs instead. So in February 1776 he was placed on a committee with Adams and George Wythe of Virginia to draw up instructions for an embassy going to Canada.[53] This embassy, consisting of Franklin, Samuel Chase, Charles Carroll and his brother John, a Catholic priest, was the most important of several that attempted to woo the Canadians to the colonial cause. Its instructions were a matter of considerable importance, and it is a measure of Sherman's stature that he was given a share in writing them. The mission was a failure, of course; the Frenchmen of the North were tired of fighting colonial wars, and refused to be involved this time.

The instructions need no detailed treatment here, therefore, but it might be pointed out that the New England-dominated committee included an interesting sentence: "You are further to declare that we hold sacred the rights of conscience, and may promise to the whole people, solemnly in our name, the free and undisturbed exercise of their religion." And the clergy was to remain in control of its estates, all other matters of religion to be "left entirely in the hands of the good people of that province," excepting only that all civil rights and the right to hold office were to be extended to persons of any Christian denomination. This is not surprising, however, for the authors were practical politicians, and Sherman, who would not be called the most liberal of the three, was reasonable on matters of religion.*[54]

L'Affaire Silas Deane

During the winter of 1775–76, the relations between Sherman and Deane rapidly disintegrated. Silas Deane had never been trusted by some of his fellow politicians, and by this time Sherman must have known of Deane's attempts to block his election as a delegate to Congress in August 1774. William Williams had feared that Deane might use the public business to further his own private interests, and there is evidence to support his suspicion. "The Congress have also appointed a Secret Committee," Deane wrote Thomas Mumford in October '75, "for Supplying the Continent with certain Necessary Articles. of this I am one, and wish I could see you, or some other of my Connecticut Mercantile Friends here, as it would be in my power to help them, and in theirs to serve their Country. this hi[nt is a]ll I can give on this head, and if you will come down, the sooner the better." Even among his partisans, Deane did not give the impression of a straight and sound character; James Duane, who had been an ardent supporter of Deane in the factional politics of Congress, wrote that he "was not surprised to hear that Silas Deane had turned traitor since he wanted a 'dignity of soul.' "[55]

Deane was diligent in his country's behalf, however, as well as his own. Indeed, that he was one of the hardest-working members is not only the conclusion of historians, but his own as well. "My Dear," he wrote his wife, "I rise at six, write until seven, dress and breakfast by eight, go the Committee of Claims until ten; then in Congress till half-past three or perhaps four; dine by five, and then go either to the Committee of Secrecy, or of Trade until nine; then sup and go to bed by eleven." But these efforts were not appreciated in all quarters of his home state.

The elections to the Assembly in October 1775 boded ill for him, and perhaps he suspected it.

I suppose Connecticut politicians have been busy, and that the Nomination will be varied, but I hope not very greatly, as I wish for the old steady plan of the Colony, in preference to any private view, either for myself or friends. I am a little surprised that Col. Seymour missed his

---

*In 1778 when at Silas Deane's suggestion Ezra Stiles hired a French professor for Yale, a great hullabaloo was raised in New Haven at the intrusion of a papist in the town. But Roger Sherman, satanic religious libertine that he was, thought that there would be no danger, and even went so far as to welcome the Catholic Monseigneur Martel to the campus. Stiles, *Lit. Diary*, II:296–98.

election for Hartford, but duplicity and haughtiness are two of the worst ingredients in nature for a Connecticut statesman.[56] In the same letter he indicated that his relations with Williams remained quite cool.

At any rate, re-election to the Congressional delegation was not granted to Deane and Dyer. Oliver Wolcott and Samuel Huntington were chosen to return with Sherman, with Titus Hosmer and William Williams as backers-up, the delegation not to exceed three paid members, but any one of them authorized to vote for the colony. Ezra Stiles gave the reason for the defeat of Deane and Dyer that the Assembly "think Liberty most secure under frequent changes of the Delegates—and they determine to set an early Example & Precedent."[57] But rotation was not the only motive. Deane himself admitted that he had behaved equivocally. Dyer had so energetically pushed Susquehannah claims as to antagonize important Pennsylvania congressmen. Deane, believing that the western settlers had acted "in a most shocking manner, . . . persued quite a different plan. . . . I avoided the dispute wholly and when forced upon it express'd my warmest wishes for a friendly Settlement. by this means I stood with The most dispassionate of the other party, . . ." His hopes that this would not hurt his influence with the Susquehannah people to whom he "wrote in the most peremptory stile to keep quiet . . ." were ill-founded. Mumford had other explanations, which he outlined to Deane: "your true friends found the Junto had levied their artilery [sic] & strongly fortified against you by securing a large majority of the present members in favor of both Col. Dyer & you being recalled." He blamed the trouble on "the class at Munson's," the New Haven radical Whig organization. Deane himself contributed the name of Williams, "that little malevolent prig in buckram," as the leader of the "rascally junto."[58] Williams, as a matter of fact, was one of those chosen in place of Deane, though he did not attend till later in the year. Williams' brother-in-law, John Trumbull, a crony of the highflown merchant, wrote unkindly:

A man of Congress asked thus
    "How comes it, Poet Tombel,
Your State doth send a Fool to us
    Whose Name is William Wimble?"
The Poet did this Speech relate,
    "From honest views we sent him.
The Fools are many in our State,
    He goes to represent 'em."[59]

Sherman, too, was obviously involved, and when he returned to Philadelphia in January, having paid a visit to his family, Deane could not contain himself: "of my old friend Sh---n," he barked to his wife, "suffice it to say, that if the order of the Jesuits is extinct their practices are not out of fashion, even among modern New Lights Saints, or some of them, for I never particularize any Sect." There was no hiding his feelings, and his fellow sufferer, Dyer, wrote to Joseph Trumbull that Deane "is confoundedly Chagrined at his recall. He is really Very Usefull here and much esteemed in Congress." For himself, Dyer wrote that he was "happily relieved in a most important critical situation of Congress." At this time Deane told his wife that he gave up his seat "with pleasure," but less than two years later he wrote Governor Trumbull "I will confess to you that I was hurt in the manner in which I was dismissed from being a delegate."[60]

John Trumbull, the Hartford Wit whose *M'Fingal* was soon to make him the darling of the literary Whigs, had condolences for his connection, however. His pen could stab Sherman as well as Williams. "You have heard of our Assembly's Choice of Delegates for next Congress. Have you heard what motives they proceeded on?" he wrote to Deane.

> It is dangerous, they say (I am going to write a vindication of them). It is dangerous to trust so great a power as you now have, for a long time in the hands of one Set of Men, least [sic] they should grow too self-important and do a great deal of Mischief in the end. Very well; there may be something in that. On the other hand, they say, it is not best to change all at once, least the new men should not know whether the others broke the thread, & so be unable to find the end. Good again. Nor was there even a better expedient to avoid all danger on all sides, than to drop all those who are capable of doing mischief, and at the same time send one who is as well able to keep his finger on the place where ye left off, as the best of you? For my part, viewed in this light only, I take it for a master-stroke of Connecticut policy. But there is yet more in the matter. You know, Sir, we esteem it a matter of some consequence to the Colony, to send to the Congress men of politeness & gentility, as it may give other Delegates a better opinion of our Goodbreeding in Connecticut. Can it then be wondered at, that we should chuse again a Man, allowed on all hands to be the Politest Gentleman of our Age? As this last paragraph is a little obscure, I beg leave to explain it in a few words. It is allowed that we thought yourself and Col Dyer tolerably polite men, when you were first chosen Delegates to the Congress; yet it was observed on all hands that, on your return, you did not seem at all altered, either in your manners or your dress; you made no proficiency in Gentility. We considered the Congress as a school of politeness, at which you seemed incapable of learning. You must pardon us, therefore, if we gave you up as unteachable or incorrigible. While your Colleague returned so bodwigg'd, so short-skirted (new Ideas require new terms), so silk-stocking'd,

so small-hatted, in short so universally bemacaronied, that nothing since the last Comet has glittered with so much splendor, or been stared at with such amazement. And then his Sulky, in which he rode last to Philadephia—what wheel-carriage, since Ezekiel's version, could ever equal it? You know he turned off an old honest Chair-box to give it admittance, & fixed it on between the wheels in such a manner that it looked like an overgrown Go-cart, for Newberry's Children six feet high; & when he came to set it agoing, it had more different motions than the earth—backwards, forwards, progressive, digressive, here a little & there a little, playing up and down, like the balance-wheel of a watch; so that he appeared in it like Addison's Angel 'riding in the whirlwind,' & went forwards with more dashing and plunging than Arion on the back of a Dolphin. Nor did his internal accomplishments fall below the glory of his outward appearance. Who has not heard of his honesty and his Almanackmaking [sic]? All panegyric must sink beneath the inimitability of his eloquence, Demosthenes only can be compared to him; when haranguing on the seashore, he filled his mouth with pebbles, to aid the natural impediments of his speech. And could we wish his sun to set when it had but just fairly arisen? when we only began to cry out with Virgil

Hu, miserande Puer, si quo fata asper
rumpas. Tu macaroni eris.
No, cried the Genius of Connecticut
(if it have any) I decus, I, noster,
melioriches utera fatis:

and so sent him again to Congress. And this I take to be a full & true account of the matter.[61]

So John Trumbull was a man to be reckoned with! Nowhere else is there a trace of insinuation that old Roger is vain or pompous; nowhere else is he treated with a lack of respect—even by his enemies. If the picture is accurate, it is the only one from this point of view. It all sounds reasonable, plausible, and even welcome to know that the man who had controlled his passions by the time he was twenty-one was really human after all. But the only thing that might be considered substantiation for any of this is in one of Sherman's notebooks, on the blank pages of *Father Abraham's Pocket Almanack for the year 1776*.[62] Here he listed some expenditures made in Philadelphia during the April following the composition of Trumbull's masterpiece. There were some extraordinary purchases for a staid old Puritan, such as red shoes, wine-glasses, silk gloves and ribbons. But he had his wife with him, so perhaps the items are not so strange after all. The sharp quill of John Trumbull, however, if accurate is revealing.

The defeat of Deane at the hands of the Assembly may have brought on rumblings for a change in Connecticut's government. A correspondent signing himself J.R., perhaps Jesse Root, a friend of Deane's, called for a direct election of Congressional delegates in a letter to the *Courant* in June. The call is based on the best Lockean theory, holding that all authority ultimately resides in the people and they should choose their own representatives. An answer a week later put the matter to rest for a time by pointing to the need for accountability to the Assembly. Nevertheless, sentiment for direct election continued to build throughout the war, finally to be enacted into law in May 1779.[63] But if Sherman and the junto thought Deane's defeat removed him from the Congressional scene, they were soon to be disabused of that delusion. In the spring of 1776, when Sherman's committee was fighting out the question of opening the ports, two secret committees appointed Deane to conduct activities for them in France. One of these, known simply as the Secret Committee, delegated him to procure supplies surreptitiously—under the counter, so to speak. The other, known as the Committee of Secret Correspondence, sent him abroad to try to fathom the mind of the French minister Vergennes in regard to the colonies. These commissions were dated the 1st, 2nd, and 3rd of March, but Deane didn't leave the country until early April. These agencies, Adams thought, were created specially for Deane, who

> had been left out of the Delegation by the State, but instead of returning home to Connecticut remained in Philadelphia, soliciting an Appointment under the two foregoing Committees, as an Agent of theirs. . . . Unfortunately Mr. Deane was not well established at home. The good people of Connecticutt thought him a Man of Talents and Enterprize, but of more Ambition than Principle.[64]

Upon his arrival in Europe, Deane immediately became embroiled in a wrangle with the envoy already on the spot, Arthur Lee, brother of Richard Henry. The reasons for the antagonisms and the motivations of the two men are obscure, and to this date there seems to be no clear scholarly agreement on just what went on. In any event, Deane got into trouble with one element in Congress by sending to America hundreds of French military officers, some merely adventurers, others genuinely interested in the issues of the war, like the young Marquis de LaFayette. One close student writes, "he had wildly, even if with the best intentions, made agreements with French military adventurers, who had in consequence besieged Congress in such shoals demanding commissions, that native officers protested in disgust . . . ," and Congress had to send many of them back at the expense of the colonies. Deane was also charged with using his position to make large profits, misapplying public funds, and worst of all, stealing public money. This last, the most serious and apparently the most simple problem, still plagues historians, none of whom has thoroughly unraveled the web. The question was this: had the supplies sent to the colonies through Beaumarchais prior to the alliance been gifts—as Lee maintained—or had they been charged to the account of Congress? If they had been gifts, what right had Deane to charge the Congressional account? It was Lee, through his brothers and friends in Congress, who initiated the charges, and his faction pressed for an investigation.[65]

Eliphalet Dyer, back in Congress by 1777 and feeling no comradeship for his once close collaborator despite their suffering together at the hands of the Assembly in '76, wrote to Joseph Trumbull of Deane's imprudent conduct in Europe. William Williams conveyed the same information to the place where it would do the most good—to Mr. Roger Sherman, now sitting with the Connecticut Council of Safety at Hartford. Sherman had some ideas on the subject:

> I received your favor of the 2nd Instant [he wrote on August 18th] and am obliged to you for the Intelligence it contains, I want to know the final results of that affair—If the Gentleman you mention went such lengths, without any authority, what, may be expected when he has plenary power to bind in all cases—To make the matter more easy he might be Sent for, to give more full intelligence than can be communicated by writing.[66]

The Sherman-Adams-Lee forces did their work rapidly, and Deane was recalled in the autumn of that year. He delayed in Paris, however, long enough to sign treaties with France, and did not return until July.

Once again in Philadelphia, Deane found it difficult to get a hearing before Congress, and was informed by the Connecticut delegate, Titus Hosmer, that it was the aim of the junto to wear him down with delays and petty harassments. By the middle of Septmber these tactics had begun to weary the long-suffering envoy, and he complained to John Hancock that a minority of Congress was persecuting him.

> but you know that in Congress a few men can put off the decision of any Question by one means or other as long as they please, and you are not a Stranger to what a certain Triumvirate, who have been from the first members of Congress, are equall. The baseness and ingratitude of one of them you have sufficiently experienced in private Life, to know him capable of anything in public; [S. Adams] and my old colleague Roger, the Jesuit, with their Southern associate, [R. H. Lee] have been indefatigable ever since my Arrival. Roger, indeed, is at present on a Tour to the Army, and thence to New Haven, to stir up the pure minds of the Faithful there against the next Election of Delegates; he is expected back

in a few Days, when perhaps they will be ready to take the Field, after having suggested in whispers ev'ry thing that could tend to hurt the man they causelessly attack.[67]

This trio, Deane continued, has "by one circumstance or another greatly influenced the deliberations of Congress." A month later and in more politic tone, Deane wrote to Governor Trumbull: "I support myself calmly against the cabals of a junto of men, who are most assiduously laborious to injure me. . . ." He then proceeded to describe the parties that had grown up in Congress through the long continuance of some members there, whose principal object was to secure jobs for friends and relations. These are men, he said, "who by long and assiduous attention are become skilful in such kind of management . . . ," and he recommended that the delegates be required to report regularly the proceedings of Congress. Deane was less than candid. He had been Connecticut's principal spoilsman while at Congress, and it had been the Governor's own family that had benefited most. Three of Trumbull's sons had been given high-level positions, but all found petty fault with the arrangements, wrote carping and disagreeable letters to Congress, and ultimately resigned in pique. Oliver Wolcott wrote his wife that the three boys' "claims on the Head of Merit I believe have rendered them a little ridiculous." [68]

Typically, Sherman tried to stay out of the messy patronage business. The first he knew of his own son Isaac's military adventures was through a letter from Joseph Trumbull to Eliphalet Dyer. And typically he wrote not to his son, but to Trumbull, thanking him for sending on word "that [Isaac] was well, I have not heard from him since the Battle of Charlestown—when you write again should be glad you would inform wether he was in that Battle and what Place he sustains in the Army, I did not know he was there till you mentioned it. . . . I should be glad you would mention my sons State of health when you write to me or Colo Dyer."[69]

It is clear that affairs in both Congress and Connecticut were solidifying the connections between the young, nationalist and progressive mercantile faction consisting of Deane, the Trumbulls, Thomas Mumford, Deane's stepson Samuel Webb, Jeremiah Wadsworth, and others. At the same time the older patriots who had provided the merchantile dynamic of the sixties were maintaining a strong grip on political office. A third element, agrarian and provincial, and probably a majority of Connecticut's yeomanry, was rumbling and beginning inchmeal to move from inchoate to organized. When a combination of these forces pushed through a law providing for direct election of congressmen, Sherman was to be shelved temporarily to re-emerge as a compromise candidate for the Constitutional Convention of 1787.[70]

The matter had not been resolved by the following summer, and the ranks of the anti-Deane men were shrinking. A member from Massachusetts wrote in June: "R. H. Lee is gone home resigned. Mr. S. Adams goes on Monday, to resign. But there are some hardy watchmen in this political Camp besides the veteran Sherman." By this time "the whole affair had degenerated into a struggle between the partisans of Lee and the partisans of Deane, with the welfare of America all but lost sight of." This is not surprising, since the roots of the fracas were personal to begin with.[71]

Deane finally lost all patience with Congress and went to the people with his case in an address published in the *Pennsylvania Packet* in December 1778. This public airing of the controversy so infuriated President Laurens that he resigned his chair and gave a speech that heated the debate to a temperature yet unequaled.[72] Ultimately both factions took to the newspapers, and by the time Deane was permitted to read his prepared narrative in December, there was hardly a member who had not made up his mind on the issue. The whole imbroglio was most unproductive of good; Deane was discredited and Arthur Lee lost prestige, and unnecessary personal antagonisms kindled and smoldered between the two factions for years afterward.

The root of the controversy was the antagonism that had developed between Deane and his fellow Connecticut politicians in the years before the actual outbreak of the war. One of Deane's biographers has said:

> This mission [to Europe] he was the more willing to assume, since the Connecticut General Assembly had not again elected him to the Congress. Although held in high esteem at Philadelphia, Deane was not on good terms with Sherman and Dyer. He had objected to several items in the Accounts of Connecticut against Congress, and had strongly supported Putnam for a generalship in the Continental Army, and thus antagonized the friends of Spencer; besides he had neglected local for national politics.[73]

To these can be added his objections to Wooster, and his connivance in an attempt to keep Sherman out of Congress in the first place. When Sherman discovered that he could get support from the powerful Lee brothers, and through them from Sam Adams also, the junto was set. That these men were members of the radical faction on the independence and trade questions cemented the alliance, and the breach with Deane began to widen. There can be no doubt that these connections, rather than the substance of the issues, determined the votes of some members on more than one occasion.

The Articles of Confederation

Almost from the first sitting of the Second Congress in 1775 the problem of confederation lurked behind much of the debate on independence and foreign affairs. As Washington attempted to assemble an army in New York in the spring of 1776, Congress could give little attention to politics. But by June the General had collected about 19,000 troops, and on June 11, 1776, the first official moves in the direction of confederation were made. On that date Congress resolved to prepare a plan of confederation and chose a committee of one member from each state to do it.[1] Sherman, assigned the previous day to the committee to write a declaration of independence, was put on this new Grand Committee as well. The only other member who served on both of these supremely important bodies was Robert Livingston of New York. Sherman was also a member of the Board of War, thus gaining position on the three most significant agencies of this session, if not the whole Congress.

The Grand Committee gave the actual drafting of an instrument of union to John Dickinson, and his report was debated in committee and on the floor over a period of six years before final adoption. The discussion again and again crashed headlong into the basic question of the division of sovereignty with its corollary, the basis of representation and taxation. And when this double trouble was not standing in the way of progress, the delegates found themselves snagged on the thorns of western lands. Sherman ultimately developed the final solution to the question of representation, and he was instrumental in clipping the thorns of the dispute over western lands.

Western Lands

The snags of western lands were the first to catch at the drifting debaters. Earlier Benjamin Franklin had offered a proposal for union, respectfully but unenthusiastically recieved, which included a phrase giving Congress exclusive right to purchase land from the Indian tribes. The Dickinson draft gave Congress powers of "Regulating the Trade, and managing all Affairs with the Indians—Limiting the Bounds of those Colonies, which by Charter or Proclamation, or under any Pretence, are said to extend to the South Sea . . ." and ascertaining new or undetermined boundaries, setting up new colonies from lands already owned by states or later purchased by Congress and disposing all such lands for the general benefit. "The language of the clause wriggles rather widely," writes one historian, "but its principal bomb was in the phrase, 'are said to extend to the South Sea.' " [2]

The debates between the states claiming western lands and those with fixed boundaries were the most bitter and durable aspect of the struggle for acceptance of confederation. Connecticut's western lands claim was somewhat extraordinary, since much of the land lay within the fixed bounds of Pennsylvania.

Already this was beginning to upset intercolonial relations, and cause some hard feelings between the delegates from Pennsylvania and their cousins from Connecticut. At the end of the first Congressional session the Pennsylvanians had evidently asked the Yankees to calm down their obstreperous wersten appendage in the Wyoming Valley. Dyer, Deane, and Sherman wrote to Colonel Zebulon Butler, the western leader, just before they left Philadelphia in August 1775. "It has been represented," the letter reads, "to ye Continental Congress that there is great danger of discord and Contention if not Hostility & bloodshed between the People setling [sic] under Connecticut Claim & those under Pensylvania [sic] which would be attended with the most unhappy consequences at this time of general Calamity & when we want our whole United Strength [—?—] our common enemy. We are therefore desired" (and at this point was added the line, apparently as an afterthought, "by ye Congress"), to request that the Pennsylvania settlers be left alone, especially those families who have members fighting in the rifle companies at Boston; make no new settlements, and do nothing to give offense to Congress because they may have more to do with this affair. Again it was emphasized that this letter was written at the request of Congress. The letter, though found among Sherman's papers and signed by all three delegates, is in Dyer's handwriting.[3] Congress would have more to do with this affair; there is no question about that.

In October the frontier was still in ferment. On the 7th, Ross of Pennsylvania submitted a resolution laying the "Connecticut Intrusion before Congress that something be done to quiet their minds." But the issue was not clear; one of Ross's fellow Pennsylvanians, Thomas Willing, indicated that there were two sides to the question, and suggested the need of an umpire. Sherman, taking advantage of the opening, said that he thought agreement might be made on a temporary line of separation. But Dyer was the major *bête noire* of the Pennsylvania land holders, waxing so hot that he ultimately destroyed his effectiveness in the issue. Deane, involved in other western speculations and courting the favor of powerful Pennsylvania interests, had opposed the Connecticut settlers, calling their activities a "mad frolic."[4]

Now, a year later, and with Dyer and Deane replaced by Samuel Huntington and Oliver Wolcott, Sherman, the predictable pragmatist and a member of the drafting committee, saw the absurdity of trying to support every charter claim of every state, so many of which were overlapping. While attempting to protect the Wyoming settlers already on the spot, he nevertheless supported the Dickinson phrase. Not so his even more provincial-minded Connecticut colleagues. Huntington insisted on the claim all the way to the Pacific and brought Wolcott along with him. Sherman was outvoted, so Connecticut took her place in the camp of the landed states. The Dickinson draft recognized by implication that land existed that belonged to no state, and that the general government would control it. Obviously this would be unacceptable to the landed states, especially when a release to Congressional control really meant surrendering the claims to speculators, already organized and functioning, most of whom were residents of the landless states.[5]

Sherman's interest in giving Congress control over the Indian tribes in 1776 illustrates his liberality toward them. But in context another reason for his suggestion seems equally important. Jefferson wanted to nail down the assumption that charter boundaries "to the South Seas" were valid, and at the same time undercut the stand of the speculator interests in Congress. To this end he proposed an amendment to the Dickinson draft that "No purchases to be made by the individual states or persons of lands on this continent not within the boundaries of any of these United States, shall be valid . . . ," that all such purchases were to be made by Congress, and the lands should be given to any permanent settlers. Sherman seconded this motion of July 25. The next day, however, the Connecticut politician offered something to members who approved of the original wording by moving that, despite the location of Indians—in state bounds or out—Congress should have "superintending power to prevent injustice to the Indians or Colonies."[6]

One more complication grew out of the efforts of settlers in land disputed by New York and New Hampshire to separate from both governments. These Vermonters later sent a petition to Sherman, who introduced it on June 25, 1777 asking for statehood and representation in Congress. Sherman, the principal agent of the Vermonters, most of them former Connecticuters, really wanted both disputes put off till after the war.[7] It was not a propitious time for an interstate squabble. General Washington sat on Manhattan with less than twenty thousand half-trained, ill-equipped militia and one-year Continentals facing a growing force of over thirty thousand seasoned professionals of His Majesty's army.

In August 1776, when the debate was renewed, Sherman was willing to meet the landless states halfway, particularly Pennsylvania, which, with Maryland, had held up the major portion of her side in the debate. He agreed that the boundaries should be resolved, but moved that "No lands be separated from any State, which are already settled, or become private property."[8] Behind this stipulation lay the double motive of attempting to protect the Connecticut people in the Wyoming Valley who were already on the spot, and retreat with dignity from the untenable position of pushing Connecticut's claims all the way to the South Sea. Sherman gave away a good deal with this inconsistent stand, but it was the only practical solution to the western lands question from the Connecticut point of view.

Despite the American defeats at Brandywine Creek and Germantown, and the occupation of its home base, Philadelphia, Congress continued to plan postwar unity. No doubt Burgoyne's surrender at Saratoga gave some heart to the relocated Congress as it continued debate at Lancaster and then York in the fall of 1777. The landed states then received strong protection from the landless states and from speculators by a provision "that no State shall be deprived of territory for the benefit of the United States." But ratification lay ahead and "The history of the ratification of the Articles of Confederation is almost entirely the history of the continuation of the struggle [over western lands]."[9] Sherman was at home during the fall debates, but his side won, both in protecting western claims of the states and in limiting the power of the central government. He, no doubt, was satisfied. The question had to be resolved in some final way through ratification by the states, and by February 22, 1779, all had ratified except Maryland. This little province feared complete subordination to her large sister to the south unless Virginia's land claims were limited.

The matter was taken up in the Connecticut Assembly some time during the early months of 1778, apparently without resolution, and again between then and the spring of the next year.[10] By the fall of 1778 Sherman was pushing his home state to work out some sort of compromise. He wrote Governor Trumbull:

> The Assembly of New York in their late session did not ratify the Confederation, nor has it been done by Maryland and Delaware States.

These and some other of the States are dissatisfied that the western ungranted lands should be claimed by particular States, which they think ought to be the common interest of the United States, they being defended at the common expense. They further say that if some provision is not now made for securing lands for the troops who serve during the war, they shall have to pay large sums to the States who claim the vacant lands to supply their quotas of the troops. Perhaps if the Assembly of Connecticut should resolve to make grants to their own troops and those raised by the States of Rhode Island, New Jersey, Delaware and Maryland in the lands south of Lake Erie and west of the land in controversy with Pennsylvania, free of any purchase money or quit rent to the Government of Connecticut, it might be satisfactory to those States, and be no damage to the State of Connecticut. A tract of thirty miles east and west across the State would be sufficient for the purpose, and that being settled under good regulations would enhance the value of the rest; these would not be claimed as Crown lands, both the fee and jurisdiction having been granted to the Governor and Company of Connecticut.[11]

Sherman was proposing what eventually became the final settlement, with the exception that Connecticut ultimately assumed no obligation to provide for the troops of other states. It is typical of Sherman's political style simultaneously to continue the claim of Connecticut to the territory, while making the land available to the landless states—to grant and withhold at the same time.

In May 1779, Maryland's euphoniously named delegate, Daniel of St. Thomas Jenifer, wrote his governor that "Connecticut is now I am told by Sheerman disposed to allow Congress to settle the Dispute about the Back lands. That State has empowered its delegates to confederate with the other States, but on the express Condition that Maryland shall have the power at any time hereafter to accede to the confederation on equal terms with the other States." Then in November the North Carolina delegates reported that Connecticut was indifferent about its "claims to Lands westerly."[12] Nevertheless, it was a year later before Connecticut's position on the issue became generally known.

The Assembly, reacting to a Congressional resolution of September 6, 1780 requesting a speedy end to the claims, declared itself willing to do whatever was necessary for the "liberty and independence of this rising empire. . . ." On this basis they gave to the United States the authority to survey and sell Connecticut lands west of Pennsylvania and east of the Mississippi River. The amount of land given up was to be in proportion to that ceded by the other states, and was to remain under the jurisdiction of the Connecticut government.[13] This was, then, an effort to give Congress a revenue without losing political control over the area. But Congress was not interested. Thus in November, Madison could write only that Connecticut had ceded *some* of her territorial claims. She still reserved to herself certain jurisdiction, "and clog the cession with some other conditions which greatly depreciate it, and are the more extraordinary as their title to the land is so controvertible a one."[14] This was not the last word that Madison was to have on Connecticut's manipulation of her "extraordinary" and "controvertible" claim to the west.

Finally, Oliver Wolcott spelled out Connecticut's position in a letter to President Laurens in December, 1780; in the interest of cementing the union, Connecticut had ceded all unlocated lands west of the Susquehannah Purchase provided other states claiming unlocated territory should cede a proportionate amount of land.[15] The action was welcome, and sufficed to satisfy Maryland of Connecticut's good intentions. So when Virginia made some concessions, too, Maryland ratified, and the Articles of Perpetual Union became effective.

Ratification, however, marked only one stage in the struggle between Connecticut and Pennsylvania over the constantly simmering Susquehannah question. The issue was to boil forth again in the early years of the 1780's, not to be finally resolved until the eve of the inauguration of the Federal government. The Articles of Confederation included a section that set up a "means for the settlement of disputes over private rights to soil claimed by two or more states under different grants made prior to any settlement of jurisdiction in such cases." The dispute between New York and Vermont, as well as the Wyoming controversy, were examples of issues to be settled through the use of this machinery.

Pennsylvania had always been eager to take advantage of this judicial establishment for the settlement of the dispute. In November 1779, before the Articles had been ratified, she had proposed that this provision be utilized. Since both she and Connecticut had ratified the Articles, why not adjudicate? But the Connecticut Assembly put off the proposal, holding that many of the relevant documents were in England and unavailable. In spite of attempts to bring about agreement between the Pennsylvanians and the Susquehannah interests in Connecticut out of court—or out of doors, in the parlance of the day—the issue was finally taken to a special court provided under the Articles.[16]

This Court of Commissioners was set up in 1782 on petition of Pennsylvania, thus instituting the only action between two states occurring under the old Articles of Confederation. Despite delaying tactics by Jesse

Root and Eliphalet Dyer, the Court was finally chosen and met at Trenton on November 18, 1782. Again the Connecticut commissioners, now with the addition of W. S. Johnson—who were technically only agents of the state at court, and not delegates to Congress—attempted to delay action.* Even partisan Dyer granted that the Court was fair, but after hearing arguments for a month, it handed down a decision entirely in favor of Pennsylvania, holding that "the State of Connecticut has no rights to the lands in controversy." The question of private rights still remained, however; did the individual settlers have legal title to their holdings in the Valley?[17]

At this point Roger Sherman stepped to the forefront of the settlers' cause. His son William had gone west the previous summer on some scheme or other—more than likely looking for work as a surveyor—and wrote back that things were bad; in particular, the Indians were burning houses and killing livestock with impunity. The Assembly of Connecticut had passed a number of resolutions of support and encouragement for the westerners, and Sherman apparently was the prime mover in these. In November 1783, the Settlers appointed him their agent at Congress, presumably assuming he would be re-elected a delegate, which he was. Sherman's commission, signed by Zebulon Butler and eighty-eight others, gave him full discretion in determining the progress of the petition through the court.[18]

On January 13, 1784, Sherman arrived in Annapolis with Butler's petition, and the Pennsylvanians were immediately suspicious. Edward Hand, writing to John Dickinson, then President of Pennsylvania, said, "notwithstanding the irregularity of the form, bad Orthography etca. would at first view lead a person to believe it to be the offspring of those people [at Wyoming] I apprehend your Excellency will without much difficulty trace it to another source."[19] That the "other source" was thought to be Roger Sherman is beyond doubt. But while Sherman might well have suggested the petition, it certainly was not written by him. There would be no need for him to disguise his handwriting or style, and he would not have been inclined to do so. He arrived at Congress both as the state's delegate and as the settlers'

---

*Philip Jordan contends that a deal was in fact struck between the Connecticut commissioners, especially Johnson, and the court. This was suspected at the time by the Susquehannah Company members in Connecticut. Julian Boyd believes no deal was made with the court, but discusses fully the evidence that points to a Sherman–Jefferson settlement later. Jordan, "Connecticut Politics," pp. 236–41; Boyd, *Jefferson Papers*, VI:474–87. The most recent and most thorough student of the Trenton settlement believes that "No evidence supports the notion that the trial was a sellout or that an honest effort was not made on each side." If Johnson's efforts seemed feeble to some observers it must have been because he was ill during the trial. Taylor, "Trial," ps.545, 543n79.

agent. Among the papers he carried with him was a proclamation by Governor Trumbull asserting a claim to the lands between Pennsylvania and the Mississippi River.

Trumbull's proclamation was read before Congress and given to a committee of which Jefferson was the leading member. Jefferson wrote a report that immediately snuffed out any attempt Connecticut might make to reopen the case on its own behalf. A second report authorizing a court to hear the claims of individual settlers was passed on January 23. "It is plain," writes Jefferson's editor, "from the nature of the reports and from the alterations made in them by Jefferson and by Congress that a tug of war was in progress between Jefferson and Sherman." In the backwoods the settlers were now faced with ejection suits brought by the Pennsylvania speculators, and by late June blood had again been shed when the Pennsylvanians attempted a brutal, forcible dispossession of men, women, and children from the area. Correspondence between Sherman and John Franklin, who had become the Wyoming leader, shows that Sherman tried to quiet the westerners by settling the case out of court, either by a deal with the speculators directly or through the Pennsylvania Assembly, though he had little hope of success.[20]

At the same time Sherman suggested to Governor Griswold, who had succeeded the venerable Trumbull, that Connecticut petition Congress on behalf of the settlers, who were plagued not only by Pennsylvania militia and raids by unorganized Pennsylvanian settlers, but by floods and Indians as well. He also went further than any of the commissioners to the court had been willing to go in pressing the legality of the Susquehannah claims. While Dyer, Root, and Johnson had only asked for a fair grant by Pennsylvania to the Wyoming settlers, Sherman wrote John Franklin, agreeing with him that even Company members still residing in Connecticut should get some sort of settlement. Franklin was the leader of the extremists among the Susque-hannans, those who would hold out for compensation to Connecticut speculators in addition to granting the claims of the actual settlers.[21] Sherman believed that the presence of the Pennsylvania militia violated the Articles of Confederation, and that the case should go to both Congress and the Supreme Court of Pennsylvania. This plan would at least delay action, as it couldn't come up until the next session. On Sherman's return to his home state, the upper house resolved to raise an army to go to the contested lands. The measure evidently met with reluctance from Governor Griswold, and was not submitted to the House. By 1784 Sherman remained one of only three members of the Council, once the Susquehannah stronghold, to support the western lands company. The other two, Williams and Wolcott, were shareholders, which Sherman was not.[22]

The court that was to hear the petition of the settlers as private citizens sat on June 28, and Sherman kept Franklin informed of the procedures to be followed. It was necessary for at least one of the petitioners to appear, but since they were busy laying siege to the fort of the Pennsylvania forces, no one came. Finally the court was discontinued, and despite a report on the matter by William Samuel Johnson wholly favorable to the petitioners, it was never held. This was "a flat denial to the Wyoming settlers of the machinery provided by the national constitution" for a fair adjudication of their claims.[23]

A year later Sherman was authorized by Connecticut to give up all claims. to western lands from a point 120 miles west of Pennsylvania to the Mississippi, thus reserving the territory from the Pennsylvania border 120 miles by 60—a large tract of what was thought by most states to be the public domain. Hardly coincidental was the fact that this tract, about half the size of the Susquehannah claim, was almost exactly the same size as Connecticut herself.[24] The cession was accepted by Congress, and the Wyoming settlers believed themselves abandoned by their Connecticut brothers, a sacrifice to other interests. To this point Sherman's activities had been the legitimate operations of the legal agent of the settlers, who were attempting to work through the regularized channels set up under the Articles. His later conduct is somewhat obscure. He was working toward the acceptance of the public domain by Congress, and principally toward the acceptance by Congress of the Virginia cession. He was chairman of the committee that recommended the acceptance of the terms of Virginia's cession and as such wrote the report.[25]

But Sherman had a more difficult problem to solve than merely gaining acceptance of the various state cessions. He had at the same time to protect the claims of his state to sufficient land in the west to pay off its debt to the militia, an objective complicated by his general feeling that land should go to those who use it, and be kept out of the hands of speculators—unless, of course, the speculators were Connecticut holders of Susquehannah shares. He may have alienated some of his most likely allies when he voted to commit the petition of the Indiana Land Company, which had been brought in by a group of New Jersey speculators and supported by Sherman's unfriendly colleague, Jeremiah Wadsworth. In protecting Connecticut's claim, however, he was temporarily successful in taking away from Jefferson the writing of a general report on the land cessions. Jefferson would have the report develop a plan for dealing with all land presently ceded or to be ceded in the future. Sherman—who replaced Jefferson on the committee, and though not chairman, wrote the report—merely asked the landed states to authorize their delegates to make liberal cessions. He also attempted to expedite such a solution by having the delegates confer with Congress before the states drew up their cessions. Thus some mutual agreement could come about without the three years of wrangling that preceded the acceptance of the Virginia grant.[26] Though this report was then referred to a committee headed by Jefferson, the victory ultimately was Sherman's, for in 1786 Connecticut's cession was agreed to, and the rocky Yankee state was able to hold its Western Reserve.

Evidently Sherman managed to get Pennsylvania's crucial vote in favor of this report by assuring the delegation that Connecticut would not reopen its claim to the Wyoming Valley.* There is also evidence that he connived at the abandonment of the court set up to hear the private claims of the settlers in exchange for Pennsylvania's vote in favor of letting Connecticut keep the Western Reserve. William Grayson wrote to Madison in 1786 that the Connecticut "cession was nothing but a State juggle contrived by old Roger Sherman to get a side wind confirmation to a thing they had no right to. Some of the States, particularly Pensylvany, [sic] voted for them on the same principle that the powers of Europe give money to the Algerines."[27]

The final cession of the Reserve was far from certain when Sherman left Congress in June 1784. However his replacement was William S. Johnson, no less astute than the doughty old politician, and far more accomplished as a jurist. Johnson carried the cession through a series of tight legal maneuvers and a number of crucial votes. His final success gave him a popularity in Connecticut exceeded by no one there, and is no doubt responsible for his attendance at the Constitutional Convention of 1787 and for his selection as the state's first U.S. Senator.[28]

It was Sherman's method to give and take away at the same time, and for the progress of practical politics it has never been surpassed. It was by such maneuvers that Sherman put into effect one of the most important measures of the Confederation period. With the acceptance of the Virginia and

---

*The available documentary evidence would indicate that W. S. Johnson, at Congress for three years after Sherman's last appearance there, was the prime mover of the Reserve cession. However, Sherman's propensity for backstage politicking and statements like Grayson's, seem adequate evidence for the view put forth here. Taylor, *Susquehannah Papers.* Ms. copy of introduction to volume VIII:21-28. See p. 144n above, and Taylor, "Trial," *passim.*

Connecticut cessions, the sharpest point of contention was removed from the staggering union, a union that Sherman thought vital to the national welfare. At the same time it assured his own constituents, to whom in this confederation his first allegiance unquestionably belonged, that the future payment of lands to their militia could be carried out without large expenditures of public money. To have refused to bargain would have meant further attempts to push to almost sure failure what never had been a very tenable claim. Moreover, it would have intensified bitterness and interstate rivalry on the eve of the great Federal Convention, and made impossible the establishment of any kind of public domain.

In addition to Sherman's major effort in settling the western lands question between 1781 and 1786, he also played a part in the development of the various Northwest land ordinances. Though the idea may not have been original with the Connecticut delegate, he suggested in a Congressional report as early as October 10, 1780 that states to be carved out of the public domain enter the United States on equal terms with the original members. And he reiterated this in April 1784, when he moved to amend Jefferson's report of April 20 in order to provide for the new state parity, with Jefferson concurring. Thus Sherman appears to have been one of the prime movers of the anti-imperial commitment of the Founding Fathers. New Englanders generally were responsible for the six-by-six township surveys, and Sherman spoke for this aspect of the ordinances in the Federal Congresses of the nineties.[29]

When Sherman's earlier biographer says that such dealing "is unsupported by any known facts and is absolutely at variance with all we know of Sherman's character," he misses on two counts;[30] he has failed completely to see that Sherman's success was due in very large measure to his willingness to perform the necessary pick and shovel work of politics—sometimes called the "dirty work." He has further neglected to see that Sherman operated in the larger—even largest—interest. Indeed, if Sherman had any measure of greatness, it lay in his capacity to compromise and his uncanny ability to mold the contending forces around him into a solid, cohesive, functioning unit.

Connecticut's Congressional course in the crisis over lands was not dictated solely by territory lying to the west. Northern frontiers, too, were important to the New Englanders, and as James Madison pointed out in the spring of 1782, "the two great objects which predominate in the politics of Congress at this juncture" are western lands and—Vermont. The eastern states, except New Hampshire, desired Vermont's admission into the

Confederacy, Madison explained, for three reasons: their traditional jealousy of New York—a claimant to the area; the investment many New Englanders had there; but most of all the added Congressional strength it would bring to that part of the nation. Pennsylvania and Maryland, both landless states, welcomed another such member in hopes that their hand against Virginia's western claims would be strengthened; and Rhode Island, New Jersey, and Delaware liked small states. The southern states opposed Vermont's admission for the reverse reasons, and also out of fear of establishing precedent for the dismemberment of established governments.

Madison went on to assert that Connecticut and Massachusetts were really more interested in keeping the Vermont issue alive in order to maintain the support of the other eastern states in the western lands controversy. If Connecticut got her western claims settled, Madison said, she and Massachusetts "would instantly divide from the Eastern States in the case of Vermont." This is much to be doubted, however, in view of Sherman's efforts on behalf of his Green Mountain friends right up to the moment of their statehood.[31]

Our Brothers to the North

The frontier of New England in the late eighteenth century was the area north of Massachusetts, sandwiched between the Connecticut River on the east and long Lake Champlain on the west. It was claimed by New York and New Hampshire, and occupied by a band of farmers led by the ambitious Allen boys. This land, known variously as New Connecticut and the New Hampshire Grants, finally entered the union of states in 1791. Behind that lay a long, rough story of conflict on the field of battle and on the floor of debate. Roger Sherman, Connecticut's senior delegate to the Confederation Congress, had no small part in the bitter congressional wrangling over these green mountains and fields. The area was dominated by settlers from Connecticut, and some of them were friends of Sherman from New Milford and New Haven.[32]

Sherman's first reported remarks on the Vermont affair are noncommittal enough. He wrote to his governor in April 1777 that

The people on the New Hampshire Grants have Petitioned Congress to be acknowedged [sic] an Independent State, and admited [sic] to send Delegates to Congress. The Convention of New York has also remonstrated against their proceedings requesting Congress to interpose for preventing the defection of the people on the Grants from that State. Nothing has been yet acted on the affair.[33]

But Sherman's disinterested remarks belie the part he took in debate just two months later when the question came before the Congress.

Indeed, rumors, largely false, of Sherman's involvement in the New Hampshire Grants had been current in New York for some time. William Smith of that state reported that there were:

> Proofs that the Scheme of that Seperation from NY, was concerted by Roger Sherman. . . . This Sherman had an Interest in the Wioming Scheme as well as Dyer, and Capt. Ledlie says for a finesse to elude Objections to their Councils, they parted with their Interest, & then published what they had; but it was found out that the Conveyances were to their own Children.[34]

Of course Sherman had no financial interest in the Wyoming lands, and seems never to have had any in Vermont either. True, in 1779, he was listed along with sixteen others on a petition to purchase eight townships, each six miles square there, but his name lies with several other delegates to Congress, two from Connecticut—Ellsworth and Andrew Adams—so it is quite possible that it was included for political purposes, perhaps even without his knowledge. Later, a delegate from Virginia was to charge "it is beyond a doubt that [John] Witherspoon [of New Jersey] and some others have received large tracts of land, at least grants of them, from the Vermonters, to support their claim in Congress." However, the largest single group of speculators in the wild northern lands was a collection of New Haven merchants, some of whom were business connections of Sherman's.* It was he who spearheaded the drive for Vermont statehood; on June 25, 1777, as General Burgoyne moved toward Fort Ticonderoga, Sherman introduced the petition from the Grants. The Vermonters wanted recognition as an independent state and representation in Congress, and based their demands on the Congressional resolve of May 10, 1776, which called upon the colonies "where no government sufficient to the exigencies of their affairs have been established, to adopt such government as shall . . . best conduce to the happiness and safety of their constituents in particular, and America in general."[35] The New York members took immediate and intense umbrage at what they regarded as an attempt to dismember their state. James Duane, a New York speculator and, according to John Adams, a man of "sly, surveying eye, a little squint-eyed . . . very sensible . . . and very artful," took the lead in the debate that began with a motion by Sherman, who brought in the

---

*Bradleys, Munsons, Leavenworths, and Bishops, all Sherman business connections, were involved.

Vermonters' petition. Duane held speculations in the west, but he was particularly interested in the Vermont lands, and was New York's major authority on the question. Sherman became unusually animated, and Duane wrote this account to Robert Livingston:

> Yesterday the Committee of the whole House finished their proceedings concerning our Revolters and reported them to the House. An unexpected field of debate was opened and some of our neighbors (R. S. in particular) discovered an earnestness and solicitude that did not belong to Judges between a State and its discontented members. But it was of little avail to object to what had been agreed to by the Committee of the whole House on the most solemn argument and debate of which I have been witness.[36]

Resolutions confirming New York's right to the territory had little effect on the determined and independent-minded real estate operators of the Green Mountains, and the New Yorkers knew it. Especially would the Vermonters balk at the action of Congress when they knew that they possessed such a powerful ally as Connecticut's senior delegate. Intrepid but tactless Yorker William Duer worked fast, but was already behind his wily opponent. "May we be permitted to suggest," wrote the New York delegates to their Council of Safety,

> the Propriety of dispatching Commissioners without delay to circulate explain and enforce among our too aspiring Countrymen [in Vermont] — these Resolutions of Congress, and to seize the Advantage which the first impression of unexpected disappointment, and Condemnation from the only Tribunal they fear, may make on their Minds, in order to induce them to a Submission to your Jurisdiction. This appears to us to be the more necessary as Mr. Roger Sherman of Connecticut, who brought in the Petition for these People to Congress, and has all along acted openly as their Advocate and Patron, and in the last Debate plead their Cause with a Zeal and Passion which he never discovered in any other Instance, and which in a Judge between a State and some of its own members was far from being commendable. This Gentleman, we say, immediately on passing the Resolutions, procured Copies, and having obtained Leave of Absence, is already set out on his Journey to the Eastward. What may be his Views with respect to our Dispute, we know not; But to his Enmity and officiousness you ought not to be Strangers.[37]

Sherman was unable to persuade Congress that New York should give up her claim to the eastern lands, perhaps because he was busy most of the month with the tremendously demanding War Board. Failing in Congress, he obtained leave of absence on the thirtieth of June, though apparently he stayed in Philadelphia till July 2. Just a month earlier Duer had crossed swords with Sherman over the question of a general for the Northern

Department, and may have been unduly prejudiced. He seemed to relish Sherman's defeat and wrote again to Livingston on July 9:

> I believe no matter has ever been more solemnly argued in Congress than this. The house were in Committee for three days, and very warm opposition was given to [sic] by some of our Eastern friends against the resolution for dismissing the Petition of Jonas Fay etc and that answering Dr. Youngs incendiary production. Mr. Sherman was quite thrown off his bias, and betrayed a warmth not usually learned within the Walls of Yale College.*[38]

Sherman's job was made even more complicated by divisions among the Vermonters themselves. As the controversy ground on (only New York considered anything settled by the resolutions of June), an anti-Allen party gained some strength in eastern Vermont. Elisha Payne, recently moved to the Grants from New Hampshire proper, looking for "the sweets of liberty and government in the greatest simplicity and freedom," found only various kinds of distressing politics. "We have not only N.Y. and N.H. to defend against," Payne wrote, "but that which is worse than boath (viz) the old Green Mountain constitution (cloathed under the name of civil Government)." Payne asked Sherman to try to delay any action that would confirm the present Vermont government under the Allens, and insisted that the respectable people were opposed to the present ruling clique. He further charged Ethan Allen with duplicity in dealing with the legislature.[39]

Sherman wrote him a letter dated three days later which must have crossed Payne's. He discussed the action of several towns on the east side of the Connecticut River—that is, in New Hampshire proper—that had revolted and were attempting to join the freer government of Vermont. After disclaiming an opinion as to the disposition of the Grants, and mentioning that this matter would have to be adjudicated later, he continued:

> But for the people inhabiting within the known and acknowledged boundaries of any of the United States, to separate without the consent

---

*Sherman, of course, had not attended Yale, but he typified the characteristics New Yorkers saw there. Gouverneur Morris' father, while wishing the boy "the best education that can be furnished him in England or America," insisted that "under no circumstances shall he be sent to the Colony of Connecticut for that purpose, lest his youth should imbibe that low craft and cunning so incident to the people of that country and which are so interwoven in their constitution that they cannot conceal it from the world, although many of them, under the sanctified garb of religion, have attempted to impose themselves upon the world as honest men." Gipson, *Ingersoll*, p. 254n. The boy was sent to King's College, but would have learned better morals at Yale. After Sherman attacked him on the floor of Congress in 1792 as "an irreligious and profane man," Morris wrote a friend that though "Virtue which scorns to entrench itself in gravity and Form, but comes naked into the Battle, is soon driven off," he would dress himself "like other Folks, so that Prudery may not be scandaliz'd. . . ." King, *King*, pp. 421–22.

of the State to which they belong appears to me a very unjustifiable violation of the social compact, and pregnant with the most ruinous consequences. Sir, I don't know whether you live in one of the revolted towns, but as you are in that vicinity, I trust from acquaintance with your love of order and regard to the welfare of your country, you will use your influence to discourage everything that in your opinion may be prejudicial to the true interests of these States. If the present constitution of any of the States is not so perfect as could be wished, it may and probably will, by common consent be amended; but in present circumstances it appears to me indispensably necessary that civil government should be vigorously supported.[40]

By May 1779 the Yorkers were pressing for more substantial Congressional action on their account in the disputed lands west of the Connecticut River. On June first a resolution was passed declaring that Congress was duty bound to preserve the rights of the several states, and on the second a committee of five, three of them Connecticut men, was sent to the Grants to inquire why the inhabitants insisted on their own jurisdiction.*[41] Sherman did not serve on this committee, though he was present in Congress at the time of its appointment, and it can be easily surmised that the New Yorkers would never have allowed his selection. In September, incidentally during Sherman's absence, Congress pledged that it would determine the dispute according to equity and would support the decision of the committee on the spot. A hearing was scheduled for February 1, 1780. But by the time that the interested parties had assembled, the required presence of nine states could not be obtained, so the question continued to dangle. This was probably just as well, for a decision unfavorable to the Green Mountain Boys almost certainly would have brought on a small war.[42]

By the fall of 1780 after Gates' humiliation at the hands of Cornwallis at Camden—"the most disasterous defeat ever inflicted on an American army"—the obstreperous Vermonters were threatening to make a separate peace with England if their claims were not soon recognized by Congress. In the face of this piece of blackmail, and in view of new encroachments east of the Connecticut River and west of Lake Champlain on lands clearly those of New Hampshire and New York, Congress began to worry. This worry suddenly turned into action in August 1781, when evidence came to hand that the Vermonters were actually in negotiation with the King's agents; Congress quickly agreed to deal with the wild men of the north on their own terms. A committee had been set up in July 1781 consisting of Varnum, Madison, McKean, Carroll, and Sherman to weigh the question. The report,

---

*The Connecticut men were Pierpont Edwards, Jesse Root, and Oliver Ellsworth.

which came to the floor on July 20, suggested that New York and New Hampshire follow the earlier example of Massachusetts and surrender their claims to the region. Sherman added to the original report, which was in Carroll's hand, that the townships east of the Connecticut should cease their revolt against New Hampshire and rejoin their mother government or be considered enemies of the United States. The remainder of the controversy, he insisted in his separate report, should be adjudicated by Congress.[43]

Sherman made his position clear in a letter to Josiah Bartlett of New Hampshire on the last day of July. He enclosed the resolution of Massachusetts and told of the report that recommended its example.

> What will ultimately be done in Congress is uncertain; some gentlemen are for declaring Vermont an independent State; others for explicitly recommending to the States aforesaid to relinquish their claims of jurisdiction; others only for referring it to their consideration as reported by the committee, and some few against doing anything that will tend to make a new state.
>
> I am of the opinion that a speedy and amicable settlement of the controversy would conduce very much to the peace and welfare of the United States, and that it will be difficult if not impracticable to reduce the people on the east side of the river to obedience to the government of New Hampshire until the other dispute is settled, that the longer it remains unsettled the more difficult it will be to remedy the evils—but if the States of New Hampshire and New York would follow the example of Massachusetts respecting the grants on the west of Connecticut river the whole controversy would be quieted very much to the advantage and satisfaction of the United States, and that the inhabitants of New Hampshire and New York living without the disputed territory would return to their allegiance.[44]

He then discussed the matter of an alliance between the Vermonters and the British, which he hinted might be a possibility. Finally it appears that Sherman's attempt to get the question adjudicated by Congress in his report of ten days before was either a matter of empty procedural form or merely an intentional delaying action.

> I think it very unlikely that Congress can attend to the settlement of the dispute by a judicial decision during the war. For though the parties were heard last fall respecting their claims, yet it cannot now be determined upon the right without a new hearing, because there are many new members that were not then present. I am credibly informed that a great majority of the members of the Legislature of the State of New York at their last winter session were willing to relinquish their claim of jurisdiction over that district, and that they should be admitted to be a separate State, but the governor for some reasons prevented an act passing at that time.

It might be recalled that it was at this time that Connecticut was attempting to get adjudication of its own land dispute put off till after the war.[45]

This approach, a bundle of hinted threats and promises, may have had some effect, for on August 7 Sherman's report instead of Carroll's was accepted by Congress. The report defined the boundaries of Vermont, and provided for a committee of five to meet with representatives from New Hampshire, New York, and the Grants to settle the question of admission as a state. Sherman was not appointed to the committee, which consisted of a member each from New Jersey, Maryland, Delaware, Pennsylvania, and Virginia, but the final settlement was according to the lines he had laid out in his report of the seventh. He confidently wrote home that Vermont would soon be admitted to the Union.[46]

But still Vermont had not been admitted, and Sherman wrote in September to Governor Trumbull, "I have heard nothing from the State of Vermont since their agents left this place in August, but expect delegates will arrive from thence to Congress, in case they comply with the only condition of their being admitted into the union, which is to relinquish their claims to the encroachments lately made on the States of New Hampshire and New York." But to the surprise of everyone at Philadelphia, intrepid Vermont refused to give up the east-of-the-river claims. This discommoded Sherman and the other Connecticut delegates no end, and Congressmen from some other states began to think about reversing their previous favorable attitude toward the Green Mountaineers. Further efforts to settle the matter were blocked by southerners, who saw Vermont as one more northern vote, and by Yorkers and Pennsylvanians, who liked neither the principle of dismembering a state nor the precedent it might set.[47] So by this time the Vermont question had become entangled with the western lands controversy, and its resolution had to await settlement of the larger question of the national domain. As a result Vermont was not admitted to the United States until 1791. At the Constitutional Convention in 1787 Sherman moved specific provision for the admission of Vermont, and her ultimate statehood depended upon these phrases.[48] It cannot be said that he did less than his best for the northern settlers, however. He was acknowledged by New York to be the archenemy to its claims, and his correspondence with men of New Hampshire shows him to have worked consistently for a settlement that would make the Connecticut River a permanent boundary.

It would be natural to question Sherman's disinterestedness in the controversy, especially considering the large financial investments made by other Connecticut speculators in Vermont lands. But his efforts in the cause seem to have been pure enough. In the seventies and eighties Sherman had no real investment in the profitable lands to the north, and never did get on the speculative bandwagon. Nevertheless, he was fully aware of the value of his services which, in his old age, he was not above calling to the attention of others. Jeremiah Mason wrote that he:

> was once surprised by [Sherman] stopping and kindly greeting me, requesting me to call at his house before I left the city. When I called, he received me most courteously. . . . He then told me that being a member of the old Congress of the Confederation during the time Vermont . . . was asserting against New York its claim to independence, believing the claim just, he had been an earnest advocate for it; that during the pendency of the claim, the agents of Vermont often urged him to accept grants of land from the State, which he refused, lest it should lessen his power to serve them. Now, as their claim was established, and the State admitted into the Union, if the people of Vermont continued to feel disposed to make him a grant of some of their ungranted lands, as his family was large and his property small, he had no objection to accepting it. . . . [influential Vermonters that Mason spoke to] readily recognized the merits of Mr. Sherman's services, and he said he ought to have a liberal grant. But I never heard that anything was done in the matter, and presume his case made another item in the history of the ingratitude of republics. The time the Vermonters needed his services was passed.[49]

This must have happened no more than three years before Sherman's death, and there is no mention of Vermont lands in his will or inventory. Thus there is every reason to believe that Mason's assumption that nothing was done for the old man is correct. But Sherman's work on behalf of the sturdy, if somewhat disorderly boys of the Green Mountains was important, and his steadfast support during times when the northerners were almost without other friends deserves to be recognized.

Representation and Taxation

The conflict in the Continental Congress over the double question of representation and taxation is much better known than the difficulties regarding western lands. Representation was again thrashed out in the more intensively studied Federal Convention, while the western lands question had been largely settled by the time that Convention met. If both of these problems had remained, any success of the Philadelphia delegates in 1787 would have been a greater miracle than it was.

Sherman's part in the debates over representation and taxation was considerably more direct and open than in those involving western lands, but no less influential, and productive of just as large results. He was, of course, a representative of a medium-sized state, but Connecticut was one of the most provincial-minded. It is probable that Sherman at first took the position that was finally adopted, one-state-one-vote. But very early in the debates, in 1776, he proposed an entirely new approach to the matter. It was a compromise, of course, and in the heat of the summer it received no real consideration. Three modes of representation had been offered. One was that of the large states, represented in debate by Adams and Franklin. They wanted votes in proportion to numbers. A second mode was that most forcefully supported by the arch states'-rights spokesman, John Witherspoon of New Jersey, who wanted, naturally, an equal vote for all states. A third proposal was that of South Carolina that the vote should be according to the size of the contribution to the general coffers.

All of these proposals had their day on July 30 and 31, and on August 1 Sherman made his suggestion. "Sherman thinks we ought not to vote according to numbers. We are representatives of the States, not individuals," Adams recorded in his diary, and Sherman cited the case of the states of Holland. "The consent of everyone is necessary. Three Colonies would govern the whole, but would not have the strength to carry these votes into execution."[50] This is the pragmatic Sherman at his best. Who else in these debates looked beyond the mode to its execution? If the impression has been given that Sherman was a manipulator of second-rate intellect, this insight into the essential connection between theory and method should establish his claim to real intellectual strength.

Thus the seed of the Great Compromise that was to flower in the Federal Convention eleven years later was sown. Adams records Sherman's words, "The vote should be taken two ways; call the Colonies, and call the individuals, and have a majority of both." Here lay not only the idea that would finally develop into our differentiated Senate and House, but also form the basis of Calhoun's doctrine of concurrent majorities some sixty years later. Apparently, however, no one gave it the slightest consideration at the time. Perhaps this was just as well, for with a single house of delegates, the method would have been cumbersome and complicated in the extreme.

On the business of taxation that became so intertwined with representation, Sherman was again pragmatic in his approach. He was primarily interested in seeing the Confederation work, as his attitude on taxation indicates. Some members wanted taxes levied on the states according to the value of property, and others according to the number of inhabitants. In both cases southern slaves became the *bête noire* of the debate. Should they be counted as property or as people? When in 1777, Congress finally approved the Articles with taxation on the basis of property, Sherman wrote:

> The mode adopted by Congress for proportioning the Quotas of the several States according to the value of their land I think impracticable. The number of Inhabitants I think will be the best that can be devised. The wealth of a people I believe will generally be found to be nearly in proportion to the numbers that can be supported in a State, and wealth principally arises from the labour of men. As to the negros I should be willing to do as appears equitable. If for the present it should be agreed to exclude all under ten years old or any other age that may be devised, and not make a perpetual rule at present would it not answer better than to have confederation delayed, for I am persuaded that the States can neither agree to nor practise the mode voted by Congress. . . . [51]

Confederation was uppermost in his mind in that letter, and in one written a month earlier to William Williams, who was then unhappily in Congress.* "Confederation of the States would add much to the public credit," Sherman wrote from Lebanon, where he was sitting with the Council of Safety. "What will become of the continental Securities if the States can't agree how their Quotas Should be proportioned—I see not why it may not now be settled as well as hereafter."[52] This last phrase, in contrast to the later letter to Lee in which he says "and not make a perpetual rule," shows his willingness to compromise in order to hasten confederation.

Union and Sovereignty

During the debates centering on the division of sovereignty in the Articles, Sherman very early tipped his hand in favor of states' rights. In October 1775 he had insisted that provincial conventions should retain control over the appointment of their own military officers, and the next February he declared that "Long enlistment is a state of slavery. There ought to be a rotation which is in favor of liberty," and that difficulty in getting new recruits had resulted when Congress took over the power to nominate officers. In 1777 Sherman wrote that inhabitants of a state who commit crimes against the Continental army should not be tried by courts-martial, but by the court of their own state.[53]

---

*After William Williams left Congress and returned to Connecticut he commented on the occupation of the Congressional seat: "I expected from the former conduct of Providence toward us since the beginning of this Contest, That Philadelphia so much the Mistress of Iniquity would be taken, and Corrected; and that this event will finally prove the Overthrow of the Enemy—However God is righteous—and His ways tho' dark and intricate to us, yet they are just and faithful—." CHS, "Jonathan Trumbull, Sr. Papers," Vol. IV (October 14, 1777).

It should be remembered, however, that if this narrow states'-rights attitude seems myopic, Sherman represented a jealous province, more used to self-government than any other. In December 1777, when the Articles were first up for ratification, a New Haven town meeting objected strenuously to them. The meeting was opposed to troop quotas based on white population only; and it was against the tax on land and improvements. Sherman tried to nudge them along as fast as possible to a wider view. In 1780 he was charged by the state's upper chamber to try to persuade the Assembly to agree to open a "Free Trade and transportation by land from one state to another."[54]

The part that Sherman played in the construction of the Articles of Confederation, and the attitudes that he displayed at the time, are laid out here in detail because of the light they shed on his part in writing the Federal Constitution. He was to be influential in the final convention, and any clues to understanding his views at that time are worth study.

Connecticut Confederates

Copies of various drafts of the Articles began to arrive in Connecticut as early as the late summer of 1776. The final draft was submitted to the states by Congress on November 17, 1777, with a request that it be acted upon by the following March 10. Governor Trumbull received his copy in December and on the 18th submitted it to the Council of Safety, which ordered that three hundred copies be printed, one sent to the selectmen of each town in the state and rest to the Assembly.[55] By late December, forty-seven out of Connecticut's seventy towns had received their copies, along with a letter from the Governor requesting that the selectmen get a speedy reaction from their townsfolk. No town is known to have rejected the draft, and forty-five voted explicit endorsement. New Haven's town meeting objected to provisions of the Articles prohibiting states from laying duties or taxes on property of the United States and in determining shares on the basis of white inhabitants only. "We object," the meeting protested, "to furnishing troops in proportion to the white inhabitants only, as we hope the time may be when the black man may be a freeman,* and the owner of property and then he ought to bear his share of military burdens." The lower house took up the draft at the January session and quickly approved it. The Council, however, was not so precipitous and delayed till the next month, at which time the Governor asked that the matter be speedily finished.[56]

---

*At this time New Haven County Connecticuters held five hundred slaves, twice as many as any other county.

There seems to have been general agreement in principle on confederation. The Articles, in the opinion of the Assembly, "in general appear to be well adapted to cement and preserve the union of said States, to secure their freedom and independence and promote their general welfare. . . ." However, all was not quite right, and amendments were proposed. Proportionate expenses should be based upon population, not the value of land and buildings because "Trade and manufacturers, . . . [are] sources of wealth to a State as well as the produce of lands"; and besides a just estimate of relative real-estate values would be impossible to determine. A second proposal would qualify Congressional regulation of the army by prohibiting the maintenance of land forces in time of peace or pensioners except for military disability.[57]

The instructions to the delegates, however, were ambiguous. That other ratifications might also be qualified by proposed amendments was recognized but it was "highly expedient . . . that the Articles of Confederation be finally concluded and ratified as soon as possible." Connecticut, the second state to do so, empowered her delegates to Congress to ratify "with such amendments, if any be, as by them in conjunction with the Delegates of the other States in Congress shall be thought proper." Presumably this gave leeway to adopt the draft as it stood or with amendments of any kind. On June 23 the Connecticut Congressional delegates, Sherman and Titus Hosmer, dutifully presented their amendments, but along with all other proposals for alteration at this time, they were rejected. Nevertheless the Connecticut delegates, with those of all the other states except Delaware, Maryland, and New Jersey, signed the ratification on July 9, 1778. Since unanimity was required, final ratification didn't come about until three years of wrangling over western lands had gone by.[58]

Financial Problems

ROGER SHERMAN always thought of himself as an emissary from his state to the Continental Congress, which to him was a sort of international organ of diplomacy. Though he spent as much time at Congress as any other member, and far more than most, he never forgot that his primary responsibility was to Connecticut. He made frequent trips back to New Haven, some of them of fairly long duration. But these visits were not for rest and rehabilitation. He had much hard work to do in connection with his duties as a member of the upper house of the Assembly, as a judge of the Superior Court, and above all, as a member of the Council of Safety.

This select committee of nine, to which Sherman was first appointed in May 1777, had almost complete power to act as the government and military staff of the state when the Assembly was not in session. The commission of that year, for instance, read that the committee shall have

> full power and authority to order and direct the militia and navy of this State and the marches and stations of the troops that have been or shall be inlisted and assembled for the special defence of this or the neighboring States. . . . and to give all necessary orders from time to time for furnishing and supplying said militia. . . . with full power and authority to fulfill and execute every trust. . . .

And the Governor was expected to "convene the whole of said Council on all important occasions and business which shall be before them," or a small number if haste is required.[1] This important committee usually met in Lebanon at Governor Trumbull's house on the Cambridge-to-Philadelphia riders' route, and Sherman spent a good many days there—for which he claimed expenses, ultimately dutifully paid by the state.

The New Haven Raid

One trip back to New Haven Sherman had not planned, but it was perhaps the most eventful of the lot. On July 13, 1779, Cyrus Griffin of

Virginia wrote to Jefferson, "The Enemy with a body of five thousand men have plundered and destroyed New Haven in Connecticut; they carried off the wife and children of old Shearman the member of Congress; yesterday he left this City full of anxiety and trouble; I pity the Lady and Children exceedingly, but I have no tender feelings for the old fellow on many accounts." He added that the report is not "ascertained to satisfaction," but it was enough to get Sherman moving northward in a hurry. The report was inaccurate as to the kidnapping of Rebecca and her brood, for there is no indication that she was ever carried off.* Sherman's son, William, however, did have his house ransacked as his wife and seven children fled the rapacious lobsterbacks with only what they could carry, and so William was left with "Seven helpless children naked to clothe and to feed." A letter to Governor Trumbull from an unidentified correspondent says of the British raid, "I cannot enumerate all the houses that were rifled—Mrs. Woorsters, Parson Edwards and his Brothers—Mr. Todds—Deacon Lymans—Mr. Shermans. . . ." were the worst damaged.[2] But Roger's as well as William's house was broken into.

The attack had taken place on the 5th of July in the midst of preparations for the Fourth of July celebration (the Fourth being a Sunday) and the damage, mostly to private homes, amounted to about £15,660.** Sherman's share was twenty-six pounds and nine pence which was paid to him by the state in October. His son, William, who desperately needed the money, was not so lucky. While the ruins were still smoking on the 6th, he petitioned for a bit over forty pounds as losses due to the raid, which was not paid until after his death. The damage to Roger Sherman's estate did not destroy his morale, however, for less than two weeks later he was off again to Lebanon for meetings of the Council of Safety, and by the end of September he was back for Congress.[3]

As usual, Sherman took up lodgings at Mrs. Cheeseman's on Fourth Street, near the corner of Market Street. Among his fellow boarders were Samuel Adams, Matthew Thornton of New Hampshire, and Sherman's New Haven ex-political rival, Jared Ingersoll. A frequent visitor from Third Street was John Adams, who wrote his wife that cousin Sam would have a curious time of it among these "characters, as opposite as North and South. . . .

---

*An Adonijah Sherman, no relation, was taken prisoner by the British. Goodrich, "Invasion," p.79.

**This is the official figure. Estimates at the time put it at over £25,000. Stiles, *Lit. Diary*. III:111-12.

Between the fun of Thornton, the gravity of Sherman, the formal Toryism of Ingersoll." And Mrs. Cheeseman herself gave a lift to the group as well. She "has buried four husbands, one tailor, two shoemakers, and Gilbert Tenant, and is still ready for a fifth, and still deserves him too."[4]

The Tribulations of Public Finance

It could well be that one reason for Roger Sherman's failure to receive the fame that came to many of his Revolutionary brothers was that his chief contribution lay in a field both highly complicated and drearily pedestrian. Financing a war without money is a painful concern, a heartbreaking one in this case, and yet the workers in this vineyard of frustration wrought perhaps the greatest miracle in a war in which miracles were almost commonplace. It was here that Sherman labored most ardently during the years of the Continental Congresses. Two major financial problems developed; how to raise money in the first place, and how to maintain its value in the second.

In the late summer of 1775 Congress had in mind only a short campaign to force Parliament to change its colonial policies and thus saw no need of a permanent domestic currency. But as the conflict deepened, a constant supply of cash was found necessary. Politically it was impossible to tax, and realistically it was impossible to borrow at this early stage. So Congress turned to the emission of bills of credit, which were popular though admittedly dangerous.

In July 1775, three million paper dollars were issued, and by the end of the year the figure had been doubled.* This was but a drop in the torrents that were to flow in the next five years.[5] Sherman was early put on committees dealing with the troublesome question of revenue. In April 1776 he served with a group to determine the value of several species of gold and silver in relation to Spanish milled dollars, for which he drew up the table of valuations. He worked with another group later that month to look into the counterfeiting of Continental bills. But his first major appointment in the

---

*The Spanish milled dollar, also known as pieces-of-eight, was in general use and was adopted by Congress rather than the English pound because of the differing values given the latter in various colonies. The dollar was divided into ninety pennies until Sherman—with the aid of Secretary of State Jefferson—introduced the decimal system as a congressman in 1790. The Pennsylvania penny, when Congress was sitting there in the seventies, was further divided into eight farthings. Bronson, *Currency*, p. 87n. Congress had Sherman and James Duane draw up a table of values showing the paper dollar in relation to specie. Gold was to be worth $17.00 per ounce troy weight sterling alloy; silver was 1 1/9 dollars per ounce—or just the same as an English crown. A shilling was to be worth 2/9 of a dollar. *JCC*, IV:382–83.

area of financial policy put him on the committee assigned the Alice-in-Wonderland task of raising ten million dollars. Sherman's views on the issuance of unsupported paper are clear: he opposed it as best he could. He had obtained a copy of George Whatley's "Principles of Trade . . . Containing Reflections on Gold, Silver and Paper passing as money," in 1776, and it no doubt strengthened the commitment to hard money that he had developed during his old mercantile days.[6]

It would be politically disastrous, of course, for Congress to tax individuals directly, for this "would give a disgust that might ruin all their measures. . . ." The states could do it if they were willing, which, however, most were not. But Connecticut tried as Congress continued to flood the Continent with more and more paper in wave after wave. By 1779, when Congress finally cried halt, 241.5 million dollars had spilled off the national presses. Another hundred million or so had earlier gushed from the states when Congress asked them to stop the flow in 1777.[7]

Sherman believed in "taxing high and often to defray the expenses of the war," and he added his opinion that the "people in general are convinced of the necessity of it." Though taxes were already high—at two shillings eleven pence on the pound compared to a mere one pence in 1776—Connecticut's Assembly voted new taxes totaling forty-eight pence on the pound between December 1776, and October 1777.[8] In May of the latter year the treasurer was authorized to borrow £72,000 and issue 6 percent notes in exchange for either Continental or Connecticut bills. The Assembly dealt peremptorily with efforts to thwart these inflationary measures, and a pamphlet attacking the loans was suppressed while still on the press at Hartford.[9]

When Congress resolved in November 1777 to request the states to refrain from further emissions, the Assembly responded by declaring Connecticut bills no longer valid in private transactions and calling them all in by July 1778. The treasurer, however, was authorized to exchange the old bills for new 6 percent notes up to £235,000. At the same time the Assembly levied two one-shilling taxes to make up the state's share of a new £600,000 Congressional requisition.[10]

But Sherman was always opposed to such financial flights. He wrote with delight to Robert Paine in February 1778 that the Connecticut Assembly, at which he was in attendance, had promised no new emissions. His satisfaction was short-lived, however, for no sooner had he returned to Philadelphia than the state slapped out another large sum in bills of credit. "I am very sorry," he wrote Governor Trumbull, "that the State of Connecticut have had occasion to emit so large a sum in Bills of Credit . . . but am glad to hear that they have laid so large a Tax to be paid in the New Bills. . . ." Connecticut's emissions only slowed down when the plates were worn out and had to be remade.[11]

Sherman's views on paper hardened even beyond what they were in 1778, and by 1780 he was writing that the state should "speedily . . . draw in those bills by taxes, and not suffer them on any account to reissue. . . . The credit of the State is scrupled and depreciation ensures. The people lose their confidence in Government. The laws are enervated, military operations prevented, justice impeded, trade embarrassed, the morals of the people corrupted, men of integrity in office abused and resigning, whilst peculators ride in coaches. . . ." Only real taxation, and destruction of the paper by the state—all states—could avert this horrendous fate. "I am full persuaded that no way can be devised in our circumstances to support the value of paper currency but by taxing to the full amount of our expenditures after having emitted a sufficient sum for a medium of trade . . . ," he insisted to his Governor.[12] Despite Sherman's strong stand, however, the presses were not stopped.

The principal question was then, not how to get the money, but rather how to make it worth something once it was printed. Thus the issuance of paper created something of temporary and rapidly diminishing value. Congress, and Sherman in particular, turned, then, to the maintenance of the national credit. The system adopted was that of requisitions on the states by quotas, and its administration was as troublesome as any other problem tackled by the infant body. Congress first seriously considered the matter during the discussion over Dickinson's draft of a confederation in October 1777. Apportionment of quotas could be made on the basis of population or value of land or general property values, or even some complicated formula that combined them. Henry Laurens wrote about this debate, "Two days have been amused in conning it [the mode of taxation], some sensible things have been said, and as much nonsense as ever I heard in so short a space."[13]

The method of assessment adopted at this time—with New England in the negative—was based on land and improvements. But in actual practice population estimates became the base employed. To Richard Henry Lee, Sherman pointed out the impossibility of ever obtaining agreement among the states on relative valuations. "The number of Inhabitants I think will be the best that can be devised." The problem of determining the relative value of property in the various states was never overcome, and quotas were set throughout the whole length of the war on the basis of population of all ages, black, white, and mulattoes.[14]

Sherman was immediately concerned with the currency problem and worked at getting as much of the paper withdrawn as possible. As early as February 1777 he was put on a committee to chase the chimera of sound currency; "to devise ways and means of supporting the credit of the Continental currency and supplying the treasury with money." Sherman reported for the committee a week or so later. This report recommended that the interest for loans to the Congress be increased to 6 percent; that five million dollars more be emitted; that the states tax to make up their quotas rather than print their own money; that earlier emissions be called in; and that a mint be established which would coin half-ounce copper pennies, at seventy-two to a dollar. Most of this report was passed on February 26, with Sherman bringing over his Connecticut colleagues to the rise in interest which they had opposed at first. This is a hard-money report, but it rested largely on the hopes of state taxation, and the sinking of earlier emissions. Neither of these developed, though Sherman wrote Samuel Adams in August that the people had plentiful crops and now, not only could pay, but seemed quite willing to pay higher taxes.[15]

Sherman kept plugging away to get as much paper withdrawn as possible. Even while at home in the fall of 1777 he wrote a set of instructions to the Philadelphia delegates and tried vainly to have the General Assembly endorse them. After this failure he took to direct communication with various Congressmen. "The affair of the paper currency is a very important matter to be immediately attended to by Congress," he wrote to Williams at Philadelphia from Lebanon, where he was attending the Committee of Safety. "People cant purchase the common necessaries with money here—If we could Sink about one half or one third of the currency, the Credit of the other might be Supported and the Treasury supplied by taxes and loans. . . . If we could have a foreign loan of 2,000,000 Sterling, and apply part of it to pay our foreign Debt and to import necessaries Supplies [sic] and the residue to lessen the quantity of paper currency it would in good measure . . ." stablize the currency. But, he added, "taxing for near the whole of future expenses will be the best expedient to preserve Credit and keep out of Debt. . . . Confederation of the States would add much to the public credit."[16]

A few weeks later he suggested to R. H. Lee that Congress recommend that all states sink their own paper and tax themselves a sufficient amount for carrying on the war. Further, about three million dollars should be set aside annually to be burnt. "Such provision being made and published would have an immediate effect to give credit and stability to the currency." And to Williams, Sherman voiced a more common complaint: the activities of speculators and manipulators, or "inimical and avaricious persons," in Sherman's words, were partly responsible for the collapse of the currency.[17]

As the emissions continued to pour from the state and Congressional presses, the value of paper fell. In Philadelphia it took $1.25 to buy a dollar's worth of specie in January 1777, and by April 1781, the same amount of specie would cost an incredible $167.50 Continental. Sherman became more and more ardent in his attempts to restore the credit. Writing in July 1778 to Governor Trumbull, he said, "I am fully persuaded that no way can be devised in our circumstances to support the value of paper currency but by taxing to the full amount of our expenditures after having emitted a sufficient sum for a medium of trade," which was to be limited by Congress to ten million dollars.[18] The next month Connecticut's delegate Andrew Adams wrote a friend that "one particular Member . . . is extreamly urgent to have something effectual done to appreciate the Currency; this indeed seems to be the full Determination of Congress and accordingly three days in each Week . . . are now set apart to attend to our Finances." It seems most probable that "one particular Member" was Roger Sherman, who was away for "about six weeks on the business of arranging the army, which, so far as it is accomplished, has occasioned less dissatisfaction than I feared it would." When Sherman returned to Philadelphia, he found Congress in hot debate over the most recent financial report.[19]

The report had been drawn up by Gouverneur Morris, and it contained some new and different suggestions. It called for immediate negotiations for a foreign loan of five million sterling, and the sale of bonds, twenty million dollars on the credit of the Congress at 4 percent and ten million on Loan Office certificates at 6 percent. Only the first of these three suggestions was accepted.[20] Sherman arrived on October 1 for most of the debate, and reported to Governor Trumbull:

> There is a report lately made on the subject of finance, not acted upon, which I think will not be an adequate remedy for the evils. I think a reasonable time ought to be fixed for sinking all the outstanding bills, and sufficient funds by annual taxes provided for bringing them in. That would fix their credit by letting the possessors know when and how they are to be redeemed, and would in some good measure do justice to the public, as the bills would be collected in at about the same value they were issued out. The first part of the time people would obtain them at a cheap rate to pay their taxes, and they would gradually appreciate till restored to their original value.[21]

He added that legal tender laws should be altered so that people to whom the Congress owed debts and salary would not have to accept Congressional money at par. Sherman, then, appears financially harder than even Gouverneur Morris.

Another provision of this report would have the states cede some of their western lands to the Congress for sale as a source of revenue. The members were sworn to greater secrecy than usual. Sherman, perhaps because he was not present when the ban was set, let some of the financial secrets out, apparently the only one to do so.[22] On October 27 he again wrote his governor:

> The affair of the currency is to be further considered today. The members in general seem to be at a loss what can be done to restore its credit. The plan that appears to me most probable to be adopted is to recommend to the legislatures of the several States immediately to pass acts to raise by taxes five or six million dollars annually for eighteen or twenty years, as a sinking fund sufficient for the redemption of all bills and Loan Office certificates, to take out of currency about fifty million dollars by loan, to lay a tax of about twelve or thirteen million dollars for the expense of next year; and if further emissions are necessary that additional funds be provided for sinking them within the time limited for those that are now outstanding, so that the possessors of the bills and the lenders of money be able to make a just estimate of the value of their securities. . . .[23]

This plan was very similar to one that Sherman had offered for a committee on finance that reported the previous February, and now in October 1778 he tried in debate and by amendment to obtain its adoption.[24]

By the middle of November he thought he could see only a small measure of success approaching, and wrote Trumbull that, since a foreign loan seemed out of the question—because of the "warlike appearance in Europe"—taxing and sinking to make way for further emissions was all that was possible at the time. He wrote William Williams early in December, after reporting that he had found Williams' letter interesting and had destroyed it according to instructions, that the time seemed bad for a foreign loan, but that one was not so much to be desired until "we can make remittance in Country produce—What we owe and pay interest on among ourselves does not empoverish the states taken collectively." And he added hopefully, "If we could disband our army we could easily redeem our bills." The final report was not adopted until January 2 and by that time Sherman had gone home to attend to his affairs there.[25]

But report or no report, the Congress continued to crank out paper as fast as it could vote to do it. An issue of fifty million was immediately approved, and then in rapid succession a number of others totaling about thirty-five more, and by the end of the year when redemption time arrived, the issues of 1779 equaled 140 million dollars Continental. By this time Congress was in general agreement in principle that the presses should be stopped and heavy taxes levied for the sinking of the nearly worthless Continental paper. A report of June 14 in Sherman's hand would have Congress stop emissions shortly, call on the states to do the same immediately, and redeem Continental bonds in gold or silver. But the proposals failed of passage in a six-to-five vote, with Spencer and Huntington driving Connecticut's vote against their colleague.[26]

However, Sherman continued for the next year to take every opportunity to push for the collection of the quotas owed by delinquent states. He had been appointed to the Committee on the Treasury on September 30, 1779, replacing William Carmichael, and had immediately taken on the thankless job of apportioning the state quotas in both October and January. His honest position did his state no good, for Connecticut's quota was larger than Governor Trumbull thought fair. Sherman had to defend the levy in several letters during the fall and winter.[27] But he was sure that state quotas were the only way out. The demands on the states seemed small to him, and he had figured in 1778 that at that time, with only ten million of Continental currency outstanding—though over one hundred million had been circulated—a tax across the whole United States of only one shilling on the pound would pay the entire debt in twelve years.[28] But an annual levy of 5 percent on property was not happy news for the colonists who had gone to war against taxes. Sherman was obliged to fight his battle almost alone, and it would seem that he had lost his political sensitivity in even dreaming that money could be actually raised by the quotas.

In Connecticut, however, he was more successful. He convinced the Assembly that further paper of any kind was useless and higher taxes must be laid. Connecticut, always more willing than the other states, was won over to Sherman's position and acted promptly and efficiently. Indeed, Washington singled her out in 1779 as being the only state to live up to her responsibilities in this regard.[29]

By the beginning of 1780 the Congress had to acknowledge its monetary policy a complete failure, and even the old Puritan himself was forced to face up to repudiation of the debt.[30] A report by his junior colleague, Oliver Ellsworth, effected the dirty work. Adopted on March 18, it called for the redemption of the old debt at 1 to 40. Redemption was to be brought about by the states' acceptance of Continental bills as taxes, the states then to turn them in for new money at 40 to 1. But even this failed, and by 1781 the old money was passing away at 150 to 1 and even worse. It was a sad ending to a sad story, and an epilogue of later depreciations of the inevitable new issues added no joy to it. But, though considered a failure at the time, it was still a miracle when looked at in light of the overall success of the war. "Common consent," wrote Thomas Paine about the Continentals, "has consigned it to rest with that kind of regard, which the long service of inanimate things insensibly obtains from mankind. Every stone in the bridge, that has carried us over, seems to have a claim on our esteem, but this was a cornor-stone and its usefulness cannot be forgotten."[31]

Despite the defeat of Sherman's attempts to keep the money serviceable, and especially to permit a fair return to public creditors, he would not forget the issue. Much, much later, as a representative to the Federal Congress in 1790, he drew on his memory of this period to support assumption of the state debts. In notes for a debate of that year he wrote, "The support of the public credit by a provision for doing justice to the public creditors was one of the great objects that led to the establishment of the present government, and if it should fail of doing that justice it would lose the confidence of many of its best friends."[32] Thus debts owed to individuals for goods and services provided to the states or the general government should be paid. In 1790 he was more successful.

By 1784 Sherman saw the possibility of another source of income in an import duty. With the tradition of state cooperation well established during the course of the war, it now might be possible to get unanimous agreement on such a levy. In January he urged states to permit their delegates to ratify the impost so the Congress could begin to collect the duties, that

> being a matter of utmost importance for supporting the national credit of the United States, and doing justice to the public creditors both at home and in Europe; and I apprehend it will be impracticable to raise a sufficient revenue in the ordinary way of taxing. Raising money by imposts takes it at the fountain head and the consumer pays it insensibly and without murmuring.

And to William Williams several months later he wrote, "It appears to me that a general impost will be the best way for raising a revenue for the interest of the national debt, though I never wish to have the power in Congress to raise money extended beyond what may be necessary for the present debt, but never to raise any for current expenses."

Writing to W. S. Johnson who was at Congress in April 1785, Sherman asked if New York and Georgia had complied with the impost. "If they have not, I wish the other states would consent to the levying it exclusive of them, and to prohibit the importation of any of the dutied articles from those states into any of the other States." Johnson responded that Georgia had complied and that New York would allow the impost if her state government could appoint the collectors and if new New York money could be accepted in payment, a qualification not acceptable to Congress. Sherman's plan, he agreed was a good one, but "it is so bold & decided a measure that I fear we are not at present sufficiently in Spirits to adopt it." Sherman thought the New York request a reasonable one, the difficulty of using state money "may be remedied by ordering that the creditors in each state shall be paid out of the monies collected in the state. . . ." Further—and it is a measure of Sherman's anti-national view—he thought that each state should "make suitable provision for payment of their quotas of the foreign debts, by supplementery funds."[34] Ultimately, an impost had to wait for a new, stronger government where unanimous votes were not required.

Personal Shortages

Roger Sherman had even greater trouble, but also more success, with his personal finances than with those of the public.* Beginning in 1777 and continuing throughout the entire Confederation period he was in financial straits because of the failure of Connecticut to pay him in valuable money, or indeed sometimes at all. During the winter of 1776–77, Sherman was not well. He had gone home in October and had remained there until early in January. He had expected to return to Congress almost immediately, his primary reason for going having been only to pay a short visit to his wife. The fifty-six-year-old work horse had been engaged in some business for the colony in regard to the army, when he was suddenly taken ill and confined for some time. He returned to Baltimore, where Congress was sitting at the time, but was not up to the work and suffered a relapse that kept him in his quarters for four months. He then wrote to his governor, saying that he had to leave Baltimore whether replaced or not, "for my constitution will not admit of so close an application to business much longer. . . ." He stayed on, however, remaining until the second of July, when he was given a leave of absence by the Congress.[34]

---

*The state of Sherman's finances is of interest primarily to establish his position among the economic factions so much discussed by historians of the Confederation period. Sherman's interests were highly diffused: he was a large landholder, principally as a landlord rather than as a speculator; he was a usually solvent merchant with no debts to British factors; he was a hard-money price-fixer not inclined to inflationary policies; lastly, he was a creditor to a significant degree of both the U. S. and Connecticut governments, with the balance probably lying with the latter. See below, Chs. X and XII.

It was during these difficult days that the erstwhile merchant was deeply afflicted by financial worries. In March 1777 he penned a letter quite out of character for the dour stoic, in which he berated Governor Trumbull and spoke bitterly of the raises just given the state troops. The letter is much crossed out and written over; no doubt it gave the compromising old fellow a good deal of trouble. He had not received any money and his chest was empty. "I have had the Mortification to see an augmentation of wages and Subsistence to *almost* all the Officers in the Army whilst I am—I had almost said singly—excepted. Suffer me to ask what is the Reason of this singular Treatment. . . ."[35] The Governor's reply vaguely discussed the shortage of money, but gave no real answer to Sherman's plaint.

The failure of the state to make its payments to Sherman hit especially hard at this time because of the inflation that was beginning to make a strong impression on the economy. In April he complained that prices were high and going up all the time; board was up a third and horses' keep doubled. But the inflation at this date was nothing to what he would experience in the coming years. One hundred dollars printed in September of 1777 was worth only twenty-four a year later and but four in 1779. By March 1780 it took $3732 to buy what could have been bought for $100 in late 1777. Sherman had run up a bill of $99 at the barber's; he owed for eight bottles of wine at $58 each and two barrels of "cyder" at $100 apiece; "washing for self and servant $639; for 15 w[eeks] 4 days board self & waiter, $8330; 1 pair silk hose, $300; mending watch $210; 1 pair leather breeches, $420." In all, a formidable account. Cash from his business was hard to come by, too, and his agent in Boston, the redoubtable Thomas Cushing, could collect nothing there. By March 1781 he was forced to admit his state's inability to pay him his salary in useful money and was willing to accept notes instead. This plea was granted, and he was paid for his services for the previous year.[37] But notes could buy nothing, and in July he wrote for something hard.

> I was obliged to use a part of the £100 furnished me last May to provide some necessaries for my family and I have occasion for some clothing. Living here is very expensive, board is as high as ever, tho' the prices of provisions have fallen in the market . . . I must entreat your Excellency and the Hon'ble Council of Safety to order the Pay Table to draw on the Treasurer to furnish me with the sum of fifty pounds at least, (a greater sum would be more acceptable). . . .

At the end of August he was still without funds and had to repeat his request.[38] By January of 1782 things were getting desperate for the old patriot, and he petitioned his government. He had not received much of the money due him, and had taken notes not payable till after the war for much of the rest. And, he continued in the third person,

> what money he had due before the war have been chiefly lost by depreciation or expended for the support of his family, and the residue put into the continental loan office for which at present he can receive neither principle or interest except small sums payable in bills of exchange. That your memorialist is now wholly destitute of money to pay his necessary expenses or to pay some small sums borrowed by his family for their necessary support while he was away at Philadelphia.

He asked for some cash and the rest in notes. This pathetic plea was granted quickly.[39]

Nominally, Sherman received substantial sums of money for his services in Congress, and more on a per diem basis for his work at the Council of Safety, in revising the state statutes and for attendance at a number of financial conventions. He drew over $40,000 in either Continental currency or interest-paying state bonds between January 1777 and September 1780. He also received a number of payments in pounds during his various stays at Congress. In addition to this, much of which was of little value to him or anyone else, he received over £2172 for expenses, including those of his servant during the years 1775 to 1781. The wages of the delegates, exclusive of expenses, were 18 shillings per day computed in silver at 6 shillings 8 pence per ounce, with adjustments made if the pay was in bonds. It is impossible to know just how well he fared, however, for frequently there is no indication of the kind of money that was given him. As late as 1789, for instance, he was still petitioning his state for about £775 that was owed him for services between 1775 and 1780.[40]

Roger Sherman would never have to fear the poorhouse, however. It is true that there were too many lawyers in Connecticut, and most had a hard time supporting themselves. But Sherman's common sense was very highly respected. Time and again he handed down decisions from his bench seat with such notations as, the objective is "substantial justice, any circumstantial defects or informalities notwithstanding"; or that "the law regards the substance more than the form of a contract." Besides, as a Superior Court judge he exerted certain leverage when appearing as an attorney in the county courts. Thus when hard pressed in 1787, he went back to his old love, the circuit, and did £37 worth of work in October and November 1787.[41]

Roger's son John also held some considerable sum in Congress money. He had been appointed by Congress to disburse Pierce's final settlement notes to the officers and men of two Connecticut regiments which had served in the

Continental line. These notes were to liquidate back pay, commuted officer's pensions, a soldier's bonus of $80, and various claims for clothing, rations, and other items. The difficulty of locating the men and straightening out their accounts was an extremely complicated one and time-consuming. Finally, it was too much for John, and burdened with his own debts, drinking too much and in the midst of marital problems, he used the money for his own purposes. A U.S. Assistant Paymaster came to Connecticut, but John had fled, his soldiers unpaid even as late as 1794, when they were still petitioning for their money. He explained himself in a most pathetic letter to his father in 1790. "I found them [Pierce's notes] daily falling and no general government established, which induced me to take the measures I did, and by advice not from my friends who always held up an Idea of their being funded, but from other Gentlemen which prompted me to the Action. It is done I cannot help it," he wailed. But he added that he had no resources, and though liable to arrest, could give no property, no gold or silver, for he had none.[42]

The Mirage of Steady Prices

Sherman's valiant attempts to support the paper of the Congress through heavy taxation have already been described. This was one of the two major failures of the master politician to recognize the political realities of a situation. On this and one other occasion he allowed his hard mercantile outlook to overbalance his hard political outlook, and both times failure resulted. The second of these battles was his attempt, as a wartime measure, to maintain price controls.

In the middle of December 1776 Congress was forced to depart in unexpected haste from Philadelphia as King George's troops approached. The delegates moved to Baltimore and in bad spirits set about debate once again. But there were few members left to debate, as wet, cold Baltimore was not to the liking of most. "I have the melancholy Prospect before me," complained John Adams to James Warren, "of a Congress continually changing, until very few Faces remain, that I saw in the first Congress. Not one from South Carolina . . . only one from Connecticut. . . . Mr. S. Adams, Mr. Sherman, and Coll. Richard Henry Lee, Mr. Chase and Mr. Paca, are all that remain. The rest are dead, resigned, deserted or cutt up into Governors, etc. . . ."[43]

One of the principal topics of discussion there was that of price-fixing; and the debates were bitter contests, too. There had been a convention of the New England states at Providence in December that dealt among other things with inflation, and this convention was the immediate subject of discussion. Connecticut had already passed some price legislation in November 1776, the first state to do so.[44] Blaming the high prices on "monopolizers, the great pest of society . . . who threaten the ruin and destruction of the State," the Assembly proceeded immediately to curb the wages of laborers. But grain, meat, molasses, rum, and other necessities were covered, too. Price controls were in general popular with Connecticut's agricultural class, and managed to remain so until 1780. One writer to the *Courant* categorized the profiteering traders as "GREAT BUGS whose eyes stood out with fatness, and who have collops of fat on their flanks." But merchants protested, claiming at one time that price lists had been drawn up by farmers, tavern keepers, and lawyers who drown out the voices of the merchants; and at another time that the farmers, lawyers, and physicians dominated the lower house, where they outnumbered merchants and urban artisans by fifteen to one. The price fixing act was brought up for repeal the next year "by Gentlemen in Trade and Seconded by Farmers who have no Avertion to Money nor Ways of Gitting of it." Army supplies, they said, "would alwayse be Scarse untill the Poor Farmer and Honest Importer Could be Encouraged to their Several Employments. . . ." But the repeal bill drew the support of only ten or twelve of the 150-odd deputies "to the Great Mortification of the Mammonites. . . ." Opposition, however, came not only from potential profiteers, but also from those who accepted laissez-faire principles—price-fixing to them was unworkable and illusory. But they remained a minority until 1778, when the various Connecticut Acts were repealed.[45]

The Providence Convention endorsed the action of Connecticut, and on January 2, 1777 reported out a recommendation for stern price regulations which was laid before Congress on the 20th. The argument in Philadelphia centered on the cause of the jumping prices. Some blamed inflation on speculators and counterfeiting enemies, and others held that it was all the inevitable result of the flood of paper. In general, however, support for price-fixing was cold to lukewarm, as most Congressmen believed the "Hacknied Maxim, that Trade Must alwais Regulate itself." [46]

Roger Sherman, who had earlier investigated the counterfeiting of Continental bills, was put on a new committee with R. H. Lee, Wilson, Chase, and John Adams to consider the proceedings of the Providence Convention. The Providence report had already been discussed in the committee of the whole for several days, but there was a procedural question of even greater importance than the substance involved. This was the propriety of two or more states taking up problems that might properly fall under the survey of the Congress. Debate was long and acrimonious, but no final conclusion was drawn. At last, however, Congress accepted most of the Providence report and recommended that the other states take into consideration price and wage-fixing.[47]

As a result of this recommendation a convention was held at York, Pennsylvania, late in March 1777, and a second one for the New England states and New York on the last day of July in Springfield, Massachusetts. At Springfield Roger Sherman was a dominant figure. The delegates of New England and New York were determined on hard money. The Convention recommended sinking bills of credit of the states either by exchanging them for Continental or buying them with tax monies, and called for an end to further state emissions. It suggested that state taxes be levied at least four times a year; "tax often and high," in the Connecticut tradition. It recommended the repeal of acts regulating prices, speedy sinking of state paper, and expeditious provisioning of troops.[48]

Sherman wrote William Williams on August 18 that it seemed to him that prices could be held if the states would sink their paper—which he was apparently naive enough to consider a possibility. The Continental money could be supported if this were done, and if the states would pay their own war costs by frequent high taxes. Almost all dealing, he continued, was by barter, and the people in general were convinced of the necessity of high taxation. A few weeks later he wrote Thomas Cushing in Boston that though the Connecticut Assembly had not ratified the Springfield report yet, it probably would do so in October. His guess was only partly correct. The Assembly did pass new legislation to prohibit monopolizing and hoarding, but did not, in 1777, remove the price controls.[49]

The following January Sherman was a delegate to another price-fixing convention, this one in New Haven—a trip he made at a cost to the colony of over twenty-four pounds, despite the fact that the meeting was in his own home town. He was in this convention from January 15, 1778 to February 1, and on January 28 was appointed with Robert Treat Paine, Nathaniel Peabody, and Benjamin Huntington to draw up its report.[50] Sherman was elected chairman, and his notes are the only available source of information about the New Haven meeting. In spite of the generally approved recommendation of the Springfield Convention that price-fixing be done away with as futile, Congress had directed this meeting to draw up a table of prices and wages for common necessaries and services, this table to be adopted throughout the northern states.[51]

Sherman had written in one of his Almanacs almost twenty-five years earlier that "Reason and Passion answer one great Aim, / And true self love and social are the same." Now he was involved with hoarders, engrossers, and monopolizers. But bravely, if somewhat apologetically, he wrote,

> When we see self-love, that first principle planted in the humane breast by the all wise Creator for our benefit and preservation, through misapplication and corruption, perverted to our destruction, we feel the necessity of correcting so pernicious an error and directing the operation of it in such a manner as that our self and social love may be the same.

The Calvinist and the man of Enlightenment at odds—and compromised as only old Sherman could do it. What amounts to a sermon on Sherman's adage follows with the lesson, ultimately, that paper emissions must be stopped and prices must be fixed. "Must the lunatick run uncontrouled to the destruction of himself and neighbors merely because he is under the operation of medicines which may in time work his cure?" Appended to Sherman's report was the list of prices, which applied as a rule of thumb the idea that they ought to be three-fourths again of what they were in 1774. The prices were filed with a table of relative values which was kept up, altered, and readopted in Connecticut month by month. Sherman reported to Robert Treat Paine that a prime consideration in Connecticut's adoption of price regulation was the difficulty of recruiting soldiers who were paid in a depreciating currency. The people in general favored price control, he continued, though some speculators opposed it.[52] He may have sensed right, for his vote in the nominations for Assistant in May 1778 placed him third from the top—the highest he ever reached.

But by 1778 Congress had become convinced of the folly of price-fixing and recommended the repeal of all such legislation. Oliver Wolcott in Philadelphia wrote his wife that Congress was expected to suspend the controls. "No Regard is paid to any Act of this Kind in this State No such Act to the Southward of it Exists nor never will. If Connecticut maintains a Regulation of this kind, they will be the only State in the Union that will do so. . . ." Be that as it may, Connecticut tried to force at least its little neighbor to the east to pass such legislation. When Rhode Island pleaded for badly needed troops, Connecticut refused to send them until the regulation was passed. But the staunch and independent "Isle of Rogues" refused to budge even then.[53] Even in Connecticut, price-fixing by law never worked. It had always been marked by "the most flagrant Violations," as Governor Trumbull claimed in a proclamation notable for its lack of effect, and evaded by merchants who practiced "Many Arts, dissimulations, & Subterfuges in their manner of bargaining and dealing. . . ." People would barter or refuse to sell at all; farmers would grow only what they needed for themselves; and the shrewd Yankee pedlar would sell the regulated commodity at the legal price and then charge what he could for the bag or box or barrel that contained it. Indeed, it was the refusal of Connecticut farmers to sell any beef at all at regulated prices that drove Congress to ask the state to suspend or repeal its troublesome laws.[54]

In October 1779, however, another convention was held in Hartford in the face of a dizzying downward spin in the value of paper money. This convention again recommended price controls, but evidently a majority in the state was no longer behind the policy. In November Sherman was assigned by the Connecticut Council to deal with the lower house, which wanted to remove the controls that had been on the statute books since 1776. Apparently he was unable to persuade them, for the next month he was forced to go back to the Council and recommend that the ceilings be eliminated.[55]

But the desperate Congress sitting at Philadelphia again wanted something to be done. Finally it recommended to the states that they regulate prices at rates not to exceed twenty times those current in 1774. Sherman wrote his governor that the act passed "nem. con.," so it is to be assumed that the idea of regulation had regained Congressional respectability. He continued that the expectation was to reduce prices to an equal level in all states, and then to keep them reasonable with increased taxation to sink old emissions. He still believed in price-fixing as a measure worthy of consideration and in January wrote Andrew Adams that he saw no reason why, with presses stopped, prices could not be fixed. He admitted, however, that there were many who scoffed at the idea.[56]

In the winter and spring of 1780 new attempts were made to hold conventions in Philadelphia aimed at further regulation of prices. Sherman took a keen interest in the progress of these efforts but finally modified his position to suggest that if further enactments were recommended, Connecticut should not put them into effect until other states made a move. It would be better, he said, to have a stable currency and make price-fixing unnecessary. A Philadelphia Convention finally collected, with John Hancock in the chair, but got nowhere, and closed a week later with Virginia and New York not yet in attendance. The attempt of the previous fall was a complete failure; with prices set at twenty to one they promptly rose to sixty to one. It was at this time that Sherman was paying $99 for a haircut; no wonder he was worried.[57]

The Philadelphia failure in 1780 was the death knell of price control, which during the whole war had been ineffectual anyway. "In general even advocates of such regulation looked upon it as a temporary expedient and palliative, while taxation and retrenchment in government expenditures, no further emissions of irredeemable paper currency, and the sinking of such paper already emitted were considered as the true cure for inflationary prices."[58] Thus writes a scholar on the subject generally, and this could be said of Sherman specifically. Sherman worked harder than most, perhaps harder than any other, for the attractive but doomed cause of price regulation.

Indeed, 1780 marked one of the periodic high tides of agrarian strength in Connecticut. Frustration over the course of the war and final defeat of efforts to re-establish regulated prices coupled with deep disagreements over taxation also helped split the mercantile and agricultural interests among Connecticut's freemen. As early as August 1777, with taxes taking precipitous climbs, a committee of the lower house called for heavier assessments on merchants' property and profits. The demands were not met at the time, but the Assembly did provide for higher rates on interest on loans and more local authority over assessing merchants, traders, and professional men. But antagonisms were sharpened as the war began to bear down on poorer folk. "Since the commencement of the present war," held a petition from hilly Litchfield County," a remarkable change of property & circumstances has taken place, and some men have had the good fortune amids[t] the calamities of their country to amass prodigious sums which still lies in money and money unless on loan is not taxable." Other petitions called for a reduction of the poll tax (levied on all males over sixteen), which was an "insupportable Burthen on the poor," and taxes on personal property. Dissatisfaction was widespread, and the Assembly finally passed a comprehensive tax reform bill in May 1779, which reduced the poll tax for men under twenty-one, diminished rates on farm real estate, and laid taxes on savings over £50, coaches and carriages, clocks, and household silver. Lands, barked one protesting trader, "have a powerful patronage and the merchant hath none."[59]

Nevertheless, the farmers were not happy. Governor Trumbull, who had been an open opponent of price-fixing since 1778, became their special target. A cabal operating out of Windham in the northeast engineered the popular defeat of the Governor and his son-in-law Councillor William Williams in 1780. Though the mechanics of Connecticut's archaic election laws permitted the lower house to continue Trumbull in office, Williams remained out of the Council, being replaced by Oliver Ellsworth. The same agricultural groups were able in 1781 to limit Congress' request for a 5 percent impost to three years, and to beat back efforts to have it extended through the Assembly sessions of the next year. Finally, however, the mercantile and nationalist interests prevailed, and Connecticut granted Congress the authority to levy an impost until all the U.S. debts had been paid.[60]*

---

*The yeomanry was suspicious of long-time office holding. The anti-Trumbull sentiment of 1780, '81 and '83 washed off on Sherman, too. In those years of direct election of Congressmen, the people denied re-election not only to their governor, but to their senior U. S. delegate as well. See below, pp. 183, 189, 215.

CHAPTER IX

The Last Days of Congress

WITHIN the Connecticut congressional delegation, relations had not always been smooth. In particular the urbane, young* and aggressive mercantile members such as had traveled in Deane's train were unhappy about the niggling and deliberate precision with which Roger Sherman insisted matters be arranged. A particular cause of disgust with the old Puritan was his officiousness in the establishment of the Commissary Department. Sherman had always been looking for inexpensive ways to equip and feed the army, suggesting as early as September 1775 that soldiers could depend on their folks at home to send them clothing, and other provisions could be sold to them by suttlers at the camps. When this scheme received no support and a commissary was established, he insisted on a constant audit of the accounts and called for committees to check for frauds.[1]

Commissary Politics

Sherman found himself on numerous bodies set up to provide supplies, or to find ways for the Commissary General to provision the troops. When in the fall of 1776 the soldiers at New York were found to be starving, he made up a committee with Elbridge Gerry and Francis Lewis to investigate. The Commissary General was none other than Joseph Trumbull, a member of the anti-Sherman cabal of 1774. Though no fault was found in Trumbull, it was

---

*For fifteen most active Connecticut politicians before 1775 the average age was fifty-eight in that year; for fourteen who became active during the war the average age in 1775 was about thirty-six. Joseph Trumbull and Silas Deane were thirty-eight, and Jeremiah Wadsworth was thirty-two. Sherman was fifty-six. His future antagonist, Pierpont Edwards, was twenty-five. The list of politicians with their ages is in Loucks, "Connecticut in the Revolution," p. 153 n55. I have moved William Williams from the Revolutionary to the pre-Revolutionary list.

clear that abuses were rampant in the purchase and distribution of supplies. A new system was needed, and Sherman took the lead in writing its report. The final product is about one-quarter his with the rest contributed by Gerry, Lansing, and Schuyler. The point particularly offensive to Trumbull and other commissary officers was the provision of salaries rather than commissions. Gerry disavowed this part, and Trumbull's successor Jeremiah Wadsworth was to blame Sherman for it. Wadsworth, indeed, had been suspicious of the old man all along. When a commission as a deputy commissary officer had been delayed early in 1776, Wadsworth accused Sherman.[2]

In short, the young Yale graduates just didn't like the crusty old cracker. As tight-fisted and small-minded as Sherman appeared to be, his instincts were right. In dealing with people like Joseph Trumbull and Jeremiah Wadsworth, he was confronting men whose scope was wide and vision and imagination informed more by potentiality than practicality. They were nationalistic rather than provincial, and aristocratic rather than republican. There was merit on both sides, but Wadsworth had constantly to be reminded that he "would have less difficulty in obtaining money if Congress had it to give you," and that he could not expect grants without some proof of expenditure. Wadsworth was the kind of fellow who could urge Henry Knox to accept the secretaryship of the army for nothing less than $2500 a year, and a week later remark that he thought $5 a month enough for the soldiers. "It is true," wrote Nathanael Greene to Wadsworth once, "you are rather high toned; but the exercise of a little patience and moderation will correct this inconvenience."[3]

Certainly the commission system had to be an improvement on salary payment. But the obvious interest that commissaries would have in paying top prices when given a percentage of the money spent brought doubters over to Sherman's side. Indeed, he felt constrained to admonish Trumbull that one of his deputy commissioners was actually posting notices that he would pay top prices for goods needed by the army. "Your credit," he wrote the Governor's son, "and I fear the public Interest has suffered much from your employing a Gentleman in this place to purchase provisions. there are great Complaints against him that he gives very exorbitant prices and that prices of articles have been much increased by his indiscretion. . . . it will not do to . . . purchase on Commissions unless you limit the prices: For the greater prices they give the more will be their profits, which is such a temptation as an honest man would not wish to be led into." Yet Sherman's good friend R. H. Lee wrote Washington after about five months' trial of the system that "It was most evident to discerning men that the change in the Commissariat, at the time it was adopted would produce most mischievous consequences, yet such was the rage of reformation, that no endeavors to prevent the evil could avail. . . ."* And Governor Trumbull wrote in June 1778, "The Army and old Commissary feel the bad Consequences of the Regulations made in that Department—Hope and trust both will recover the shock."[4]

If the army recovered from the shock, Joseph Trumbull did not, and, despite a prescription for "a deccoction of strong soot with the yolk of an egg," from his brother-in-law, he died in late August. He was succeeded by Roger Sherman's secret enemy Jeremiah Wadsworth. Wadsworth, with Nathanael Green, the Quartermaster General, kept up the pressure for a commission system.** But in turn these men, who were running a private business on the side, came under heavy criticism. Both threatened to resign, and in Wadsworth's case it was Sherman who persuaded him to remain.[5]

The two supply officers were sure that Sherman was behind all their troubles, and in December 1779, Wadsworth resigned again. He tried to close out the government accounts but had to write one agent, "the Bearer brings you all the Money . . . I expect to Obtain. . . . Mr. Shermans Influence is too powerfull for any representation I can make . . . I am told Mr. Sherman says the State of Connecticut will furnish the Cattle, if they do not, I am sure the Army must live without flesh meat, or subsist for themselves . . . my fears are the Army will disband; what can be Mr. Shermans motives Heaven knows, but he is busy in, and out of Congress, to prevent my having Money, ..." Wadsworth on his part was busy, too; for he and his friends brought about Sherman's defeat at the Connecticut delegate elections, for the first time by direct vote of the freemen. "I feared the Influence of R. Sherman," Wadsworth wrote a provisioner, "wou'd prevent the grant passing but his Villany will not allways Prosper." Wadsworth had to report, though, that

---

*Joseph Trumbull wanted ½ per cent for himself and 2½ per cent for each of his deputies. Burnett, *Letters*, II:365n.

**Nathanael Green (1742-1786), a Rhode Island Quaker with military inclinations, enjoys a reputation for battlefield success second only to Washington. He organized a militia company in 1774, but was denied officer status in it because of a bad limp. He served, however, as a private and was promoted from that rank to brigadier-general the next year by the Rhode Island Assembly, of which he was a member. He showed a talent not only for military strategy, but for supply as well. He was a particularly trusted advisor of Washington, and at one time was even charged with dominating his commander. He saw considerable action as a brigadier and major general, and served as Quartermaster General from 1778 to 1780 while maintaining his command rank. His wartime financial involvements, public and private, ruined him and he died a young man in the midst of attempting to salvage his estate.

Sherman had been again appointed to Congress to fill a vacancy by "the few people in our Assembly that love Sherman [and had] influenced the rest to appoint him again. . . . " In April Wadsworth actually went before the General Assembly and told the deputies that Sherman was obstructing the payment of bills to provisioners. Sherman had done this, Wadsworth claimed, by pressuring members of the Treasury Board and by other acts of "art and deceitful cuning."[6]

Finally in March 1780, a congressional committee was established to study the whole matter and reform the entire supply system. Sherman, of course, was a major figure and was given credit—or rather, blamed—for the report, which ran to eighteen printed pages.* Greene reported to Washington that "The best people in Congress think the new system for drawing supplies from the States, will be found totally incompetent to the business . . . The scheme is too complex and tedious. . . ." He added that even committee member "General Schuyler and others think it will starve the Army in ten days."[7] But Schuyler had known that it would turn out badly. He had written Washington that he would have nothing to do with "a Business which I forsee from the Manner In which It will be Conducted, will neither redound to the honor of the agents or the service of the public. . . ." Washington responded with little faith in Sherman's work, giving Greene orders to ignore the committee system "which Roger Sherman is at the head of." "I cannot think he would put it upon avery [sic] eligible footing if he had ever so much time," wrote Greene to his commander, "as his main object is to keep the Army as weak as possible, having said last spring that he thanked god the Army was no stronger. You may see his principles and wishes, from the Sentiments he sports. I believe him to be the wickedest, and worst politician, that ever disgraced the American Councils—Thank god that his race is but short. . . ."[8] It is true that Sherman wanted to keep the army in its place, "We cant be too careful of Military incroachments," he wrote once.** But this was not unusual in New Englanders, as Rhode Island's Nathanael Greene knew very well.[9]

---

*Modern historians generally ascribe authorship of the new plan to Greene's predecessor as Quartermaster General, Thomas Mifflin, and to Timothy Pickering of Massachusetts, Greene's successor.

**Sherman continued that "it is easy to accuse any person with being a Spy and so put his life in the power of a Court Martial if that is allowed—The case of Molesworth who was tryed and executed in this City [Philadelphia] was approved by Congress, but it was from necessity, because there was no Civil Courts established in this State." This is

But Philip Schuyler, Wadsworth, Greene and others thought the whole system was at base an effort to embarrass Washington and to force themselves into resignation. Though the chief villian was Thomas Mifflin, coauthor with Sherman of the plan, and notorious anti-Washingtonian, Sherman came in for his share of abuse. When Greene refused to continue as Quartermaster General under the reorganization an attempt was made to dismiss him from the army. "Roger Sherman," he wrote bitterly,

> is doing all the mischief he can in Congress; he is at the head of this affair. It appears to be his intention to get our public affairs in as bad a train as possible at the time he leaves Congress; that the confusion and disorder that will follow, may appear to be owing to his having left the house. I am of the opinion that he is one of the most wicked and ignorant politicians that ever disgraced an Assembly or that had such an extensive influence.[10]

These were hard words and unkind ones to write to Wadsworth, one of the principal architects of Sherman's first removal from Congress since its inception six years before. But worst of all, they were untrue words, too. Embarrassedly—one hopes—Greene had to correct himself.

> In my last I wrote that Congress were about to suspend my command. They attempted more, they pushed hard to dismiss me [from] the service altogether, so great was their resentment for my daring to oppose their tyrannical steps. Six days the matter was under warm debate. . . . Can you believe it, or do you think it possible that Mr. Shearman was my fast friend in all this affair. . . . I have this from the best Authority.[11]

---

interesting for its very early application of principles applied during the Civil War in *Ex Parte Milligan* and other cases.

Perhaps Sherman went too far in his naive, even romantic militia policy. Once he objected to a War Committee report that would have permitted delinquents from the army to be given five hundred lashes by the courts-martial. His technically successful opposition was based on the principle laid down in Deuteronomy (xxv:3) that "Forty stripes he may give him, and not exceed: lest, if he should exceed, and beat him above these with many stripes, then thy brother should seem vile unto thee." Whereupon General John Sullivan wrote to Washington in great disgust that this principle was "strongly urged by Roger Sherman Esqr and Co and though a Great Majority of Congress were for it the Question was Lost for want of the assent of Seven States: This relation," Sullivan continued bitterly, "will Convince you of the Incompetence of Some Members in the American Senate as well as the Absurdity of Some parts of the Confederation." It must have been aggravating, indeed, to be treated as Benjamin Rush was when he reported the retreat of the American forces from their entrenchments on some Long Island hills. Sherman's sprightly comment was taken verbatim from Jeremiah (iii:23), "Truly in vain is a salvation hoped for from the hills." If there were those who doubted the pious Yankee's military sagacity, perhaps they had cause. Burnett, *Letters*, VI:133; Corner, *Rush*, p. 145.

The system never worked, of course, and the army was ragged and hungry, with the chief supply officers resigning or threatening to resign. With Congress at a total loss, it turned the job over to the states: maybe they could procure provisions and clothing from their people on a barter basis. But, wrote Governor Trumbull, this had failed, too: " 'Tis difficult, and ever will be, for Governor and Executive Councils to be Commissaries and Quarter Master Generals. . . . The winter I think will be employed in systemizing still further—." Nor would Connecticut's hard-pressed yeomen support such expenses. Trumbull rejected the idea of a special Assembly session to raise the necessary funds because he "was not sure the Assembly, if called, would lay on a further tax immediately—rather—I believe not."[12]

The commissary squabble was only one aspect of a much larger conflict—that which set a burgeoning nationalist faction against the old provincials. A series of letters between Wadsworth and Greene in the winter and spring of 1780 illuminates the relationship of the narrow fiscal policies of the pecunious provincials in Congress to the frustrations of the young nationalists, many of whom held executive posts. In his third year as Quartermaster General, and under attack from his predecessor, Thomas Mifflin, Greene's discouragement grew as the winter deepened. "The business of my Department is growing more and more desperate every day," he wrote Jeremiah Wadsworth. "The Congress are calous to all our representations. The people are pressing for payment to pay their taxes. I expect total revolution in the course of a fortnight or three Weeks. Confusion, disorder, complaints and murmuring will be the consequences. . . . "[13]

The Congress, said Greene, just didn't know how to act; it was only good for philosophic conversation. What was needed in Philadelphia was men of action—like Wadsworth, who had recently resigned his commissary generalship. "Is your object private or Public? If the latter I wish you to go to Congress. I think you can do more good there than a hundred Almanack makers or Lawyers," wrote Greene taking a swipe at Sherman. "It is men of business is [sic] wanted in that house more than Men of [intellectual] Speculation. the first are useful, the last are perplexing to all transactions out of their walk of life. They are always in the Clouds upon the wings of imagination, with minds too exalted, to discent to the dull [—?—] and laborous forms of business."*[14]

---

*But if Wadsworth scorned public business and should "think of going a privateering, I should be happy to become an Adventurer in the bottom," wrote Greene. "I am sure you are a child of fortune," he added in accurate prophecy. Yale, Hist. Ms. Room, "Knollenberg Collection" (March 17, 1780).

As the bitterest winter of the war drew to a welcome close—with weather worse than Valley Forge and little more to eat—Greene again congratulated Wadsworth on his absence from the scene. "I have many things to say to you," he wrote, hungover on an early March morning.* "Our political concerns grow worse and worse. . . . I cannot help thinking you made a happy and seasonable retreat. You will come off with flying colours. The distresses that must follow from the present mismanagement of public affairs, will reflect no small honor upon you, as it will be attributed altogether to a change of men, and not measures." Two weeks later, Greene's disgust with Congress was even greater. "The folly and injustice of administration is so obvious notorious that the minds of the people seem to be prepared for any kind of revolution that design or accident may throw in our way."[15]

The executive orientation of the young men—a year apart in age, Greene and Wadsworth were about twenty years younger than Sherman—gave them no patience with either Congress or its Boards. The latter were at a standstill, Greene reported in May 1780, and "The Congress are a Chapter of expedients, and a body of little things; and without they mind their manners, and change their policy, they will soon have the honor of entailing slavery upon us."**

It is a maxim of wise politics, Greene said,

> to employ only such men as have wisdom, devise and spirit to execute whatever may be committed to their management. And tho such may appear dear in the first instance, yet like the purchase of cloth of the first quality the wear will sufficiently compensate for the price. It has been more the policy of our government to get men upon very moderate conditions than get such as are capable of conducting the business to advantage.[16]

"The National strength is so torn to pieces," Greene lamented,

> and divided with the different views and [interests?] of the different States, that little or no attention or support is given to the great object, the common opposition. The Army is ready to disband this moment for

---

*Greene "was at the Assembly last night and feel not a little fatigued and clouded. We are merry at Camp, but have little to eat either for man [sic] beast." Yale, Hist. Ms. Room, "Knollenberg Collection," NG to Jeremiah Wadsworth (March 2, 1780).

**Here Greene was implying that shadowy element of the Confederation period—the fear of a military dictatorship. In 1943 Charles A. Beard noted that

> Leaders among the framers of the Constitution regarded the resort to constitutional government instead of military dictatorship as their greatest triumph. . . . What I am referring to is a movement . . . for a permanent military dictatorship, or rather a number of underground movements or demands looking in that direction, which took form during and after the war. Beard, *The Republic*, pp. 21-22.

want of proper provisions. The Soldiery are neither fed or paid; and are getting sour amazingly fast. Such a temper never appeared in our Army before. God knows how it will end.

It was not merely a lack of men of vision and ability, however, that was impeding the war effort. Indeed, men of large views should look beyond the war to the condition of the states in victory and independence. Movement toward a more unified government was in danger of being reversed, Greene wrote in March 1780. "There is a sentiment creeping into existence in political life that looks like putting all the States upon a total indepdent footing of each other, with regard to raising, paying, viticulling and clothing the Army."[17]

By May he was in a state of near panic. Though pleased to congratulate Wadsworth on his election to the Connecticut General Assembly, he still was "more and more convinced" that "a revolution of some kind" was imminent "both from the inclinations of many, and the necessity of the thing." He was thinking, apparently of the possibility not only of a rebellion from below, but also of a coup from above. "Many members of Congress," he wrote in May 1780

> confess that in the present state of things, with such restricted powers, under the present plan of confederation, with the loss of the confidence of the people, and in the manner they conduct the public business, they are altogether unequal to the task. . . . [Congress should] call a Convention of the States and for them to form a plan of confederation upon such liberal principles as shall give to the body . . . powers of general jurisdiction and control over individual States to bind them in all cases, where the general interest is concerned. Unless something of this sort takes place, it is morally certain we are a ruined people; and that is not very distant.[18]

The dispute over the Commissary and its operation was not only troublesome to Congress and the army, but overturned Sherman's political fortunes at home, too. There had long been an anti-Sherman faction, and now it pressed the drive to remove him from Congress. The old politician had been away too much of late and his fences were broken and gaping.* In addition, the freemen were beginning to resent long tenures and dual office holding. So in May 1779 the Assembly passed an act for direct election of Congressional

---

*He served a total of at least 1543 days in the nine years he went, eight of them consecutive. [Note 12.] He was statutorily eligible to serve continuously until March 1, 1784, under the rules of the new Confederation. See Chapter X below for the Connecticut background of the politics and economics of this Congressional session.

delegates, in the manner and at the time prescribed for Assistants: twelve to be nominated in September and seven elected in April, with not more than four nor less than two to represent the state. Sherman, it seems, was in trouble with the freemen. Though never failing appointment by the Assembly, he ranked tenth in the first nomination under the new law, and was not elected to go to Congress for the first time since its earliest convening in 1774. He served out his time in 1780, failed of election again in May of 1781, but was appointed by the Assembly to fill a slot opened by the death of Titus Hosmer. The freemen responded to this by dropping him to twelfth—or last—in the January nominations in 1783 that year, and the previous one saw Sherman kept at home.[19]

But in October 1783, Connecticut's delegates ran their statutory limit and resigned, and Sherman was one of the four appointed by the Assembly to fill their places. That his several appointments had been imposed by the upper house upon the lower is to be suspected, and in this last case it becomes clear. The House resisted Sherman's appointment and tried to substitute its speaker, Charles Church Chandler, but as usual the Council prevailed, and Sherman went to Congress. He attended Congress under the Confederacy for the last time during the first six months of 1784. His record is unequaled, only four other men serving as long as he or as continuously.*[20]

Indeed, this constant participation in national affairs was undoubtedly a contributing factor in Sherman's loss of support among the freemen and in the lower house. The provincial farmers were extraordinarily jealous and ever watchful of their elected delegates. At the same time that popular election was established, the legislature resolved to hold congressmen "accountable and answerable to this Assembly for their conduct from time to time, and be liable to be recalled in case said Assembly shall judge fit." Sherman, after all, had spent about six months of each of the eight years, 1774–81, at Congress. When one recalls that a reason given for leaving Silas Deane and Eliphalet Dyer out of Congress in 1775 was that the Assembly "think Liberty most secure under frequent changes of the Delegates. . . . ," it is a testament to Sherman's political ability that he hung on so long. Of course, he was never popularly elected to the Confederation Congress, depending on interim appointments during 1780, 1781, and 1784. After 1784 he was seen no more till the reorganization of government in 1789.[21]

---

*The other four were Samuel Adams, Thomas McKean, Francis Dana, and Theodorick Bland.

The Withering Away of the State

Late in 1783 Congress languished for lack of a quorum, despite the necessity of debating the treaty of peace that ended the war with Great Britain. And as soon as that job was completed and only ratification yet remained, members began to steal away in groups until it became almost impossible to muster the nine state delegations necessary to transact business. On but three days between November 4 and March 1 was there a quorum. Connecticut's delegation could have helped, and letters were dispatched to Hartford and other capital cities pleading for members. On January 13, 1784, Sherman and James Wadsworth, country cousin to the cosmopolitan Jeremiah, arrived.[22]

The appointment had been a surprise to the old trooper, who supposed that he might be free from the burdens of public business away from his family. But there is no doubt that he wanted to go. The anti-Sherman party was still active in Congress and its Connecticut contingent. The old politician did not get the appointment without at least a hint that he desired it. Nevertheless, Sherman had to cancel a trip to visit his wife's relatives in Salem planned for the early spring, though he hoped only to put it off for a month or so. Even this small two-man representation put a strain on the state treasury, for Sherman and Wadsworth had to delay their departure because "they could not get money for our expenses, and have not but a Scant Supply." Sherman intended to start out the day after Christmas, but was held up by the important business of rechartering his town as an incorporated city. Perhaps reluctantly, then, he left for Annapolis, the current seat of the mobile Congress. James Wadsworth had departed on December 23 by ship, but the two arrived in the muddy little city on the same day.[23]

There were six important items that required action, and a quorum was necessary. Treaties of commerce needed to be set in motion; the general government was sadly lacking in organization; arsenals and military posts were required; Indian affairs were troublesome; the western lands question still plagued; and finally the eternal problem of finance pressed as always on the shoulders of a slender Congress. And of course, the treaty of peace still awaited ratification with the March 3 deadline assigned by Great Britain coming on apace.[24]

The arrival of the Connecticut delegates was augmented by the return of Richard Beresford of South Carolina, who staggered in from a Philadelphia sick bed, and a quorum was achieved on January 14. Twenty-three delegates ratified the treaty and sent it on its way back to England immediately on assembling. The ratification merely reduced the willingness of the impatient delegates to remain any longer, and after the sixteenth no quorum could be raised again for six weeks. Life in Annapolis must have been frustrating for the businesslike and unfrivolous Sherman, used to the intense Congress of earlier times. The "polite Attention of the Gentlemen of the Town, Engages all our leisure hours in Visits and Amusements. The Players Exhibit twice a week and there is a Brilliant Assembly or Ball once a fortnight to which We have Standing Cards of Invitation," wrote a New Jersey member, and the old Puritan, who refused to use a ferry on Sunday, must have squirmed. Certainly he took no time out for "plays, Balls, Concerts, routs, hops, Fandagoes and fox hunting." He agreed, no doubt, with David Howell of Rhode Island that neither his education and taste nor his pocketbook admitted of such activity.[25]

But some fruit was harvested from the Annapolis meetings. The cession of Virginia's western lands was as important as any other Confederation accomplishment, aside from winning the war itself. Here at Annapolis the last major contention was stifled; contention which if continued would have made it impossible for the deeper cooperation among the states that was to culminate in the Constitution of 1787. Sherman's part in bringing about this settlement has already been detailed. At this session he continued to press the claims of the Susquehannah settlers for private rights to the soil they had cultivated. He was up against Thomas Jefferson, who wished to see no precedents established giving squatters any rights at all, but by this time accommodation between Connecticut and Pennsylvania was in the works, and Jefferson could not have things all his own way. The settlers never received a report favorable to their demands for a second court, but neither were they explicitly rebuffed at this time. Delay was a good tactic, and it gave time necessary for a political solution ultimately worked out in 1786.[26]

Sherman was the man in charge of credentials at this session. This legal underbrush became more than a bit thorny when Congress decided that the three-year limit on consecutive membership would become effective on the first of March, 1784. In this capacity Sherman wrote the opinion that his friend Samuel Osgood of Massachusetts could no longer sit, an opinion that Osgood contested wildly but vainly. He finally left the chamber storming that he would slam "farewell [to] all Connection with public life . . . [for he was] inexpressibly disgusted with it."[27] Gunning Bedford and James Tilton of Delaware and Howell and Ellery of Rhode Island also fell under the legal eye of the perhaps overconscientious Sherman. The former pair left delightedly, but the Rhode Islanders, who strangely questioned their own right to stay, brought on a long debate lasting six days. Later on Sherman evidently had a change of heart and fought for the right of Howell and Ellery to remain and vote.[28]

But it was a nasty debate, Howell later wrote:

> Some young men in Congress pursue the object of taking away our Seats in Congress as if it was of the first magnitude. . . . P.S. I have been in hot water for six or seven weeks. . . . I have received two written challenges to fight duels; one from Col. Mercer, of Virginia, the other from Col. Spaight, of No. Carolina. . . . I answered them that I meant to chastise any insults I might receive and laid their letters before Congress.[29]

Credential-searching, then, was a job that no sensible person would want; it could produce nothing but hard feelings and interrupt the work of the Congress, and it really might have been better left undone. But if it was to be done at all, Sherman was the kind who would do it.

In the Annapolis session of the Congress Sherman continued his work on the problems of finance; dull, dreary, and very necessary work it was too. He was assigned to a whole series of committees, to act on letters from the Superintendent of Finance, the Paymaster General, and various private petitions, for many of which he wrote the reports. He even held a place on the grand committee of a member from each state whose pathetic job it was to wail again for the still tardy state levies. The national debt, after all, did have to be paid. Another committee to deal with the depressing insolvency was organized in March, and Sherman found himself on that one, too. But generally he worked with the New England delegates, who sought to cut expenses to the very marrow, even to reduce the size of the Continental army to less than five hundred men—or better still, to eliminate it entirely. Limiting expenses would have the dual benefit of keeping the debt small and constricting the area of activity of a central government that Sherman at this time saw as a necessary evil.[30]

The main constitutional issue that plagued the slender Congress during this period was the matter of an interim government. Interims apparently were going to come often and last long, and some kind of skeleton was needed to run the ghostly Confederation. The most frequently suggested plan was to set up a Committee of States, consisting of one member from each province. The previous September James Duane had submitted a report dealing with the construction of such a body, and the report was handed to a committee consisting of Jefferson, Osgood, and Sherman, though the last was not present in the Congress at the time. Jefferson reported in January, 1784.[31] In its original form his report would have given the interim committee almost complete executive power. But debate in the house whittled away all of the authority except that which would normally fall to Congress when seven states were present, though representatives of nine were required for even these actions by the Committee of States. It mattered little, though, what the powers were to be, for the nine-member quorum was present on only one day in the Committee's career, which its leading scholar dismisses as brief, checkered, and ending in fiasco.

Jefferson was not around when the Committee was established, for Congress melted away in the early summer sun, but Monroe was there to keep him advised:

> the Committee consists of Mr. Blanchard, Dana, Ellery, Sherman, DeWitt, Dick, Hand, Chase, Hardy, Spaight and Reed; for the states not represented on the floor any member who produces credentials may take his seat. the members may also relieve each other at pleasure . . . the powers of the committee are confin'd so that no injury can be effected. Sherman and Dana will necessarily govern it.[32]

But Monroe need not have worried about the influential Yankee, for five weeks earlier plans had been made by both Connecticut delegates to depart as quickly as possible. In April they had written home requesting relief and declaring their intentions to leave as soon as Congress adjourned.[33]

The Committee of States met and organized on June 4, the day after adjournment, and Sherman stayed long enough for that and no more. He was in evidence no longer at Congress either at this session or any other. His next national mission was in behalf of a stronger, more virile government for the jealous, liberty-loving little republics. His departure from Annapolis was at a most desolate time for the Confederation; in its last vestige of power, the Committee of States was unable to raise a quorum even to adjourn, and all that remained of the government was its civil service—a few clerks and secretaries.[34]

Sherman's service in the Congress had been great. Patrick Henry is quoted as having said that when he was a member of the old Congress, "the first men in that body were Washington, Richard Henry Lee, and Roger Sherman." At a later date Henry said that Roger Sherman and George Mason were the greatest statesmen he ever knew. Jefferson was more reserved in his comments, made long after Sherman's death, but paid tribute nonetheless. Sherman, he wrote, "was a very able and logical debater. . . . [in the old Congress] Steady in the principles of the Revolution, always at the post of duty, much employed in the business of committees. . . ." But, "Being much my senior in years, our intercourse was chiefly in the line of our duties. I had a very great respect for him. . . ."[35]

Constitutional Revision—Connecticut Style

During these years on the national scene Sherman always maintained firm connections in Connecticut. He returned there frequently, attended meetings of the General Assembly, the Committee of Safety, and occasionally went the rounds of the Superior Court. He was a majordomo in the state's politics, and by 1784 held four important posts. He was a member of the Council of Assistants, the Superior Court, a deputy to the Continental Congress, and was elected New Haven's first mayor.

His local prestige had been growing almost without setback through the more than two decades of his residence in New Haven. Now in 1783 he capped a long legal career with an assignment to codify the laws of the state, a task he had discharged once before in 1768. This was done with the help of a much younger, but no less able colleague with the fitting name of Richard Law. The work took all the summer of 1783 and most of the fall, and then at the direction of the Assembly had to be corrected and further revised during a part of the winter. The draft of this code is preserved at the State Library and deserves thorough study for the light it sheds on changes then taking place in Connecticut government, economics, and society. Everything from Adulterers (they still should be branded with an A on the forehead) to Quakers (they needed to be watched carefully) affecting the people and communities of the state is precisely systematized.*

That Sherman's view of things was not wholly in accord with the still predominantly provincial and agrarian-minded freemen of the rocky coastal state is evident. Indeed, very few of his revisions were accepted without debate, while virtually all of Richard Law's were left just as he wrote them, many with no objection at all.**[36] In three areas in particular did Sherman's revision run into trouble in the General Assembly's lower house. These were executive authority in Connecticut, relations with the Confederation government, and state mercantile policies. While Sherman retained, with minor

---

*Some indication that the periodically revised law code was considered the basic organic document of Connecticut government is attested not only by Connecticut's desire that the U. S. Constitution be ratified by state legislatures rather than conventions of the people, but also by statements referring to pre-1784 practice as being "under the old constitution." Philadelphia Debates, July 23-26; *SR*, V:407; "House Journal 1787-1788," p. 28, whence the quotation. But see also Purcell, *Connecticut in Transition*, pp. 114-16; Wood, *Creation*, pp. 276-78.

**A significant revision of Law's section was the addition by the lower house of a paragraph granting freedom at the age of twenty-five to all persons born into slavery after March 1, 1784. "Mss. Code." p. 360; "House Journal," pp. 94–95 (January 30, 1784).

changes in wording, the statement of independence of 1776, he altered the preamble. To the original statement, "The people of this state being by the providence of God free and independent, have the sole and exclusive right of governing themselves as a free, sovereign and independent State and as such to exercise and enjoy every power, jurisdiction and right," Sherman added, "not by them expressly delegated to the United States in Congress assembled," which was struck out in the lower house.[37]

The deputies also negatived Sherman's addition that all treaties made by Congress "with any foreign nation agreeable to the powers with which they are invested by the Confederation shall be duly observed." And although Sherman would allow U. S. commissioners and auditors to come into the state and call witnesses, the House added that no state officer could be required to allow examination of records of money or property even if it belonged to the United States and had been placed in his charge by Congress! The provincials of the lower house, however contradictorily, did allow Sherman's proviso "That due obedience shall be paid by the several courts, officers and inhabitants of this State, to all orders and ordinances of the united States in Congress assembled, made by virtue, and pursuant to, the powers and authorities vested in them by the articles of confederation."[38]

A second major concern was a revision of the court system that would both centralize it and add many executive powers to the Council. These changes are found in the longest section of the new code, "An act concerning the Supreme executive power of Government in this State." Apparently Sherman was following the wartime practices developed by the Council of Safety, which was slated to end its existence in October 1783. The Governor and Council in his new code would be "for the time being . . . the Supreme executive authority of this State, with power to Superintend the prudential affairs thereof, and the execution of the laws which concern the public weal, especially such as relate to the revenue and the collection of Taxes and debts due to the State." The Council would also be given authority to issue orders to all subordinate officers, to remove them if necessary and appoint others in their place. Sherman was careful to leave the judiciary independent by explicitly exempting judges and justices of the peace from removal, but the whole section was negatived by the lower house, though quite naturally acceptable to the Assistants. With the failure of this provision the upper house attempted to continue the Council of Safety with its wartime powers, but that, too, was struck down by the wary yeomen of the House.[39]

Sherman also added sections establishing the Governor and Council as a Supreme Court in any matter over £50, giving County and Superior Courts authority to license all attorneys pleading before them, and granting county courts admiralty jurisdiction under laws of both the state and the United States; all of which were temporarily negatived by the lower house, to be enacted in part as a separate act. Provisions giving original jurisdiction in some cases to the Superior Courts and permitting county courts to levy taxes on towns in proportion to their lists to pay court expenses were also postponed by the deputies.[40] Here Sherman was attempting to streamline state judicial practice. Matters of equity were heard in the last resort by the Assembly, with that body acting as judge and jury by majority vote. The amount of this business and its obstruction of the normal legislative function had long troubled Sherman. Over a decade earlier he had written that as such equity proceeding "increases it becomes very burthensome and expensive for the whole Assembly to sit to hear them." He added that the erection of a court of chancery was being considered and wondered how that system worked in Massachusetts. Sherman's effort to put this into practice in 1784, though held off for a while by the lower house, was implemented at the October session.[41]

Several acts proposed by Sherman to aid merchants were also rejected by the House of Representatives. For instance, a law requiring the clearing of all private debts after seven years on the books was first turned down and then passed by the lower house after a section omitting the war years was added. Another provision—this one accepted by both houses—permitted creditors to sue people not inhabitants of the state, and to enter suits against groups of people even though only one of them is known. Sherman's old-fashioned Calvinism is evident in a section of the declaration of rights holding that life, property, wife or children could not be taken away except under laws of the state or "by some clear plain rule warranted by the word of God." The lower house substituted for this last part "unless clearly warranted by the Laws of this State."[42]

In general, Sherman's revisions—which included "all the laws from the beginning to Letter L inclusive and several that were afterward passed under other Letters"—attempted to centralize the judiciary, give the Council executive powers, strengthen the judicial aids to merchants, and sanction Congressional authority. He was beaten back on most of these by the lower house, but his was the more progressive mode and theirs the more conservative. The lower house just opposed change, especially centralizing innovations. By October Sherman was able to send in his bill for the assignment, which he estimated had taken about thirty-eight work days. He billed the Assembly for "all the time that I can't redeem from other public business from the 1st of August in revising comparing and correcting . . . [the laws] wherein I examined and compared that part of the Laws which Mr. Law had prepared and noted for amendments, etc." At twelve shillings a day plus the cost of paper, postage, and clerical help, the total came to seventy-eight pounds, paid in two installments. This was not excessive for the labor involved.[43]

The Incorporation of New Haven

In the immediate pre-war period New Haven had been Connecticut's leading center of trade, and the colony's wealthiest town. But for a number of reasons it declined greatly between 1776 and 1783. For one thing, it was not thought secure to march soldiers along the coast, and so inland towns in general, and Hartford in particular, became provisioners to the army. Another cost of the war was the loss of New Haven's Tory population, larger than any other Connecticut town. Population declined by three hundred during the war, though not all of those were Loyalists. New Haven had had a good West Indian trade in the early seventies, sending out one hundred ships in 1774; but only fifty went in the first three war years together. Then the British raid was costly, amounting to well over £15,000.[44]

In general Connecticut flourished during the war. Hartford was known as the "Grand Focus" of Continental bills of credit in New England, and more money circulated than ever before. Connecticut moved more and more away from a barter into a money economy, a trend started during the French and Indian War. The flourishing of this trade in paper and provisions brought about the rise of businessmen and the solidification of their political influence.[45]

After 1783 New Haven regained its prominence as Connecticut's most important trading center. Indeed, the town underwent what one commentator has called a "nearly complete metamorphosis." By the end of the war one lone sloop was all that remained of her shipping facilities, but by 1787 there were sixty-one vessels sailing out of New Haven, mostly to New York, but many to the West Indies as well.[46] Its seven or eight retail shops remaining in 1783 had risen to an amazing 103 by 1787. But it was largely a prosperity based on circulating paper, and when tax levies called for specie, troubles arose. Farmers, in particular, felt the pinch, and class animosities became exacerbated. New Haven's outlying districts, East, West, and North Haven, Amity, Bethany, Mt. Carmel, and other sections began to see the commercial part of town as dominant and self-centered.

Thus the ground was prepared for a revival of the incorporation movement that had been started back in 1771, when Sherman headed a committee set up to investigate the implications of city government, but had been laid aside for the duration. In 1780 a series of petitions for self-government came in from the suburban parishes with their agrarian interests*. They were opposed then, but when more joined the next year, New Haven proper, dominated by merchants, acquiesced, and a body was established to lay out boundaries and regulate financial affairs.[47]

New Haven's merchants were only too happy to keep the movement going. Incorporation as a city would get rid of town meeting government, which had been dominated traditionally by the agrarian interests of the outlying areas. An important objective of incorporation was the establishment of New Haven as a free port. "Our merchants," wrote Noah Webster, "are now mere retailers who collect money for our sister states. What a generous compliance do we show our neighbors! The scene is indeed changing—New Haven sets a laudable example—and we trust that the Legislature will give other towns the same advantages and that the merchants do not want a disposition to improve them." At the May session following incorporation, this special status was granted to New London and to New Haven. Webster was forced to report, however, that this action accomplished little. A petition laid before the Assembly in October 1783 demonstrated the merchantile impetus of the drive. Dated September 22, 1783, and signed by 215 of New Haven's leading figures (though unaccountably not by Sherman), it opens by stating that the petitions "have been obliged to turn their Attention to commerce. . . ." and need new governmental institutions to aid its development.[48]

Both major factions were agreed on the desirability of incorporation, so the town meeting, with Sherman in the chair, expressed disappointment that the Assembly did not act in 1783. It instructed its deputies to push for a speedy conclusion of the business at the January session in 1784. It was not easy to overcome the suspicions of the House, where every new town meant two new members, and local self-government came at the expense of Assembly control. It voted to continue the bill for further consideration not less than four times. The Assembly ultimately complied, however, and in

---

*The increasing mercantilization of Connecticut's economy apparently tended to sharpen the differentiation between town and country interests. In 1776 there were 74 towns; by 1796 there were 106. New Haven's incorporation as a city set off a rash of such town-splitting ventures. Twenty new towns were incorporated between 1785 and 1789, and then none in the next five years. *SR*, VIII:xx, VI:xi-xii.

January 1784 incorporated not only New Haven, but New London, Hartford, Middletown, and Norwich as well. Thus city government came to Connecticut in a rush. The new charter provided for a mayor, four aldermen, up to twenty members of a common council, and various other municipal officers. The mayor and aldermen were to have considerable judicial, appointive, and executive authority.[49]

Aldermen and council members were elected annually under New Haven's new city charter, but the mayor was to be chosen once and then remain in office at the pleasure of the General Assembly. The logic behind this is obscure, to say the least, but apparently incorporated cities were to be agents of the state the same as any other kind of chartered entity. The first elections were held in February, 1784, and the outcome demonstrated the domenance of the mercantile faction. Businessmen held all four aldermanic seats and sixteen of the twenty seats on the council.[50]

The Return of the Tories

But the elections were not all that simple. The Treaty of Paris ending the war was signed on April 3, 1783, and word of it arrived in New Haven on the 24th. At sunrise thirteen cannon were discharged on the green; there was a repeat performance at three in the afternoon, when twenty-one more were fired for France and seven for Holland. In the evening "Skyrockets & fireworks,. . . a great Bonfire lighted up at VIII½ & burnt down by IX, when 3 Cheers finished the whole and all broke up & retired peaceably home. Tho' there was Liquor served to the multitude, yet thro' the great care & discretion used, there was little, very little Excess and in general great Decorum." But at Hartford—where the schoolhouse had been blown up to celebrate the repeal of the Stamp Act sixteen years earlier—the fireworks got out of hand and this time burnt down the courthouse.[51]

Peace meant political problems, and the most troublesome of these was the return of the Tories. Articles V and VI of the treaty provided that Congress would recommend to the states that Tories be permitted rehabilitation and restitution of property. This was a much debated aspect of that generally controversial treaty and in all states created factions of pro-and anti-Tories. Connecticut was no exception, and a newspaper battle over the issue had begun the previous January. Citizens of Norwalk reminded the Assembly that these "Villains . . . have been the cause of so much Destress, Conflagration and Bloodshed . . . [who] flew to the assistance of our Murderers and displayed their Talents against us in the most vigerous and

Savage-like manner possible to be invented. . . ." When sentiment favorable to permitting return became manifest in New Haven, a town meeting in March instructed its deputies to prevent rehabilitation, and a writer to the *Gazette* urged citizens to consider carefully that they do not elect Tories, for though these people had lost the war they had "insidious designs" to win over the government.[52] But it was in New Haven and Middletown that one sees the strongest efforts to bring the Tories back. One sympathetic correspondent wrote that he thought the issue "must jolt some folks out of the Saddle," and it no doubt did when in May the Assembly's first act was to repeal some of the nine Tory-restraining measures passed during the war.[53]

The Council had moved to repeal some twenty-three wartime laws, including the anti-Tory acts, but the House left four on the books, including one for punishing high treason aginst the state or the United States, and another for confiscating estates of "inimical persons." And in Fairfield County, where feelings ran most bitter, at least six towns refused to readmit Loyalists anyway. Indeed, a large number of outraged citizens from Norwalk, recalling the Tory raid on their town, begged the Assembly not to let them return "especially while you are sensible that the ties of humanity obliges near two thirds of the people to declare war against those Villians the instant they set foot on this shore, also that the dying Groans of our Parents, Children and Friends (murdered by them in cool blood) must force us to pursue and slay them whereever they are to be found. . . ."[54]

In New Haven there was a concerted effort by the commercial interests to lure certain wealthy Tories into the city. Ezra Stiles reported a petition inviting "about 120 Tory Families of the City of New York, of which 40 are Merchants of Property, to come & settle in New Haven, as they cannot tarry in New York. They offer to bring Two Thirds of the Mercantile property of the whole City into this town." A similar petition made the rounds in New London, but New York allowed an amnesty, so few if any of the Yorker Tories came to Connecticut.[55]

The February elections under New Haven's new Charter were fought out, Ezra Stiles wrote, "in an Endeavor silently to bring the Tories into an Equality & Supremacy among the Whigs. The Episcopalians are all Tories but two, & all qualified on this Occasion, tho' dispis[in]g Congress govt before—they may perhaps be 40 Voters." Stiles reported that the certified freemen of New Haven numbered 343,* but that only 261 were sworn for the election on the 10th. Of these only 249 actually voted. "This day," he wrote

---

*Stiles reported the amazing fact that 55 of these were college graduates. *Lit. Diary*, III:107.

on February 10, 1784, "was held the first Meeting of the Citizens for the Election of the first Mayor, Alderman &c of this City." The votes for mayor were Sherman, 125; Thomas Howell, 102; and Thomas Darling, 22. "So Mr. Sherman was elected & proclaimed Mayor, the first time going round." The elections continued for two more days, and on the 12th Stiles reported, "This day the Election of City officers completed. Mr. Sherman the Mayor-elect is absent at Congress. Mr. Howell is the present Head of the City [as he was chosen 1st Alderman]. We elected thirteen Common Council Men yesterday & 7 today. There was a great Struggle. About 100 Freemen Voters present." So even in a red-hot controversy only about a third of the qualified electorate bothered to vote. Stiles' editor suggests that the reason Sherman, "unquestionably the most distinguished resident of the new city . . . did not carry a larger vote may have been due to his personal characteristics; that natural shyness and reserve of manner which some of his juniors mistook for aristocratic *hauteur* may well have stood in the way of popularity." [56]

Yet there must have been other reasons for the split vote. Howell was an old rival of Sherman, and a member of the First Church—the house of the "Old Lights" that had provided so much conservative spirit in the town ever since the days of the Great Awakening almost half a century earlier. Darling, a lawyer of Yale, class of '40, was the son-in-law of the Reverend Mr. Noyes, and thus very much of the Old Light party, and well known as a quasi-Tory. Howell and Darling split the Tory vote and took some twenty or thirty Old Lights with them. Stiles guessed that perhaps a third of the citizens were "hearty Tories, one third Whigs, one third Indifferent." His analysis of the election was "Mayor & two Aldermen, Whigs; 2 Ald. Tories. Of the Common Council 5 Whigs, 5 Flexibles but in heart Whigs, 8 Tories. The 2 Sheriffs & Treasr Whigs—the 1st Sheriff firm, other flexible." [57]

But even with the election safe in the Whig column, there were doubts that Sherman would accept the office. It was strictly a post of honor, with no pay other than a few fees, and two dollars a day when the town court was in session. The pastor of the mayor-elect, Jonathan Edwards, Jr., a close friend, wrote him a week after the election, "If you refuse it . . . Mr. Howell would certainly be chosen." The conservatives and Tories were so strong that only Sherman could beat them. "I cannot bear that the first Mayor of this infant city should be a tory," Edwards pleaded,

> The disgrace which would be brought on the city, the mortification to every real whig, the triumph of the tories, all come into view on this occasion. . . . I hope the Place will produce some little profit to you. It will be entirely in your way to attend the business when you are at home, and the fees will be something.

In the end, of course, Sherman accepted; indeed the question was probably never in doubt. The costs of public honor were something, too, for Sherman's amiable Rebecca "received some addresses on the subject of the election and by way of answer has fed some hungry bellies whilst others wanted money to buy powder to fire in honor of the Lord Mayor elect. Thus the emoluments of office are felt by her in your absence. The cannon are this moment firing in a most tremendous manner on the subject. I wish you could hear it." And Sherman's old friend Benjamin Huntington added that little Oliver, Roger's seven-year-old son, "hearing that his papa was chosen Mayor was concerned and inquired who was to ride the Mare?" Roger Sherman could run his adopted town almost as he saw fit. His position, according to one historian, was nearly autocratic, though his influence was acquired by pure force of character.[58]

Incorporation was, however, only a manifestation of more fundamental changes in Sherman's town. By 1787 it was the seventh largest city in the United States; even stripped of its suburbs it had a population of 3400, and nearly 900 buildings, including 103 retail stores. A governmental agency for the dissemination of medical knowledge was established, a library and fire department organized, and a program of city beautification with trees and fountains was planned. And in 1785 an English traveler found a "very elegant" inn where diners could dance "cotillions, jigs and Scotch reels till one o' clock in the morning" in stolid Sherman's old Puritan town.[59]

CHAPTER X

Who Should Rule at Home?

PSYCHOLOGICAL factors such as a reluctance to face change, suspicion of authority, fear of losing status, and other historically unprovable attitudes no doubt underlay the factional division of Connecticut's freemen in 1787 as in the forties, the mid-sixties and in 1776. Historians not prone to psychological speculation so long after the events can, however, identify more openly manifested tendencies driving men to one position or another. Somewhere—perhaps a stratum between the psychological subsurface and the identifiable political issues—economic factors condition the thoughts and actions of men. A discussion of Connecticut's economy during the Confederation therefore is useful to an understanding of her political history.

Confederation Commerce

Colonial military conflict had always heated up the Connecticut economy, and in particular the French War and the Revolution hastened the change from the largely barter business Sherman had conducted in the old days back in New Milford to a predominantly money system. Hartford was known as the "Grand Focus" of Continental bills of credit in New England, largely because of the activities of Jeremiah Wadsworth as Commissary General through most of the war. Connecticut people held well over four million dollars in Continental bonds worth about 1.3 million specie dollars, exceeded only by Massachusetts and Pennsylvania. In addition, state certificates of nearly four million dollars were still held by individuals, as were large amounts of Pierce's final settlement certificates given to Continental soldiers and suppliers in 1782–83. Of course, much of this paper did not circulate in trade, and much that did was badly depreciated by 1786.[1]

Despite the shortage of specie and a really reliable paper currency, trade boomed throughout the period. Privateering during the war had been Connecticut's most important mercantile activity, with about 400 prizes, totaling over 21,000 tons, brought to Connecticut ports, mostly New London and Norwich. After 1781 New Haven, which had suffered such a disastrous collapse of trade after 1776, enjoyed a vigorous revival. In 1784 a hundred ships were built in Connecticut, and in each of the next three years New Haven alone sent twenty-five new bottoms into Long Island Sound bound for the West Indian and New York trade. And by 1787 the state's shipping had regained its 1774 level of between 15,000 and 20,000 tons.* At its peak Connecticut's shippers had over three hundred vessels sailing the Sound and the Caribbean. But European restriction of the West Indian trade hampered business after 1785, and a sharp decline set in, reducing the fleet by one-third in 1790. In particular 1786 saw foreign nations tightening their controls, and merchants began to decry the decline in trade to the Indies.[2]

A New Haven citizen wrote a friend in England that unless trade between the two nations were opened, British merchants would not be paid. Easy credit from the former oppressor was at the bottom of the trouble, he thought. "Oeconomy and industry, like honor and virtue and religion have fled from among us, and our traders, by the unbounded credit of the English merchants, are enabled to credit almost any person, while all ranks of people seem fond of parting with all they have to purchase foreign fripparies." Joseph Hopkins of Waterbury brought a bill into the lower house that would have required all state civil officers to be dressed only in clothes of domestic manufacture. And in New Haven the ladies formed an "Oeconomical Association" promising not to buy ribbons, lace, feathers, and other luxuries, except for weddings and funerals. To another correspondent, the scarcity of cash "proves nothing more than that the balance of trade is against us, and that we eat, drink and wear more foreign commodities than we can pay for in produce—that is, we spend more than we earn, or in other words, *we are poor.*"[3]

---

*Saladino reports the 1774 figure at about 10,000 tons for the colony, but New Haven and New London claimed more than that (7170 and 3247 tons respectively), so obviously his figure is too low. See reports of David Wooster and Jeremiah Miller in CSL, "Trumbull Papers," IV:2ab, 8ab. There were 108 vessels employing 756 seamen at New Haven; 72 West Indian traders, and 20 coasters with 496 sailors at New London. For dutied goods alone, New London had a clear lead. Sutherland, *Population Distribution*, pp. 276-93. This would indicate that New Haven's shipping was largely coastal—with Boston, Newport and New York.

The nature of the West Indian trade caused distress not only for merchants, however. By 1785 Connecticut was the largest exporter of livestock to the Indies, and the shift from a formerly grain-dominated agriculture had painful implications for farm labor. Some people would have to look for livelihoods elsewhere. Nevertheless, Caribbean commerce was essential as a source of specie with which to carry on even more important interstate trade.[4]

New York dominated Connecticut's interstate commerce, and commissions and imposts raised prices and hampered business in the Yankee state. Estimates as to the amount of Connecticut specie left in New York ranged up to $100,000 a year, but the most accurate is probably about half that. New York City's merchants knew that the dependence was reciprocal, for their eastern neighbor took about one-third of all their imports.[5] Efforts to encourage deep-sea sailing out of New Haven and New London were furthered by the legislature, which made these two ports "free cities" in 1784.[*] The Assembly also granted tax relief to any Connecticut ships trading to Europe, Asia, or Africa. Merchants—providing they had not been Tories—who would move to New Haven and New London and bring either three thousand pounds' worth of oceanic import business or two thousand pounds in cash could take profits tax free for seven years. But these incentives availed naught. And when New York fought to continue its advantage by refusing to allow Congress an impost, both farmers and merchants in Connecticut would join in railing against the "unchristian Jews" to the south of Byram River.[6]

Connecticut's Council had evinced great foresight in 1780 by calling for a quasi-free trade area of all the states by "opening a Free Trade and transportation by land from one state to another." But the suspicious yeomen of the lower house blocked so daring an action at that time. Most Connecticut merchants continued nationalist and favored granting Congress exclusive authority to levy imposts. But the agrarian-dominated legislature was opposed to such a grant, their leader James Wadsworth holding that "it would lay the foundation for the ruin of the Liberties of the U. States."[**][7]

---

[*]This term does not imply duty free status to importers. It meant, rather, that the ports were open to all traders whether they were Connecticut residents or not. *SR*, V:325-26.

[**]The division between Connecticut's mercantile element and those oriented more toward property in land is pointed up by a vote in Congress on February 19, 1783. On an amendment to the impost bill to limit the authorization to twenty-five years, Eliphalet Dyer, the land promoter, voted for the limitation, while Oliver Wolcott, principally mercantile, voted against. Hutchinson, *Madison Papers*, VI:261.

Fairfield County, next to New York bore the brunt of that state's import duties, and naturally deputies from the towns of that county favored an exclusive grant to the national government. In 1784 Fairfield County deputies voted fourteen to one in favor of the Congressional request, while the rest of the members of the lower house went three to one against. The commercially-minded governor and Council, of course, supported the national impost.* The farmers would compromise by passing a grant limited to three years, and then only for the purpose of paying the existing debt. Fear that U. S. revenue would be used to distribute pensions among former Continental officers also caused Connecticut's suspicious yeomen to block compliance for an unconditional grant to Congress for the 5 percent levy. Connecticut, wrote a member of Congress, "is at present in too great a pet with the Commutation to comply [with the impost], but possibly may in time agree to it." William S. Johnson at Congress asked a Connecticut friend to send him "the sentiments of you Politicians in Connec't . . . whether to invest Congress with the Power of regulating their Trade as well with foreign Nations *as with each other.* . . . to prevent Dissentions between State and State which might endanger the Union. The latter might probably overturn the System Connt has adopt'd relat[iv]e to N Y which it is said she will counteract by regulat[ion]s of her Assembly. . . ."[8]

Meanwhile the General Assembly took steps to stimulate local enterprise and to share in the import profits of neighboring deep-water ports by levying duties on their goods.[9] Finally Connecticut granted Congress its 5 percent levy, but only to be effective when twelve states had complied, an effort to force Rhode Island into a universal scheme. A delegate from that state wrote his Governor, "I think we ought not to be scared into it, by the inefficacious acts of Connecticut," but the Massachusetts General Court sent a circular letter to Governor Griswold protesting the excise and impost laws and urging "the propriety of their making such alterations and amendments as shall render them, not only conformable to the Spirit of the Confederation, but consistent with those principles of reciprocity which in a national view ought to be adopted." Nathaniel Gorham of Massachusetts reported that only the Congress, weak as it was, prevented bloodshed over the differences between New York and her two irate neighbors.[10]

---

*My analysis would support Main's statement that "Agricultural Connecticut was primarily responsible for rejecting the impost." Main, *Antifederalists*, pp. 90-91. It was not, however, an exclusively agrarian-commercial division. Anti-aristocratic and provincial, the farmers objected to the uses to which the money might be put—payment of officers' pensions—and the fiscal independence that the impost would give the national government.

Connecticut made up for its mercantile dependence on other places by moving toward an industrial economy. By the late eighties foreign observers were coupling it with Pennsylvania as one of the principal manufacturing areas in the United States, and Alexander Hamilton thought that industry rather than agriculture or commerce would soon "distinguish" the province. Simeon Baldwin, Sherman's son-in-law, with brilliant—if commercially biased—insight, analyzed the Connecticut situation as one of equipoise. Though far from flourishing, the state seemed

> to have arrived to the turning point, between a commerce in wh the balance has long been against us, & the introduction of manufactures among ourselves whh will supercede the Necessity of such a commerce—The fact is we have too many inhabitants for the extent of territory—considering . . . our mode of cultivation & the employments of the people—All have not farms nor can they obtain them—of course untill manufactures are introduced, the people must be idle, or crowed into those professions which do not immediately depend on the soil—The people thus employed, consume the produce of the farmer—till nothing is left for a remittance for those articles which our stage of Society has to a Degree rendered necessary.

In 1785 New Haven enterprisers even asked the General Assembly to levy a tariff against foreign imports, claiming that manufacturing would increase the general wealth and create thousands of jobs, especially for women and children. With legislative encouragement, a private mint was established in New Haven, which turned out over £39,000 worth of copper pennies between 1785 and 1787.*[11]

Despite the pennies, the lack of a sound, sufficient circulating currency was a real problem, made more troublesome by the heavy taxes laid on Connecticut people during the period. Private debtors were being pressed. Peter Colt wrote that "a gentleman can hardly go out of his door but what he hath a Catch-Pole at his heels watching for an opportunity to grab him. . . ." The Assembly ceased taxing hard and high, and also made provision for various kinds of relief. Soldiers' notes, largely in the hands of the small farmers, were accepted in payment of taxes. In 1784 the levy for paying the state civil officers was cut in half, and other acts removed cattle under two years and all swine from the tax lists and permitted only six instead of seven years for merchants to sue for book debts—a change Sherman had fought in his code revision of the previous year.[12] An act of 1786 permitted farmers to

---

*Sherman was appointed one of the five inspectors for these coins which, though not legal tender, continued to circulate until at least 1860.

deduct a percentage of their sheep from the tax lists, and well over a quarter million woolies went tax free. Other acts declared that Continental loan office notes, script given to Continental soldiers, and all notes given by the state treasurer "shall be received promiscuously" for payment of taxes, duties, and excises. An attempt in the House to exempt land from being taken for taxes was beaten back 124 to 22, but selectmen and tax collectors were permitted to grant modest abatements in cases of destitution.[13]

Taxes Turned Around

Tax policy, as a matter of fact, provides a good indicator of the relative strength of agrarian and mercantile influence. As early as August 1777, when an act introduced levies against incomes of professional persons, efforts were made to shift away from an almost total reliance on poll and land taxes. In January 1779 men between sixteen and twenty-one were listed as liable to only half the regular poll tax; and buildings, with the significant exception of barns, were to be taxed as well. In addition, income resulting from interest on loans was assessed. The greatest revision was passed in May 1779, when efforts were made to equalize the burdens. The size and construction of buildings were to be considered in evaluation, and deductions could be made for those "decayed by age"; the quality and profitability of land were taken into account; watches, clocks, household silver, and carriages were assessed, as well as money in possession; and engrossers were taxed punitively. This revision, however, reversed some of the modest gains made by the agrarians in 1777. Luxury and carriage rates were reduced, as were levies on profits of various kinds. Erastus Wolcott, an agrarian spokesman, considered the principal beneficiaries the professionals and tradesmen.[14]

Agitation continued, and the period 1783–1786 in general saw agricultural interests dominant in the House, so the worst financial pressures were alleviated legislatively knocking the wind out of any Shaysite storms that might begin to brew. In May 1783, Sherman, Richard Law, and five deputies had been made a committee to review the state's entire fiscal position: what was still owed to the U. S.; how much was due in back taxes; what taxes had been levied; how much did the state owe in notes and interest; and finally to recommend how to raise some money and resolve the situation. The outcome of all this concern was an act the following May declaring that since so many of the wartime taxes were still unpaid and that "it would be extremely burdensome to the People if not Impracticable to pay at this Time new Taxes to any considerable amount, . . ." the treasurer was directed to suspend collection of most taxes entirely.[15] New levies were generally low—far lower than the wartime rates. Indeed, Alexander Hamilton in June 1787 remarked to Sherman that he thought that the Connecticut government of late "had entirely given way to the people, and had in fact suspended many of its ordinary functions in order to prevent those turbulent scenes which had appeared elsewhere." Hamilton even challenged Sherman to say whether Connecticut "dare impose & collect a tax on ye people."* And William Grayson of Virginia wrote in April 1787 that Connecticut would have erupted like Massachusetts had she laid taxes to fill the Congressional requisition.[16] But Connecticut agrarians still felt aggrieved. Their position on tax policy was laid out by Erastus Wolcott in a set of letters to the *Courant* in February 1787.[17] The poll tax, which represented half of all taxes collected, was unfair, wrote Wolcott, because it lay equally on rich and poor. So were taxes on land by quantity instead of use and quality. A tax on grasslands was a double tax because farmers paid once on the pasture and once again on the animals. To lay the burden more equitably, houses should be taxed by number of fireplaces, and luxuries such as silverplate should be taxed.

No merchants and not all farmers advocated paper money as a solution to economic distress. Instead, spokesmen of both types might rant against Rhode Island, whose paper was nothing more than "contemptible trash."

Hail Realm of Rogues, renown'd for fraud and guile
All hail, ye knav'ries of yon little Isle[18]

wrote a Hartford wit. Some, however, caught the fever from Rhode Island. And William S. Johnson admitted that Connecticut had a pretty strong party partial to paper, only controlled by the misery of other states that had given in to the "iniquitous System." "A Citizen of Connecticut," writing to the *Courant* in April 1786, called for a £100,000 emission of state paper. Land, he claimed, was not fairly appraised and was being taken for a quarter of its value. Something must be done, he wailed, or thousands of farmers will leave "and bid farewell to a country which holds out nothing but poverty and prisons."** A New Haven merchant reported that there was not $40,000 in all of Connecticut and that the 541 houses advertised to be sold for taxes in November 1785 went untaken for lack of cash. A petition was circulated calling upon the Governor to convene a special session of the Assembly in the

---

*Either Hamilton did not know that town and state taxes were continually levied in Connecticut, or—more likely—the implied meaning of his remark was that the General Assembly dared levy no taxes for the purpose of paying the U. S. quota.

**A later correspondent disputed the one-quarter land valuation figure. *Connecticut Courant*, March 26, 1787.

spring of 1786 to discuss the emission. "Plenty of money is a powerful means
to make everything else plenty," wrote a MODERN WHIG. Money, he said,
"is a powerful friend to all good business, and every thing that is generous,
commendable and wholesom in the state. . . ."[19] Town meetings in Sharon,
Killingly, Lebanon, and Windsor called for emissions in the fall of 1786, and
bills for printing paper were brought in both the 1786 and 1787 sessions of
the legislature. LYCURGUS, battling the effort in the *Middlesex Gazette* and
other papers, pointed out that

> The whole force of emitting paper money and public securities is but an
> imitation of the child's play of Robins alive—The legislature light the
> straw, which everyone knows must be quickly consumed. The subjects
> pass it round in quick circulation, and only guard against it dying in their
> hands, and the unfortunate man in whose hands it perishes, submits to be
> saddled with the loss, as the natural consequence of playing at the
> game.[20]

A paper money bill was to have been introduced in May 1787, and it was
passed around among the deputies during the early days of the session. But
just as it was about to be entered, a bill making Connecticut money legal
tender for Rhode Island debts was laid before the House. Sharon's Jonas
Gillet objected when asked to bring his paper money bill out at the same
time, because, he said, "both read at once would give so great a shock that
the house would not be able to bear it." So the tender bill was voted on and
defeated 122 to 20, and Gillet was scared off.* "The disdain of honest men
struck the spirit of paper money with terror and dismay," gloated the
Courant's correspondent, who suggested the Litchfield jail as a good place for
such Shaysite fellow-travelers. The Reverend Elizur Goodrich's opening
sermon and prayers against the "vileness & impolicy of a paper medium"
were answered.[21]

Nationalists and Provincials

The ambiguous economic situation—rising levels of living in the face of
specie shortages, the public debt comprised of insecurities rather than
securities and everyone a debtor, including the creditors—provides some
insight into the factions of Confederation politics in Connecticut. But clues
can be found elsewhere, and the psychological differences between city

---

*The *Connecticut Courant* and the *Connecticut Journal* reported the vote as 124 to 22
(June 11, 1787). The twenty-two names listed in the *Connecticut Journal*, June 13,
1787, represent the hard-core agrarian faction.

slicker and country cousin might shed greater light. Granting the impossibility
of such analysis two hundred years in retrospect, it is possible to generalize
on a more superficial level about Connecticut politics during the Confederation.

Lines were drawn between conservative and dynamic, farmer and
merchant, town dweller and rural rustic. In general the mercantile class
favored movement toward a better articulated local and state government,
with increasing authority passing to the national government. It desired also
economic policies which would add the expansion of commerce, in particular
private corporations. The provincially minded picked up support in opposition to two closely related issues: the payment from a national revenue of
pensions to officers of the Continental army, but not to state militia officers;
and the payment of the national debt in precedence to the state debts.

The first question arose in January 1778, when at Washington's insistence
a report was presented in Congress calling for a half-pay pension for life for
Continental officers. The men just wouldn't stay on the job, the General
claimed. "Without it," he wrote, "your Officers will moulder to nothing, or
be composed of low and illiterate men void of capacity for this, or any other
business." Congress divided into two camps: those who thought that such a
provision would produce a military establishment, or at least an aristocracy of
pensioners, and those who agreed with Washington that "the salvation of the
cause depends upon it."[22] Connecticut's aristocracy, a pale shadow relative
to that which prevailed in the states south of New England, voted republican;
the measure lost, and a compromise of half-pay for seven years was passed,
though Oliver Wolcott cast one of the two individual dissenting votes.* This
act threw a bone to noncommissioned officers and men who, if they served
till the war's end, would receive a bonus of eighty dollars.[23] Sherman and
Huntington were embarrassed and wrote their Governor, "It is almost
impossible to give a clear and full representation of the difficulties attending
this debate, on both sides of the question, to any gentleman who was not
present. . . . If the inclosed Resolve is not the best measure the nature and
circumstances of the case would admit, it is certainly the best that could be
obtained." But a few days later they moved unsuccessfully to forbid both
standing armies and pensioners, except for the wounded.[24]

---

*It should be recalled that the Connecticut General Assembly in 1778 had wished to
amend the draft of the Articles to provide "that no land army shall be kept up by the
United States in time of peace, nor any officers or pensioners kept in pay by them who
are not in actual service, exept such as are or may be rendered unable to support
themselves by wounds received in battle. . . ." *SR*, II: 532-33.

The Connecticut Assembly received the news of the pensions with disgust. Town meetings passed antagonistic resolutions, Lebanon's declaring "such an establishment is contrary to the Genius of this State, is unconstitutional, injurious, impolitic, oppressive and unjust." To the degree that it could, the state obstructed the pension plan. In 1782, when it granted Congress authority to levy a 5 percent impost, it explicitly provided "that no part of said Monies to be used and applied for the Payment of any Pensions or half Pay to discharged Officers, or to any Person or Persons whatsoever . . . not then in the Actual Service of the United States," a provision the Council had tried to modify when it sent Sherman on one of his rare failures to the House to dicker.[25] Dyer reported from Congress that the restriction "was particularly pleasing to some." Other Congressmen, pointing out that Connecticut was rapidly retiring and replacing officers in its Continental Line so that there was "nothing to prevent the State from putting every man in it on the half pay establishment . . . ," rejected Connecticut's 1782 list of new appointments.[26]

Nevertheless, the question continued to exacerbate Connecticut politics and became especially troublesome when prospects of peace appeared. The Continental officers grew more and more restive and dangerously insistent on postwar pensions. Congress took up the matter again, but Jesse Root insisted that Connecticut "people would not brook the paying of annual pensions, that they could not bear to see men strutting about their streets in the part of masters who had a right to demand of the people a part of their annual labour and toil to support them in idleness. That they chose to pay their officers at once after the war and then see them descend into the class of citizens." But the Connecticut delegates were pressured into assenting to the proposal to commute the pension to a lump sum equal to five years' pay, though Dyer put up a good fight first. Dyer, indeed, cast a vote which deadlocked the Congress. "On the question for paying the army," wrote James Madison,

> we had eight States; it required nine. It turned on the vote of Connecticut. These representatives were Dyer, a man of gentlemanly manners, who had seen the world (he had been to England) but not of very sound principle. Wolcott, an honest man. Wolcott determined he would brave the storm that awaited him at home. Dyer hung back. He was of course very much pressed. At length, he consented, on condition that it should be referred to a committee, and that he should be allowed to write a preamble. In this he was indulged.

The measure was then voted on again. Dyer's preamble provoked a good many criticisms and the Connecticut delegate "was kept for an hour as pale as a sheet" for fear that it would be defeated.[27]

As passed, the ordinance provided that "officers who shall continue in the service to the end of the war" would "be entitled to half pay during life," a direct violation of General Assembly actions of 1778 and 1782. Apprehensively Dyer wrote home, "How it will be received I know not, but hope for the best." Again the towns rose up in protest; eleven passed resolutions against the plan, and Killingworth's citizens attacked its constitutionality as the power of granting pensions "was not expressly delegated to Congress, or even by implication, the States are not holden to pay." Dyer, was not returned to the seat he had held on the Council since 1762. He did manage to get his town of Windham to send him to the May session, however, and the lower house took advantage of his connections and experience by electing him speaker.[28]

But by this time the nationalist faction had begun to articulate its point of view. Patriotism, sanctity of contracts, obedience to constituted authority, and the necessity of establishing trust and faith in the Confederation government at home and abroad all required that the promised commuted pensions be fulfilled. The debt must be paid "to maintain a good character as to justice and integrity. Righteousness exalteth a nation." The Assembly that refused to grant Congressional requisitions in 1786 and 1787 was nothing more than a "Massy body." It was not the requisitions that provincials objected to, however; it was the use to which they were to be put. In general anti-nationalists favored requisitions as a better check on the central government than giving it an independent revenue.[29] In January 1783 one group of Continental officers had sent Major William Judd of Farmington to Congress to collect, which he did. On his return a band of his townsmen attempted to intercept him and confiscate the securities, but he managed to dodge them. The next day a town meeting was held at which he was denounced, and at which a committee of correspondence was set up for the purpose of organizing a statewide convention at Middletown to investigate methods of protesting or preventing the Congressional action.[30]

But the Middletown Convention was an expression of much more than opposition to the pension question only. It grew out of frustration brought on by years of heavy taxation, envy of special privilege, fear of Congressional encroachment on state prerogative, and resentment toward returning Tories and those who tolerated them. Of course, the pro-commutation people— whose leaders were also the leaders of the Connecticut Cincinnati—in turn, accused the Conventioners of being pro-Tory. Had not their leader William Worthington of Saybrook promised "to open the back door to let old George in to ravish" the state, wrote a nationalist wit. As town after town sent delegates to the Convention, the *Courant* at first explained that "the body politic is often liable to paroxisms of madness and is as subject to be seized by them at town meetings as an e[pi]leptic at the change of the moon," but later became more concerned and turned sarcastic. "I perceive we have secured to ourselves the liberties we desired and ought to have persued—a liberty of doing what we please, and of obeying any law we approve and opposing any law we dislike." [31]

The first convention drew representatives from an insufficient number of communities, but a second got responses from forty-two of Connecticut's seventy-seven towns. "The Devil has been dancing," wrote Colonel John Chester, "Commutation is the jig—and the whole country almost seem to be joining in it." The Conventioners were not without wit, however, and one wrote ironically that of course it would be convenient for those now in office to stay there.

> They surely are able to tell what is best
> And carve out the rules and the laws for the rest:
> Its a folly for the farmer that pays all the rates,
> To meddle with the police or the expence of the states.
>
> . . . .
>
> 'Tis strange that till now we could ne'er see the mistery,
> That is held up to view in the records of history,
> That most men were made to be slaves to the rest
> Most distinguish'd in titles the society is best
>
> . . . .
>
> Forbear noble statesmen give up your estates,
> And establish Cincinnati by paying your rates;
>
> . . . .
>
> But rejoice in this, that your children are free,
> And may work all their days to support a grandee,
> With pride exult, in his elevated station,
> That he may be menial to a plunderer of his nation

These conventions were patronized largely by the rural towns in the north and western parts of the state. About a third of the membership had been deputies in recent Assemblies, and many, of course, were state militia officers. A resolution was adopted calling for an investigation into the constitutionality of Congressional pensions; asking the Assembly to oppose all encroachments on the sovereignty of the states under authorities not expressly voted in Congress; and demanding that delegates to Congress reject the appointment of expensive ambassadors to foreign nations. Later on they also attacked the Society of Cincinnati as secretly promoting the pension plan.[32]

The nationalists were not unaware of the democratic implications of the movement. Some even feared that constitutional alterations were the ultimate objective. The *Middlesex Gazette* reported that the farmers were saying "openly that if they can get rid of the upper house of Assembly, they can do as they please. First however they are attempting to change the members. . . ." The Conventioners, entering directly into politics in a way then considered in poor taste, drew up a slate of nominees for the Council, an action reminiscent of the old Stamp Act days. The nationalists controlled the press throughout the state, so the nomination lists had to be printed in New York. Though the *Courant* blustered that "the glaring impropriety of such measure must occur to every person," ten new men were nominated for the Council. No Middletown list survives, but the new nominees, though old political figures from the lower house and Council of Safety, were mostly militia officers and all anti-pension men.[33]

Some immediate success was realized when the new legislature met and the lower house passed a report asking for a remonstrance to Congress. But the Council, unchanged by the elections, refused to endorse it. The House then ordered that a circular letter of protest be sent to all the other state legislatures. This letter would criticize not only commutation but also the multiplicity of Congressional officers and their high salaries. Under this threat of exposing dirty Connecticut linen, Governor Trumbull transmitted the remonstrance without his signature.[34]

At this point two other local events occurred that aided the Connecticut provincials in their efforts. Governor Trumbull, upon whom much of the opposition to national and centralizing policies had centered, resigned. He was seventy-three and had spent fifty-one years in public office, but that he left under pressure is beyond doubt. The farmers were distrustful of the mercantile class generally, and sighted on the long-insolvent Trumbull as the most visible mark to shoot at. Rumors were rampant that he profited by trade with the enemy, that he protected Loyalists in whose business he had an interest and accepted bribes to influence court decisions on their behalf. The rumors, though dashed by official investigations demanded by Trumbull himself, were so damaging that the doughty governor failed to claim his usual majority of freemen's votes in 1780, 1781, and 1783, though placed in office by the Assembly when no other candidate received a majority either. Finally, the old warrior was wearied enough to call it quits and in October 1783 declared his decision to withdraw from public service the following May.[35]

At the same time the Congressional terms of Oliver Ellsworth, Samuel Huntington, Richard Law, and Oliver Wolcott ran their statutory limit, and they had to be replaced. The successor delegation consisted of three Convention sympathizers, James Wadsworth, William Hillhouse, and William Williams; and Roger Sherman, who was insisted upon against the desires of the lower house, where their secretary C. C. Chandler was preferred.[36] For Sherman, election came as a surprise, as he thought himself well out of national duty.

Connecticut was not the only state where half-pay upset provincial politics. Throughout republican New England the issue raged. In Massachusetts, in the summer of 1783, the pro-commutation Congressmen were thrown out of office and a new delegation composed entirely of antis was sent to Philadelphia with a memorial that James Madison reported as "pregnant with the most penurious ideas ... which concern the national honor and dignity." The Rhode Island legislature did not even consider the measure, and her delegates saw the Bay State memorial as "plain a language as they formerly spoke to Great Britain. . . . They remind Congress that they inherit republican principles from their ancestors, and that it is necessary to attend to the voice and abilities of the people." James Madison commented that the half-pay opposition in New England had increased to such a degree by the fall of 1783 "as to produce almost a general anarchy. . . . those who are interested in the event look forward with very poignant apprehensions."[37]

Sherman and Wadsworth, each representing a Connecticut faction, arrived at Congress on January 13, 1784 and took their seats the next day, on which they joined the other delegates in signing the treaty of peace with Great Britain.* Immediately Sherman was assigned to a number of committees, most of them having to do with finances. One of these committee assignments put him in a position where he could no longer dodge the question of commutation of lifetime pensions to a lump sum half-pay for five years. Though the Assistants had never accepted the remonstrance against half pay, the lower house had submitted it to the Governor, demanding that he forward it to Congress, which he finally did on November 1, 1783. When Sherman arrived at Annapolis to take his seat, he found the petition tied up

---

*It was not until May 1787 that Connecticut acted to repeal all acts contrary to the Treaty of Paris of 1783.

in committee. Significantly, Sherman rather than Wadsworth was placed upon a new committee to review the work of the old one.[38]

When the committee reported in March, Sherman wrote to Trumbull at length on both the constitutionality and expediency of the measure.[39] He took at this time an unequivocal "implied powers" position.

> The question is not whether Congress are vested by the Confederation with a power to grant half pay for life. This need not be enquired into. It is whether by the 12th article* of the Confederation they can do otherwise than to acknowledge that a debt was created by the resolution of the 21st of October 1780 which resolution was agreed to by persons having plenipotentiary powers from their respective States, to do whatever appeared to them necessary and expedient for opposing the then enemy effectually.

Not only was Sherman pointing out that the United States under the Articles was obligated by contracts entered into by the old Continental Congress, but more significantly that if debts are contracted, Congress may use whatever powers are necessary to liquidate them. As to the expediency of the measure, Sherman became his more usual politic self, writing, "we have great reason to distrust our own competency to judge in this matter, none of the delegates present having been in Congress at that particular time." But, he added slyly, "a proper degree of respect to the States obliges us to suppose that they appointed persons most worthy of the trust and confidence placed in them." He closed by suggesting that a candid examination of the question by Connecticut's House of Representatives would bring it to support the Union "in this as in all other federal matters." And he wrote William Williams, who as secretary had signed the remonstrance, that "I don't find any members [of Congress] that think that the commutation can be rescinded, or avoided without a violation of public faith, a majority approve of the measure."[40]

Back in Connecticut the provincials had not been idle. After Sherman's removal from the local scene, the lower house pushed through a new measure opening up more opportunities to break the grip of the establishment. Picking up one of Sherman's previously rejected provisions in the new law code, the Assembly made the Governor and Council a Supreme Court of Errors for the state, a centralizing measure, as up to this time the whole Assembly had been the court of last resort. But in doing so the act provided that no person could

---

*Article XII holds that "All bills of credit emitted, monies borrowed and debts contracted by . . . Congress before the assembling of the United States, in pursuance of the present confederation, shall be deemed and considered as a charge against the United States, for payment and satisfaction whereof the said United States and the public faith are hereby solemnly pledged."

be a Judge of the Superior Court and hold any other high state or national office. This meant that Sherman, Oliver Ellsworth, William Pitkin, and Richard Law had to decide where to serve, and all of them chose to remain on the Court rather than the Council.*

The Middletown Conventioners met once again in March 1784, but their cause was dragging. Nevertheless, they put up a bold front and posted their list of nominees for the April elections. Of course they took Trumbull at his word as having resigned and endorsed Matthew Griswold and Samuel Huntington for the top spots, and most of the other previously nominated men as well. Omitted, however, were the two Olivers, Ellsworth and Wolcott, Benjamin Huntington, and Roger Sherman. Though Trumbull's resignation and the hopelessness of the provincial cause in Congress took most of the wind out of the sails of the anti-establishment group, the breezes were not all blowing the other way. Griswold, who as Lieutenant Governor should have sailed into office, did not even appear among the top twenty on the nomination list, nor did Assistants Dyer, Davenport, and Adams. Five new men arrived on the list, three of them from the east, and two of these were chosen delegates to Congress.** But since none received a majority vote, the Assembly was able to install Griswold as Governor. Samuel Huntington, a former president of the Congress, was elected by the freemen as Lieutenant Governor, receiving 2752 votes with 2708 divided among other candidates.*** But the party got up by what Noah Webster called "that Nest of Vipers" took

---

*The act provided that the judges serve at the pleasure of the Assembly, which Sherman and the others probably interpreted to mean unless impeached, as was the case with his mayoralty. But the lower house insisted on appointing each spring "for the year ensuing" only. Three years later the Council was still trying to repeal this separation of office, but the House was adamant. "House Journal 1787–88," p. 13. The law was passed in May 1784. The judges affected at that time were Samuel Huntington, Richard Law, William Pitkin, and Sherman. Huntington was made chief justice of the new Supreme Court of Errors and Oliver Ellsworth was appointed to the Superior Court on which Law became chief in place of Huntington. This occurred in May 1785, the same session at which the judges resigned—including Ellsworth, whose appointment and resignation are reported on the same page of the records. Treadwell, Sturges, and Wolcott were appointed first, and Wadsworth later to replace Ellsworth. *SR*, V:323–24, VI:5.

**The five new men ranking 16-20 were John Treadwell of Farmington, Increase Mosely of Woodbury, Dyer Troop of East Haddam, Samuel Mott of Preston, and Charles Church Chandler of Woodstock. Chandler and Treadwell were elected to Congress, though neither attended and Chandler resigned in October. *SR*, V:313, 318, 444; Burnett, *Letters*, VIII:lxxxiii–iv.

***The title Deputy Governor was changed to Lieutenant Governor the year before. Huntington was President September 1779 to September 1780.

severe losses in the lower house. Except for Dyer, who had alienated his agrarian constituency by his vote for commutation but came in as deputy from Windham and was elected Speaker of the House, all of the old Assistants were re-elected. The *Courant* gleefully announced "departed this life in the eighth month of his age, Mr. HOBBY CONVENTION . . . with violent spasms and convulsions. . . ."[41]

In the May General Assembly the House chose Eratus Wolcott* and William Hillhouse, convention selections, to be Superior Court Judges, but the Council vetoed them. Despite this modest show of agrarian strength in the lower house, a grant of authority to Congress to levy an impost, soundly defeated the previous January 78 to 36, was finally voted through 93 to 42, with the Council concurring, of course. The farmers, clearly no longer dominant, had to content themselves merely by insisting that the revenue be used only for paying the wartime debts and "on no Account be diverted to any other Use," and to limiting the whole authorization to twenty-five years.[42] Thus the provincials won out in Connecticut on the question of half-pay pensions.

But if, as REPUBLICAN later claimed, "their real design was to take advantage of [the issues] to ride into office," they failed badly. The provincials had lost their most committed leaders in the April elections when Wadsworth failed of reappointment to the Council, and losses in the lower house brought self-congratulations from the nationals who were pleased with the outcome.[43] Provincial strength, then, was on the wane, shortly to fail almost totally at the crucial moment of national consolidation, but there were more cards to be played out and one more trick to be taken by the rustics.

The Western Reserve

The question of commutation involved expanding the powers of the Confederacy, establishing a quasi-aristocracy, favoring national over state debts and in general creating suspicions about the old establishment in Connecticut on the part of the agrarian and conservative-minded freemen.

---

*Erastus Wolcott (1722-1791) is an enigmatic figure. He was a son of the colonial governor Roger Wolcott, brother of the later governor Oliver Wolcott, highest of nationalists. Erastus apparently did not attend college and shared the sentiments of the provincial yeomanry. He was a lukewarm revolutionary whose moderation cost him influence thereafter. He was a holder of state notes. Zeichner, *Controversy*, p. 197; AAS, "Sherman Papers," Nathaniel Sherman to RS (March 14, 1789).

But there were other issues that split off the mercantile group from the major part of the populace, the provincials from the nationals. One of these was the disposition of the Western Reserve.

After giving up land claims in Pennsylvania, Connecticut hung on to a vast tract of land south of Lake Erie, in theory reserved to provide for payment of outstanding war debts, principally to her militiamen.[44] The Assembly appointed a western lands committee in May 1786 to see "what ought to be done respecting the Support of the claims thereto or Disposition thereof."[45] In October the committee reported out a plan that would offer the land in lots of not less than 5000 acres at fifty cents an acre, payable in either Continental or state paper, or specie. This arrangement, obviously, was of no benefit to the homesteading farmer in Connecticut, at that time very unlikely to possess money of any kind at all. Indeed, hundreds lost portions of their farms for taxes and thousands left Connecticut for other places where land was more plentiful. Despite a growing mercantile influence in the state as a whole, the agrarians still had numbers on their side, and had been aided in the lower house by the incorporation of seventeen new towns, all rural, during the previous two years. Thus they were able to reject the committee plan and propose instead that the territory be surveyed into townships six miles by six miles, sold in much smaller lots and paid for only in state money. But this, in turn, was blocked by the Assistants.[46]

The General Assembly confidentially considered the Western Reserve a *fait accompli*, but at Congress in New York William Samuel Johnson still found himself defending the holding against Virginia's William Grayson, the leading opponent of the deal. But the Pennsylvania delegates had been bought off already, as they wrote Benjamin Franklin, by Connecticut's removal of support for the Susquehannah settlers. The Virginians knew also that Connecticut was preparing to open a land office for the whole of its former claim all the way to the Mississippi. When the cession was accepted by Congress on May 26, Charles Pettit of Pennsylvania wrote Jeremiah Wadsworth that "It is understood that the State of Connecticut will on her part give no further Countenance to the Claims of the State or of her Companies within Penn[sa] but on the Contrary use Means to induce these Companies to relinquish their Pretensions to such Claims. That Penn[sa] will take the Actual Settlers on the late disputed Territory under protection as Citizens and treat them with Generosity as well as Justice as to their Private Rights. That the implied Right of Connecticut to the 120 Miles not ceded will not be questioned by Pennsa. . . ."[47]

Stephen Mix Mitchell wrote Johnson in September 1786 that "The Disposal of our Western World, will be a Subject of some Altercation at the next Session of Assembly; some are for selling it for continental, others for state securities. Your and my best friends are of the former Class, I confess myself rather of the latter, but not unalterably fixed: Your assistance with Mr. Sturgiss will be indispensibly necessary. . . ."[48] It was at this point that Judges Sherman, Pitkin, Ellsworth and Law were compelled to give up their seats on the Council and were replaced by John Treadwell, Jonathan Sturges, Erastus Wolcott and James Wadsworth,* the last two firm provincials. And Councilor William Williams, though son-in-law to former Governor Trumbull, came out for the agrarians with a series of newspaper pieces signed AGRICOLA.**[49] The result was a new compromise proposal that was enacted by the General Assembly in October 1786. The land was to be surveyed into six-by-six townships and sold for not less than three shillings in specie or state paper. This was a victory for the agrarians, but in fact, the land ultimately was sold to large speculators. The Act closed:

> That measures not inconsistent with the principles of the confederation of the United States shall from Time to Time be taken by order and under Authority of the General Assembly of this State for the preservation of the Peace and good Order of the settlers in said Towns, untill this State shall resign its Jurisdiction of the Same and Government be settled amongst them upon Republican Principles.[50]

---

*Wadsworth was temporarily removed in 1786, but when Oliver Wolcott was elected Lieutenant Governor, the Assembly put Wadsworth back on. "House Journal, 1785-1786." (May 12, 1786).

**Williams sent his pieces to Joseph Hopkins, another agrarian leader, to insert in the Hartford newspaper. Williams knew the Governor was of the opposite view and asked that his name be kept secret. Samuel Holden Parsons, a major land speculator, got hold of Williams' letter and forwarded it to the Governor with the note, "I wish in Turn that my Name may be as Safe as Mr. W. wishes his own to be kept." CHS, "Oliver Wolcott, Sr. Papers," IV:23,25, Williams to Hopkins (August 12, 1786) and SHP to OW, Sr. (September 11, 1786). For further illumination of the Williams-Parsons feud see *Connecticut Courant*, April 2, 1787.

CHAPTER XI

E Pluribus Unum?

IRREPRESSIBLE Benjamin Gale, writing in February 1787, was outraged by what he interpreted as a strong aristocratic trend in the formerly republican agrarian province. Attempts had been made in the General Assembly, he wrote heatedly of Sherman's law revisions, to give complete power to the Governor and Council; to grant the power to tax to the central government under the Articles; to permit Congress to have its own army; and in general to subordinate the state government to the general one. Congress, Gale said, had plenty of land to sell if it needed money, but it was trying to dignify itself with ambassadors and needless pomp. It should cut staff and salaries; "if they do not *Lower Sail* they will Certainly over set the *Ship*. . . ." Revolution had broken out in Massachusetts, and in Connecticut "People at Large are more ripe for a Revolt against Government; than I Conceive our Rulers are Generally Apprized of. . . ."[1]

These views, conveyed by Gale to Erastus Wolcott in a twenty-seven-page letter, were reinforced by that recently elevated Councilor. Wolcott looked to reform at home as the best way to assure "that a democratical government may exist" as it had for over a century and a half "unruffled through the most trying scenes." Though execrating the Shaysites, at that moment in flight from western Massachusetts, Wolcott urged tax reform at least. Expanding and increasing taxes on personal property could reduce the rates on land and shift some of the burden to mercantile and professional people. And indeed Wolcott had sponsored a bill to accept tax payments in state securities as early as 1784.[2]

As the new agrarian attack launched by Wolcott in January grew hotter and hotter, more and more rumors of an impending change in the Articles were fed into the political firebox. The newspapers printed long letters in a series from LYCURGUS, probably Josiah Meigs, who rode hard on the necessity for a reformed government in the state. In response to Wolcott's defense of Connecticut's good record in paying off its debts, nationalists pointed to the large amounts of money paid to New York as goods passed through that state on their way to the local consumer. And what about Pennsylvania's attempt to dispossess the Wyoming settlers; and the refusal of New Jersey to pay its Congressional levy; and New York's hostility to the impost desired by the general government? The union was in a bad state, correspondents had long pointed out, and now something must be done.[3]

Politics in Balance

Noah Webster reported later that the opposition which had developed over the commutation "measures of Congress gave rise to the democratic party in Connecticut. It proceeded from honest motives, an extreme jealousy of power in the hands of rulers, ..." It constituted, he said, "about one third or one fourth of the citizens."[4] The battle over altering the Articles of Confederation, wrote a correspondent to the *Courant*—probably the same Noah Webster—was merely a continuation of the old debate. Commutation and noncommutation were now federal and anti-federal men. The antis, he said, were indifferently educated and "think as they have been bred . . . on a small scale." Furthermore, "most of them live remote from the best opportunities of information, the knowledge they acquire is late, and is longer in producing conviction in their minds." If they got out and around and conversed "with men who understand foreign policy" they would become federalists.*[5] It was true, of course, that the antis came from small towns, with little strength in mercantile centers. One lampoon of the antis had a farmer praise the provincials as "poor mens politicianers" who "dont intend to pai the public debt: and a peny saived is as good as a peny arned,—so I tel my nabors these are the rite men for us and so we'd better to voat for um at nectx proxying."[6] Noah Webster, writing from Rhode Island under the pseudonym TOM THOUGHTFUL, represents the views of Connecticut's high nationalists in late 1786. In articles that later were to influence Alexander Hamilton's fiscal reforms, Webster came out against stay laws; "tendry" laws making new paper emissions legal tender for past debts;

---

*Webster's point was not a new insight. Puritans had always found it difficult to convert farmers because, as Richard Baxter pointed out a hundred years before, "Plowmen . . . are so wearied or continually employed, either in the Labours or the Cares of their Callings, that it is a great Impediment to their Salvation," whereas town dwellers and tradesmen were "allowed . . . time 'enough to read or talk . . . or edifie one another." Quoted in Simpson, *Puritanism*, pp. 116–117n13.

luxury; and weakness in the central government, which he said was "a devil." He was also against mobs and conventions, but subsequent action indicates that he opposed conventions only when dominated by provincials.* [7]

It was a see-saw battle. As Suffield's agrarian Abraham Granger put it, "This is a time of jealousy: all men are on Tiptoe, the waters are troubled and the people are just ready to jump in and be healed." In October 1786, the Assembly had refused, in a close 68-to-61 vote, to comply with Congressional requisitions of money, and the nationalists chose to bide their time till new support could be returned in the April elections.[8] Governor Huntington refused to call a special session to respond to the Annapolis invitation to a new constitutional convention. That invitation had been on tap at the October session, but the provincials desired a negative response, and the nationals thought time was on their own side, so action was put off until May. The Council had agreed unanimously with Governor Huntington that a special session of the Assembly was not necessary, but his Excellency suggested that the deputies get to the election of a delegation immediately on convening in May. In March 1787 David Humphreys, writing from New Haven, reported to Washington that he doubted the Assembly would send delegates. "And if they do," he added, "my apprehension is still greater that they will be sent on purpose to impede any salutary measures that might be proposed." Conversations with many people in New Haven, he said, gave little hope for a "successful issue of the meeting." Connecticut, in his exasperated view, was "under the influence of a few such miserable, narrow minded & I may say wicked Politicians."[9] The situation looked desperate to New Haven's contingent of U. S. bond holders, who were now watching their stock sell for two shillings on the pound. They called for a meeting in May of original holders of Continental securities in Hartford County and suggested that the other counties do the same. The gathering—which would have seemed much like a convention of nationalists—was not held, probably because the Philadelphia Convention encouraged enough optimism to delay further efforts at organization.[10]

Echoes of the Shaysite animosity toward courts reverberated through Connecticut. The papers were filled with anti-lawyer polemic throughout 1786, and in Windham County William Williams shut down the Court late that year. He was charged with saying at the time that the great scarcity of money and resultant foreclosures were the cause for tumults in Massachusetts, and attempts to hold courts there had resulted in a "scene of *blood* and

---

*See note on page 227 below.

carnage." Williams admitted closing the court, with the remark that money was scarce and that the people would no doubt pay their debts before the next session. But he insisted that the reason for not meeting was a violent snowstorm.[11] A minor Shaysite incident in Preston in Connecticut's southeast was exploited by the nationals, who linked the democrats not only to the Shaysites, but also to the Rhode Island paper-money people, widely reprobated by Connecticut's freemen. The debate this time illuminated one more facet of the complicated fiscal situation. Abraham Granger of Suffield on the Massachusetts line opposed granting money to the U. S. government to pay *bond* holders because he felt that such creditors should suffer depreciation to the same degree as did holders of Continental *paper money.* The outcome of the April elections gave neither side much comfort. All the provincials were returned to the Council, and a test vote in the House on the Governor's call for U. S. requisitions fell 79 to 70 against the United States.[12]

The May session opened with a sermon by Elizur Goodrich of Hartford, who pointed out the "Necessity of National faith to the Happiness of a State."* When debate opened, the opponents of revision, and therefore the opponents of sending a delegation, based their fight on the aristocratic tendencies that such changes might bring about. They were against giving up any more state power, especially in the area of taxation. These were the same men generally who had opposed increases in land taxes in the state and a reduction in the size of the General Assembly, and who had shouted against the aristocratic Society of Cincinnati.[13] Amos and Abraham Granger led the democrats, aided by Hosea Humphrey of Norfolk and Daniel Perkins of radical Enfield, who feared that the "State would send men that had been delicately bred, and who were in affluent circumstances, that could not feel for the people in the day of distress." And, he added, "if we send we will be under double obligation to adopt what the convention shall recommend." Abraham Granger feared "arbitrary power and the destruction of the poor, and says we shall become asses—This State may well be compared to the strong ass, crouching down not only under two, but twenty burthens, and will finally crush us out of existence." Granger liked the Articles. They were, he said, "sufficient for every purpose." Power enough was already delegated to Congress, and a strengthened constitution "would be disagreeable to his

---

*James Davenport, one of the more flamboyant House clerks, also noted that "in compliance with custom the usual address to the Governor &c. were made, which a Man of a tolerable degree of modesty would blush at if it were not sanctified by long habits. . . ." "House Journal 1787–1788," p. 1.

constituents," for it might tend to "produce a regal government in this country," thus endangering "the liberties of the people."[14]

From the topside of society, however, it was the poor themselves who were to blame for their difficulties, though they were learning the evils of borrowing. Stephen Mix Mitchell wrote from Wethersfield in the summer of 1786 that "The States have sufficient Ability to do great things, we are fast recovering from the fatigue of Warr, and like a young Man who by sleep recover'd as to run into every kind of Luxury and Extravagance and not so much by Credit as formerly. New Buildings are errecting in every part of the Country; and no striking Marks of penury appear."[15] Even nationalists such as William S. Johnson, delegate then at Congress, initially opposed a new convention—though for opposite reasons. He was afraid that changes might bring a weakening, rather than a strengthening of central government.*[16]

Perhaps most nationally inclined Connecticuters would have agreed with Sherman's friend over at Yale. President Stiles doubted the expediency of the convention because he didn't think "our wisest Men had yet attained Light eno' to see & discern the best, & what ought finally to prevail . . . Neither did I think the People were ripe for the Reception of the best one if it could be investigated. And yet . . . I did not doubt but Time & future Experience would teach, open & lead us to the best one." Jeremiah Wadsworth, writing to Rufus King from his seat in the House toward the end of the session, was "persuaded a good Government is wished for by the majority of our House of Assembly—but whether the people at large will be prepared to receive such an one as you & I wish, is uncertain: but I hope the Convention will be united in something that is not so totally unfit for our purposes, as the present system, for I consider that at an end."[17]

Nor did the old Middletowners fail to point out the ironical fact that the very men who were now urging a national convention were those most damning of state conventions three years earlier. Indeed, James Madison told Thomas Jefferson at the time of the Annapolis meeting that Connecticut refused to go "not from a dislike of the object, but to the idea of a Convention, which it seems has been rendered obnoxious by some internal

---

*There is no evidence in the Connecticut experience to support the view that the move to strengthen the Articles derived as much from the problems of the state governments as from the weakness of the Congress. No one in Connecticut, no matter how much they disparaged the deputies, would refer to the state system as "vile," as had Henry Knox of Massachusetts. Indeed, high nationalist Noah Webster believed that Connecticut's stability in the mid-eighties resulted from the fact that "the Legislature wear the complexion of the people." The view I am contesting here is stated in Gordon Wood's *Creation of the American Republic*, ps. 467, 474-75, where the Knox quotation is found also. Webster's statement is on p. 413 of the same work.

Conventions which embarrassed the Legislative authority." Now he reported again that though "Connecticut has a great aversion to Conventions, and is otherwise habitually disinclined to abridge her State prerogatives ... her concurence nevertheless is not despared of." In 1787 Stephen Mix Mitchell found his former objection to conventions so embarrassing that he would not attend Congress when the Constitution was under discussion because it had emanated from a convention—and one that he had explicitly opposed.* [18]

An Old Man Is Sent to Revitalize the Government

In the end a delegation was sent. Two elements seem to explain why this should be so when the provincials were still strong in the state. The first is the feeling among many that the Philadelphia Convention was no threat to state sovereignty. Indeed, there was even the possibility that new restrictions might be thrown around the central government—especially if the right people were chosen to represent the state. The second element was the increasing concern of the merchants and progressives in the cities. They needed foreign treaties to permit them to expand their West Indian trade, and to open British ports in the Caribbean.** They wanted the national debt—a good deal of which they held—paid, and paid in a sound circulating medium. But more than these enlarging aims caused them in the end, to agitate for the Philadelphia meeting. They had seen the strength of the agricultural majority develop sufficiently to push through tax reform that shifted burdens from farmers to large personal property holders. They had felt tremors in Connecticut of the Shaysite uprising so close to their own borders. They had witnessed reversal

---

*Roger Sherman had always frowned upon extralegal conventions, and took part only in those officially supported by the General Assembly or the Confederation Congress. See above, p. 52. But one's feelings about such gatherings seems to have depended largely on whose interests were being promoted. In 1784 Samuel Adams, of all people, wrote Noah Webster that "popular Committees and County Conventions are not only useless but dangerous." Against royal government they were excellent but "as we now have constitutional and regular Governments and all our Men in Authority depend upon the annual and free Ellections of the People, we are safe without them." Cushing, ed., *Writings of Samuel Adams*, IV:296, 305–306, quoted in Wood, *Creation*, p. 327. Connecticut, of course, had always had annual or semiannual elections, so in theory extralegal conventions had never served any good purpose.

**A figure for 1787 is not available, but in 1789 coastal and foreign imports divided at about 55 percent for the former and 45 percent for the latter. Syrett, *Hamilton Papers*, VI:415. Connecticut ranked third in amounts of U. S. loan office debt owned by her citizens. Only the very much more populous and commercial states of Massachusetts and Pennsylvania held more. Connecticut held $1,269,677 out of a total debt of $11,400,485--about 11.1%. Hutchinson, *Madison Papers*, VI:292, 297 n46.

after reversal in Sherman's attempts to strengthen their own central government at home. Certainly a stronger United States could be counted on for foreign commercial treaties and a sound currency. And maybe it would make possible the retention of aristocratic dominance at home so manifestly threatened since the end of the war.[19] No doubt a second Shaysite cabal—this time in Sharon near Shay's stomping grounds, and instigated, it was alleged, by his agents—also played a part.* Word of it reached the Assembly on May 16 and two legislators and a couple of sheriffs were dispatched to quell "the Massachusetts Rebels and other Subjects of this State in the northern Parts abeting them. . . ." And though the threat was thus "happily crushed in the Head," it probably scared a few more votes into pro-convention column, which had won its initial victory four days earlier.[20]

The democratic element sought to insure itself against too much centralization or aristocracy by naming their principal leader, Erastus Wolcott, as one of the three-man contingent and providing that at least two delegates must be present to commit the state. But cagey old Wolcott was not so easily involved, and resigned, and anyway the Council had insisted that any one of the delegates be authorized to represent Connecticut.** Wolcott's refusal to serve seems to have been a shrewd move. At the next elections for the Council he collected more votes than any candidate except Benjamin Huntington, and over twice as many as the ultra-nationalist Jeremiah Wadsworth.[21] Wolcott's resignation left only William Samuel Johnson, shortly to be named President of Columbia College, and Oliver Ellsworth, neither agrarians, though not known nationalists, in the delegation. Wolcott's place was a hard one to fill, for the men of property would not permit one of the "wild" democrats to go to Philadelphia, and the democrats on their part would never turn the entire delegation over to the "aristocrats." Finally the vacancy fell to Roger Sherman. Perhaps the most notable aspect of the

---

*Ironically, only the previous October the Sharon town meeting had resolved "that there be no *deputy sheriffs* in this state." The meeting also called for a paper money emission, a demand renewed in February 1787. Sedgwick, *Sharon*, p. 80.

**The lower house decided to send delegates "after a long discussion," and chose William S. Johnson, Oliver Ellsworth, and Erastus Wolcott in that order, or any two of them, on May 12, a Saturday. They reconsidered and, at the request of the Council, allowed only one delegate to represent the state on the 14th. Wolcott resigned the next day, and Sherman was chosen on the 15th, and the final authorization was passed on May 16, 1787. Authorization of funds for the expedition was not made until May 19, further delaying departure of the delegates. "House Journal 1786–1787," ps. 3, 5, 6, 16.
    The uncharacteristic provision that a single delegate be authorized to represent the state was shared only by Maryland. The other states required two or three delegates to act officially, and Pennsylvania insisted on four.

delegation, however, is its moderation. Not only were all three men of a temporizing pragmatism, but all were well disciplined in mind and temperament. No hotheads like Eliphalet Dyer or William Williams would represent Connecticut. The moderation was not only one of character, but also of politics. The high nationalists such as Jeremiah Wadsworth or Noah Webster were without representation, and so were the rockribbed provincials of the likes of James Wadsworth or the brace of Grangers from Suffield. The near equilibrium in state politics had occurred at just the right time for the destiny of the nation.

At that time no one knew what Johnson's views were. On the question of strengthening the national government he "proceeded with his usual moderation, experimented with unworkable palliatives, and tactfully avoided making his own views a matter of public record." And Ellsworth had played no part in efforts to strengthen the central government, nor had he even made public his views. His private opinions remained completely unknown.*[22]

As for Sherman, he too appeared enigmatic. He had kept out of the debate on the issue, presumably following his usual political tactic of waiting to see how the wind blew. In early June supernationalist Jeremiah Wadsworth wrote Rufus King that "our delegates had set out. I am satisfied with the appointment—except Sherman who, I am told, is disposed to patch up the old scheme of Government. This was not my opinion of him when we chose him. He is as cunning as the Devil, and if you attack him, you ought to know him well; he is not easily managed," said the Colonel in what might be the understatement of the century, "but if he suspects you are trying to take him in, you may as well catch an Eeel by the tail. . . ." Wadsworth reported the same views to Henry Knox, adding that if Sherman "is stubborn he will influence too many others."[23]

Retrospect, however, permits a sketch of Sherman's position at this time. His proposed code of 1784 introduced the concept of granting aspects of sovereignty to the central government, and permitting its officers to operate in the states. He also would require individuals in the states to obey all ordinances of Congress made under authority of the Articles and he would have made Congressional treaties with foreign nations binding upon the states and, by extension, upon individuals as well. However, he wished the central

---

*Later on, of course, Ellsworth became one of the highest of Federalists. That crusty Pennsylvania democrat, William Maclay, hated him for it. "I can with truth pronounce him the most uncandid man I ever knew possessing such abilities. I am often led to doubt whether he has a particle of integrity; perhaps such a quality is useless in Connecticut." Maclay, *Journal*, p. 229.

government to be representative of the states rather than the people directly and proposed to return to Connecticut's old system of Assembly election of delegates, the method employed everywhere else but Rhode Island. Of course he would grant Congressional authority to levy duties, but probably only in order to pay the wartime debt. On this program Sherman would be classified as an anti-nationalist when cast in the context of opinion throughout the United States.[24] But in Connecticut, he appears to be just slightly on the national side of center.

The Connecticut Constituency

Though Sherman always maintained that legislators were free agents subject only to their own conscience and wisdom, he seldom operated without one eye cocked toward his constituents. The state of politics in Connecticut could never have been too far from his mind when he rose to speak at the Convention—which he did more than any other member but Madison. Three other factors helped determine the direction of Sherman's efforts at Philadelphia. One was his experience in national Congresses, starting in 1774 and continuing regularly for ten years. No one at Philadelphia had more national political experience, and this, when coupled with his two decades of provincial public office-holding, gives him an edge shaded only by Benjamin Franklin. A third, but weaker, constituent of Sherman's character in the spring of 1787 was a set of political principles drawn largely from experience but also from reading and discussion. The fourth element shaping Sherman's actions was his absolute determination that the union of states would not only continue, but would continue stronger. His pragmatic—even expedient—temperament permitted him to mix the convictions of his constituents with the needs of union without violating his political principles.

This same amalgam was present, no doubt, though with varying emphases, in every one of the fifty-five who showed up in Philadelphia. In the case of Connecticut, all three delegates were very similarly affected by these elements—though Johnson and Ellsworth were far more intellectual than Sherman. Of course, too, one's concept of one's constituency depends largely upon whom one talks to.

The more aristocratic Ellsworth and Johnson were higher in their federalism than Sherman, and also perhaps somewhat less concerned with their constituents. This would have been especially true of Johnson, whose appointment to the presidency of Columbia College was reported in the press in May during the debate over sending delegates, but before his election as one of them. He would be moving to New York City immediately. Furthermore, Johnson had been opposed to the Revolution and had withdrawn to his Stratford farm during the war years, 1774 to 1784. Only his astute legal efforts on behalf of Connecticut's land claims gave him the genuine popularity he held in 1787. Ellsworth was one of the "young men of the Revolution." He entered law practice the same year Sherman retired from it, and first came upon the public scene as a justice of the peace in 1777. He enjoyed the unique experience of being chosen a delegate to Congress before ever serving in the state Assembly, and actually served in the national body before standing in the state halls.[25] The nationalizing effect of this background should not be underestimated.

Sherman alone was a professional politician skilled in drawing strength from his constituency when in intercolonial negotiations, but at the same time sensitive—almost hypersensitive—to the demands of the folks back home. Men like him in other states wanted no truck with the suspiciously aristocratic and centralizing prospects of the Philadelphia Convention. In Massachusetts Sherman's old friend Samuel Adams refused to attend, and so did Patrick Henry of Virginia and Governor Clinton of New York. Sherman was cut from their stamp, and his selection as a replacement for arch-provincial Erastus Wolcott would indicate that he was expected to represent the states'-rights viewpoint. Sherman alone could be counted on to consider his constituency in every case.

The Connecticut constituency probably gave its delegates more trouble than anything else in their background. The people of Connecticut didn't really want much alteration of the Articles. They were not discontented, and initiative for changes would not have originated among her yeomen had it not been for the money crisis. And only Rhode Island's bad example convinced most Connecticuters that they could not handle that problem alone. The mercantile contingent yearned for free trade through New York and Massachusetts, but agitation by this group only excited suspicion on the part of the agrarians. What all factions in Connecticut wanted was an ample supply of sound circulating currency. The provincials hoped to avoid contributions by the state, and national direct taxation was beyond the pale of polite conversation. Most Connecticut farmers would support the merchants in their efforts to deprive states of the right to levy international and interstate duties. These considerations all led to a single solution—the right of the central government to exclusive authority over imposts, with interstate duties to be forbidden entirely. The revenue from such an impost would be used to provide a national currency as the sole paper medium.

An exclusive national impost to support itself and provide a circulating currency was the only point on which most Connecticut factions would agree—and there were those such as Erastus Wolcott and James Wadsworth who would not even go that far. But there were other issues that provided the delegates with some support for nationalist principles. Shippers to the foreign West Indies wanted an effective treaty-making power. Public creditors wanted their notes redeemed, though holders of state issues were ambivalent; a national assumption would get them paid, but at the same time would be too highly centralizing in its tendencies for their tastes. Sherman, incidentally, held thousands of dollars' worth of state notes, most of it given as payment for various state and national services. But of course he also held large amounts of Continental notes as well, so he was a public creditor in general rather than decisively either state or national.[26] Four small groups saw a stronger national government as providing a surer safeguard to Connecticut's hold on the recently acquired Western Reserve. These were the land speculators; the soldiers of the militia, who were to be given lands or money derived from their sale; citizens who had suffered damages during British raids, who sought similar compensation; and state creditors in general, who saw their best hope for a revenue lying among the streams and forests of the northern backlands.

The list of what the great majority of Connecticut's citizens did not want is much longer. Beyond all else they wanted no tampering with their internal government. It had withstood the Revolution and they had no desire to see it altered now. By 1787 they would willingly surrender the right to levy imposts if all others did,* and if necessary give up authority to print their own paper money; but nothing else. Connecticuters would insist upon an equality of representation among all states in the national government. They would oppose national courts below one supreme bench. An efficacious and coercive executive was an anathema to the hardy yeomen—"the very essence of tyranny," in Sherman's words. A standing army, direct taxation, and anything at all that would interfere with the domestic police powers were absolutely to be avoided if Sherman and his colleagues were to answer unembarrassedly to the people back home. Though the Connecticut delegates time and time again may have wanted to yield to the nationalist tide at the

---

*On March 11, 1783 both Connecticut delegates to Congress, Dyer and Oliver Wolcott, voted no on the resolution, "Shall any taxes to operate generally throughout the States be recommended by Congs., other than duties on foreign commerce?" The resolution lost six to five. Hutchinson, *Madison Papers*, VI:322.

Convention, they knew they would hazard all by straying too far from their constituents' expectations.

It is abundantly clear that economic reforms were all that Connecticut called for. Even treaty-making powers were to be granted out of commercial rather than either political or military needs. The agrarian faction too, though founded on distrust of power and resentment toward authority and other anti-aristocratic modes, was primarily concerned about economics. The provincials opposed giving the central government an independent revenue, and saw no reason to surrender the right to print money or enact stay laws. They would agree, though, that states ought not to levy duties against each other.

A Steady Trio Tunes for Debate

Virginia was the first to appoint delegates to the Philadelphia Convention. That was in October 1786, and by April of the next year all the states but Connecticut and Maryland had followed. It was not until the middle of May that Connecticut answered the call for delegates; only Maryland was more tardy. Because of strong opposition, Connecticut chose to act on the official call promulgated by Congress on February 21, rather than the earlier Annapolis proposal. With Huntington barring a special session of the General Assembly, this May meeting was the earliest opportunity to elect delegates, and their selection was the first order of business.

The official appointments furnished to Johnson, Sherman, and Ellsworth authorized any one or more of them to "Act in said Convention and to discuss upon such Alterations and Provisions agreeable to the General Principles of Republican Government as they shall think proper to render the federal Constitution adequate to the exigencies of Government and the preservation of the Union." The charge included the phrase, taken from the February act of Congress, "for the sole and express purpose of revising the Articles of Confederation." This was the same phrase used by several of the states that had chosen delegates after February, and it paralleled the words, "special and sole purpose" in the Annapolis call.[27] The aim of the Annapolis delegates to "devise such further provisions as shall appear to them necessary to render the constitution of the Federal Government adequate to the exigencies of the Union" is a broader object than merely "revising the Articles of Confederation," and it certainly was the understanding of the Connecticut delegates that a revision was all that was called for.

The Convention was scheduled to open on the fourteenth of May. The Connecticut authorization had not been passed until the 16th, so they were directed to proceed to Philadelphia "without delay," but they had to wait three days for their travel money. None of them was able to get there before May 28, when the Convention finally opened. Indeed, Sherman didn't leave New Haven until the 25th and arrived on the 30th. He found that Ellsworth had preceded him by two days, while Johnson didn't appear until June 2.*[28]

Oliver Ellsworth was more than twenty years younger than Sherman, but had been a leading man of the Connecticut bar for some time. He was a member of one of the old families of his state, a Yale graduate and married to a Wolcott. He served in various offices of government, the Council of Safety, and several times was among the Connecticut delegates to the Continental Congress. Ellsworth was a great admirer of Sherman, and is reported to have declared that he took the older man for his model, on which John Adams remarked that it was praise enough for both.[29] He was later to be one of Connecticut's first senators, a Chief Justice of the Federal Supreme Court, envoy extraordinary under Adams to France, and finally Chief Justice of the Connecticut Supreme Court in 1807, the year of his death.

William Samuel Johnson had been Sherman's mentor in law, and frequent political companion for over a generation. He was six years younger than the more rustic Roger and was the outstanding figure of the Connecticut bar. He had worked against even greater handicaps than the self-educated, Massachusetts-born Sherman. Johnson, an Episcopalian, had been a semi-Loyalist. During the Revolution he had retired to his Stratford home, for he could not bring himself to fight against either his king or his countrymen. Despite these

---

*Of the Connecticut delegates, Ellsworth was present from May 28 to about August 23; he did not sign the Constitution, though he worked for its ratification in his home state. Sherman took his seat on May 30, and Johnson three days later. Sherman and Johnson made one joint trip back to Connecticut. Sherman went to see his daughter Rebecca married to Simeon Baldwin and to attend the funeral of Chauncey Whittelsey. He and Johnson left Philadelphia at eight o'clock on the morning of July 20 on the mail stage, stopping overnight at Brunswick, New Jersey. The following evening they spent with several gentlemen of the Congress at the home of their old merchant colleague, the conservative Samuel Verplanck. On Sunday, evidently without objection from the old Puritan, they embarked by ship for Connecticut. The travelers had "Fair wind, and agreeable Passage Tho' Mr. Sherman sea sick." They arrived in New Haven in the rain, and a week later the *Courant* reported Sherman's arrival, but was blocked from further news of the Convention by the ban of secrecy. Meanwhile the Convention had adjourned until August 6, the day that Johnson and Sherman returned. Sherman, then, attended the Convention for ninety-three days, two more than Johnson, and about six more than Ellsworth. Yale, Beinecke Library. "Sherman Papers," *Gaines Pocket Almanac for 1787*; CHS, "Johnson Papers," Diary for 1787; *Courant*, July 30, 1787; Stiles, *Lit. Diary*, III:271.

WILLIAM SAMUEL JOHNSON (1727–1819). Portrait by James Weiland after an original by Gilbert Stuart. Courtesy of the Connecticut State Library.

OLIVER ELLSWORTH (1745–1807). Courtesy of the Connecticut State Library.

ordinarily insurmountable barriers to political success in the rigidly Puritan
patriot hills of Connecticut, Johnson achieved great political prominence. He
had been one of the state's three members to the Stamp Act Congress, and
served on the Council of Assistants from 1766 to 1776. He represented
Connecticut in England, and was one of Connecticut's first U. S. Senators,
serving concurrently as president of Columbia College. This last position he
resigned in 1800, the year of his second marriage, and lived in retirement at
Stratford until his death in 1819 at the age of ninety-two. He had received an
honorary doctorate from Oxford and was usually referred to as Doctor.

Of the three, Sherman had by far the longest and most continuous
political career. Of course he was much older too. Benjamin Franklin, at
eighty-one, was the only delegate older than Sherman's sixty-six, among a
group of comparatively young men. Dayton of New Jersey was forty years
younger than Sherman, and five others were under thirty-one. Only twelve
were over fifty-four. Together with Daniel of St. Thomas Jenifer at
sixty-four, Sherman and Franklin were regarded as the "three Nestors." But
of course the Convention contained members far more prestigious than the
Connecticut politician. Washington was there, and Edmund Randolph, John
Dickinson, and others of greater national fame than the provincial Sherman.

The Connecticut delegation was a very strong one, and was recognized as
such at the time. A pair of observers have given characterizations of the
members that further color the picture already drawn of the simple, steady
Yankees. William Pierce, delegate of Georgia, often quite caustic, gave the
three members his respect.

> Dr. Johnson is a character much celebrated for his legal knowledge; he
> is said to be one of the first classics in America, and certainly possesses a
> very strong and enlightened understanding. As an Orator in my opinion,
> there is nothing in him that warrants the high reputation which he has for
> public speaking. There is something in the tone of his voice not pleasing
> to the Ear,—but he is eloquent and clear,—always abounding with
> information and instruction . . . . Mr. Elsworth is a . . . Gentleman of a
> clear, deep, and copious understanding; eloquent, and connected in public
> debate; and always attentive to his duty. He is very happy in a reply, and
> choice in selecting such parts of his adversary's arguments as he finds
> make the strongest impressions,—in order to take off the force of them,
> so as to admit the power of his own.
>
> Mr. Sherman exhibits the oddest shaped character I ever remember to
> have met with. He is awkward, un-meaning, and unaccountably strange in
> his manner. But in his train of thinking there is something regular, deep
> and comprehensive; yet the oddity of his address, the vulgarisms that
> accompany his public speaking, and that strange New England cant which

runs through his public as well as private speaking make everything that is connected with him grotesque and laughable;—and yet he deserves infinite praise—no Man has a better Heart or a clearer Head. If he cannot embellish he can furnish thoughts that are wise and useful. He is an able politician, and extremely artful in accomplishing any particular object;—it is remarked that he seldom fails. I am told he sits on the Bench in Connecticut, and is very correct in the discharge of his Judicial functions. In the early part of his life he was a Shoe-maker;—but despising the lowness of his condition, he turned Almanack maker, and so progressed upwards to a Judge. He has been several years a Member of Congress, and discharged the duties of his Office with honor and credit to himself, and advantage to the State he represented. He is about 60.[30]

G. W. Otto, the French Chargé d'Affaires, who kept in close touch with American politics, sent to his government a number of informed and astute letters dealing with the Convention. One of these was a collection of sketches of a number of the delegates, probably written several months after the debates began.

Monsieur Ellsworth, heretofore a member of Congress, is a man absolutely of the same temperment and of the same disposition [as Benjamin Huntington who had just been described] (i.e.) a man simple in his manners, but wise and infinitely reasonable; never having followed any faction and desiring the best without consideration of personal motives. One can say the same of M. Sherman. The people of that state have in general, a national character that is seldom found in other parts of the continent. They clothe themselves with the greatest republican simplicity; they are all comfortable without knowing opulence. . . .[31]

The republican character of Sherman had been remarked by other observers, including Benjamin Rush, who had known him as a member of the old Congress. Rush recalled some years after Sherman's death that "he was so regular in business and so democratic in his principles that he was called by one of his friends 'a republican machine.' "*[32] The true nature of Roger Sherman's republicanism is hard to define, but the best place to observe it is in the debates of the Federal Convention.

---

*This remark may have had pejorative overtones, for its author, Benjamin Rush, had written the year before that "It is possible to convert men into republican machines." The republican pupil must "be taught that he does not belong to himself, but that he is public property." Quoted in Gordon, *Creation*, p. 427.

The Constitutional Convention

THE great Constitutional Convention opened on May 25, a Friday, when a quorum of seven states had finally rallied. On that day Washington was elected chairman and Major William Jackson, formerly an Assistant Secretary of War, was chosen secretary. The only other act of the first day was the appointment of a committee to prepare a set of rules of procedure. On Monday the rules were reported out, and on Tuesday they were adopted. Seven states were to be considered a quorum, each having a single vote, and all proceedings were to be secret. Also on that day Edmund Randolph set forth his statement as to the faults of the present Confederation, and proposed a plan for a new government. Sherman took his seat on Wednesday, May 30. The New Haven to Philadelphia excursion could easily be made in three days, but Sherman had stopped in New York to buy an umbrella, some silk hose, breeches, five and a half yards of haircloth, and a number of other things for himself and his family; ordinarily, he did not travel on Sunday. Presumably he arrived in Philadelphia on the 29th, so the trip took five days.[1] In any event he missed the vote on the rules, and the original presentation of Randolph's new plan.

Revise or Rewrite

It is convenient, and perhaps not too great a simplification, to divide the delegates into "nationalists" and "federalists." The nationalists wanted a radical rewriting of the old document, which would give the general government power to act directly on individuals as citizens of the United States. The federalists were those in favor of a less radical change, amendments only, to the existing system, with power clearly divided between the general and state governments, the balance lying on the latter. Though appearing somewhat nationalist in the context of Connecticut's provincial politics, Sherman immediately established himself as federalist when compared with the strong unionism of many other delegates. On the first day of debate on Randolph's Virginia Plan, Sherman indicated that he was not in favor of making too many changes in the old system—though he admitted that additional powers must be given to the Congress. He may have been in advance of his constituency but he could not ignore it. Thus, he suggested that it would be a mistake to lose every amendment in an attempt to do more than the states would agree to accept. On the very first vote of the debate he and Ellsworth made Connecticut the only state to go against the establishment of a "national government"; they favored merely a "more effective government" as proposed by Read of the little state of Delaware.[2]

Clearly Jeremiah Wadsworth was not far off the mark in his estimate of Sherman as wanting only to "patch up the old system." But the Connecticut delegates were contending with domestic politics as well as their own convictions, neither of which would satisfy the high federalism of the Hartford speculator. By June 5, there was a fairly general acceptance that the delegates were at work on a new system, not a revision of the old one. Nevertheless, Sherman spoke against state ratifying conventions on grounds that the Articles already provided for amendment with the assent of Congress and the state legislators. Ten days later Madison was still lamenting that "Cont & N.Y. were agst. a departure from the principle of the Confederation, wishing rather to add a few new powers to Congs. than to substitute a National Govt." A showdown vote came on the nineteenth by way of a motion by Dickinson to the effect that the job of the Convention was to revise and amend the old system. Connecticut voted aye and was supported by New York, New Jersey, and Delaware, but the nationalists claimed six states, with Maryland divided. After a long speech by Madison, however, the question was reset in terms of preferring Randolph's plan over Paterson's, and Connecticut alone switched its vote. The next day, however, Ellsworth moved again to strike out the word "national" before government, and he continued to press the view that the convention should suggest amendments only.

The Connecticut delegation began to move away from its fixed position in regard to leaving the Articles basically intact when on June 21 it voted with the large states to make the legislature bicameral.* But on the major

---

*The relative size of the states can be shown by indicating their percent of the total population:

Virginia	16.5	New Jersey	5.5
Massachusetts	14.8	New Hampshire	4.5
Pennsylvania	13.9	South Carolina	4.5

issue, the delegation voted against changing the mode of representation in the lower house from that established in the Articles (June 29). But by July 14 Sherman was fighting a losing battle and seemed to know it. During the debate over the method of voting in the Senate he remarked that he cared "not so much for the security of the small States; as for the State Govts which could not be preserved unless they were represented & had a negative in the Genl Government" in the Senate. His statement was especially important because by now, despite warnings from Governor Huntington against "attempting too much," Sherman believed in a somewhat broader general grant of power to the national legislature.[3]

On August 30, Sherman suggested that perhaps the new constitution might be brought into force after ratification by only ten states. On the 31st, he wandered briefly back to his allegiance to the rules of the Confederation, saying that it would probably be improper to authorize the activation of the Constitution without unanimous concurrence. But he also saw the improbability of unanimous adoption, perhaps recalling a 1779 Connecticut resolution suggesting that the Confederacy be activated without Maryland, with the proviso that the little state be admitted when she wished.[4] Finally, on September 10, he supported a proposal that the new plan be submitted to Congress, nine states required for acceptance, and that the act arranging for such acceptance not be part of the constitution itself. In other words, he was resigned to treating the new constitution outside of provisions for amendment in the Articles.

Cutting the Pie of Sovereignty

Sherman, in concert with his constituents, wanted to keep the state governments firmly in control of political matters: police powers and the execution of state laws, and, in most cases, even the national law itself. His was a long tradition of confederation dating far back to the early days of the Continental Congresses. He had consistently opposed phrases or actions that would tend to unify the thirteen states. In 1779 in debate over the New

North Carolina	10.3	Rhode Island	2.2
New York	10.1	Georgia	1.7
Connecticut	7.5	Delaware	1.6
Maryland	6.9		

Adapted from Roll, "We, Some of the People," p.24. The figures are the 1790 and do not include slaves. As recently as 1783 Connecticut had been thought to be larger than New York. An estimate gave the former 206,000 as opposed to New York's 200,000. Hutchinson, *Madison Papers*, VI:432.

Hampshire Grants, he had voted with the majority against changing the word "several" to "United" in the phrase, "Congress are . . . duty bound . . . to preserve the rights of the several states. . . ." As late as March 1784, he joined the minority to strike out of the instructions to foreign ministers the phrase, "That these United States be considered in all such treaties, and in every case arising under them, as one nation, upon the principles of the federal constitution." And about the same time he had moved to strike out of a motion dealing with new western states the phrase that they should be subject to "the government of the United States in Congress assembled," thus leaving the new states subject only to the Articles of Confederation.[5]

In the Federal Convention he continued this stand, starting from his first day of attendance. He opposed the term, "national government," preferring "a more effective government" instead. He divided Connecticut's vote on the question, should the general government be given legislative power "in all cases to which the State Legislatures were individually incompetent." He believed apparently that the grant was too vague and thus too general, so he voted no, while Ellsworth with all the other states voted aye. On June 6 in one of his fullest statements on the division of powers, Sherman said the objects of the union should be few: foreign defense, internal defense against disputes and resort to force, treaties with foreign nations, regulating foreign commerce and drawing revenue from it, and perhaps a few lesser objects "alone rendered a Confederation of the States necessary. All other matters civil & criminal would be much better in the hands of the States." Thus, he asserted, it was not necessary that the people directly participate in the national government. "The right of participating in the National Govt. would be sufficiently secured to the people by their election of the State Legislatures." This same reasoning better explains his oft-quoted statement that the people "immediately should have as little to do as may be about the [national] Government" (May 31) than the one usually given: that he was anti-republican or aristocratic. Besides, popular government implies representation by population—an end to equality of the states.

Sherman's determination to maintain the integrity of the provincial governments is evident in Connecticut's vote on June 11 against requiring state officers to swear to observe the national Constitution and laws. He remarked at the time that such oaths would intrude unnecessarily into local jurisdictions. This view extended even to providing that the national legislators be paid by the states rather than by the national government, though he later modified this stand (June 12, August 14). Sherman sometimes saw the difficulty of making the division of authority precise, and on July 17 was willing to make the grant to the United States general so long as it was accompanied by the reservation that it would not "interfere with the Government of the individual States in any matters of internal police which respect the Govt. of such States only, and wherein the general welfare of the U. States is not concerned."

Sherman at this point read from a paper he had prepared for such an impasse.[6] He suggested enumeration, rather than a general grant of the powers to the national legislature. On June 8 he had opposed giving Congress power to negative state laws contravening the Constitution or treaties under it, and he restated his position on July 17 with the comment that the local courts would invalidate any such legislation. He repeated these objections on August 23, but with the admission that the laws of the general government would be supreme and paramount. However, the idea that there could be a clear division of power through enumeration persisted in Sherman's mind. During the debate on jurisdiction over treason on August 20, Sherman stated quite baldly that treason against the laws of the United States as distinguished from treason against the laws of a particular state could form the line of jurisdiction. Sherman's colleague Johnson, however, declared that treason against one state would be the same as treason against the United States, and the power to punish treason was left concurrent, with national power limited, as Sherman wished, to punishing treason against the United States exclusively.

By August 24 Sherman knew he was fighting a losing battle to maintain state sovereignty. Nevertheless he still hung on. In the debate on the election of the executive by the legislature Sherman insisted that the two houses ballot separately because a joint ballot would deprive "the *States* represented in the *Senate* of the negative intended them in that house." On the 30th Connecticut's delegates in a series of votes indicated their desire that the national government be enjoined from sending troops into disordered states without prior request. Right down to the conclusion of the Convention, Connecticut's delegation, then consisting of only Johnson and Sherman, insisted on the rights of the states. In a series of votes on August 31 they demanded that the method of ratification be set individually by each state, with accompanying concurrence of the old Congress, where an equality of vote prevailed; and this was the method finally adopted.

Besides these general considerations on the division of powers, Sherman was opposed also to such actions as permitting the national government to build canals or establish a university (September 14). Perhaps the extreme of the old politician's states'-rights feelings were expressed as a last gasp in the final hours of debate on September 16, the last day of substantive discussion. Here he stated his antagonism to permitting three-fourths of the states to pass amendments to the Constitution because "three fourths of the States might be brought to do things fatal to particular States, as abolishing them altogether or depriving them of their equality in the Senate." And twice he vainly sought to include as part of the amending machinery the proviso that "no State should be affected in its internal police, or deprived of its equality in the Senate." Sherman's states'-rights views prevailed about half the time. He was no mere obstructionist, however. The old confederate was not dedicated to the principle of a weak general government, so his states'-rights views must be further explored.

Sherman was a republican through and through, and his strong provincial position was an aspect of that attitude. He saw the states as the best protectors of individual liberty. In fact, Sherman often used the term "states" and "people" interchangeably. He was really pro-states, not anti-national. On June 7 he observed that it was important that the states support the national government; that harmony prevail rather than contention. The states were willing to trust Congress with every power that was necessary to carry out its general purposes, he said on the 20th. Further power must be granted to the national government (June 20, and 30), even to making laws "binding on the people of the United States in all cases which may concern the common interests of the Union," but only so long as there was no interference with local police power (July 17). Thus Sherman's attitude was in concert with that of most of his fellow delegates in that he wanted to add considerable powers to the general government.

Sherman's opposition to anything like a bill of rights was also a function of his states'-rights position. Certainly it was in no sense anti-republican. On August 23 he opposed a statement reserving to the states the right to organize their own militia because he thought it unnecessary: "The states will have this authority of course if not given up." It was probably on these same grounds that the Connecticut delegation earlier that day had opposed including a prohibition of *ex post facto* laws in the Constitution. (Johnson gave as his reason that such a prohibition implied "an improper suspicion of the National Legislature.") The same reasoning would also explain why Sherman on August 27 spoke in favor of forbidding the states to issue paper money, but would not support prohibitions against bills of attainder. On August 30 he thought that prohibitions against religious tests for national officers were unnecessary, "the prevailing liberality being a sufficient security agst. such tests." On September 12 he explicitly stated that "The State Declarations of Rights are not repealed by this Constitution; and being in force are sufficient," and two days later opposed a statement protecting the press on grounds that it was unnecessary: "The power of Congress does not extend to the Press." Preserving state integrity was his aim, not opening the door to abridgments of liberty.

Perhaps the clearest example of Sherman's insistence on state sovereignty is his attitude toward control of the militia. Way back in 1775 he had begun his campaign to keep military control out of the hands of the general government. He insisted at that time that the appointment of officers in New Jersey battalions should be left to the provincial conventions. Even after the war's lessons concerning the inefficiency of separately controlled militias, he fought against giving the Confederation government anything but the most meager military arm. In May 1784, for instance, he had supported a motion that the states rather than the general government enlist troops for western defense.[7] By 1787, however, he had learned a little and was less determined to have his own way on the issue. Again he fought hard and successfully to maintain state control of the militia. Finally he and his federal colleagues were forced to agree to a standard code and discipline and to U. S. command of the militia only when in actual service of the general government.

Thus when the archnationalist Madison tried to push his advantage and take away from the states the power to appoint general officers, Sherman's slow temper warmed up. This, he said, was "absolutely inadmissible . . . if the people should be so far asleep as to allow the most influential officers of the militia to be appointed by the Genl. Government, every man of discernment would rouse them by sounding the alarm to them." Strong words to use against James Madison, who was then beaten back. Thus the states retained full control over their own troops, submitting only to a uniform set of regulations. Sherman was still not fully satisfied. On September 5 he remarked that he would like to have a "reasonable restriction on the number and continuance of an army in time of peace." He hoped that a two-year limit on appropriations might help in this regard.

In the end, then, Sherman was far from unsuccessful. Though the general government gained the power to make rules for governing, arming, organizing, and disciplining the militia, the training of the troops and the appointment of all officers was kept to the states. And though the Congress could call up the state militias for specified purposes, the president was to command them only when in the actual service of the United States. It was an impressive demonstration of political skill. Later on, of course, Congress was given the authority to raise armies independently of the states, which undid a good deal of Sherman's work.

By July 16 the large and small states were at loggerheads over the question of voting in the Senate—usually referred to by them as the second house. On that morning an equal vote for each state was provided for in that chamber, and the populous states were outraged. Randolph of Virginia declared during the hot afternoon that the vote "had embarrassed the business extremely," and proposed that the body adjourn till the next day so that the two factions could caucus. This was agreed upon, but conversations then and the next morning yielded no new proposals from the large states.

It had been put forth that the small states might not be so timorous about granting powers to a proportionately constructed Congress if there was agreement on the areas of authority. Since no one else had a plan, Sherman moved to amend the resolution granting Congress authority to legislate in all cases "in which the harmony of the U. S. may be interrupted by the exercise of individual legislation." He had earlier objected to the phrase "individual legislation," and had voted to establish a committee to specify "the powers comprised in general terms," but to no avail. Now he was ready with his own plan. The general grant to Congress should read:

> to make laws binding on the people of the United States in all cases which may concern the common interests of the Union; but not to interfere with the Government of the individual States in any matters of internal police which respect the Govt. of such States only, and wherein the General welfare of the U. States is not concerned.

High-nationalist James Wilson liked the statement and seconded it, but Gouverneur Morris objected, so Sherman read to them his own idea of the powers Congress ought to have.

The plan called for further grants of power to the general government, and some additional restraints on the states, most of which ultimately found their way into the Constitution. The first of Sherman's proposals would give Congress the power to make laws regulating interstate and foreign commerce, to impose a tariff and apply the income to the payment of the debts of the United States. Next, a trio of amendments would make laws of the United States directly binding on the people of the states, in all cases "which concern the common interests" and the "general welfare" of the United States, but without interference in the general police power of the states. The judiciaries and the executive officers of the several states would be obliged to uphold and execute the laws of the United States. Furthermore, Congress would have the power to establish and set powers and jurisdictions of a supreme court and any other courts it thought necessary; this last a concession to the nationalists.

The right to emit bills of credit, to make tender laws or to obstruct the recovery of debts would be taken from the states. Contributions to the national treasury would be based on population rather than value of land.

Perhaps the most radical clause provided that if any state refused to pay its levy, the national legislature would have the power to lay taxes on the individual citizens of the erring state. This was followed, significantly, by a proposal that Congress be given the power to call forth the assistance of the people in order to enforce the laws of the nation, and to punish those who refused. But prosecutions were to be pressed only in the state where the crime was committed, nor could anyone be deprived of the privilege of trial by jury. This plan represents a tremendous concession to the nationalists, and is clearly something that would have gotten Sherman into very hot water at home. But it was given short shrift, and after a scant minute or two of debate was rejected, with only Maryland joining Connecticut in support.

The Supreme Will of Society

Roger Sherman's adherence to the republican principle of the supremacy of the legislature is one of his most easily identifiable trademarks. As early as June 1 the old Connecticut deputy had stated his position that the legislature was the "depository of the supreme will of the Society," and therefore should control the executive. It followed, of course, that as in the Connecticut system, the executive should be denied veto power over actions of the legislature (June 4). Sherman's opposition to restraints on the legislators was voiced on July 11: "We ought to choose wise & good men, and then confide in them," he said. He also set himself against Elbridge Gerry's motion directing that taxation and representation should be in the same proportion, on the same grounds that if the legislature were left at liberty to do what it thought was right it would no doubt conform to correct principles without instruction (July 13). At this time he protested that the legislature should be trusted, without orders, to publish its journals (August 11). But Connecticut's legislators published no journals, and the debates there were not even recorded except by an occasional newspaper reporter. That very fall had seen a flurry of adverse comment in the *Courant* about this neglect; Sherman's alleged faith seems ingenuous at best. He seemed more candid when the day before he had protested against recording the individual yeas and nays because "They never have done any good, and have done much mischief. They are not proper as the reasons governing the voter never appear along with them." He had voted against the recording of yeas and nays back in 1780, too.[8] He would also permit secrecy in discussions of foreign affairs (August 11).

Typical, but unfortunate, however, was Sherman's statement on August 17 that the power to *make* war, not merely to *declare* it, be left to the legislature. In view of his long firsthand experience with the difficulties involved in such an operation, he seems not to have learned much, and was determined to push the militia policy. He explained his view on the 24th during a debate on the powers of the executive. Sherman was against giving away too much appointive power, and believed that most appointments should be made by the legislature, especially general officers in time of peace; "herein lay the corruption in G. Britain," he said. "If the Executive can model the army, he may set up absolute Government; taking advantage of the close of a war and an army commanded by his creatures."

If the military was to be kept under Congressional control, so was the purse. On September 14, Sherman insisted vainly that the legislature appoint the treasurer (the Connecticut system). He added, significantly, that the appointment be separately voted in each house rather than jointly, so that the power of the states would have full play in the Senate. Even during the final debate of September 12, Sherman continued his battle for the supremacy of the legislature. "In making laws regard should be had to the sense of the people, who are to be bound by them, and it was more probable that a single man [the executive] should mistake or betray this sense than the Legislature." The people trust Congress, he said at one point (June 20). Almost all the states had agreed to give Congress an impost and let it dispose of its own revenue; ". . . money matters being the most important of all, if the people trust [Congress] with power as to them, they will trust them with any other necessary powers."

The Very Essence of Tyranny

Another way of looking at Sherman's attachment to a strong legislature and a strong states'-rights position is to examine his views on executive election and limitation. In the early days of the debate, June 1 as a matter of fact, the doughty old republican had favored no fixed executive, holding that since the legislators "were the best judges of the business which ought to be done by the Executive department . . . he wished the number [of executives] might not be fixed but that the legislature should be at liberty to appoint one or more as experience might dictate." He continued that the executive ought to be appointed by the legislature, and be "absolutely dependent on that body, as it was the will of that which was to be executed. An independence of the Executive on the supreme Legislature, was . . . the very essence of tyranny if there ever was any such thing." Certainly, he concluded, the legislature should have the power to remove the executive at pleasure (June 2). But if there were to be a single executive, he preferred short terms and re-eligibility as in the Connecticut tradition. On June 2 he voted with Johnson and Ellsworth to permit re-eligibility and on July 17 he seconded Houston's motion to that effect. But he wanted short terms. A seven-year tenure he considered "by no means safe or admissible." A re-electable executive "will be on good behavior as far as will be necessary. If he behaves well he will be continued; if otherwise, displaced, on a succeeding election."

At one point in his fight to weaken the possibility of a strong man, Sherman attempted to institute an executive council without whose advice the first magistrate could not act. This was rejected, and the Connecticut delegation voted with the majority to establish a single unencumbered executive. An executive veto was, of course, anathema to the old Connecticut salt. "No one man," he said on June 4, "could be found so far above all the rest in wisdom," and should not be permitted to "overrule the decided and cool opinions of the Legislature." He had the support of at least one of his colleagues on this account, and the delegation ranged itself against an absolute executive negative—a position Sherman reaffirmed on August 15. The delegation then, however, was willing that three-fourths instead of two-thirds of the legislature be required to override such a veto.

Further executive limitations were pushed during the discussion of the legislature's power to "make" war. Sherman wanted the term left as it was, thus permitting the Congress to conduct war rather than to declare it only. But Ellsworth believed that the power to conduct war was an executive function and shifted his vote. Sherman was overruled, and Connecticut voted to permit Congress to "declare" war, but not to "make" it. The old republican was opposed to executive appointment of military officers in time of peace, but he would give the president command of the militia in time of war. He even wanted the power to grant pardons and reprieves dependent on Senate confirmation, and voted all alone on his motion to put this into effect. On the matter of presidential election, his desire to keep the executive appointment in the hands of the national legislature voting as states further emphasizes Sherman's deep distrust of strong unitary executive authority (August 17,24,27,25).

Electing the Executive

It had been agreed on June 2 that the executive should be chosen by the national legislature, and the Connecticut delegates wanted it kept that way when the subject came up for reconsideration on the 8th. They also wanted the president to be free from direct controls by the state governors and therefore opposed election by them (June 9). Connecticut's desire to keep the election of the national executive in the legislature must be understood in terms of a legislature with each state an equal. On July 17, when Gouverneur Morris suggested election by the people at large, as prevailed in New York—and in Connecticut, too, he slyly pointed out—Sherman insisted that the legislature would be more expressive of the will of the nation than the people themselves. The people, he insisted, "will never be sufficiently informed of characters. . . . They will generally vote for some man in their own State, and the largest State will have the best chance for appointment." His colleagues agreed, and Ellsworth restated the view during Sherman's absence on July 25. The delegation voted then with the majority against election by the people at large and also against electors chosen by the state legislatures.

It was Ellsworth, however, acting alone on the first day of Johnson's and Sherman's absence, who took the lead in transforming the election of the executive. He was able to cast Connecticut's vote on his own motion for selection by electors chosen by the several state legislatures, a method earlier opposed by Sherman, and recently negatived. Ellsworth was also willing to accept a six-year term, twice the three years that his senior and more republican colleague had been pushing for. The final composition of the executive at this point was a single magistrate, elected by the national legislature for one seven-year term. Three of the four provisions were distasteful to the absent Sherman.

When the question of executive election came up again on August 24, Sherman fought off attempts to make the selection a joint legislative affair on the grounds that such a method would deprive the "States represented in the *Senate* of the negative intended them in that house." When the vote was called he had the support of only New Jersey, Maryland, and Georgia, with New York absent. Further maneuvering, with Connecticut divided, showed that Johnson (Ellsworth was now absent) favored selection by electors.

August 31 saw the appointment of a Committee of Eleven, of which Sherman was one, to draw up acceptable compromises on a number of still troublesome provisions. It reported on September 4. Sherman took responsibility for the proposal regarding the election of the executive, which was to be by electors chosen in a manner directed by each of the state legislatures. He said that one aim in taking the election out of the national legislature had been to make it possible for members of that body to be eligible. He pointed out the next day that the large states would have an advantage in selecting the candidates, while the small states, assuming no majority among the electors, would have an advantage in picking one of the top five. He wanted to give even more leeway to the Senate by permitting it to choose an executive from among not five, but seven or thirteen candidates, and he would give up the whole plan rather than reduce the number. He reiterated his desire to see that the election, when thrown into the legislature by absence of a majority in the electoral college, be made by states even if it came from the House instead of the Senate. That was on September sixth, the day when debate on the election of the executive reached a climax.

Finally Sherman moved that instead of the Senate, "The House of Representatives shall immediately choose by ballot one of them [tied candidates or candidates not having a majority] for President, the members from each State having one vote." That ardent democrat George Mason, immediately declared that he liked this best "as lessening the aristocratic influence of the Senate," and the measure was passed with only Delaware dissenting. Sherman had intended the votes to be cast in the House on a one-state-one-vote basis, but he didn't say so, and Madison pointed out that a majority of the House voting per capita could consist of only two states. A number of cumbersome attachments were made that day and also the next, attempting to avoid any possibility of election in the House by less than a majority of the states. The final result was the present system—election in the House with each state having one vote. Thus the outcome was almost as Sherman proposed.

It is likely, in view of the interest and authority with which Sherman spoke on the method of electing an executive, and the acceptance that his final system received, that he was largely responsible for the method first suggested by the Committee of Eleven. If this is the case, it is clear that he had compromised his determination to make the executive dependent on the legislature. However, it was generally believed that most elections would be decided not by the electoral college, but by the House in the manner Sherman prescribed. Therefore, he thought he had maintained the power of the states. His intent, and his ultimate accomplishment, was to protect the states, rather than to keep the executive dependent on the legislature. This suggestion gains even more credence when viewed against his 1784 efforts to establish a strong, though plural, executive in Connecticut, and failing that, to continue the Council of Safety with its extraordinary executive prerogatives. Sherman was not opposed to strengthening the institutional executive so long as individual power was restricted. He certainly was not trying to develop a democratic electoral system. In any event, the present method of presidential election seems to be as much or more Sherman's creation than anyone else's.

A Diffusive Judiciary

Sherman's states'-rights stand carried into the discussion of courts also. That the judiciary should have inferior courts was agreed to without debate on June 4. But Rutledge of North Carolina moved on the 5th that no inferior courts be established, since the state tribunals were adequate to decide all cases in the first instance, "the right of appeal to the supreme national tribunal being sufficient to secure the national rights & uniformity of Judgmts." Sherman, who had protested federal interference in the states as early as 1779, seconded him. When it came time for the old Puritan to speak, he "dwelt chiefly on the supposed expensiveness of having a new set of Courts, when the existing State Courts would answer the same purpose." The expense argument must have caused a few of Sherman's colleagues to suspect some lack of candor in the old man, but Rutledge's motion against inferior courts was passed five to four, with two states divided. Then came a quick reversal when Madison moved to permit rather than to oblige the national legislature to establish inferior courts. Connecticut stood against even this, with South Carolina her only partner.

Sherman continued to think of the state courts as quasi-federal in that they would be bound to prefer federal over state laws. He had added to the Connecticut statutes in his revision of 1784 that "due obedience shall be paid by the several courts, officers and inhabitants of this State, to all orders and ordinances of the united States in Congress assembled, made by virtue, and pursuant to the powers and authorities vested in them by the articles of confederation." For his state, the Articles were already the supreme law of the land. On July 17 he remarked that he saw no need to give the national legislature the power to negative state laws, for the "Courts of the States would not consider as valid any law contravening the Authority of the Union. . . ." Anyway, the self-trained lawyer pointed out, giving the national legislature a negative on state laws "involves a wrong principle, to wit, that a law of a State contrary to the articles of the Union, would if not negatived, be valid & operative." He, along with many of his colleagues, assumed judicial review as an operative principle. The next day he had weakened and was willing to give the power to establish inferior courts to the legislature, but "wished them to make use of the State Tribunals whenever it could be done, with safety to the general interest." So Connecticut joined in the unanimous vote for inferior courts. Sherman's principle that state courts should owe allegiance to the general government remained, and thus the old federalist provided one of the keystones of the national plan.

The method of appointing the various judges worked out more successfully for Sherman. In Connecticut, until 1784, the highest court had consisted of the Governor and Council, called the Superior Court and elected by freemen. A law of that year changed its name to Supreme Court of Errors and gave it jurisdiction only when a new Superior Court had erroneously applied rules of law or principles of equity. The Superior Court, on which the Governor and Assistants were no longer permitted to sit, was chosen by the lower house to hold office at its pleasure.[9]

The problem was first discussed on June 5, when Madison moved that the legislature be denied the selection of judges. Only Connecticut and South Carolina voted to keep judicial appointment in Congress, and they lost, two to nine. A week later Pinckney, with Sherman seconding, moved to re-establish the power of the legislature to appoint the judges of the supreme court (June 13). But when Madison proposed to rest appointment in the hands of the Senate alone, the two men happily withdrew their motion, and Madison's method was approved without further debate. When Paterson brought in the small-states plan on the 15th, it called for appointment by the executive, a suggestion not seriously discussed until July 18, when Gorham of Massachusetts recommended executive appointment with the advice and consent of the upper house—the method used in his state. But Wilson moved to omit Senate participation. Luther Martin, the most ardent states'-righter of them all, wanted appointment by the Senate alone, and Sherman agreed, "adding that the Judges ought to be diffused, which would be more likely to be attended to by the second branch, than the Executive." By the term "diffused" he apparently meant geographic distribution; the Connecticut custom was to choose judges of the state courts from different counties. Thus in 1784, upon the establishment of the new Superior Court, its four members, including Sherman, in fact represented four counties.[10] Sherman restated his views again as Wilson, Gouverneur Morris, and Madison pressed further for executive appointment of judges. Madison reported that Sherman "was clearly for an election by the Senate. It would be composed of men nearly equal to the Executive, and would of course have on the whole more wisdom. They would bring into their deliberations a more diffusive knowledge of characters. It would be less easy for candidates to intrigue with them, than with the Executive Magistrate." These were the same views presented by Madison on June 5, when the Virginian had also hinted at appointment by the Senate. Randolph and young Gunning Bedford of Delaware rallied to Sherman's cause, and the attempt to give appointment to the president failed, with only Massachusetts and Pennsylvania in favor.

The fight was not over yet, however, as Gorham promptly moved the method used in his state and there ratified, he said, by "the experience of 140 years"; that is, executive appointment with the consent of the Senate. Sherman gave the only speech against the measure, remarking mildly that he found this "less objectionable than an absolute appointment by the Executive; but disliked it as too much fettering the Senate." After further brief debate the matter was left to the Committee of Eleven, whose number included Sherman, which recommended the system favored by Gorham and Madison. Thus a clause providing for appointment by the executive with the advice and consent of the Senate was accepted by all the states on September 7 without significant new debate. No specific provision for the removal of judges was provided, but when the question had come up earlier Sherman had seen no impropriety in a suggestion of Dickinson's that magistrates be removable by the executive on the application of the Senate and House (August 27).

As to the functions to be performed by the national courts, Sherman had not come to the Convention without ideas on that. In 1780 he had voted with the Congressional majority that U. S. Courts of Admiralty should follow the law of nations, and not use juries, a surprising view considering the use that the British had made of their Admiralty Courts on the eve of the Revolution. Indeed only six weeks earlier he had insisted that jury trials be guaranteed in domestic courts (July 7). And for over twenty years Sherman had been one of the principal members of the Connecticut Superior Court. The Connecticut delegation voted with the rest on June 13 to give the national judiciary authority over cases involving the national revenue, impeachments of national officers, and "questions which involve the national peace and harmony." But Sherman set himself firmly against admitting the judiciary to the veto power. When Madison moved on August 15 that all laws be submitted to the judiciary as well as to the executive for revision, Sherman remarked that "he disapproved of judges meddling in politics and parties."

Sherman envisioned the great role for the judiciary in settling disputes between the states. On August 24 he seconded William Johnson's motion to strike out the cumbersome mechanism proposed for settling such disputes without recourse to a supreme court. This machinery had been suggested by the Committee of Eleven and had followed generally the pattern fashioned by the old Congress and used in the Susquehannah dispute. Sherman's concurrence in abandoning this mode of settling land controversies was significant; probably, with Johnson's help, he could have made the old system stick if he had fought for it. Sherman, however, wanted an explicit statement of jurisdiction over land disputes similar to the one that had been written into Article IX of the Articles. Thus, he moved to specify in the Constitution that the national judiciary would have authority over cases involving citizens and foreigners; citizens and other states; and citizens of different states. But to protect the private claims of Connecticuters still living in Pennsylvania's Wyoming Valley he also added the phrase, "Citizens of the same State claiming lands under grants of different states." This was accepted on August 27 without debate. On September 8 he attacked Madison's proposal to empower the supreme court to try presidential impeachment cases, for judges appointed by the executive might not give him an unprejudiced trial. Sherman favored leaving impeachment trials in the Senate.

In sum, it might be said that the national judiciary emerged fairly close to Sherman's hopes for it. Though its dependence on the legislature was virtually nonexistent, Sherman had always expressed his view that there should be a clear separation between the two branches. The method of appointment was acceptable to him, though second best because the states would not have original nominating power in the Senate. The fact that inferior tribunals were left discretionary and not mandated gave him hope that the state courts would retain their importance, a hope which he saw fade under Ellsworth's Judiciary Act of 1789. Land disputes could be settled by a relatively unprejudiced body with no legal or institutional ties to the states. No doubt Sherman was well satisfied with the national judiciary. But the executive and the judiciary were the two branches that Sherman considered of secondary importance. The crux of the business at hand, as Sherman saw it, was the power to be granted to the national legislature—and on this central question attention must now focus.

The Powers of Congress

Just what did Sherman have in mind for the national legislature? It goes almost without saying that he wanted an augmentation of the economic powers already held by Congress. The first thing he said on taking his seat on

May 30 was that "the Confederation had not given sufficient power to Congs. and that additional powers were necessary; particularly that of raising money which . . . would involve many other powers." He was in favor of an enumeration rather than a general grant, and at first he held that in no case should jurisdictions be concurrent (May 30). His great faith in the legislature, which inclined him toward giving it the power to appoint various executives and judges, has already been demonstrated.

The main area of authority to be entrusted to a national body, in Sherman's mind, was that of economic policy: commerce, revenue, and currency regulation. The thinking of the old merchant, himself a victim of paper money, followed a very clear pattern. He wished to gather economic authority to the national government while most jealously guarding state control over the police power. This was manifest time and time again throughout the Great Debate. He sometimes admitted, however, that keeping these two areas of economics and politics separate was no easy problem.

The power to raise a revenue, said Sherman, "would involve many other powers," but at this time he held that none should be concurrent. In his maiden speech Sherman mentioned the revenue, the first time the subject had been brought up at all. In a major departure from his republican commitment he favored the right of both houses to initiate money bills. The Senate with its greater wisdom was "particularly needed in the finance business," he said on June 13, and besides, this was the system successfully tested in Connecticut. He pushed this idea further still on the 20th by pointing out that since nearly all states had agreed to let Congress set an impost, "it appeared clearly that they were willing to trust Congs. with power to draw a revenue from Trade. There is no weight therefore in the argument drawn from a distrust of Congs. for money matters being the most important of all, if the people will trust" Congress with such power they will trust it "with any other necessary powers." These "other" powers would include—from Sherman it is a surprisingly radical suggestion—authority to levy taxes directly on the people of a balky state and to make the collection of them a federal matter (July 14).

The taxing power is the surest measure of Sherman's intention to press for real economic responsibility for the national government. While he ordinarily insisted on the integrity of the states in matters of civil government, he was willing to accept federal authority to coerce states that would not pay their taxes. The national government, he thought, "ought to be empowered to carry their own plans into execution if the States should fail to supply their respective quotas" of taxes (July 14). This would be done by authorizing Congress to call "forth such aid from the people . . . as may be necessary to assist the civil officers in the execution of the laws of the United States; and annex suitable penalties to be inflicted in case of disobedience." He thought, however, "that authority need not be exercised if each state will furnish its quota."*[11]

On August 21 the Connecticut delegation came out against a very similar proposal made by Luther Martin, but it is not known how Sherman voted. Direct taxation, however, was hardly one of Sherman's main objectives. He omitted any such provision from his amendments, hoping that income from imposts and post office revenues would be sufficient, though he admitted on July 17 that he supposed that other sources of income would become necessary. Apparently it was the lack of a direct taxation provision that brought the defeat of Sherman's amendments during their brief discussion on that day; only his own state voted to accept any of his ideas.

Rufus King of Massachusetts pointed out that much of the opposition to federal imposts came from holders of state notes. It would not only be just for the general government to assume these debts, but also politic. In a Congressional report of 1780, Sherman had called for cessions of western lands tied with federal assumption of states' wartime debts.[12] Now he saw the political wisdom of placating the Connecticut provincials, who tended naturally to be state rather than national creditors. He considered the assumption as just, he said, and thought "it would have a good effect to say something about the Matter." Ellsworth thought not; if the debts were just, they would be paid (August 18).

The subject was referred to a committee on which Sherman served (August 18). When the report was released on the 21st Gerry objected that Congress was only authorized and not obligated to pay the state debts, and Sherman pointed out that the plan was merely to continue to follow the method of the old Congress. This was a subject about which Sherman could speak with authority, for his 1780 report had provided for the reimbursement

---

*An example of how differing interpretations of the same Constitutional clause could justify one states'-righter's acceptance of the new system while another rejected it, is this one relating to taxation. While Sherman chose to see the laying and collecting of taxes as incidental and occasional and said so in letters urging ratification of the finished document, George Mason declared that this "clause clearly discovers that it is a national government, and no longer a Confederation . . . The assumption of this power of laying direct taxes does, of itself entirely change the confederation of the states into one consolidated government." Quoted in Ferguson, *Power of the Purse*, p. 290. Sherman, however, wrote that though direct taxation was provided for, "that authority need not be exercised, if each state will furnish its quota." Quoted from a letter to Governor Huntington in Elliot, *Debates*, I:491–92.

of all "necessary and reasonable expenses" which any state incurred in the war. He now moved to bring the new assumption more in line with the old system by crediting to the states' accounts all supplies, services, and monies advanced to the United States. This allowance had been made under the old Congress on Sherman's recommendation, and he wanted this express power given to the new government. He withdrew the motion, however, on other considerations.

Sherman tried once again on August 25, vainly and with the support of his own state alone, to make an express connection between the federal taxing power and the payment of the debts, old or new, "incurred for the common defense and general welfare." Ultimately the clause was included. Sherman's intent here was twofold: to get the state debts assumed and to limit national taxation to the payment of the current debt only. It was distinctly his intention that the monies raised by Congress were to be used for the payment of the national and state debts incurred in providing for the general welfare. Sherman's economic nationalism is somewhat qualified in that he was not of the mind that Congress should have the power to raise money for the future general welfare of the nation. He had said in 1784 when the question of federal impost was under discussion that "I never wish to have the power in Congress to raise money extended beyond what may be necessary for the present debt."[13]

Control over commerce was of major importance to Sherman. As long ago as 1780 he had been part of an attempt in the Connecticut Council to open a "Free Trade and transportation by land from one state to another."[14] He spoke with authority on this subject, and his views generally prevailed in the long run. He consistently opposed giving Congress the power to tax exports because such a tax would be prejudicial to the noncommercial states, and not being accepted by the people, might "shipwreck the whole" (August 21). Connecticut, of course, carried on an extensive export trade to the West Indies, though her imports came largely through New York. Thus a national government vested with power to regulate foreign and interstate commerce was desired by Connecticut's merchants, as Sherman emphasized on August 16.

His understanding of commerce was appreciated in the Convention, for on August 25 he was assigned to a committee to deal with a number of commercial problems still unsettled. He reported for the committee on August 28, though discussion had to wait three more days. Sherman's recommendations forbade Congress to prefer any ports over others or to require vessels in interstate commerce to pay duties in any state, and would enjoin that all Congressional duties, imposts, and excises "shall be uniform throughout the U. S." Coupled with the prohibition on export taxes, the report thus set up a free-trade area consisting of the whole United States. The committee recommendations were all accepted, and Sherman must have been well satisfied.

Despite his tendency to bestow large economic powers upon the national government, Sherman indicated on August 28 that he would prefer to retain in the states the power to lay embargoes "to prevent the suffering & injury to their poor." It was his understanding that control over commerce was to be concurrent, but that no danger was to be apprehended because "The power of the U. States to regulate trade being supreme can controul interferences of the State regulations when such interferences happen. . . ." (September 15).

On the question of currency the senior Connecticut delegate was equally influential. On August 16 with most of the other delegates he voted the conservative way—to prohibit the emission of bills of credit by the national government; and on a series of votes the next day the Connecticut delegation joined the majority in providing for punishment of counterfeiters.

Sherman's most important contribution in this area was characteristically an economic limitation on state power. On August 28 James Wilson moved, with Sherman seconding, an addition to the restriction on the states not to coin money. They moved to add, "nor emit bills of credit, nor make any thing but gold & silver coin a tender in payment of debts," making these prohibitions absolute, instead of making the measures allowable. This phraseology, nearly identical to the language used in Sherman's proposed amendments, was adopted verbatim in the final draft of the Constitution. Nathaniel Gorham protested that such a prohibition would alienate too many people. But Sherman, long ago author of *A Caveat Against Paper Money*, remembered his constituency, where in May tender laws had been ridiculed out of the Assembly.[15] He replied that he "thought this a favorable crisis for crushing paper money. If the consent of the Legislature could authorize emissions of it, the friends of paper money, would make every exertion to get into the Legislature in order to licence it."

Western Lands Again

Connecticut citizens would have considered it disastrous if anything in the new constitution jeopardized her claim to the hard-won Western Reserve. William Samuel Johnson was included in the delegation, no doubt, because of his legal expertise in this matter, and Sherman had long been a friend to western settlers. Sherman was concerned about other matters regarding western settlement. He would insist that the states there be guaranteed a republican form of government, and that they enter the union on an equal footing with the original members. In 1780 Sherman had written a Congressional report providing that lands ceded to the United States be "formed into distinct republican states . . . members of the federal union [with] the same rights . . . as other states. . . ." Again in 1784, he moved to alter Jefferson's important report of that year to remove new states from the authority of Congress and put them under the Articles of Confederation only. Even Jefferson voted to allow this anti-imperialist alteration.[16]

Sherman did not believe that western states would ever outnumber those on the Atlantic coast. He pointed out in the convention on a couple of occasions that there was nothing to fear, anyway, because the new states would be settled by the offspring of the present population. Though he had a majority with him, he did not persuade Ellsworth and Johnson, who voted to limit the western representatives to a number less than the "originals" (July 14). He was so concerned about eastern progeny in the west that he attempted to get an explicit guarantee of equality of treatment written into the constitution. But on this, only Virginia and Maryland agreed, Sherman losing his Connecticut colleagues again (August 29).

When a question relating to the Wyoming settlers arose, Sherman answered the call to arms. On August 29 Gouverneur Morris moved that no new state could be erected within the limits of an old one without consent of both the state and national legislature. Sherman opposed this motion, he said, because it was unnecessary; "The Union can not dismember a State without its consent." Johnson agreed and tried to steer the discussion in the direction of Vermont. But Wilson of Pennsylvania was not willing to let the matter drop. He charged that Sherman was attempting to put the general government on the side of a minority within a state, for a majority could always decide to divide if it wished. Debate was cut off by adjournment at this point, but the next day Sherman moved to give the legislature power to "admit other States into the Union" as well as new states formed by the division or juncture of present states. He explained that "other states" referred to Vermont, but he got the support of only New Hampshire, Massachusetts, and Pennsylvania. Johnson, however, was more successful in phrasing a motion that would save Vermont from a dependence on New York's assent.

The major concern of the Connecticut delegation, however, was the maintenance of the Western Reserve agreed to by Congress the previous September. There was not much danger that the arrangement would be upset, however. Congress always knew it would have to provide for Connecticut in some way. In May of '86 as the Connecticut Assembly was writing the final cession with its reserve provision, Congress, acting upon the Land Ordinance of '85, ordered a survey of the Old Northwest. A proviso essential to Connecticuters was added, however: the survey was to be confined to the area south of the point where the Ohio River leaves Pennsylvania—about forty miles south of Connecticut's sea-to-sea claims. Each state was to contribute a surveyor to aid in the work, and after Samuel Holden Parsons, nominated by the State, accepted another Congressional appointment, the job fell to Isaac, Sherman's third son. Congress accepted Connecticut's cession in September, '86, and the Assembly immediately went to work arranging for its disposal.[17]

It was well understood at the Convention that Connecticut would countenance no rough handling of her darling Western Reserve. Surely this was her *sine qua non* for acceptance of a new government. There were, however, a number of sneering remarks by Madison and others about land "dealt out to Cont. to bribe her acquiescence" in the Trenton decree. On the other hand, Pennsylvania was firmly behind Connecticut by the terms of the 1786 agreement. In a sense, Connecticut held Pennsylvania hostage to the good behavior of the Wyoming settlers.

If Connecticut would insist on her land holdings, South Carolina would demand that her slave holdings be guaranteed, too. In fact, the circumstances surrounding debate on the two issues lead one to believe that Sherman may have made another one of his famous deals. Outright efforts to deprive Connecticut of her western lands and South Carolina of her slaves are really conspicuous by their absence except for a tirade by Virginia's Mason attacking Southerners for owning slaves and Northerners for shipping them. But the mutterings sounded ominous to delegates who could not in good conscience support either of their pets. In addition, South Carolina was determined to see that authority to levy duties on her exports was denied Congress. What may have happened is that the Connecticut delegation agreed to help fight off abolitionists and work toward prohibiting export duties if South Carolina would assist in guaranteeing Connecticut's western conquest.* It is unlikely, however, that Sherman and his colleagues would give up much that they really wanted to get what they already thought was pretty well secured.

---

*This is an assertion made by both Richard Barry in *Mr. Rutledge of South Carolina* (pp. 330–35) and Forrest McDonald in *E Pluribus Unum* (pp. 176–77, 298–99n48), but since McDonald relies on Barry and Barry provides no specific documentation and is inaccurate in a number of details, I cannot accept their accounts as definitive. An effort to locate the Rutledge diary upon which Barry apparently bases his account of the affair has proven fruitless. The more generally accepted interpretation is that the northern states got their commercial provisions by promising no interference with the slavery of the deep south. Farrand, *Records*, II:449,449n.

When the Constitution came out of the Committee of the Whole on June 13, it provided that the national legislature have all the powers held by Congress under the Articles. Presumably this included the cumbersome process for settling land disputes which had resulted in the disastrous Trenton decision of 1783.* But the draft also provided for a national judiciary with jurisdiction over "questions which involve the national peace and harmony," which might have applied also. This was substantially the form in which settlement of land controversies remained when referred to the Committee of Detail on July 26. But when that committee, on which Ellsworth represented Connecticut, reported after a recess ending August 6, it had included almost verbatim the Articles' procedure: submission to a commission chosen by the contesting parties as in the Trenton case (which went unanimously against Connecticut); or nomination by the Senate of three commissioners from each state, the contesting parties to choose thirteen of which the Senate would designate seven to nine to adjudicate the claim. The Connecticut delegation may have had some faith in the Senate, where they had equality of votes, but they certainly had little love for a procedure that had cost them so dearly in 1783. Thus when Rutledge moved to strike out this whole complicated procedure as "rendered unnecessary by the National Judiciary now to be established," Johnson quickly seconded and Sherman concurred. But the Reserve was never questioned again and stayed with Connecticut until she voluntarily ceded it in 1801.

---

*The Trenton court sat from November 12 to December 30, 1782 and laid its report before Congress on January 2, 1783. Burnett, *Congress*, p. 546. See also Taylor, "Trial."

E Pluribus Unum!

Roger Sherman was the consummate politician. His instinct for the possible was not always precise, but it was usually near the mark. His sense of direction inevitably led him to the center, and he spent most of his political life edging from one side of center to the other. His method was compromise, the stock in trade of every successful politician; to give and to take away; to trade and dicker.

These were the elements that brought about his successful shaping of the Connecticut Compromise to fit the Constitutional edifice. In fact, this great keystone of the Constitution is so much his work that a recent historian has suggested that the most accurate name for the proposition would be the Sherman Compromise.[1] All of the ageing statesman's characteristics stand out in their strongest colors in the development of this major contribution—his gift to the generations of Americans who have lived under the Constitution.

The Connecticut Compromise

The Connecticut Compromise was no sudden stroke of brilliance inspired by the Convention. Nor was it a scheme tacked together for the specific time and events of the summer of 1787. This "Great Compromise" was almost the climax of a career in national politics for the Yankee republican. It did not emerge as the easy outgrowth of earlier political development. No similar system existed in Sherman's Connecticut, nor had the system been attempted in earlier general congresses. It was, then, neither new nor old, neither forged on the anvil of experience nor produced in a stroke of sudden inspiration. It had been molded over a long period of time.

The crucial debate went on periodically from the end of May to the 5th of September, and involved two questions: how were the members of the legislature to be chosen, and on what basis was suffrage to be granted? Since choice of congressmen by the state legislatures implied the federal principle of state equality, the two questions became inextricably enmeshed. Thus it is hardly possible to treat them separately. Side issues crept in and compounded the confusion. For example, the number of houses—should there be one or two? General agreement was on the side of two, and drives for a unicameral house were scarcely a problem, though had Franklin been twenty years younger we might have had one.

Like many of Sherman's ideas, the inception of the Connecticut Compromise can be traced back to his early years in national politics. During the debates on the method of voting in the Second Continental Congress, in August 1776, Sherman had suggested that "The vote should be taken two ways; call the Colonies, and call the individuals, and have a majority of both."[2] He gave two reasons for this proposal: one was that the delegates were representing states, not individuals, thus the vote should be by delegations; second, if voting were done on the basis of representation by population alone, then the three largest states could "govern the whole, but would not have a majority of strength to carry those votes into execution." So voting according to population was not only unfair, it was also impractical. There should also be a vote by states.*

Sherman had come to the Convention assuming that the method of voting would be the same as under the old Confederation, but before May was out it was obvious that it would again be a major point of contention. As early as May 31 Sherman suggested that Congress consist of one member from each state. On June 6 a motion by Pinckney that the lower house be elected by the state legislatures reopened debate, and Sherman again insisted that unless the states were to be abolished entirely, elections to the national legislature should be by the states. This would ensure harmony between the state and national governments and at the same time let the people participate in the national government by virtue of having elected the state legislature.

Mason and Madison were on their feet immediately, calling for a national legislature elected directly by the people. Dickinson also "considered it as essential that one branch of the Legislature shd. be drawn immediately from the people"; but he added that it might be "expedient" that the other be elected by the state legislatures, a view he had voiced on June 2. William Pierce of Georgia agreed with Dickinson, and on the vote only South Carolina and New Jersey supported Connecticut in accepting election of the lower

---

*Taxes, however, should be based on the relative populations of the states, an inconsistency attributable to the high value of Connecticut real estate. *JCC*, XI:639–40.

house by the state legislatures. The next day the debate was renewed, this time on Dickinson's motion that the state assemblies should choose the members of the second branch of the legislature. Sherman seconded this motion and remarked that it would give the particular states an interest in supporting the national government even though the two ought to have separate and distinct jurisdictions.

The debate now began to turn to the essential question of proportional or equal representation. Hugh Williamson of North Carolina hinted that different modes of representation might be adopted for the two houses. "Mr. Butler was anxious to know the ratio of representation before he gave any opinion," and James Wilson opposed any idea of representation other than that based on the people at large. If one branch were chosen by the legislatures and the other by the people, the different bases would give rise to dissensions between the houses. At this point Madison declared that a departure from proportional representation in the Senate would be inadmissible, adding in a footnote that election by the state legislatures would involve a surrender of the proportional principle. Madison did not believe that the best men would be elected to the Senate any more often by the state legislatures than by some other mode. Sherman replied with the opinion that it was by election in the legislatures that the best men would be produced.* When a vote was called, the motion to refer election of the Senate to the state legislatures was passed unanimously.

On Saturday, June 9, the question of the mode of voting in the legislature was brought to the floor by Paterson and Brearley of the little state of New Jersey. Both men gave long, strong speeches on the evils of changing the old system of equality. Wilson and Williamson spoke, but when the question was about to be put, Paterson called for postponement and the house adjourned. The activities of Roger Sherman on Sunday, June 10, are of prime interest, but they are not easily discovered. Apparently he spent a good deal of time in conference with Paterson and other small-state delegates, and perhaps he talked to others as well. At any rate he decided during the day that compromise was necessary and the best he could hope for was equality in one house only.

On Monday, June 11, Sherman proposed what was to become the basis of our present system of national federalism in the general legislature. Suffrage

---

*Sherman knew whereof he spoke; three times he had been chosen a delegate to Congress by the Assembly after the people in general election had failed to recognize his worth.

in the first branch should be based on the respective proportions of free inhabitants, while in the second branch each state would have "one vote and no more." To force some kind of action on at least part of this idea Rufus King moved that the suffrage in the first house ought not to be equal. A short debate followed, consisting mostly of a long speech of Franklin's read for the old man by his colleague Wilson. Franklin wished the legislature to be representative of the people, but could see that it would never be agreeable to the small states to be put at the mercy of the large, nor would the reverse be possible. He then endorsed Sherman's proposal: "An honorable gentleman," said Franklin, "has, to avoid this difficulty, hinted a proposition of equalizing the States. It appears to me an equitable one, and I should, for my own part, not be against such a measure, if it might be found practicable." But he suggested also that if the votes be equal, then so should the contributions to the national treasury. The speech was passed over without debate, and the question was called on King's motion. The vote to change the method of suffrage from equality, as practiced under the Articles, passed with New York, New Jersey, and Delaware on the losing side and Maryland divided. Connecticut's vote to give some kind of a proportional voice in the lower house presupposed that the upper house would conform to Sherman's suggestion of equality.

Sherman then moved the second part of his proposal, that in the upper house each state should have one vote. Ellsworth, speaking in the Convention for the first time, seconded the motion. To Sherman this was the single most important decision to come before the entire Convention. "Every thing he said depended on this. The smaller States would never agree to the plan on any other principle than an equality of suffrage in this branch." The vote was called for without further debate and the division was straight down the party line, New York, New Jersey, Delaware, and Maryland voting with Connecticut in favor, and the majority of six voting against. The same division prevailed on the vote to make the suffrage in the upper house the same as in the lower, and for the time being, Sherman was defeated. It is doubtful, however, that the dogged old politician considered the matter closed. If there had been no hope of maintaining at least one strong arm of state control, then his whole attitude toward the Convention would have changed. He probably would have remained, but only as an obstructionist determined to weaken the general government at every opportunity. There must have been some impression of weakness in the nationalist bloc that persuaded Sherman and his supporters to believe that the issue could be reargued and reversed at a later time. So they acquiesced temporarily.

On the 13th of June the measures were brought together in a report that recommended a bicameral legislature with the lower house elected by the people directly and the upper house elected by the various state legislatures. The suffrage, however, was to be based on population in both houses. At Paterson's request, debate was suspended for a day so that members could have more time to study the report. On June 15 the New Jersey plan was brought in. No change in the mode of voting from the equality prevailing under the Articles was suggested, and the legislature was to remain unicameral.

When Sherman spoke next it was in the long, far-ranging debate on the two conflicting plans. His particular concern at this time was the problem of a unicameral legislature. Lansing of New York moved on June 20 that in accordance with Paterson's plan a single house be continued. Sherman seconded the motion, for with the failure of his compromise proposal he was looking for new methods of securing the primacy of the states. A single-chambered congress had carried the nation through the war perhaps as well as any government could have, he said. "The complaints at present are not that the views of Congs. are unwise or unfaithful; but that their powers are insufficient for the execution of their views." Certainly it could not be argued that the people do not trust Congress, he continued, for it has been given power to draw a revenue from trade. And, since money matters are the most important of all, it must be agreed that a people willing to trust Congress with those powers would certainly trust them with any others thought necessary. A second house was not only unnecessary, but would be downright embarrassing. A few designing men from the large districts could get control and undermine the people's faith in the general government.

> The disparity of the States in point of size he perceived was the main difficulty. . . . If the difficulty on the subject of representation can not be otherwise got over, he would agree to have two branches, and a proportional representation in one of them; provided each State had an equal voice in the other. This was necessary to secure the rights of the lesser States. . . . Each State like each individual had its particular habits usages and manners, which constituted its happiness. It would not therefore give to others a power over this happiness, any more than an individual would do, when he could avoid it.

Sherman's point was clear; either the Convention would accept his compromise or it would leave the present construction of Congress unchanged. James Wilson challenged some of Sherman's assumptions, reminding him that on many occasions it had been the obstructions of the small states that had damaged the public interest. And, Wilson continued, "The success of the Revolution was owing to other causes, than the Constitution of Congress." Finally only three states, Connecticut, New Jersey, and New York, with Maryland divided, could be found in favor of even taking a vote on Lansing's motion for a single house.

The next day (June 21), Connecticut's Johnson spoke at length to the point that if New Jersey were guaranteed the inviolability of states' prerogatives, her delegates might be reconciled to a vote by population in at least one house. Wilson and Madison spoke again for two houses, and a vote was called. Here Connecticut deserted her small friends, leaving only New York, New Jersey, and Delaware with the split Maryland in the minority. The legislature would be two-chambered. Exactly why Connecticut talked unicameral and voted bicameral is not clear. Sherman's vote is not known, nor is Ellsworth's. Johnson almost certainly voted with the large states, and maybe both his colleagues did, too. If Sherman did, however, it was probably because he expected success at a later date.

Later the same day a new attempt was launched by Pinckney to transfer election of the lower house from the people at large to the state legislatures (June 21). Sherman said that he favored the proposal but inexplicably claimed he would be content with the plan as it stood; i.e., proportional suffrage in both houses. But certainly he had not given up his battle for states' rights. Perhaps he was waiting for a more opportune chance to strike. On the vote, however, Connecticut supported Pinckney and stood with the small-state minority. Then she promptly reversed herself in harmony's name and voted with all but New Jersey for a lower house elected by the people. The pace of the debate quickened, and by June 25 the Convention was ready for a vote on the construction of the upper house. The timing was right, and election by the state legislatures passed with only Virginia and Pennsylvania dissenting.

While the wind was blowing fairly on the small-state forces, this was surely the time to sail into the seas of suffrage again, and on the 27th a new proposal for equality in the upper house was taken up. Williamson and Madison, particularly the latter, spoke at great length on the unfairness of an equal vote, and finally Wilson compared the small-state position with that of the British rotten boroughs. At this point Sherman made his most precise and telling argument on behalf of the small states. It was the climax of his part in the Convention duel, and went to the heart of Madison's and Wilson's discussion of principle. "The question is not what rights naturally belong to men; but how they can be most equally and effectually guarded in society," he said.

And if some give up more than others in order to attain this end, there can be no room for complaint. To do otherwise, to require an equal concession from all, if it would create danger to the rights of some, would be sacrificing the end to the means. The rich man who enters into Society along with the poor man, gives up more than the poor man, yet with an equal vote he is equally safe. Were he to have more votes than the poor man in proportion to his superior stake, the rights of the poor man would immediately cease to be secure.

The last word seemed to have been spoken, but New York asked that the question be put off for a day, and Franklin took the opportunity to move that a moment of prayer be instituted each morning before debate. Sherman seconded the motion and supported it against a number of objections. A vote was never held, however, and the suggestion of prayers died with the day's adjournment.

On Friday, June 29, Johnson once more pointed out that if the states were to continue to exist at all, they must be given enough influence to protect themselves. States were both districts of people and separate entities, he said, and the two capacities should be combined in the general government. The Connecticut lawyer proclaimed his support for Sherman's compromise; in one branch the people ought to be represented, in the other the states. Madison replied with his usual strong opposition to equal suffrage among the states; such a principle was unjust, could never be admitted "& if admitted must infuse mortality into a Constitution which we wished to last forever." On a pair of votes to determine the suffrage in the lower house, Connecticut, New York, New Jersey, and Delaware were for equal suffrage, with Maryland divided, and the majority for proportional suffrage.

But Johnson, with Ellsworth seconding, now moved successfully for an immediate consideration of the resolution providing for an equal vote in the upper house. Ellsworth made the major speech, again presenting the Connecticut view that a proportional suffrage in the lower house would be wholly acceptable if equality obtained in the upper. "We were partly national; partly federal," he said. The significance of Ellsworth's speech lies in the emphasis he placed on the necessity of compromise on these grounds. "And if no compromise should take place, our meeting would not only be in vain but worse than in vain." All the eastern states but Massachusetts would "risk every consequence rather than part with so dear a right."

Madison's response was one of his least commendable efforts of the Convention. He pointed to alleged errors in Ellsworth's reasoning, and in his facts. He even went so far as to charge Connecticut with bad faith in its obligations to the Confederation. Ellsworth responded in kind, retorting that Connecticut had more troops in the field during the late war than had

Virginia. Sherman now stepped in to bring Madison back to his usual good sense. The senior Connecticut delegate observed that Madison had set about name-calling when he should have been showing the faults of the present Congressional suffrage. "Congs. is not to blame for the faults of the States," said Sherman as he steered the discussion back to safer ground. National "measures have been right, and the only thing wanting has been a further power in Congs. to render them effectual."

Now Wilson had a compromise to offer. Let there be one representative in the upper house for every hundred thousand people in the state, with every state guaranteed at least one. King and Madison found this attractive, but Luther Martin did not. Franklin had his own solution. There should be one house with states having equal votes on questions of sovereignty, authority, and appointment of officers, but proportional suffrage in all other legislation. King did not comment on Franklin's proposal, but announced, "The Connecticut motion contains all the vices of the old confederation. . . . And should this convention adopt the motion, our business here is at an end." (June 30, Yates' Notes)

Young Gunning Bedford then poured forth a tirade that was as embarrassing as it was revealing. He charged the large states with assuming a dictatorial air, and attempting to aggrandize themselves at the expense of their small neighbors. Further, he threatened that the small states would find some foreign ally, if the large states failed to compromise. Ellsworth was infected by Bedford's passion and spoke sharply about the importance of the states as protectors of individual rights. If his reasoning, he concluded, "was not satisfactory, he had nothing to add that could be so." Another fiery speech by King, and the house thought best to adjourn and bring to an end the bitterest day of the Convention which, fortunately, was a Saturday.

Early Monday morning there was a division on Ellsworth's motion for an equal suffrage in the upper house. Five states voted for and five against with Georgia split, Connecticut-raised Abraham Baldwin casting his lot with his former neighbors. C. C. Pinckney proposed the election of a committee to resolve the impasse. Most speakers, with the notable exceptions of Wilson and Madison, supported Pinckney. Sherman's comment that "We are now at a full stop, and nobody he supposed meant that we shd. break up without doing something," seemed to express the general sentiment.

The committee was appointed, consisting of one man from each state, and heavily stacked with federal rather than national spokesmen. Gerry, Ellsworth, Yates, Paterson, Bedford, and Martin were among the front rank of those pushing the federal view. Mason, Davie, and Baldwin were more federal in their leaning than national, though the Virginian was "a friend to proportional representation in both branches." Even Rutledge was not an extreme nationalist. Benjamin Franklin was very much inclined toward nationalism, but was more of a conciliator and at eighty-one was not much of a fighter. It would seem that the outcome of the committee deliberations was a foregone conclusion, but to make the result even more certain, Ellsworth became "indisposed" and gave up his spot to Roger Sherman. That was on the 2nd of July. The committee was to report back on the 5th, leaving time to attend the celebration of the anniversary of Independence.

The committee thus constituted did not have things all one way, however.[4] Despite the preponderance of federally oriented members, the split was about even for proportional representation in both houses on one hand, and equal representation in both on the other. Probably these initial positions were taken for bargaining purposes, because the reason for the committee's existence was compromise, not disruption. At one point Franklin revived his arrangement that would give control over finances and appointments to a majority of the people, other questions to be decided by equal state suffrage. Sherman resurrected his ancient plan of 1776, that a vote be taken twice, once by states and once by individuals, a majority on both counts necessary for passage. The new version would have no act passed unless the majority of states voting for it also compromised a majority of the inhabitants of the United States. But no one showed any particular interest.

The compromise ultimately produced by the committee provided for a lower house with suffrage based on relative population—one member for each 40,000—and an upper house in which the state suffrage would be equal. This was almost exactly Sherman's proposal of June 11. Franklin's views prevailed only on finance, and it was provided that all money bills and regulation of salaries must originate in the lower house and were not to be amendable by the Senate. Very much in line with Sherman's thinking and earlier proposal was the condition that each of the provisions was mutually conditional on the acceptance of the others.

The report both in the form of its presentation and, of course, its substance, was received stormily by the nationalists. Debate of the next two days was warming rather than enlightening; a new committee was appointed to reconsider the 1 to 40,000 ratio; and individuals were rent by conflicting pressures for and against concessions.

On Saturday, July 7, the question of equal suffrage in the second house was taken up. Gerry rightly pointed out that this was the critical question, and he for one was willing to accept the committee's report rather than have no agreement at all. But he would prefer to wait until the committee on ratio of representatives to population, appointed on the day before, had made its statement. At this crucial moment Sherman spoke for the first time since the Gerry Committee reported. He asserted, somewhat tactlessly, that the small states had more vigor than the large ones, and that it was easier to "collect the real & fair sense of the people" in the smaller. "Fallacy & undue influence will be practiced with most success" in the large states, he continued with uncharacteristic pugnacity, "and improper men will most easily get into office." Therefore the small states must be given at least equal influence in the national government if it were to have any real vigor.

Sherman then made it clear that his understanding of the compromise report was essentially what he had proposed first in 1776 and then at the Convention. "If they vote by States in the 2nd branch, and each State had an equal vote, there must always be a majority of States as well as a majority of the people on the side of public measures, & the Govt. will have decision and efficacy." It was a practical matter of making the government work; "If this be not the case in the 2nd branch there may be a majority of the States agst. public measures, and the difficulty of compelling them to abide by the public determination, will render the Government feebler than it has ever yet been."

Only Wilson challenged the old compromiser, and a division showed a majority for equal suffrage in the upper house. But Madison notes that several votes were aye or divided because the question was to be taken on the whole proposition later. Sherman and Ellsworth moved successfully to postpone the final vote until the committee on ratio of representation had reported. That report came in on July 9, but was unacceptable to Sherman and others, so he proposed a new committee upon which he sat. This committee, in turn, reported the next day, and its sixty-five-member house was accepted. The next several days were taken up by a consideration of the basis of representation in the lower house, in particular the status of Negroes. Connecticut supported the three-fifths concept, though Johnson believed that it would be proper to count all Negroes, since they represented property which was worth consideration in the suffrage.

Slavery, of course, later on came to be the dominant issue of the nineteenth century, and the status of blacks has profoundly influenced American historiography in the mid-twentieth century.* However, the

---

*Efforts by historians to tie slavery and western lands together as aspects of various deals, while interesting and not improbable, are greatly invested with conjecture and informed by the predictable political predilections of their proponents. Lacking more

Connecticut delegation was not seriously concerned with the issue. There were a few thousand slaves in the state in 1787, between 1 and 2 percent of the population, and gradual emancipation had been provided for without significant debate in 1784. There were no slave shippers in the state. Sherman opposed slavery, though he was hardly emotional about the issue. He "disapproved of the slave trade," he said on August 22.

> yet as the States were now possessed of the right to import slaves, as the public good did not require it to be taken from them, & as it was expedient to have as few objections as possible to the proposed scheme of Government, he thought it best to leave the matter as we find it. He observed that the abolition of slavery seem to be going on in the U.S. & that the good sense of the several States would probably by degrees Compleat it.

It was better, he said, to let the southern states import slaves than to try to do without those states. But he was opposed to duties on slaves because it would imply that they were property. And, presumably on moral grounds, he thought that if given the authority to prohibit importation, the general government ought to exercise it. He said again during the First Congress in 1789 that slaves ought not to be taxed by import duties because he "could not reconcile himself to the insertion of human beings as an article of duty, among goods, wares, and merchandise." He wrote three years later about the West Indian uprisings that "Congress will not interfere. . . , by assisting either party—I wish it may be a means of putting an end to the Slave trade and to Slavery—I hope the revolution in France will contribute to that event." Sherman was not much concerned about slavery, since he believed it an

---

substantial evidence for these accounts, for which I have sought, I cannot report them as part of what I hope is a factual narrative. See McDonald, *E Pluribus Unum*, pp. 176–77, 298 n48; Barry, *Rutledge*, pp. 329–32; Lynd, "The Compromise of 1787," in *Political Science Quarterly*, June, 1966. McDonald's case is considerably weakened by his belief that "Connecticut had no carrying trade" for her delegates to protect.

The generally accepted interpretation that the northern states traded off their abolitionist sentiments in order to get the states of the deep South to acquiesce in national trade regulation seems best supported by the evidence available. Farrand, *Records*, II:449, 449n.

But all three, Farrand, Lynd, and McDonald—to say nothing of Charles A. Beard—greatly oversimplify the issue. Slavery, western lands, and trade regulation all were important elements in the compromise. But so, too, were questions of representation, taxation, payment of war debts, the funding of state and national securities, and even personal relations among the delegates. See, for instance, James Madison's immensely complex analysis of the interrelationships of these issues four years before the Convention in Hutchinson, *Madison Papers*, VI:290-92, 441 n6, and the editors' notes, pp. 292-97. If, however, for some, slavery was the central issue, for Sherman, it was not.

expiring institution. He could become far more passionate about western lands or paper money.*

The dominating factors in determining the positions taken by Sherman and his Connecticut colleagues—one of whom was a slaveholder—in the Convention were the will to compromise in order to give new economic powers to the U. S. government while maintaining most of the rules of the old Confederation. The proportion of Negroes to be counted toward taxation and representation had come up in 1776 and continued to arise sporadically thereafter. In the old Congress, in March 1783, the discussion on rating slaves took place within the context of relative evaluations of state property. It was therefore to Connecticut's interest that slaves be rated as high as possible. A committee report recommended a ratio which would count half the slaves. Oliver Wolcott moved to alter this to three-fourths, and he and Dyer would have accepted two-thirds. Both voted against the three-fifths compromise at that time. When the ratio came in as part of the tax package of April 18, 1783, Ellsworth, a principal author of the bill, had replaced Wolcott, and he and Dyer—a slave holder—agreed to accept three-fifths.[5]

On Saturday, July 14, Convention debate began again on Martin's motion that a vote take place immediately on the July 5 report in its entirety. Sherman agreed that there was no point in debating the compromise plan any longer. But tempted by an acrimonious exchange between blunt-spoken Luther Martin and James Wilson of Pennsylvania, and an attempt by Charles Pinckney to reintroduce proportions in the upper house, the old campaigner risked one more foray. His support for equality in the Senate, Sherman vowed, grew out of his desire not so much to protect the small states as such, but rather to protect the states as states—large or small. It was necessary to make this clear now, for though Sherman's basic conviction throughout the Convention had remained constant, he had frequently used small-state-large-

---

*By 1790 the number of slaves in New Haven was down to not much over eighty, including four or five children born since the emancipation act of 1784. An anti-slavery society, usually referred to as the African Society, was established in 1790, drawing membership largely from Sherman's church, Jonathan Edwards Jr. himself a member. The leading figure in the Society was Sherman's son-in-law, Simeon Baldwin, who drew up a petition the Society sent to Congress in January, 1791. The aims of this group were not abolition, but rather the prohibition of slave trade and the enforcement of the Connecticut statute of '84 freeing at age twenty-five all those born into slavery after that date, and of '88, prohibiting any connection with the slave trade to citizens of Connecticut. I do not find that Roger Sherman was a member. Baldwin also promoted a colonization society in 1818, but with no success. In 1772 Baldwin had inherited a twenty-one-year-old black man; there is no evidence that he manumitted him. Baldwin, *Baldwin*. pp. 311-17; *Journal*. September 8, 1790, February 9, 16, 1791. See also Logan, "Slavery in Connecticut."

state terms in the debate over his compromise. He also made it clear that he had no objection to a plan just suggested by Gerry that there be two senators from each state instead of one, and that each be permitted to vote separately. Later he reiterated his belief that though the general legislature would ordinarily act on the *federal* principle of requiring quotas of tax monies, it should be given *national* power to collect taxes itself if the states failed to comply.

At last on Monday July 16, the whole report came to a vote, and it was carried successfully. Massachusetts was divided, but the other large states with Georgia made up a minority of three. The report called for a proportionally constructed house of sixty-five members, with constitutional requirements for periodic censuses and reapportionments. The power over money bills was to be exclusively vested in the lower house, and the upper was to provide equal suffrage for the states.

On July 23, Gouverneur Morris and Rufus King moved that there be more than one senator in the upper house, each with his own vote. Sherman had left for home at the end of the previous week, but Ellsworth expressed Sherman's views in supporting the proposal. On the final motion dealing with the Connecticut Compromise, that the upper house shall consist of two members from each state and the vote shall be per capita, Ellsworth voted aye with all the states but Maryland. It is not likely that Sherman's absence changed the outcome of his compromise proposal in any way. Indeed, it is not likely that he would have left the Convention if there had been any serious doubt of its passage.

One last alteration was made in the compromise plan as originally reported by Gerry's committee on July 5. On August 8 a short debate led to a vote to expunge the clause giving the lower house exclusive authority over money bills. Connecticut, with Massachusetts, New Hampshire, and North Carolina, were in the minority for preserving the compromise inviolate, and the clause was struck out. On the 11th the question was taken up again, however, with only Maryland and New Jersey voting to let the sleeping dog lie. Connecticut voted against a motion to limit Senate power over money bills, but also voted against a clause that provided for origination in the House and amendment in the Senate. Both proposals lost, and so did one that would have required appropriation bills to originate in the House, against which Connecticut also voted. Apparently Connecticut delegates were willing to renege on that part of the compromise which gave the lower house exclusive jurisdiction, though on September 5 Sherman hinted that he would give the large states their way on the revenue question if in return the states were given dominance in the election of the president. But on the 8th of September it was agreed unanimously that the Senate would have the authority to propose or concur with amendments to money bills originating in the House.

Ratification in Connecticut

Back in Connecticut the work of the Philadelphia Convention was almost universally approved. Newspapers carried only laudatory comment and once or twice had to defend themselves against charges of bias. On September 26, 1787 the Constitution was published, and on November 5 Sherman's and Ellsworth's letter of transmittal to the Governor appeared. After October 1 the towns began to petition for a state convention, with Sherman's New Haven leading the way, and on October 29 the General Assembly issued the formal call.

Connecticut was the first to take such a step, and the *Courant* complimented the people on their good sense. Though report had come to Connecticut in June that the Convention was trying to "preserve the form, but effectively destroy the spirit of democracy," the public dialogue that ensued was one-sided to say the least.[6] Virtually no anti-federal comment was printed, a circumstance that the editors of the *Courant* attributed to the fact that no opposition views were sent in. Moreover, added the editors, they saw no need to publish out-of-state essays. But their word is suspect, for the only accounts of legislative debate published during 1787, and of the ratifying convention of 1788, were written by Enoch Perkins, a young Hartford Federalist. In late '86 Perkins had written privately to a friend that the provincials were "acting a part that is unreasonable, dishonest and injurious to the public; They are likewise ridiculous objects." It was hardly to be expected that fair reporting would flow from Perkins' prejudiced pen. An old Son of Liberty, Hugh Ledlie of Windham wrote to an anti-federalist friend in New York that prejudiced newspapers were only part of the problem. Threats had been made that opponents of the Constitution would be shut out of political preferment.* Besides, the federalists had all the "best Writers (as well as speakers) on their side," and these men of "Superior rank" bullied what would have been an anti-federal majority at the convention. New York papers

---

*Ledlie was right. Sometime early in Washington's administration Federalists in Connecticut refused to approve U. S. army commissions for known anti-federalists. Joseph Jewit, for instance, "a bitter Democrat . . . must be able to show he is a federalist." CSL, "Governor Joseph Trumbull Collection," #324. "List of Officers" made up by Henry Knox and transmitted to Jeremiah Wadsworth by Uriah Tracy. n. d.

did circulate in Connecticut, and copies of Richard Henry Lee's anti-federal *Letters of a Federal Farmer* were sent to William Williams and Stephen Mix Mitchell.[7]

The job of presenting the federal argument fell largely to Oliver Ellsworth. He wrote thirteen letters signed "Landholder" that ran through November and December and then continued as appeals to New Hampshire voters even after Connecticut had ratified.[8] In the earliest of these letters Ellsworth listed the enemies of the Constitution as of four classes: (1) the old friends of Great Britain; (2) debtors "who have not resolution to be either honest or industrious"; (3) politicians "not of sufficient importance to obtain public employment, but [who] can spread jealousies in the little districts of [the] country where they are placed"; (4) men with lucrative state offices who were afraid they would be swallowed up by the larger government.

The principal weight of the argument fell in two areas. The first was the necessity to convince the people that the new plan was not destructive of liberty. Early opposition to sending delegates to Philadelphia in the first place had centered on this question, and the inland towns remained very suspicious. The second and most important basis of argument was founded on economics. Here the question was, would Connecticut gain more through free trade than she would lose through increased taxation? William Samuel Johnson reported that the power of taxing anything other than imports was the most discussed topic at the ratifying convention.

Sherman was busy around the state drumming up support for the new plan. In December, for instance, he visited Hugh Ledlie, who described himself as now just an old "ploughjogger," to talk up the document, for as, Sherman's new son-in-law pointed out, in Connecticut "the farmers are all politicians." Baldwin, indeed, had "been diverted to hear the very trifling & yet very different objections which are made to [the Constitution] by different peasants." It is generally conceded that Sherman was the most active of the three delegates in promoting the Constitution. Indeed, William S. Johnson did not even return to Connecticut until the ratifying convention in January.[9] Sherman wrote five letters published in the *New Haven Gazette* and the *Connecticut Courant* in November and December signed "A Countryman." The basis of these letters was apparently a pair of draft documents that he drew up at this time.[10] These documents are largely defensive in that they were intended to answer objections to the Constitution raised by Gerry in Massachusetts and by Mason in Virginia. As a public expression of Sherman's views of the work of the Philadelphia Convention they hold considerable interest.

Sherman made six points, all of them aimed at showing that the new plan in no way diminished the liberties of the people of the states. First, he proved the necessity of an executive separate from the legislature. The principal fault in the old Congress, he continued, was its lack of power to carry out its responsibilities, so the legislature "should be . . . vested with plenary powers for all the purposes for which it is instituted. . . ." Then, to quiet traditional Connecticut fears, he emphasized that the legislature was well checked by the mode of representation, the power of the states, and the Constitution itself. Nor would the president and vice-president threaten liberty. The mode of election and their re-eligibility will provide great security against "arbitrary government, either monarchial or aristocratic."

"There are few powers vested in the new government," he wrote to quiet the fears of the provincials, "but what the present Congress have power to do or require to be done." These new powers are exclusively, he claimed, "to regulate Commerce, provide for a uniform practice with regard to naturalization, Bankruptcies, and forming and training the Militia, and for the punishment of certain crimes against the united states, and for promoting the progress of science in the mode therein pointed out, . . . These appear to be necessary for the common benefit of the Union, and can't be effectually provided for by the particular States. . . ." Then he stated a position that, had he lived into 1798, would have given him considerable embarrassment:

> all acts of the Congress not warranted by the constitution would be void, nor could they be enforced contrary to the sense of a majority of the States.—One excellency of the constitution is that when the government of the united states acts within its proper bounds it will be the interest of the legislatures of the particular States to support it, but when it overleaps those bounds and interferes with the rights of the State governments, they will be powerful enough to check it; but the distinctions between their jurisdictions will be so obvious, that there will be no great danger of interference.

The charge that the Convention acted illegally was false because "though they have formed a new instrument including the former and additional powers, yet it is not more than an amendment of the present Constitution in those matters wherein it was really deficient." Expenditures, he assured his Yankee constituents, should not be expected to rise, and taxes would be necessary only occasionally. Sufficient revenue would be derived from import duties and sale of western lands, occasional taxes would be levied according to a fair per capita ratio. And finally in his second paper, dated December 8, he mentioned that the courts would be limited and "perhaps not one to an hundred of the citizens will ever have a cause that will come within its jurisdiction." While Ellsworth hammered away at the economic benefits of the new plan in most of his letters, Sherman gave himself to quieting the fears of the democratically inclined.

Despite the activities of the nationalists, doubts persisted as to both the efficacy and the republicanism of the new system. "I think there is not Power enough yet given to Congress for firm Government," wrote the President of Yale a week before the state ratification convention opened.

> Neither can I see how far it is safe to surrender the powers of the States to the Imperial Body, without 1. prostatg. the Sovereignty of the particular states. 2. Without laying the Founda. of the Presidents growing up into an uncontrollable & absolute Monarch. And yet I think the last as well guarded as possible: and I know not whether it is possible to vest Congress with Laws, Revenues, & Army & Navy, without endangering the Ruin of the interior Powers & Liberties of the States.[11]

With men like Ezra Stiles so ambivalent, the nationalists had cause to worry. Old Benjamin Gale, congratulating William S. Johnson on retiring from politics to assume the presidency of Columbia College, was sure that a "scene of Blood and Carnage was Approaching and I Conceived by Rapid Strides. . . ." But Columbia's trustees thought Johnson more important in Hartford than New York in January, and urged him to go to the state ratifying convention.[12]

The elections for delegates to the ratifying convention were held in accordance with the plan laid down by the General Assembly in October. Each town was permitted to choose the same number of representatives that it was entitled to in the Assembly, and unrepresented Barkhampstead and Colebrook were to have single delegates also. The *Courant* printed this information on October 22, and a week later it suggested that the best possible representatives would be members of the Superior Court, that is, Sherman, Ellsworth, Dyer, Richard Law, and William Pitkin. At least a third of the members of the ratifying convention had been members of the previous General Assembly and in many cases the towns merely returned both of their delegates.

Some opposition to aristocracy continued, for Jonathan Trumbull reported to Washington that he had not been chosen because he was "under the cloud of the Cincinnati." But the Cincinnati was well accepted by Connecticut's establishment and even wangled an invitation to march in Yale's commencement procession in September—an exercise attended by Sherman, who went to watch Roger, Jr. receive his diploma.[13] The Governor,

Lieutenant Governor, and former Governor Griswold were all selected. As a matter of fact, among those chosen were two governors, a lieutenant governor, seven assistants, the five judges of the Superior Court, and ten generals, plus numerous other lower officers and civil functionaries. It was, said Dr. Stiles, "the grandest Assemblage of sensible & worthy Characters that ever met together in this State." Almost one-third of the members had been soldiers in the Revolution. The day after convention elections were held, however, Ashbel Baldwin, an Episcopal minister, wrote his bishop in Vermont, "The new Constitution is out, the Egg-shell is broke—but 'tis impossible as yet to determine how it is relished. . . . There will be powerful opposition to it in Connecticut. . . . The Yeas and Nays in several adjacent towns [to Litchfield] were taken, and a great majority against it, and members appointed accordingly; in short we are much divided; anarchy, I am afraid, is approaching."[14]

The delegates convened on January 3 in the old State House in Hartford, where they organized and promptly adjourned to the Meeting House of the First Society, which had new stoves. The galleries were opened to the public, and attendance was good.[15] There was an immediate decision to discuss the new constitution section by section, but not to vote until the whole had been read. This was obviously a victory for the nationalists. The nationalists were led by Ellsworth, who offered the opening speech, followed by William Samuel Johnson. William Williams, who ultimately voted for the new plan, objected to the clause in Article VI that precluded religious tests, claiming that there must be an express belief in God stated in a preamble to the document.[16]

The debate ended without any serious threat from the anti-federalists, and without any reported speeches by Sherman. The old politician did not remain silent, however. His earliest biographer asserts that the success of the federalists was "owing in a considerable degree to the influence and arguments" and the "great plainness and perspicacity" of Sherman's section-by-section explanation of the document. As the more ebullient reporter for the *Connecticut Courant* put it,

> The Convention got through with debating upon the constitution by sections. It was canvassed critically and fully. Every objection was raised against it, which the ingenuity and invention of its opposers could devise. . . . Suffice it to say, that all the objections to the Constitution vanished, before the learning and eloquence of a Johnson, the genuine good sense and discernment of a Sherman, and Demosthenesian energy of an Ellsworth.[17]

In view of the evidence, it may be concluded that Sherman took on the task of interpreting phraseology and answering questions on specific matters, while Ellsworth dealt more in general terms.

Provincial strength was still strong, though nationalists were confident of ratification. Debate, however, wore down the antis, and after five days Ezra Stiles could write that "about two thirds of the Convention . . . are for the new Constitution." But James Wadsworth pushed hard. No one could ever be safe, he said, under a government that held powers of both purse and sword. The taxing and impost systems of the new government benefited the southern states at the expense of New England. And certainly the whole concept of two legislative bodies, state and national, operating within the same sphere was unworkable and unsafe.[18]

The nationalists fought back with equanimity. They never appear to have lost mastery of the situation. Perhaps their greatest gain was achieved by Ellsworth's nearly explicit promise that the state debt would be taken over by the U. S.* The fact that Sherman would support the new government must have convinced other state creditors that they would be as well, if not better off, with nationalism. Only seven towns are known to have instructed their delegates to vote against the document, and many had instructed for. The roll would be called out publicly. When it was, even William Williams, a leading provincial, broke his instructions and declared for nationalism. Though he was the only one to actually break his people's trust, the two instructed antis from Hamden remained silent, rather than vote against.[19] About a dozen other identifiable provincials finally voted for the Constitution. Even Stephen Mix Mitchell who had so opposed the idea of an extra-Congressional convention voted for ratification. Jeremiah Wadsworth, sure that the popular view would be overridden, had written three weeks before the state convention that Mitchell "is right now; as far as his popular *itch* will let him be he will vote right."**

It passed easily on January 9, 128 to 40, on Samuel Holden Parson's motion "That this convention do assent to, ratify and adopt the Constitution

---

*An authoritative, though biased, correspondent wrote in 1800 that "the funding of the [state] debt has been . . . a principal means of enriching our farmers." Beard, *Economic Origins*, p. 363.

** Mitchell's "popular *itch*" caught up with him in 1794. He had been appointed to the Senate upon the death of Roger Sherman, but being on the "borders of phrensy," resigned after one year, "unwilling to encounter another Winters Storm of Politicks. . . ." CSL, "Hubbard Collection," Chauncy Goodrich to Jeremiah Wadsworth (May 5, 1794), Jonathan Trumbull to John Trumbull (November 10, 1794).

by the Convention of Delegates in Philadelphia on the 17th Day of September A.D. 1787 and referred to the determination of this Convention by an act of General Assembly in October last."* Young Enoch Perkins, who reported the Convention at the request of the *Courant*, wrote a friend that "Upon the whole, every thing relating to this important transaction, was conducted with good policey & decorum. . . ." But ploughjogging Hugh Ledlie claimed that he had heard that debate "was carried on . . . with a high hand against those that disapproved thereof, for . . . when the [antis] were speaking . . . they were browbeaten by many . . . of Superior rank . . . together with Shuffling & Stamping of feet, caughing, Talking, spitting & wispering. . . . All their Menaces & Strategems were used by a Junto who tries to carry all before them in this State. . . ."[20]**

The antis, who had been strong enough in 1786 to block sending delegates to Annapolis, had reached their high-water mark early in '87. But the uncovering of a Shaysite plot in hilly Sharon, coupled with increased economic stringency throughout the state, weakened their hold on the agrarian citizens. The anti-nationalists in Connecticut consisted of non-security-holding farmers who had opposed the Confederation impost and the commutation of officers' bonus to one-half pay for seven years. The holders of state bonds had earlier been part of this anti-national coalition that

---

*Actually the representatives of a mere third of the population could have brought about ratification, because of the usual malapportionment of the lower house. However, since nationalists tended to come from underrepresented places, and provincials from overrepresented rural areas, it is unlikely that malapportionment worked to the advantage of the antis.

Indeed, the most accurate tabulation available estimates that the 128 delegates voting for ratification—76 percent of those present and voting—represented about 78 percent of the population (Roll, "We, Some of the People,"p. 26. But Roll seems to have figured it to be 74 percent instead of 76 percent). There is no way, of course, of knowing whether the delegates accurately represented their constituents. As is evident from the foregoing discussion, it is my opinion that many did not: I see much greater support for the anti position than the statistics alone would indicate. Recall, for instance, Jeremiah Wadsworth's statement that though the Assembly wished a stronger U. S. government, he thought it uncertain that the people did. See above, p. 226.

**Privately Perkins wrote that James Wadsworth attacked the Constitution pugnaciously, and Eliphalet Dyer did so "to shew his wisdom & importance, & to shew that other men did not know as much as *I* . . . he talked . . . till he disgusted every single soul who heard him." Perkins added, "After the grand question was decided, Gen. Wadsworth & some of his coadjutors being together, could not help expressing their chagrin at the defection of Col. Williams & Mr. Hopkins. One of them (I am told) speaking of the latter, called him a Copper [worthless]. Gen. W——th replied, don't call him weathercock." Yale, Hist. Ms. Room, "Baldwin Family Collection." Perkins to Simeon Baldwin (January 15, 1788).

dominated the lower house throughout the Confederation years. The defection of this influential group to the nationalist cause during the state convention made ratification inevitable. The major factor in anti-national strength seems to have been the leadership given by such men as James Wadsworth, for the antis' forty votes came from three local geographical areas: eight towns in Wadsworth's New Haven County, where thirteen out of twenty delegates voted no; the hill country along the Massachusetts line in the northwest; and a group of towns in the east central and northeast corner of the state.[21]

The winning combination in Connecticut was vocal opposition to the Constitution coupled with a vote for it. In the April elections Erastus Wolcott's vote was way up to second on the list, and William Williams was returned as well. In addition, Wolcott was included with a list of eleven nationalists as nominees to the last session of the old Congress. James Wadsworth on the other hand had plummeted to thirteenth, and was thus thrown off the Council. Wadsworth was deprived of his office of comptroller, the highest paying job the state had to give, including even the governorship. This act of spite so incensed the hardy provincial that he rejected appointment to the New Haven County Court the next year because it would have required him to take an oath to uphold the national constitution.* The Assembly even went so far as to oust anti-nationalist Ephraim Carpenter, William Williams' co-delegate from Lebanon, as Windham County justice of the peace. Of the forty delegates voting against the Constitution, only about half were returned to the Assembly in April.[22]

The ratification was received with apparent joy in the City of New Haven, at least by the "better sort" in town. Ezra Stiles wrote that the Constitution had been ratified at 5:30 on January 9, and that a courier got the news to New Haven before 11:00. "At XII.25' this Morng," he wrote the next day, "the four Bells in the city began and continued to ring above an hour and ceased at Ih 40' during which thirteen Cannon were discharged."[23]

---

*In October 1789, Wadsworth refused to accept the judgeship, writing that he "must . . . decline taking the Oath to support the new Constitution—with the most fervent Wishes that the Rights and Privileges of Freemen may be enjoyed by the Citizens of this and other of the United States and perpetuated to the latest Generation." But the Assembly sympathized, and, though it replaced Wadsworth with Samuel Bishop—one of Connecticut's earliest Jeffersonians—the requirement which had been enacted in January was repealed in October. CSL, "Revolutionary War," Ser. 1. XXXVII:297; SR, VII:71, 71n. Sherman had anticipated Wadsworth's objection when at Philadelphia on June 11 he had remarked that requiring such oaths was "unnecessarily intruding into the State jurisdictions."

Sherman was well satisfied with his work. He wrote William Floyd that perhaps a better constitution "could not be made on mere speculation," and it provided an "easy and peaceable mode of making amendments. If it should not be adopted, I think we shall be in deplorable circumstances." Sherman's reference to the easy and peaceable mode of making amendments is ironic when it is observed how hard he tried to make such measures difficult just the year after ratification.[24]

CHAPTER XIV

No Rest for the Weary and Aged

WITH the new Constitution safely passed and about to become functional, Connecticut voters selected a pair of Senators and five Representatives. Sherman was certainly the obvious choice for the upper house in view of his long service in the national government. But he was passed over when the Assembly balloted on October 15 in favor of the younger and more eloquent Oliver Ellsworth and the highly esteemed William Samuel Johnson, recently appointed president of Columbia College, now residing in New York.* Sherman's lack of polish again played into the hands of his high-federalist rivals and caused him to be left out. But on this occasion he could take some satisfaction in the appointments, for as Johnson had been Sherman's legal mentor some forty years earlier, so Sherman had been Ellsworth's. John Adams wrote once, alluding to Sherman's lack of formal education, "Destitute of all literary and scientific education, but such as he acquired by his own exertions, he was one of the most sensible men in the world. The clearest head and steadiest heart. It is praise enough to say, that . . . Ellsworth . . . told me he had made Mr. Sherman his model in his youth. Indeed I never knew two men more alike, except that the Chief Justice had the advantage of a liberal education, and somewhat more extensive reading."[1]

National Service Again

Connecticut chose to elect its U. S. Representatives in the same manner used since 1779 to elect delegates to the Confederation Congress. Nomina-

---

*In the Senate Johnson drew a third-class term—six years, and Ellsworth a first-class term—two years. They were chosen by the Assembly on October 15, 1788. *Connecticut Journal*, May 20, 1789; "House Journal 1788–1790," p. 8. Ellsworth was elected to a six-year term on October 25, 1790. "House Journal 1790–1791," n.p. October 25, 1790.

tions would be made at general elections in November, with the town clerks submitting all names and votes to a committee of one man from each county—individually named in the enabling act. This committee would return to the towns twelve names having the highest vote, and in December town meetings would be called at which freemen would cast ballots for five of the twelve. There were no districts, and anyone not excluded by the Constitution was eligible.[2] This could have meant trouble for Sherman, because he had never won a popular election to the old Congress. But he was chosen in this apparently uncontentious election to go to the House, fourth on the nominations and second in the election, along with the usual geographical distribution among the other four. They were Jonathan Sturges of Fairfield, Benjamin Huntington of Norwich in New London County, Jonathan Trumbull, son of the Revolutionary governor, of Lebanon, then in Windham County, and Jeremiah Wadsworth of Hartford.* The Commissary General was Connecticut's chief financial beneficiary of the war, now said to be worth between £60,000 to £80,000 sterling.[3]

The election was something of an embarrassment to Sherman, for the Assembly had prohibited the concurrent holding of Federal office and that of Judge of the Superior Court. Judges were needed on the state circuit and had been sorely missed during earlier Congresses, it was said, but of course another reason for this separation was to break up the concentration of power in the hands of the establishment. Sherman had been elected to the high court every year since 1766, and he was reluctant to leave it now.[4] He wrote Governor Huntington protesting that he had given his services to the nation for long years, and had been a good deal of the time away from home. He wished to serve the people of his state as they saw fit, but would prefer to retain the position of Superior Court Judge. Indeed, he made his acceptance of the federal office conditional on being able to continue on the bench. If the legislature would not make this allowance, Sherman would "desire a little further time to consider and advise on this matter." The legislature did not see fit to make exceptions for Sherman, but he decided finally to "abdicate" his judgeship and go to New York, anyway. He took final leave of his twenty-three-year berth on the bench after the mid-February court session.[5]

When Sherman arrived in New York on March 5, 1789, he found a congress that was to exhibit some of the oddest political switches imaginable.

---

*The other seven in nomination were: Stephen Mix Mitchell, John Chester, James Hillhouse, Erastus Wolcott, Jesse Root, John Treadwell, and Jedidiah Strong. The certification took place on January 1, 1789. *SR*, VI:496; "House Journal 1788–1790," n.p. (November 26, 1788, January 7, 1789).

The body was almost totally federalist, a point most sharply made by the defeat of archprovincial Sam Adams by thirty-one-year-old Fisher Ames in the Boston congressional elections. From Connecticut Sherman was the strongest advocate of states' rights in the delegation and even he soon became a man marked by his economic nationalism. But James Madison, defeated in his bid for the Senate, went to Congress to become Sherman's principal adversary—in the startling role of guardian of the states!

It would take a while for positions to shift, and in the meantime things looked bright and unclouded for the nationalists. Only Virginia had sent anti-nationalists to Congress, and even they were lukewarm at first. The screaming radicals of '76, John Adams, now presiding in the Senate, and R. H. Lee, elected to that body as an anti-federalist, worked vigorously, though unsuccessfully, to plaster Mr. George Washington with the title "His Highness the President of the United States and Protector of the Rights of the Same."[6] They were odd times, indeed, and Sherman, now approaching his three score years and ten, would once again be put to test. Was he still the political character capable of not only reconciling conscience with constituents, but now also with Constitution? The first test was an easy one, for the Connecticut congressman had always been an economic nationalist.

Establishing A Revenue

Naturally, the initial matter to be taken up by the First Congress was the revenue. Indeed, had the states given the old Congress authority to levy duties for a national revenue, the Philadelphia Convention might never have taken place. Sherman had been intimately involved with the problem since 1776, and actually served in that year on the first national committee ever to deal with the topic. Time and time again through the war and Confederation years he had worked to establish an independent national income through import duties.[7] Now he was to plod through the whole tedious business again—but this time successfully.

An import tax was the way to do it, he was sure. He had written his wife's brother-in-law that respecting an impost "much will depend on Gentlemen in the commercial line for supporting the public measures. You justly observe that Impost appears almost the only practicable method of raising monies for the exigencies of Government. . . . One great object that the States had in view on Instituting the new government was the advancement of justice and support of the public credit—if these objectives are not attained they will be disappointed. . . ." Over and over, beginning on the first day of debate,

Sherman rose in Congress to assert the necessity of at least moderate duties. Duties were more advisable than a direct tax because they were less felt by the people, and the people, knowing this, would approve them.[8]

It is impossible to judge how much of what Sherman wrote regarding the new government was out of genuine naivete, self-delusion, or for political purposes. He seemed to feel that direct taxes were not only undesirable, but not really intended. In referring the Constitution to Governor Huntington in 1787, he wrote that though direct taxation was provided for, "that authority need not be exercised, if each state will furnish its quota."[9] He was hardly thinking along the same lines as Hamilton. To the charge that, unlike excises, import duties discriminated against the commercial classes, Sherman replied,

> the consumer pays them eventually, and they pay no more than they choose, because they have it in their power to determine the quantity of taxable articles they use. . . . The merchant considers that part of his capital applied to the payment of duties the same as if employed in trade, and gets the same profit upon it as on the original cost of the commodity.

Sherman was also in favor of using the tariff to discourage the use of tobacco and brandy, but did not think that a ten-dollar tax on slaves would do much good in that direction. Besides, "He could not reconcile himself to the insertion of human beings as an article of duty, among goods, wares, and merchandise."[10]

Up to this point Sherman, who was one of the most frequent speakers for high duties, was in agreement with Madison, the principal Congressional advocate of the measure. Indeed, he wrote to Oliver Wolcott, Sr., on May 14, 1789, that "a Spirit of harmony and accommodation has been manifested from every part and the business has been done to the general satisfaction, except as to the duty on molasses. . . ."[11] But he parted company with Madison on the issue of discriminatory tonnage duties.

This disagreement arose from an attempt on the part of the Virginian to establish a system whereby goods imported into the United States in American ships would pay lower duties than those from other nations. Madison also wished to discriminate further against nations that refused to make commercial agreements with the United States—meaning specifically Great Britain. Sherman took the stand that such discrimination in favor of American shipping would bring reciprocal action from other countries. He noted that since Great Britain did not discriminate against the United States any more than against any other nation, Madison was inviting difficulty by proposing discrimination against her. Though the Southerner ultimately had his way in the House, the Senate cast out the discrimination against Great

Britain and made its decision stick. The bill as finally passed provided for 5 percent *ad valorem* on a long list of goods as the basic national revenue. The protective principle advocated by Madison was manifest in duties of up to 50 percent on such commodities as steel, cordage, tobacco, indigo, cloth, salt, and other domestic productions.[12]

The Public Credit

After the question of a regular revenue, the problem of the public credit loomed largest in the eyes of the new Congress. As a matter of fact, Sherman thought the payment of debts was basically more important than developing a regular national revenue. "The great object of Congress," he said on May 9,

> is to raise a sum of money adquate to supply our wants; and let us dispute as we will about the mode, the fact is it must be raised. The people have sent their representatives here for this purpose; it is for their benefit that we raise the money, and not for any particular advantage to ourselves; the objects are to pay the debts, and to provide for the general welfare of the community. The first of these objects I take to be, that we pay our debts [which had been neglected through] the imbecility of our former Government. . . . I believe it is the first wish of the people throughout the United States to do justice to the public creditors, and do it in such a manner, that each may contribute an equal part according to his abilities.[13]

It had been proposed to put the problem up to the Secretary of the Treasury by means of a Congressional order that he report on the specific needs and on ways and means. This was an apparent attempt to assert Congressional authority over Secretary Alexander Hamilton.[14] Sherman, from his Confederation background and the Connecticut experience, had spoken in favor of a single elected Treasury officer, and he now asserted that Congress had as much ability and authority to develop its own revenue plan as did Hamilton. Therefore he saw no need to force the Secretary to divulge his program at this time. However, in a tie vote, broken only by the Speaker, the Madison forces carried.[15]

Hamilton, following the old 1780 precedent, rejected any idea of scaling down the debt. He was determined to pay it all, in full and at face value. When Representative Scott of Pennsylvania claimed that Congress had the power to adjudicate the domestic debt—that is, to scale it down—Sherman rose immediately to the point. When creditors lent money based on specie value, he said, "I do not see but the public are bound by that contract, as much as an individual, and that they cannot reduce it down in either principal or interest, unless by an arbitrary power, and in that case there never will be any security in the public promises." Even a reduction in interest payments would destroy public confidence, for "Interest is as meritorious a part of the debt as the principal." Sherman was proving an even harder money man than Hamilton himself, who saw the political and fiscal necessity of reducing interest rates retroactively.[16]

Obviously the existing sources of the national revenue would be insufficient for repaying the old debt, and most Congressmen favored using the proceeds from public lands sales. Sherman was opposed to paying foreigners in land certificates because some might not want them, and conversely because others might be encouraged to emigrate here. Such emigration was undesirable because foreigners "are generally persons of different education, manners, and customs from the citizens of the Union, and not so likely to harmonize in a Republican Government as might be wished." However, he agreed that the domestic debt might be paid in either 4 percent bonds or land certificates. This would please Connecticut people particularly, he said, because "they are addicted to emigration as much as any part of the Union."[17]

Assumption and Discrimination

It being agreed that the national debt should be paid in full, the debate turned to the assumption of the state obligations. "On no part of Hamilton's schemes," writes one biographer,

> was there concentrated such a torrent of abuse, such weight of heated argument, such a maneuvering for position. Charges of bribery and corruption were tossed freely into the air, and before the smoke of battle cleared Hamilton, Jefferson, Madison and a host of minor figures had been clothed in epithets and tarred in characterizations that remained the small change of party warfare concerning them for the balance of their lives.[18]

The opposition was led by Madison, whom Hamilton charged with "a perfidious desertion of the principles which he was solemnly pledged to defend." But with 80 percent of the outstanding debt owed by northern states, Madison's political life depended on this stand.[19]

At first prospects looked good for Madison, for only Massachusetts and South Carolina, together with the majority of the Connecticut delegates, favored the plan submitted by Hamilton. But Sherman was quick to jump into the fray on Hamilton's side. In 1780 he had written a report suggesting that the old Congress assume the state debts, a report he had not forgotten.[20]

Now, in the debates of 1789, he opposed the two basic points for which Madison was contending: state debts to be paid by state governments, and in paying the national debt a discrimination between original holders of notes and present holders, i.e., speculators.

Discrimination

In September Sherman had written his governor that Congress must do something to satisfy "the just and meritorious demands of the creditors." They "have long been kept out of their dues," adding self-descriptively, "expecially such of them as originally loaned their money, or rendered services or specific supplies, and still hold their securities." If a discrimination were to be made—and he wasn't sure that it ought to be—"I think it ought not to be made for the benefit of the public, but of the original creditors who were necessitated to sell their securities at a discount." But now he spoke against any such discrimination. After all, said Sherman, speculation had always gone on and always would. A discrimination against the speculators who now were reputed to hold large amounts of cheaply acquired bonds was unprecedented, impractical, and injurious to the credit of the nation.[21] Most of the state debt in particular was still in the hands of the original holders.

> He had made particular inquiry into this circumstance, and so far as it respected Connecticut, he was led to believe it was true of nineteen-twentieths. There were one hundred thousand dollars in specie in the hands of the original holders in the very town in which he lived. He believed very little besides the army debt had been transferred in that State; and even of the army debt, it was only that portion which fell into the hands of the soldiers.[22]

In Connecticut, however, a call was issued for town, county, and then a state convention of original holders to be held at Wethersfield on March 4, 1791. There is no evidence that it ever took place, so Sherman may have accurately gauged his constituency. If little transfer had taken place, Connecticut's was an unusual condition indeed. Transfer in other states rose as high as 79 percent in Massachusetts and 81 percent in Maryland. Even Rhode Island suffered a transfer of over half her U. S. securities from original holders to speculators. More remarkable is Sherman's callous attitude toward the plight of his soldier constituents, to whom over 1.8 million dollars' worth of Continental money had been issued as of 1789.[23] He was well aware of the extent of speculation in Connecticut, where soldiers' final settlement notes sold for two shillings to three shillings, six pence on the pound in 1786 and had bounced higher and higher over the next two years. A Wethersfield

merchant estimated in '86 that there were not one-quarter of such notes left
in the state. The principal dealer in notes of all kinds in New Haven had been
none other than the firm of Sherman and Wetmore, though its Sherman
member, Roger's son John, had become an alcoholic by this time and the
partnership had been broken up in 1787.* [24]

Connecticut farmers were a generally suspicious lot. Congress, wrote one
to the *Journal*, judging "from the strong aristocratic influence which appears
in that body," will fund Continental certificates at 6 percent. If this is done,
he continued, then justice would require that not only the notes but also old
Congress *money* be raised to its face value, and that obviously would create
too great a debt to manage. There was no doubt about the activities of
Connecticut speculators: 6 per cents, which had hovered around 2/6 through
the eighties, were selling at 15/10 in mid-December and had climbed to 16/8
a week later. For the most part, rustics, with their worthless paper money
about to be settled at 100 to 1, were confused and frustrated. "Have we not
seen shocking times Mesrs Printers?" wailed one to the press.

> But the whole story is not yet told.—Script—bank script—six per
> cents—deferred stock—three per cents—assumable paper—fundable paper
> —ten days credit—pay and deliver—cash—specie—bank notes—bank bills,
> and bankruptcies, are now echoing from Portsmough to Georgia.—And
> what will the poor soldier say . . .

as he hears his money auctioned off at ten times what he sold it for? Another
charged that William Imlay was appointed Commissioner of Loans for the
state because he owed money to one of the U. S. Representatives; a charge
speedily and emphatically denied. [25]

Assumption

In 1788 Sherman, though himself a very heavy state creditor, had urged
his brother Nathaniel to hold onto his £600 worth of Continental securities.

---

*In view of what seems to me ample evidence of trading in securities in Connecticut,
I find it hard to believe that most U. S. securities remained in the hands of the original
holders. It is quite possible that Sherman's statement was true in regard to state notes,
however. A correspondent to the *Connecticut Courant* in 1800 wrote

> I was Notary Public in Hartford at the time of the funding of the debts and the great
> speculations, and most of the transfers of stocks were made through my hands. I *know*
> that much the greatest part of the certificates of this state were funded in the hands of
> the *original holders*, most of whom were farmers of the country, who thus received the
> real value of their honest debts. Some of them sold their funded stock at *twenty-four
> shillings* on the pound—others sold at par—and many yet hold their stock—and the
> funding of the debt has thus been a principal means of enriching our farmers. Quoted
> in Beard, *Economic Origins*, p. 363.

PIERPONT EDWARDS (1750–1826). Engraving after a portrait by William P. Chappel (upper left). NATHANAEL GREENE (1742–1786). Portrait by John Trumbull. Courtesy of the Yale University Art Gallery (upper right). JEREMIAH WADSWORTH (1743–1804). Detail from an engraving after a portrait by John Trumbull at the Wadsworth Atheneum, Hartford, Connecticut (opposite).

JONATHAN EDWARDS, II (1745–1801). Portrait by Reuben Moulthrop. Courtesy of Yale University Art Gallery, bequest of Eugene Phelps Edwards (upper left). SIMEON BALDWIN (1761–1851). Daguerreotype taken at the age of eighty-three. Courtesy of the Historical Manuscripts Room, Yale University (upper right). WILLIAM WILLIAMS (1731–1811). Engraving after a portrait by John Trumbull, on loan at the Worcester Art Museum (opposite).

Now in March 1789, Nathaniel wrote again for assurances that the bonds would be funded. General Erastus Wolcott, who had sold his U. S. securities, thought Sherman too sanguine in favor of the national notes. According to Wolcott, funding the whole national debt would be politically undesirable as the people would not stand for it. Thus there was a better chance of realizing a full return on state holdings than on the Continentals. "I should be glad to know your Opinion once more before I do anything about it, after you have got as much Information from the members of Congress as you can. . . . I wish you to write to me as Soon as is Convenient before any of the doings of Congress about it are published." Sherman's reply is not known, but Nathaniel hung on to his bonds, though he was forced to use them as collateral for a loan from the state for £400.[26] But Eliphalet Dyer, whose western land schemes had been crushed by the central government, wrote, "As to the Creditors, I believe 9 out of 10 will rather depend on the State to which they belong for payment & justice being done therein than to Risque it in that Ocean of Debt which will appear when all is brot in & accumulated in one National Dept. . . ."[27]

Nevertheless, a parity between state and national obligations was a cardinal point with Sherman. Not only would it be "most convenient to have the funds for payment under one direction," he wrote his son-in-law, but "the debts must follow the funds or else the State creditors will fare worse than those of the United States." "I have no doubt but that the state debts will ultimately be assumed," he opined in April, "I think it must be for the general interest in every point of view." It was a view not new to him: not only had he called for assumption of state debts by the old Congress in 1780, but also in the Philadelphia Convention of '87.[28] However, Pierpont Edwards, contesting for a seat in the U. S. House, would write Sherman publicly that people ought to pay "more critical attention to your political conduct . . . for that you have an *undoubted right* to *exchange* your *Continental* for *State Securities* whenever you discover, that the funding Bill has made a discrimination in the current value of them, and that you can make *twenty-five per cent* by the exchange."[29]

In January 1790 Sherman sent a copy of the Secretary's report to his son-in-law, Simeon Baldwin, "for your perusal and the perusal of the rest of the citizens of New Haven and especially the public creditors. Among whom are Samuel Bishop, David Austin & Timothy Jones Esquires, & Doctor Wales." Sherman himself held $6,012.84 worth of state notes at this time, about equally divided between 3 and 6 percents. The Records of the Connecticut Ledgers in the Loan Office at Washington credit him with

$7,700 at approximately the same time.[30] Benjamin Rush charged that these holdings formed the basis of Sherman's support of the Funding measure, and Charles A. Beard claims that they were the cause of Sherman's interest in the ratification of the Federal Constitution. However, the relatively small amount of money involved, and certain knowledge that some of this was purchased in 1790 serves to throw doubt on this characterization of him.*[31] Certainly, the fiscal records are too tangled and incomplete to show either that Sherman manipulated his holdings or that he did not.

Regardless of personal financial interest, from the point of view of both ideology and policy, there was no doubt in Sherman's mind of the ability of the American people to pay the entire debt, "because if the whole debt must be paid by general efforts of the State and general governments, the same money may be raised, with greater ease, by the general government alone." As to the constitutional objection that the Federal government had no power to assume the debts, Sherman said that even the old Confederation Congress had had that power. The only difference was that the old Congress had to raise money "mediately through the intervention of the State Governments"; but the debts were "to be looked upon as the absolute debts of the Union."[32]

When on the House floor, Madison moved that all claims of the states be credited to them and made part of the assumption bill itself, Sherman raised the only direct opposition. This opposition is apparently inconsistent with Sherman's more frequently stated view that the states would, of course, be given credit for wartime expenditures. However, it is explained by one student of the debate on grounds that Sherman simply was generally suspicious of "Virginia's enormous and shadowy claims," and accounts of the southern states were not accurately kept. This is probably only partly correct. Sherman was still in favor of following the plan exactly as it had been submitted by Hamilton, and he was willing to brook no delaying tactics. Indeed he had predicted to his wife in early March that the assumption would soon be passed and the whole debt paid in hard currency.[33] This last move of Madison's was just one in a long series of deliberate obstructionist actions, which the canny Connecticuter recognized at once. The Madison motion was

---

*These holdings are no doubt those Charles Beard speaks of, and which Benjamin Rush and Pierpont Edwards charged formed the basis of Sherman's support of the Funding measure. Sherman ordered his son to fund these bonds at the Hartford office in the winter of 1791. In January 1793 he bought $600 worth of 6 percent U. S. bonds. Beard, *An Economic Interpretation*, p. 142; Corner, *Rush*, p. 200; Sherman, *Sherman*, p. 198; Yale, Hist. Ms. Room, "Sherman Collection," RS to Simeon Baldwin (January 17, 1793).

passed unanimously, however; Sherman apparently was not willing to jeopardize the whole plan at this point.

Sherman had planned to leave New York on the weekend of April 10, and his presence was so great an obstacle to the foes of assumption that the vote on the measure was put off till his absence. But he saw the danger and stayed on to make, on Monday, another long speech on the subject.[34] He began, "When I see the House so equally divided on an important subject, it gives me great concern on account of the threatening aspect it has on the peace and welfare of the Government. The support of public credit," he continued, "by a provision for doing justice to the creditors of the United States was one great object that led to the establishment of the present government." Failure to provide for this debt would bring about the loss of "confidence of many of its best friends, and disappoint the expectations of the people in general." The debts of the states were not generally agreed upon, but the rule fixed by the old Congress in 1777 and 1778 should suffice. Nevertheless, in the vote which followed the conclusion of the speech, Sherman lost his point by a count of thirty-one to twenty-nine.[35]

Though some of Connecticut's Congressmen were nearly ready to give up, defeat did not daunt the old campaigner; "I have no doubt but that the State debts will ultimately be assumed," he wrote. "I think it must be for the general interest in every point of view."[36] But if Sherman was to have his way, he had to do the job himself, apparently, for no one else was anxious to assume the leadership of the plan in Congress. Hamilton was desperately scheming behind the scenes to save his program, but he would have to modify or accept defeat. The political genius of Sherman was called for at this juncture, and on April 21 he came up with a compromise that met half way Madison's demand that states be reimbursed for wartime expenses paid since 1783. He introduced a resolution that began, "the debts contracted by the States for the common defense and benefit of the Union, ought to be considered as a part of the domestic debt of the United States. . . ." Then he listed tentative amounts to be paid to each state as its share of the costs of the late war. These were to be paid whether the states had debts outstanding or not. In a sense Sherman would bribe the creditor states to go along with the assumption plan. The scheme was "opposed with as much spirit as the original proposition," was the laconic entry in the Journal.[37]

The next day Madison was ready with a full-scale counter argument. In a speech that took the entire day's session, Madison implied that Sherman's resolution was nothing more than a subterfuge to reinstitute the original proposal. The new one, he said, "was liable to all the objections of the former one, as well as to the many others that have been stated against it [in the spirited opposition of the previous day]. From the explanations given by the gentlemen from Connecticut, it is evident that this proposition may, in the result, assume the shape of the original one." The sums to be paid to each state, he said, were "very objectionable."[38] Nevertheless, the bill as finally passed in August enumerated sums quite similar to the ones Sherman suggested at this earlier time. No vote was taken, and the issue was laid aside until the next month. In the interim Sherman at last got his little visit to New Haven. He was missed, however, by his nationalist colleagues, one of whom wrote "The assumption is in danger of being finally lost, . . . and S. . . . is gone, and others of our side going, from the House, the difficulty is almost insuperable." A week later Fisher Ames was still lamenting Sherman's absence; "The Assumption is yet unaccomplished, but not quite dispared of. If S. . . . and C., had not skulked off and left us, I think we could carry it."[39]

Sherman found, perhaps, more objection to assumption in Connecticut than he expected. The dithyrambic letters of Pierpont Edwards as he lapsed into temporary insanity were published in the press. "The rights of the people may be sold and bartered by Congress, at any time," he wrote, "as for instance—the northern members may barter away the residence of Congress, for the assumption of the state debts and so *vice versa*; in which case it shall be lawful for the anti-assumptionists to be entirely silent when the question is debated." Privately Eliphalet Dyer wrote that assumption was alarming with people divided in opinions: "some seem pleased with the Idea of getting rid of a State Debt . . . & carrying of it more distant at a greater remove. . . ." To others, combining all the state debts into one appeared to saddle the infant nation with an unsupportable burden. A debt of thousands was not unusual now, but hundreds of thousands

> gave some alarm, but when the Word Millions which is the Highest Integral Number the People have been acquainted with & when applied to a Debt they have got to pay prefix to that a hundred & more, it will appear Inormous, Surprise astonishment & dispair take place, the People will loose all Patience & be discouraged from every attempt to pay ye Interest, much more to reduce the Principal Sum.

The opinions of neither the half-mad politician nor the old provincial landjobber moved the Connecticut Congressional delegation, which took its que from more nationally inclined spokesmen. From Hartford, Chauncey Goodrich wrote Oliver Wolcott that "no other political subject engrosses the public attention except the Assumption of the state debt. Men of sense, unshackled with office, who are the only ones who speak their opinions till the public opinion is formed, express themselves pleased with the plan."[40]

May opened with a legislative lull, and sometime after the 15th Sherman was unable to attend Congress because of an attack of influenza, part of an epidemic sweeping the whole seaboard and which nearly killed the President himself.[41] It may have been about this time that Ellsworth, from the Senate, wrote in discouragement to his Connecticut mentor saying, "We must give up the funding system." Sherman, it is reported, promptly replied, "They may take it from us—we'll never give it up." Young Fisher Ames, a strong supporter of the assumption measure, advised a Bay State friend on the 20th, "The assumption is not less to be hoped for than it has been for several weeks past. Mr. Sherman is indisposed, but in a day or two will renew his motion for assuming certain fixed sums. The success of it would be certain, if the Pennsylvania creditors were well disposed towards it," which they were not.[42]

Sherman was back on the job on May 25, however, and made his final appeal for Hamilton's bill. He is listed as having spoken that day, and the speech, not reported in the Journal, is published elsewhere.[43] The basis of Sherman's argument was that the debts were incurred for the general benefit by states that expected to pay from funds earned by imposts. This source of revenue having been taken over by the general government, it was now incumbent on that government to pay the debts. He praised the accuracy of Hamilton's estimate of the contributions of the various states, cited the Journal of the old Congress as to the relative fairness of taxation by impost, and quoted Adam Smith on the greater expense of collecting imposts than excises. Sherman countered, one by one, thirteen charges against the Hamilton program, but brought no new argument forward. The speech was one of summary, and it is unlikely that it changed any minds among the Congressmen present. Before the final vote was taken, Hamilton had contrived his deal with Jefferson concerning the seat of the national government, which brought over the necessary one or two affirmative votes.

Hamilton's offer to support the location of the permanent seat of the national government on the Potomac rather than on the Susquehannah or a place even more northerly was probably crucial. Sherman had opposed a southern location since his days in the old Congress. He continued the strongest and most persistent foe of the Potomac location, but he gave up what might have been a winning battle after July 7, 1790.[44] It is not known whether he did this at the request of Hamilton. But since the Secretary had been attempting the dicker since June 17, and had probably completed the arrangement with Jefferson and the Pennsylvania delegation by June 20, it is unlikely that Sherman was involved. Since Sherman finally voted against the Potomac location, it is clear that he had no part in this aspect of the maneuvers. It seems somewhat graceless that Hamilton's strong right arm in the House should be left out of the bargaining. It is perhaps a reflection of Sherman's independent ways that he was not included. This is not to say that Sherman's efforts were not crucial. It was a combination of Sherman's compromise of April 21 and the machinations of Hamilton that resulted in the final victory for the nationalist forces.[45]

Amending the Constitution

Although the Assumption Bill was the hottest subject of the First Congress, the issue of most profound significance was that of altering the Constitution. Here again Sherman played a role second only to Madison in legislative influence and lasting significance. Though a number of states had adopted the Constitution with the understanding that amendments would be made immediately, a few of the old anti-federalists continued to agitate for a new convention to rewrite or alter the newborn document. In Virginia in particular Patrick Henry worked for such a convention and got the assembly there to call for one. Sherman was opposed, and from New Haven made his weight felt in the expiring Confederation Congress then sitting in New York. As the new Federal Congressmen assembled in March, delegate Samuel Otis of the old Congress, and secretary of the new, wrote that he saw no prospect of a new convention; and, he continued, "when such men as father Sherman says 'try it first' do I expect an early attempt at amendments." A convention was avoided, and the large number of federalists elected to the First Congress made quick attention to amendments seem doubtful.[46]

But James Madison had been defeated in his drive for a Senate seat by the ardent opposition of Patrick Henry and the belief that he was opposed to a federal bill of rights, so the Virginia political realities forced the young federalist to take a stand in favor of amendments.[47] He was elected to the House and forced the issue there early in June, almost three months after Congress had assembled. In May, when Madison had originally announced his intention to bring amendments before the Congress, he had seen them as additions to the Constitution. But by June he wanted them written into the body of the Philadelphia document. Sherman had opposed the power of state legislatures to make amendments, preferring specially elected conventions in the states or new federal conventions for that purpose. And when these proposals had failed in the Philadelphia Convention, he finally moved to strike out the entire amending process (September 15).

Sherman had also opposed a bill of rights either written in or attached to the basic document. When the question arose in the Philadelphia Convention, he had declared that the state declarations of rights would not be repealed by the new Constitution and thus would remain in force. He was the only one to speak against a bill of rights as proposed by Mason and Gerry, but his point was endorsed by the Convention without a state in opposition (September 12). Besides, the pragmatic politician had written in '88, "Declarations of rights in England were charters granted by Princes, or Acts of Parliament made to limit the prerogatives of the crown, but not to abridge the powers of the legislature." The new constitution vested the powers of government in representatives who have the same interest "as that of the people they govern, and [who] are dependent on the suffrage of the people for their appointments to, and continuence in office. this is a much greater security than a declaration of rights or restraining clauses on paper."[48] Roger Sherman, then, was opposed to a national bill of rights when it was under discussion in the First Congress in June 1789.

Sherman felt so strongly about the danger of altering the Constitution that he composed a long letter for the newspapers to bring his argument before the people. This two-part letter ran first in the *New York Packet* in March, and then in the New England papers. Sherman himself clipped the articles from the *Packet* and sent them to friends in Massachusetts and Rhode Island with instructions that they be published.[49] His letter, signed "A Citizen of New Haven," outlined the arguments that Sherman was to use during the House debates of July and August. His point was that the Federal Government was a strictly limited one, and that no further explicit limitations were necessary. It was also his view that the country should wait until it had some experience with the new government before it made changes. "Attempting it [alteration] at present may be detrimental, if not fatal, to the union of the States, and to their credit with foreign nations," he concluded.

It is doubtful that these letters had much effect except among those who already shared Sherman's views. The pressure for amendments was irrepressible, a fact that the old politician very quickly recognized and accepted, as

Madison guessed he would. The Virginia leader of the pro-amendment group in Congress thought little opposition would be manifest,

> though with some, the concurrence will proceed from a spirit of conciliation rather than conviction. Connecticut is least inclined though I presume not inflexibly opposed to a moderate revision. A paper which will probably be republished in the Virga Gazettes under the Signature of a Citizen of New Haven, unfolds Mr. Sherman's opinions.[50]

When Madison made his proposal on June 8, Sherman was the first to respond. He recognized that many members intended to act on the question of amendments, but this was not the time for it. If the people wanted changes in the Constitution to come before further organization of the government, they would have rejected the document until the amendments had been written, as North Carolina had done. Sherman did not object to bringing the proposal before Congress at this time, but the executive and judiciary must be organized, and a revenue provided for before any changes were discussed. Such a discussion would alarm twenty people for every one it relieved.[51] But Madison was sure that the greatest opposition to the Constitution was based on the lack of a guaranteed bill of rights. He insisted on reading the whole list of proposals.

Even ornery Elbridge Gerry, who had spoken for a bill of rights in the Philadelphia Convention, wanted to continue the business of constructing a government before making changes in the organic document. The reaction to Madison's proposals both within Congress and outside was mixed. Sherman immediately took the lead in opposing them. He admitted in another June 8 speech that the Constitution was not perfect, but he did not expect perfection "on this side of the grave in the works of man." There was no reason to expect that nine states could be persuaded to adopt changes at this time, especially in view of the ordeal which the original document had to undergo. And no one had had any experience with the new government to guide them as to what changes ought to be made, anyway. The only real question, Sherman insisted, was how to get rid of the proposal, and he would vote with Madison to refer it to a committee of the whole.[52]

The Committee of the Whole did not begin its discussions of Madison's proposals until July 21. At that time Sherman continued his opposition, but was defeated in his attempt to kill the issue. By the 4th of August he could write about the amendments that "they will probably be harmless and Satisfactory to those who are Fond of Bills of rights." At least they were no longer "detrimental" or "fatal," but he continued, "I don't like the form in which they are reported to be incorporated in the Constitution, that Instrument being the Act of the people, ought to be kept intire. . . ." The proposals were referred to a committee of eleven, one from each state, on which both Sherman and Madison served. John Vining of Delaware reported for the committee on August 13, and the House resolved itself immediately into a Committee of the Whole.[53]

Sherman was the first to speak, for he had lost his point in the select committee. He still opposed the insertion of the amendments in the body of the Constitution. "We might as well endeavor to mix brass, iron and clay, as to incorporate such heterogeneous articles, the one contradictory to the other." And, he continued, "it is questionable whether we have the right to propose amendments in this way. The Constitution is the act of the State governments.* Again, all the authority we possess is derived from that instrument; if we mean to destroy the whole, and establish a new Constitution, we remove the basis on which we mean to build." A document ratified by the people could not be altered by the states, but merely added to. Sherman then moved that the amendments be added rather than inserted piecemeal.[54] At least by now he was willing to accept amendments.

Madison said he would not insist on his formula, and Sherman picked up support from a number of members who rose to agree. Elbridge Gerry, however, who had refused to sign the basic document, replied to Sherman with bitter sarcasm. The gentleman from Connecticut is quibbling over a mere matter of form, said Gerry, and his form will require supplements and then supplements to the supplements, finally "wrapping up the Constitution in a maze of perplexity; and as great and adept as that honorable gentleman is at finding out the truth, it will take him, I apprehend, a week or a fortnight's study to ascertain the true meaning of the Constitution." Egbert Benson reminded the House of the select committee's decision to interweave the changes. But Sherman insisted again that the basis of the original document was different from that of the proposed amendments. The vote on Sherman's motion to add rather than insert the amendments was taken and, for the time being he lost.[55]

---

*Within just a few days Sherman spoke of the Constitution as "the Act of the people" and as "the act of the State governments." Nowhere is his tendency to view these two entities as synonymous so clearly manifest. The apparent confusion lies in his conviction that the state assemblies accurately spoke for the vox populi. But later (see below) he was to object to including amendments within the Constitution because that document had been an act of the people voting directly in ratifying conventions. Only the people directly, he said, could alter the basic document, though state legislatures could *add* alterations at the end through the constitutional amending procedure.

The debate continued throughout the week. Sherman stubbornly rejected any change in the original document even when the changes would strengthen his idea of what the federal government should be. At one time or another he opposed: explicit statements confining federal activity to the enumerated powers; explicit protection against double jeopardy; prohibiting Congress from altering the mode of election of senators; an explicit statement that no one of the federal branches could exercise the powers of another; prohibitions on quartering troops, with the comment that they must be quartered somewhere, and "it ought not to be put in the power of an individual to obstruct the public service." Sherman also opposed a provision for making explicit the idea that the military should be subordinate to civil authority.[56] According to his old Confederation colleague R. H. Lee, his reason was *"that it would make the people insolent."* This extraordinary statement from what Lee called a "former respected, republican friend . . . whose person, manners, and every sentiment appeared formerly to be perfectly republican . . ." was made in committee and reported by an unidentified "honble Member of H. of R."[57]

Sherman's opposition, by far the strongest of any Congressman, was based on two points: a federal guarantee of individual rights was not necessary because the general government had not been given the power to act in any of the areas dealt with in the proposed amendments; and that the amendments, if harmless, rested on the states, not the people, and thus had no right to be included in the basic document.*

> The original was established by the people at large, by conventions chosen by them for the express purpose. The preamble of the constitution declares the act; but will it be a truth in ratifying the next constitution [meaning the proposed alternations], which is to be done perhaps by the state legislatures, and not conventions chosen for that purpose? Will gentlemen say it is "We the people" in this case? Certainly they cannot; for, by the present constitution we, nor all the Legislatures in the Union together do not possess the power of repealing it.[58]

---

*Sherman had some problems with the negative inferences growing out of a list of rights. These were the very grounds on which Madison had opposed such a bill during the Convention of 1787. If Congress were not explicitly denied authority to quarter troops upon the people, couldn't this power be implied in its authority to raise and equip armies? Sherman at this point in the Congressional debate suggested that quartering was no abuse and was willing to see it happen when necessary. However, in general his opposition to a bill of rights should not be interpreted as favoring an expansion of federal authority into state and individual rights. In view of his well-known distrust of the military, Sherman's tolerance for quartering in this instance must be viewed as aberrant.

On August 21 the resolute New Haven Congressman reintroduced his motion to add the amendments as supplements rather than insertions. He must have been busy during the week, for this time he carried his point with a two-thirds majority.[59]

The next day, Benson of New York, Sedgwick of Massachusetts, and Sherman were appointed to a committee to arrange a form for the amendments. When they reported, further debate ensued, and this time "Even Sherman was capable of offering constructive suggestions for the plan he had called superfluous, if not dangerous." On Monday, August 24, the proposal was sent up to the Senate in the form of seventeen amendments. The Senate freely edited the House product, and it was necessary to appoint a joint committee to work out a compromise. Representatives Sherman, Madison, and Vining were selected to work with Senators Charles Carroll, William Paterson, and Ellsworth. Sherman, who frequently preferred the work of the upper house over that of his own, liked the Senate version, and the final form was quickly developed, both houses readopting ten of the amendments by September 27.[60]

Roger Sherman's contribution to the development of the Bill of Rights is highly significant, though largely negative. Without his efforts the original Constitution would have been altered in wording and phraseology, and a precedent would have been established for reworking rather than supplementing it. The insistence that the Constitution was a creation of the people, established on a basis different from the amending process, was crucial. Though not consistent with Sherman's anti-nationalist views of the spring of 1787, it was essential to the social-contract basis of the federal government. It is one of the ironies of the times—and the Constitutional debates of the period 1787 to 1790 abound with personal inconsistencies—that Madison's efforts to alter the basic document in 1789 would have undermined the nationalist foundations that he had worked so hard to establish in 1787, while Sherman, the archfederalist of the earlier period, became in 1789 the bulwark of a nationally founded Constitution.

Connecticut did not pass the amendments now known as the Bill of Rights until 1941, the sesquicentennial of their ratification. When they were taken up in May 1790, the lower house agreed to Articles III–XII, omitting the first, which established proportions of people to the representatives; and the second, which provided that alterations in pay for Congressmen were not to take effect "until an election of Representatives shall have intervened." But the Council dissented, and a conference was fruitless. A week later the upper house passed all twelve, and the lower house dissented; again a conference yielded no compromise. Another attempt was made in October, but the House rejected all twelve out of hand, and the Council's vote and House's concurrence to hold them over to the following May was the last they were attended to in the Connecticut General Assembly till a century and a half later.[61]

The Wheel Turns and the Cog Wears Down

THE battle over amendments was Sherman's last great effort on the national edifice. He was shortly to move into the Senate, where debate was secret, and he may have had greater influence than is apparent. But his periods of illness were becoming more frequent, and his strength no doubt was flagging. He had used up his threescore years and ten, and was very, very tired.

The First Bank of the United States

With the funding of the national debt and the assumption of the state debts completed, and debate over amendments finished, Congress turned again to Hamilton's program for the economy of the new nation. This was the establishment of a national bank. It was fought in the House by the representatives of the agrarian interests, led, of course, by Madison.[1] Madison based his opposition on the constitutional grounds that the Federal Government had no right to establish such an institution. Sherman, who in the Philadelphia Convention explicitly opposed giving Congress authority to grant corporate charters, and in civil matters the staunchest of states'-rights men, on economic questions often expressed views favorable to a broad interpretation of the necessary and proper clause in the Constitution.

It was, ironically, in support of Madison that he once voiced this opinion in Congress. Madison had argued against an explicit restriction of the Federal Government to the enumerated powers by saying that "it was impossible to confine a government to the exercise of express powers; there must necessarily be admitted powers by implication, unless the Constitution descended to recount every minutia." Sherman rose to agree and to add that "corporate bodies are supposed to possess all powers incident to a corporate capacity, without being absolutely expressed."[2] Though stating that it was well known that Congress could extend its own "authority no further than to the bounds the people have assigned," Sherman had presented a very broad view of the Federal powers in the debate over assumption. "I consider both governments," he said,

> standing on the broad basis of the people. They were both constituted by them for their general and particular good. The Representatives in Congress draw their authority from the same source as the State legislatures; they are both of them elected by the people at large, the one to manage their national concerns, and the other their domestic, which they find can be better done by being divided into lesser communities than the whole Union; but to effect the greater concerns they have confederated; therefore everything which strengthens the Federal Government and enables it to answer the end for which it was instituted, will be a desirable object with the people.[3]

Here indeed is a rationale that might justify almost any Federal assumption of power, and it is doubtful that Sherman meant it entirely.

However, this background gave Sherman a completely clear constitutional conscience when it came time to support Hamilton's bank. A note passed from Sherman to Madison during the Bank debate points up the disagreement between the strict and loose constructionists most succinctly.[4] The note dated February 4, 1791, read:

> You will admit that Congress have power to provide by law for raising, depositing and applying money for the purposes enumerated in the Constitution and generally of regulating the Finances.
>
> That they have power so far as no particular rules are pointed out in the Constitution to make such rules and regulations as they may judge necessary and proper to effect these purposes. The only question that remains is—Is a Bank a proper measure for effecting these purposes? And is not this a question of expediency rather than of right?

Sherman had marked with an X and encircled the line "and generally of regulating the Finances," and handed the note to Madison. Madison then questioned "a bank" by writing in the words "a necessary and" before "proper" and returned it to Sherman, who responded with nothing more than a smile. Madison wrote at the bottom of this note that Sherman did give up the line marked with an X. The Bank bill was passed ultimately by a thirty-nine to twenty vote, but there is no evidence that Sherman played an important part in the effort.

The Legislative Function

It is during the various debates in the Federal Congress that Sherman's views on the legislative function were most fully developed. They provide a mature and considered outline of a still troublesome problem and are as interesting today as they were in the 1790's. Most of Sherman's comments came out of the discussion of the enlargement of the House, but some were a part of other debates. He favored a small House, not exceeding one hundred members, and at various times attempted to get the ratio of Representatives to population reduced.[5] He had a certain respect for the wisdom of the public, though more than a little qualified at times. On one occasion he said:

> Gentlemen [of the Congress] have had recourse to popular opinion in support of their argument. Popular opinion is founded in justice, and the only way to know if the popular opinion is in favor of a measure is to examine whether the measure is just and right in itself. I think whatever is proper and right, the people will judge of and comply with. The people wish that the government may derive respect from the justice of its measures; and they have given it their support on this account.[6]

On the question of instructed representatives, it cannot be admitted that the people have the right to instruct their representatives, he said,

> because it would destroy the object of their meeting. I think, when the people have chosen a representative, it is his duty to meet others from the different parts of the union, and consult, and agree with them to such acts as are for the general benefit of the whole community. If they were to be guided by instructions, there would be no use in deliberation; all that a man would have to do, would be to produce his instructions, and lay them on the table, and let them speak for him. From hence, I think it may be fairly inferred, that the right of the people to consult for the common good can go no further than to petition the legislature, or apply for a redress of grievances. It is the duty of a good representative to inquire what measures are most likely to promote the general welfare, and, after he has discovered them, to give them his support. Should his instructions, therefore, coincide with his ideas on any measure, they would be unnecessary; if they were contrary to the conviction of his own mind, he must be bound by every principle of justice to disregard them.[7]*

The second statement does not contradict the first because it is the instinct of the people to recognize and elect good men, for "people are more influenced by their feelings than by speculative reasonings, or nice calculations."[8]

The legislature should possess only certain limited powers, but within those limits it was to be sovereign. Sherman would not allow the president authority to remove executive officers, a power universally granted today, and generally conceded to the president even in 1789. The president, he said during Congressional debate, had no right to remove officers who required Senate confirmation for appointment. He felt strongly about this, but

---

*The human capacity for self-deception is infinite. An analysis of Sherman's political career, 1756–84 at least, shows him to be among the Connecticut politicians most sensitive to the views of his constituents.

Madison accused him of excessive originality and of suggesting a total rejection of separation of powers. Sherman gave two more speeches on the subject, lost his point by a vote of thirty-four to twenty, but continued to urge restraints on the president's removal power.[9] This was in line with his consistent efforts to expand the economic power of the Federal government, while limiting its civil powers, and at the same time keep the legislature paramount.

This question of the paramountcy of the legislature was given a more thorough airing in a correspondence between John Adams and Sherman during the very days on which this debate occurred in the House, that is, from the 17th to the 27th of July, 1789.[10] Adams had wished to comment on Sherman's views regarding the supremacy of the legislature, and he took the Congressman's remarks upholding the qualified character of executive veto power as a starting point. In this correspondence is one of the most explicit expositions of the difference between the old British and new Continental concepts of separation of powers. Adams would separate the government into branches based on *interests*—monarchy, aristocracy, the public. Sherman saw the branches as manifesting *functions*—executive, legislative, and judicial. Considering Adams' primacy among American political thinkers of the time, his absence from Philadelphia in 1787 is perhaps the most significant non-event of the Convention.

Adams first defined a republic as "A government whose sovereignty is vested in more than one person." He then made a case for the necessity of balance between the one, the many, and the few. Adams' republic has two governmental aspects: the legislative, of which the executive is a part, and the judicial. The legislature is composed of three branches, the executive, the Senate—representing the few—and the House—representing the many. Therefore the executive must be given the same power as each of the houses to exercise an absolute veto on legislation, and in denying them, Sherman "is therefore clearly and certainly in error." Adams insisted that the Senatorial limitations on the executive in the cases of war, treaties, and appointments, and especially the executive dependence on the legislative, "will be the destruction of this constitution, and involve us in anarchy, if not amended." The executive must be an integral part of the legislature so that "it might negative a law without much noise, speculation, or confusion among the people."

Sherman's differences began with the definition of a republic; it was, he said,

> a government under the authority of the people, consisting of legislative, executive, and judiciary powers; the legislative powers vested in an

assembly, consisting of one or more branches who, together with the executive, are appointed by the people, and dependent on them for continuance, by periodical elections, agreeable to an established constitution; and that what especially denominates it a *republic* is its dependence on the *public* or *people* at *large* without any hereditary powers. . . .I am also of opinion, that they may alter their frame of government when they please, any former acts of theirs, however explicit, to the contrary notwithstanding.

Thus the old revolutionary defined a republic as exactly that which he sought to defend, namely the form of government established for Connecticut in the mid-seventeenth century and for the United States in 1788. He further insisted on a literal interpretation of the social contract. There is no real need for a balance in America, Sherman continued, because there are no opposing forces to be balanced, all members of the society "having only the same common rights with other citizens." The wisdom of two-thirds of the legislature at least should be counted as equal to that of one man at the very least; and an enlightened executive would be unlikely to exercise his veto on legislation passed by so great a majority even if he had the right to do so. "On the whole," he concluded, "it appears to me that the power of a complete negative, if given, would be a dormant and useless one, and that the provision in the constitution is calculated to operate with proper weight, and will produce beneficial effects." He ended the correspondence with his usual temperate protestations, and perhaps a slap at the more philosophical Adams, "But I have said enough upon these speculative points, which nothing but experience can reduce to a certainty."

Another bid by Sherman for legislative supremacy occurred during the debate on the treaty-making powers of the president. Sherman, usually so practical, now proposed that foreign treaties be actually written by the Senate and president acting together.[11] At the time he made this assertion, Sherman was still a member of the House, and perhaps took too distant a view of the problem. But he certainly evinced far greater faith in the new Constitution than did the vice-president.

Although Sherman would have Congressmen exercise absolute discretion over national affairs, these affairs were limited in scope. The legislature, though supreme, was to be neither absolute nor arbitrary. "The people of the United States," he said,

are like masters prescribing to their servants the several branches of business they will each have to perform. It might not comport with their interests if the Federal Government was to interefere with the government of particular States; while on the other hand, it would injure their interests to restrict the general government from performing what the

Federal Constitution allows them. It is the interest of each and of the whole that they should be separate within their proper limits.[1][2]

"The objects of the Federal Government," Sherman said, "were fewer than those of the State Government; they did not require an equal degree of local knowledge; the one case, perhaps, where local knowledge would be advantageous, was in laying direct taxes. . . ."[1][3]

Pierpont Edwards

Roger Sherman never lost an election in which he was an acknowledged and active contestant. But elections in eighteenth-century Connecticut were not really contested on a one-to-one basis. Promotion and disparagement of individuals was confined to private conversations and very subtle backstage maneuvering. It came as a shock to the freemen, and no less to Sherman himself, when, in 1789, a bitter public campaign was launched against the old man of Connecticut politics.

The ostensible issue was the per diem pay for U. S. Congressmen, and Sherman's antagonist was Pierpont Edwards, Connecticut's most successful lawyer, and a New Haven neighbor of the old man. He was also the younger brother of Sherman's minister, and the leader of a group of young anti-establishment politicians called the Stelligeri, who would ultimately coalesce with the disestablishment people to form the Jeffersonian Party. He was not unpopular in New Haven, having received the largest vote in the 1784 election for the city's first Common Council. His was a career checkered with private and professional lapses; fifteen years earlier a movement to oust him from the Connecticut bar had been attempted by Sherman and others.* But,

---

*Edwards apparently had been involved in some suspected sexual misbehavior culminating in the death of his corespondent. See *The New England Historical and Genealogical Register,* IX (1855). p. 191 for a review of A Lady of Massachusetts (Hannah Webster Foster), *The Coquette: or the History of Eliza Whorton. A Novel founded on Fact,* Boston, Samuel G. Drake, 1855 (first published in 1796). The reviewer identifies the characters: Eliza Whorton—Elizabeth Whitman; J. Buyer—Joseph Buckminster; Mrs. Sumner—Mrs. Henry Hill; Peter Sanford—Pierpont Edwards. Edwards, indeed for decades enjoyed the reputation as the "Great Connecticut Adulterer." As late as the 1860's, John Humphrey Noyes of the Oneida Community would write, "We see that Providence frequently allows very superior men to be also very attractive to women, and very licentious. Perhaps with all the immediate evil that they do to morals, they do some good to the blood of after generations. Who can say how much the present race of men in Connecticut owe to the numberless adulteries and fornications of Pierpont Edwards? Corrupt as he was, he must have distributed a good deal of the blood of his

after all, he had been Sherman's New Haven colleague at the state ratifying convention, and was a presumed friend.[14]

Edwards began his program with a general attack on Congress and its alleged aristocratic tendencies. People in Connecticut who had to sell their notes for less than four shillings on the pound are now seeing their money given away to "salary men." "These salaries and advantages united, will in a short time render them (that is all who are employed in the public service, even to the keeper of the door and sweep) rich, independent, haughty and insolent," he wrote. They will soon subvert the Constitution and write a new one that will perpetuate their riches.[15] Sherman agreed that the salaries were too high, and should be per diem for clerks and doorkeepers, anyway. As for members' salaries, that bill "was brought in and passed while I was at home, so that it would ill become me to find fault with it." At the suggestion of a Congressional library, the anonymous Edwards wrote sarcastically that since Congress pays its servants like gentlemen, it is now going to educate them like gentlemen. We will have not only rich, but also learned doorkeepers. "it is better to be a doorkeeper in Congress than to stand in high places in Connecticut."**[16]

While constantly protesting his support of the Constitution, the unstable lawyer continued to attack Congress for procrastinating work on treaties to open up the West Indian trade which, like Connecticut's crops, had been very low the past two years. Nor was anything being done about establishing the public credit. "It was principally for these purposes that the old constitution was despised and rejected and a new system of government established." But

---

noble father, Jonathan Edwards; and so we may hope the human race got a secret profit out of him." John Humphreys Noyes, "Essay on Scientific Propagation." Wallingford, Conn., Wallingford Printing Company (for the Oneida Community), n. d. p. 22.

One can hardly wonder at Edwards' impatience with the old order; he represented a town in which half the population was under eighteen years old. Edwards' machinations also involved some long-term and very complicated efforts to reorganize the government of Yale College, principally in an attempt to bring some New Divinity ministers and some laymen onto the board of trustees and to replace Ezra Stiles with Edwards' nephew, Timothy Dwight. Stiles, *Lit.*, *Diary*, III:288, 127, and *passim*.

**The Establishment view was put forth privately by Chauncey Goodrich who wrote from Hartford in January that the enemies to the government "will not be able to make any ferment about salaries, either to the prejudice of the government or the individuals who administer it." In the very midst of the Sherman-Edwards embroglio Goodrich would write "No spirit of electioneering prevails so far as my information extends; the farmers are well pleased with the high price of corn, &c., and half of them are so great fools to believe, that the President has ordered Englishmen, French and Algerines, to come and give the high price for which grain is now selling." Gibbs, *Washington and Adams*, ps. 34, 42. To Oliver Wolcott (January 2, March 23, 1790).

though the attack was broadly aimed, the intent was clear. A response leveled a charge repeated three times, that "somebody wants to go to Congress, fairly if it can be, but at any rate must go to Congress—There must be a change of members. Can you name the men?" Another letter writer summarized the expenses of Congress and pointed out that it would take the labor of 1177 farmers or mechanics to earn what had been spent in pay for the 91 men who made up Congress and its officers. And a third admonished voters to choose for Representatives the best speakers in the state of about thirty-five or forty years old—definitely not a description of Sherman.[17]

U. S. Representatives were elected at large in Connecticut, so it was not necessary for Edwards to replace Sherman specifically. But two of the five were from New Haven, a result, according to one correspondent, of that town's greater interest in politics than elsewhere.[18] Apparently Edwards considered Sherman easier to beat than James Hillhouse, and he thought he had an issue. Besides, Edwards and Sherman's son-in-law, Simeon Baldwin, were in competition for the clerkship in the office of the new U. S. District Judge, Richard Law. Baldwin had first sought the surveyorship of the harbor, but that was snatched off by Jonathan Fitch, who had solicited letters from New Haven's leading people. "That method of pushing oneself forward, seems from the customs of the World to have become necessary for the attainment of the office, but is new to the manners of Connecticut & I did not think of it," wrote Sherman's disappointed son-in-law.[19]

The establishment of a six dollars a day per diem for Congressmen outraged Connecticut's yeomen, but it was the best that could be done, with aristocratic southerners pushing hard for eight dollars. When the vote came up in the U. S. House, Sherman took off for a week's visit to New Haven and points north. Three Connecticut congressmen voted for the compromise six dollars, and one, Jonathan Sturges of Fairfield, voted against. Considerable animosity was directed against the three, but Sherman, who wrote Governor Huntington noncommittally about it, escaped. The bill then went to the Senate, where there was strong sentiment for making a discrimination in pay for the upper house. Sherman heard that rather than increase senatorial pay, the plan was to reduce that of the House. His egalitarian instincts were inflamed, and he spoke to Oliver Ellsworth urging him not to reduce House pay.*

---

*Sherman did not prevail with the Senator, however. Ellsworth not only voted for a discrimination in pay for the two houses, but actually moved that House salaries be reduced to five dollars. Maclay, *Journal*, p. 137.

Edwards picked this up from Jeremiah Wadsworth, now a Congressman, and took it to the press in the fall of 1790. Mocking the style of a farmer, he wrote

> Old Mr. *Sherman*, our Representative at Congress (you know that we have always thought that he would not tell a fib for the world)—well, he wrote a letter to our Governor . . . telling that he Want in the house of Representatives, when the vote was taken to give *six* dollars a day wages . . . and that he believed that the northern members would have been contented with *five dollars*. To tell you the truth, I was very much pleased when I heard it; but as you live, that good old man, while the Bill . . . was before the Senate, went in person to one of the Senators and said to him "whatever you do with that Bill, don't you lower the wages of Representatives below *six dollars* a day."—I don't so well like this in our old Patriot, as it wasont quite up and down perpindicular—We farmers had a great dependence on him, and always thought he would not be twistical; however what the scriptures say will apply to him, "all flesh is grass," (altho the old man cannot be called green grass)—I am very sorry he did so, but however, I think we had better put in the old members once more; and for my part am willing to try Mr. *Sherman* again; but if I ever hear of his swiveling any more, I warrent you, I wont vote for him again; and our minister says so too.[20]

Sherman did not know the origin of these letters which he considered "illnatured and injudicious," and happening to be in Hartford when this one was published there, went to the printer who verified Edwards' authorship. Upon confrontation Edwards admitted so to his antagonist. Sherman, too, went to the press and recited the facts relevent to the issue. "I have never refrained from speaking or acting what appeared to me to be for the public good, from fear or favor of any man"; he protested,

> and I have endeavored to preserve a consistency of conduct. I shall leave to Mr. Edwards to explain to the public his motives, for attemtping to injure my character, in so extraordinary and clandestine a manner. I am not conscious that I ever did him an injury, and I trust I shall continue to do him good, as I may have the opportunity.

Edwards called on Wadsworth to write him verifying his story, for "The freemen ought to know the ground on which Mr. [Sherman should] stand, so far as the matter of Compensation is to have any weight in their minds." He had not used Wadsworth's name, but since he had "challenged Mr. Sherman to deny" the conversation with Ellsworth and since he knew Wadsworth "too honest to deal with such an old Jesuit," he needed some support.[21]

But the motives were clear. CATO, writing from Middletown, described Sherman's reaction on discovering the author to be Edwards as having

> produced a greater surprise than the publications themselves; that a man of [Edwards'] reputation should descent to such a measure. Mr. Edwards himself is in nomination for the same office; this was done two weeks before the time of the election; What was his motive? What could the young man mean by attacking a politician whose wisdom and integrity will be eternized by every step in the progress of the American revolution, and the formation of our government.

Sherman himself put it more succinctly: "You was in the nomination for a representative to Congress, and you knew you could not be elected, without one of the present members was left out. . . . That you may better know & persue your own true interest; *love your neighbor as yourself*, and *avoid vain jangling*, is the desire of your sincere well wisher."[22]

Edwards desperately replied that since "it has now become a matter of publicity in this city, that I wrote those pieces," he stood ready to "establish the truth of everything I have asserted respecting Mr. Sherman." But CATO closed this part of the debate, remarking "Instead of condemning we ought to revere the sage who carefully watches against the introduction of an aristocratic influence in the legislature."[23]

The story, however, was not yet all out. Sherman, Edwards, and James Hillhouse, also of New Haven, were elected by the freemen, bringing the city's share of Representatives up to three out of five. The excitement generated by the contest had politicized that part of Connecticut so much that the New Haven candidates got 7500 votes out of 10,500 cast.* Bitterly, the half-crazy young lawyer wrote a violent attack on the people of Hartford and at the same time divulged a plot to force a resignation from one of the New Haven incumbents to make room for a Hartford man. But in the future the river town would have to take care of itself.[24] At this point the October Assembly session opened and Edwards was elected speaker, an office he had held the previous year. The record reads that he resigned "on account of Business which call'd him out of town." But the truth of the matter was that he was elected in the morning and resigned in the afternoon, and also resigned

---

*The population of the city of Hartford was 4090 and of the county 38,129; New Haven city held 4510 (including 129 free and 78 slave blacks), and the county population was 30,650. *Connecticut Journal* (February 9,16, 1791).

his seat in the U. S. Congress. Obviously he was under tremendous pressure.[25]

Pierpont Edwards' great-grandmother Elizabeth Tuttle had been one of four out of twelve children who were insane. Two Tuttle children actually murdered other members of the family.[26] The instability showed up from time to time through the generations, and now it struck. Edwards was beginning to lapse into periods of wild, disjointed ravings centering on his battle with Sherman and other exciting events such as the recent conviction of one Joe Mountain, a Negro, for the rape of a white thirteen-year-old.* Despite the newspaper publicity given Edwards' aberrant behavior, he returned to the Assembly at a special December session and was sound enough to serve on a number of committees there. He was replaced by David Austin at the May elections, but would reappear as a Jeffersonian leader later in the decade.[27]

Meanwhile a special election was scheduled for December 16, 1790 to fill the empty House seat. The members left out by the election of Hillhouse and Edwards were Benjamin Huntington of Norwich and Jeremiah Wadsworth of Hartford. There was some feeling that a second New Haven congressman should resign so that the old policy of geographic distribution could prevail. Indeed, a notice "To the Freemen of the City of New-Haven" suggested that "Your present Mayor has been absent from the state sixteen months since the first of March 1789, and will probably be absent six months in each of the two succeeding years.—Ought he not to resign an office the duties of which he cannot execute?" Or perhaps he should not accept a job that will take him out of Connecticut so much. Agitation for districting the state for purposes of national representation had also begun to arise. A writer to the *Courant* expressing an anti-establishment view, suggested that most voters in Hartford County would support Amasa Learned of New London; and presumably so would the freemen of the eastern towns. But editors of the Hartford-based paper declared Jeremiah Wadsworth more worthy of support than Learned,

---

*Mountain had petitioned the Assembly to have his death sentence commuted to life imprisonment, which had been denied on the day Edwards resigned his speakership. Part of Mountain's defense was his statement that he had not intended to rape the thirteen-year-old; his objective had been her eighteen-year-old sister, but when the older girl ran away Joe was left with no alternative to the younger one. His hanging was witnessed by a crowd estimated at ten thousand. "House Journal 1788–1790," n.p. October 15, 1790; *Connecticut Journal*, October 20, 1790. See also Joseph Mountain, *Sketches of the life of . . . , a negro, who was executed at New Haven, on the 20th day of October, 1790, for a rape. . . .* New Haven, T. & S. Green, 1790. There is a copy at C.H.S.

who was a member of Edwards' Stelligeri, and indeed the Hartford speculator was the victor "by a great Majority."*[28]

The Cog Wears Down

The successful Sherman wrote his Governor of the "high sense of honor done me by the Free Men of this State in this repeated mark of their confidence . . . ," and went wearily down to Philadelphia, Congress' new temporary home. It would be another year before an appropriation bill would be passed permitting Sherman to collect on his funded securities, and in the meantime he needed the salary. Politics was the only work he knew now. Even law would not pay him enough to live on; his erstwhile challenger Pierpont Edwards, with the richest practice in Connecticut, earned only about $2000 in 1789. At seventy years of age the old politician was beginning to feel used up. He tried to bolster his enthusiasm by calling up the old days when he was central to the excitement of the Revolution. Why don't you write, he complained to his ancient political correspondent, William Williams, like you used to during the war? "I seldom see the papers from Connecticut or hear much of politics. . . ." Perhaps his time was up, for "young people are rising up who would be willing to crowd us off the Stage to make room for themselves," he wrote recalling Pierpont Edwards' blustering. "But they can't deprive us of the consolation arising from a consciousness of having done our duty," he closed in self-assurance.[29]

The bank bill was the only major matter Sherman had time to discuss in the House, however, for when Congress moved to Philadelphia, William Samuel Johnson resigned in order to remain at his principal employment as president of Columbia College. The old politician was chosen by the Governor and Council to fill Johnson's place.** In the Senate he continued his campaign to keep the size of the House small, even though a reapportionment gave Connecticut two additional representatives. He also worked for the funding measure, which he wished to be effected as soon as possible. He took an interest, naturally, in the disastrous efforts of St. Clair to control the western Indians, and offered some military as well as financial advice on the

---

*In 1792 Learned was re-elected, but Benjamin Huntington's interrupted Congressional career was resurrected at the same time. Huntington's son interpreted the Congressional struggle as part of a larger plan to build a party against Governor Oliver Wolcott, Jr. Huntington, *Letters*, pp. 109-10.

**This mode of replacing resigned or deceased senators was statutory. CSL, "Revolutionary War," Ser. 1. XXXVII:285.

matter. Sherman regretted the Indian war but justified it as "necessary to prevent their ravages on the frontiers" and to "induce them to a Treaty of peace, where by they might have obtained all possible justice for any past injuries. . . ." However, the recent reverses at their hands, and the memory of Braddock's defeat "ought to convince us of the impropriety, of fighting Indians in the woods by regular troops in a Body. . . ." And peace would of course make possible the reduction of defense appropriations and taxes.[30]

Sherman, the one-time lawyer and long-time jurist, quite naturally took a great interest in the organization of the Judiciary. A whole series of letters to his son-in-law, Simeon Baldwin, deal with this legislation. Sherman had been working to get Baldwin either a Federal judicial position or at least a clerkship. He watched closely the discussions of compensation for these positions, though he was not on the committee dealing with them, and reported regularly and often to Baldwin. Sherman had advised his son-in-law on the proper procedure for application to Washington, and later got Ellsworth to speak to Washington personally in Baldwin's behalf. But on the passage of the act, the position of District Judge for Connecticut went to Sherman's old colleague at the bar, Richard Law. Sherman informed him of the honor and respectfully and successfully recommended Baldwin for the clerkship that was in Law's hands.[31]

Although in increasingly poor health, Sherman stayed on until the end of the first session of the Second Congress, which closed early in May 1792. He returned to Philadelphia when Congress reconvened in the fall, and was still there in the spring. By April 1793, three months before his death, however, the seventy-two-year-old Senator was sending to Philadelphia for the journals of the Senate, apparently unable to participate in person any longer.[32]

The Federal Service—A Summation

It is difficult to assess the importance of any man's part in a thing so complex, and involving so many men and issues, as the first four years of the Federal Congress. Roger Sherman's contemporaries readily attest to his influence. Theodore Sedgwick, the hot-headed but effective Congressman from Massachusetts, said of him, "he was a man of selectest wisdom. His influence was such that no measure or part of a measure which he advocated, ever failed to pass." The accuracy of this is not borne out by close examination, but that Sedgwick had such an impression is significant. Fisher Ames, who was to become the House leader of the Federalists, said that during the First Congress, "if he happened to be out of his seat when a subject was discussed, and came in when the question was about to be taken, he always felt safe in voting as Mr. Sherman did; for he always voted right." Jefferson, it is claimed, during these Congressional years pointed out Sherman one day to a friend and said, "That is Mr. Sherman of Connecticut, a man who never said a foolish thing in his life."[33]

Senator Macon of North Carolina once said that he thought Sherman "had more common sense than any man he ever knew." He recalled that once as a young man, when about to rise in debate on the Senate floor, Sherman restrained him; "My young friend," the old man said, "withhold your strength, we are now the majority—it is possible to say too much. It is the business of the minority to make speeches." "Minorities," he said on another occasion, "talk; majorities vote." This advice might have well been sauce for the gander, for Sherman spoke more times in the First Congress than any other Representative except James Madison. More significantly, he was the last speaker before the question and the first speaker of the day with a very high degree of frequency. This circumstance is especially indicative of his cloakroom method and his success therein. He missed only three rollcall votes out of 110 taken in the sessions of the First Congress.[34] He was on the losing side of many issues: he had opposed amendments; he had asked for a restricted executive power to dismiss executive officers; he had wished to keep the House small. But more often he had won. The Bill of Rights amendments were appended, not inserted; the assumption bill was passed, and no discrimination made among the various bond-holders. The debt was paid largely through relatively high duties. He was a superb politician, an expert in the art of determining the possible and bringing it about his way.

CHAPTER XVI

A Venerable Uncorrupted Patriot

IN 1788 Jeremiah Mason, then a young clerk working in the law office of Roger Sherman's son-in-law, Simeon Baldwin, wrote that the old man had a

family of children—some near my age. I was often at the house, and very frequently saw Mr. Sherman. His reputation was then at the zenith. His manners, without apparent arrogance, were excessively reserved and aristocratic. His habit was, in his own house, when tea was served to company, to walk down from his study into the room, take a seat, and sip his tea, of which he seemed fond, and then rise and walk out without speaking a word or taking any manner of notice of any individual. In the street he saw nobody, but wore his broad beaver pointing steadily to the horizon, and giving no idle nods. Still, I fancy Roger Sherman was capable of the most adroit address when his occasion required it.[1]

The law clerk then went on to describe the kindly, courteous, and flattering attitude taken by the old man when he had to ask Mason a favor.

Sherman may have had cause to appear severe, for his personal affairs were not going at all well. The principal cause of the perennial Congressman's difficulties was his inability to manage his finances and family because of long absences from New Haven. Many men in similar circumstances could rely on sons to take hold and carry on, but Sherman was unfortunate in this respect. Before the 1780's were passed he was near bankruptcy and was further saddened by desertion, divorce, and dipsomania among the three sons of his first marriage.

The Sherman Boys

Sherman's eldest son, John, was a paymaster during the Revolution with the rank of lieutenant. His service was marred by a final inability to make his accounts balance, but he was bailed out by his father, who posted a £3000 bond for him in 1783, which was still not collected at the time of Sherman's death. In general he was just not responsible, forgetting, for instance, to deliver official correspondence, to the chagrin of Joseph Trumbull, who reported to his father, the governor, that "Sherman I fear has been very Negligent." He had some success in business before the war, but afterwards never seemed to be able to settle down. In 1783 Sherman gave John a house and sold him a shop, but he was constantly in debt and in 1788 had to mortgage the property.[2] With this business failure he wished to start anew in another place, and writing a note to his father, he left. "Most Respected Parent," he wrote,

> my departure from [New Haven] is absolutely Necessary on account of my entering into business, the Trade of this city [New Haven] at Present is not an object of importance and scarcely of Support, I am now in the prime of Life, I hope my Friends will not think me lost, my determinations are Just, that is to pay all their dues and owe no one anything: . . .

He will advise his father and his wife of his new residence when he finds one, probably Charlestown or Savannah.

> Unhappy it is tho past, I did not take your advice it would not have Obliged me to take the present measures! I think that the most unfeeling Heart would not wish to distress Mrs. Sherman & the Children in my absence I leave them to your care you will please assert their rights to be their just protector . . . my own unhappiness proceeds from myself only.[3]

Evidently nothing worked out for John in the South. He continued to try to get his public accounts paid to him, sending a petition to his father in Congress in 1790. He needed the money to get into business so as to support a large family, and had made four applications to Congress before, but without success. He found his U. S. securities "daily falling and no general government established, which induced me to take the measures I did. . . . It is done I cannot help it," he wailed pathetically.[4]

In the first years of the new government John tried to get a job as a clerk in the national government, but his father could do little. "I wish John could find some Steady business," he wrote. "It is difficult to introduce him into a public office of a clerk. So many on the spot are applying. I shall speak with one or more of the heads of departments."[5] At this point Roger was still paying off suits against his eldest son, both on account of business failures and to fill up the accounts of the U. S. government. By 1792 John was living on his father's farm near New Haven, but still unable to succeed. He wrote his father in Philadelphia asking for five dollars for oats and corn for the poultry, and Sherman asked his son-in-law, Simeon Baldwin, to advance that sum and no more to him.

In Sherman's letter to Baldwin the picture begins to clear up. "Yet I dont wish to have him think that I have any distrust of his prudence in the expenditure unless it should appear to be necessary," he wrote. "He informs me that he totally abstains from Spiritous liquors and determines to persevere." During this collapse of fortunes, John was also faced with a divorce action by his wife, the daughter of Sherman's good friend, David Austin. Sherman wrote Austin, he told Baldwin, asking him to suspend the matter and promising John's peaceable behavior. "I do not think there is a legal foundation for a Separation, for if there had been a breach of covenant (which he denies) yet cohabitation after it is known extinguishes the rights to take advantage of it." He hoped a perpetual stigma on the family would be prevented, and added at the bottom of the letter, "I dont wish to have this seen by any other person." But Austin carried out the case, and hard feelings developed between the two old friends, who were now also waging a religious war in their church.[6]

It is doubtful that John kept away from old John Barleycorn, for in January he stormed into his house where his wife and children were now living without him, and in his wife's absence made off with some furniture and rugs. The children were somewhat terrorized by the event, and wrote to their grandfather asking that he do something to keep John away from the house. Ultimately, John moved to Stoughton, the early home of his father, and remarried. He died in 1802.[7]

William Sherman, Roger's second son, fared no better, indeed a good bit worse, than John. It was William to whom Roger turned over his business in 1772, and who in three years had all but run it into bankruptcy.[8] In July 1776, he was appointed paymaster in Seth Warner's regiment, but soon after began his difficulties. He started off on the wrong foot by inoculating a civilian at camp, an act contrary to the general orders. His colonel, Samuel Safford, wrote in 1777:

> your Son . . . was brought to trial before a General Court Martial and Cashiered and turned out of Employ. His staunch Friendship to the Cause we are now engaged in and the promising prospects we entertain of the Benefits that will under his auspices accrue to our Regiment induces me to bewail his Loss which will be the more severely felt as he is a person well versed in every Branch of his Duty and has acted up to it with Honour, therefore should be very willing and very happy in his Re-establishment.

Ultimately he was "re-established," but the benefits that accrued to his regiment under his auspices are dubious at best. About two years later Seth Warner received a letter from Washington, then at Morristown; Warner had asked for more clothing for the troops, or at least for some funds to buy them. Washington replied,

> There were also 20 Watch Coats, which Capt. Woolcot says Capt. Sherman your pay Master sold and applied the money to his own use. This may have been the case [also] with part of the blankets and other Articles. I have therefor suspended giving Capt. Woolcot an order for any new Cloathing untill the old is accounted for. If Capt. Sherman had been guilty of selling the Watch Coats he should be immediately arrested.

William had been in trouble for at least six months, for earlier in the year he had attempted to resign. The Board of War refused to permit this because "he has not settled the accounts of the regiment since raised, and has in his hands a considerable sum of money which is its due." The strain was too much for the thirty-year-old William and in November of 1779 he ran off, as Washington said, "in so scandalous a Manner," and so ended his active military career, not the most glorious of the war.[9]

William Sherman's difficulties may not have all been of his own making. In July 1779, about the time he attempted to resign from the army, he entered a petition before the Connecticut Assembly for forty pounds' damages due to losses incurred during the raid on New Haven by the British. His wife and children ran away, but were able to carry little with them, he reported, and so he was left with "Seven helpless Children naked to clothe and feed." The interesting and unexplained result of this petition is that the ultimate recipient of the damages money was William's father, not the boy at all.[10] Back in New Haven, his accounts to the Army probably cleared by his father, he again entered business, running a sloop to Norwich and New London, but again ended in bankruptcy. His sloop got frozen in at New London for two months, and a scow he used to transport salt was run up against some rocks and damaged beyond repair. In a petition before the Assembly, the executors of his accounts, David Austin and James Hillhouse, claimed "he has for a number of years been engaged in Trade and Merchandizing & by a Series of inevitable Misfortunes Such as the failure of Some persons largely indebted to him, losses at Sea . . ." had been brought to this embarrassment.[11]

William formally retired from the army in 1781 and at the same time gave up his marriage as well, for he was divorced from his wife that year. He went west to the Susquehannah lands in 1782, probably expecting to find work as a surveyor.[12] His success there is unknown, but he was back in New Haven a few years later. In 1789, while trying to earn some kind of living, again in business, William caught a sudden cold and died. He was thoroughly bankrupt and his accounts, which dragged on for several years, were finally settled for about eleven pence on the pound. William's death in 1789 caused Roger to write a long letter to Rebecca, for he could not attend the funeral, being at Congress at the time. "It is my earnest Prayer that this Providence may be Suitably regarded by me and all the family—and especially the surviving children, of our family and his [William's] child—that may be excited to be always in an actual readiness for death." His grandchildren were baptized but, for those who have come of age, "it is indispensibly necessary for them to give their cordial consent to the covenant of grace and that it is their duty to make a public profession of Religion and attend all the ordinances of the Gospel . . . " It was a sad end at the age of thirty-seven to a pathetic life for William.[13]

The third of Roger Sherman's boys, Isaac, fared much better than his two older brothers, but not really well. He, like William, was a graduate of Yale, class of 1770. He later received an M. A. as well, and taught for a while at Exeter, New Hampshire. In 1774 he went to Massachusetts to engage in business, but after the 19th of April of '75 he enlisted in the Massachusetts line to fight with Washington. He wrote a long letter to his father from Sewall's Point in September. "Public difficulties which rendered it almost impossible to obtain any employment sufficient to procure a maintenance, was an inducement for me to enter the Army; but far from being the only one. The goodness of the cause a desire of being an useful Member of society and of serving my Country—a thirst for Glory, real glory, were the grand incentives. . . . " His military career was a gallant one, and when new lists of officers were drawn up, no less than Washington himself took notice of an omission; "I would also mention Major Sherman," the Commander-in-Chief wrote from Harlem Heights, "Son of Mr. Sherman of Congress, a Young Gentleman who appears to me and who is generally esteemed an Active and Valuable Officer," who should be kept "lest we should lose an officer, who so far as I can judge, promises good service to his Country." And good service he gave, too, for he marched up grade, retiring in 1783 as a regimental commander, not yet having reached the age of thirty.[14]

After the war Isaac received a commission from Congress as a surveyor in the western lands. But because of various complications the job did not pay what he had supposed it would, and he had to petition Congress again and again between 1786 and 1788 in an attempt to get a fair compensation. For Isaac the war years were the height of his career, for he never developed beyond them. By 1788 he, too, had tried his hand at business and failed, having finally to write to his younger half-brother, Roger, for sixty dollars to clear his debts in order to leave New York City. His own misconduct, he said in a whining and petty letter, made it easier for him to sink into obscurity after military glory.[15]

In 1789 he accompanied John to Georgia, where they tried to earn a living, probably as surveyors, but Isaac was back in New Haven in 1790, asking his father for money to carry him until he could find employment—his father hoped in a government office. His financial difficulties followed him for years, and he was forced again and again to borrow from Alexander Hamilton, his old military comrade—from whom he also solicited a government job—as well as members of his own family.[16] Finally, some years after his father's death, he found himself in debtors' prison and wrote his brother-in-law in New Haven for thirty dollars. Baldwin replied that he and Roger, Jr. had investigated the matter and did not believe that thirty dollars was enough, but they couldn't afford even that, anyway. But he sent along five dollars and the cheering word that young Roger would look into the matter next time he was in New York.* Isaac ultimately moved to New Jersey and died in 1819.[17]

The failure of these three boys to live up to the standards set by their father is troubling. They were born of Sherman's first wife, Elizabeth, and grew up in the days of Roger's upward struggle, a fight that certainly left him little time or energy for his children. There is the added element of a mother who was possibly not the most exciting. Elizabeth never learned more than to scratch out her name, and she came from farm stock—good yeomanry, but not among the highly literate of the age. The fate of these three boys was sad, and it no doubt cast a shadow over the last years of their father's life.

The Distaff Side

Sherman's daughters, like his younger sons, all children of Rebecca, turned out far better than the three older boys. The girls were educated in the customary manner by a private female tutor, who was paid sometimes in merchandise from the old Sherman store. Sherman commonly addressed his letters to the girls, "Dear Daughter," and referred to their mother as "Mama."

---

*Genealogists have always reported Isaac as never married. Boardman, *Sherman*. p. 334n. However, sometime around 1794 he married Isabella, a woman of scant cultivation, and lived with her for several years. Either she had previously had children or she and Isaac had some. Isaac left her about 1800, perhaps only temporarily. He apparantly shared his brother's propensity for ardent spirits, and spent much of 1797 in debtors' prison. Baldwin Family Collection, December 17, 1794, February 1, 1795, January 2, 7, March 31, 1796, March 3, 15, April 8, 19, May 23, June 9, 27, July 29, 1797, January 6, February 17, July 14, 1799, April 19, 1800.

One of them, Rebecca, was a very pretty girl and at one time was sought by both Timothy Pitkin and Simeon Baldwin. Baldwin won out in the end, possibly because of some advice from his sister that "had you rather spend an evening with a book than the Ladies if I was to give my advice I would Spend some time with the Ladies and Some with my Book. . . ." When Rebecca died and then Sturges Burr, husband of Rebecca's sister Elizabeth, died also, Simeon Baldwin married the widow in 1800.[18]

As a matter of fact, all five of the Sherman girls who lived to maturity married well. Martha married Jeremiah Day, who was president of Yale for thirty years; Mehetabel was the wife of Jeremiah Evarts of New York, though she had been briefly married first to a classmate of young Roger's at Yale, Daniel Barnes, who died on a business trip to the West Indies; the youngest of the girls married Samuel Hoar of Massachusetts. Two of these girls raised boys who grew up to be senators, and one produced a governor of Connecticut, Roger Sherman Baldwin. The girls apparently took after their quick-witted mother more than the slower-thinking Roger. There is a family tradition that when George Washington visited New Haven and stopped for tea at Sherman's house, he was let out on his departure by Mehetabel, then fifteen years old. The President said to the girl, "You deserve a better office, my little maid," to which she replied (with a curtsy) "Yes, your Excellency—to let you in."[19]

The year 1789 saw the death of a sister and sister-in-law. And in 1790 Roger's brother Josiah died. But by 1790 Simeon Baldwin was able to keep things in New Haven under control. Baldwin,* a young lawyer who had graduated from Yale in 1781, married Sherman's daughter Rebecca in 1787. This young man, who established one of Connecticut's most prominent families, served in various public offices. He was made clerk of the City of New Haven by his father-in-law, the mayor, in 1789. Sherman also sponsored him for positions as clerk of the Connecticut Federal district and circuit courts, which he held from 1790 to 1806. He later served as a Congressman and judge of Connecticut's highest court. Sherman's two sons by Rebecca, Roger, Jr., a 1787 Yale graduate, and Oliver, still in his teens, were both too young to entrust with family affairs, and the old man took Simeon on as his attorney.[20]

The Theological Sherman

Certainly one of Roger Sherman's most prominent characteristics was his compromising temper. Indeed, expedience is a hallmark of his political career.

---

*He was also a first cousin to Silas Deane.

His lapses from flexibility were few. Perhaps, however, it is to be expected that a man over seventy would develop some rigidities, especially in religion, and Sherman's part in the New Divinity fracas that rumbled through Connecticut in the late eighties and nineties is most uncharacteristic.

Jonathan Edwards, Jr. had been appointed minister to the White Haven meeting in 1769 upon the resignation over a salary dispute of the doughty but dull Samuel Bird. The ordination had been brought about only with considerable acrimony, and after a vote of 94 to 36, about 90 members, one-third of the congregation, left to form its own society, known as Fair Haven, "rather than attend ye Ministrations of Mr. Edwards. . . ." who insisted upon the abandonment of the Half-Way Covenant. Since the time of the twenty-four-year-old preacher's settlement, the leaders of the reactionary New Lights had been passing from the scene. Jonathan's father died in 1758; Joseph Bellamy, "a broken paralytic vessel. . . . in ruins," in Ezra Stiles' description, would die in March 1790. Samuel Hopkins, Edwards' cousin, was still alive and happy in Newport, but subject to fits and nervous debilitation, and slipping out of reaction into mere conservatism in his religious doctrines. Younger men like Jonathan's brother, Pierpont, were trying to push ahead to leadership in politics; and so Jonathan and others sought to claim the theological captaincy no longer mounted in Connecticut.[21]

The result of this younger, more militant leadership was a skewing rightward of the New Divinity divines ever back closer and closer, so they thought, to the strict morality of the original American saints, and even to Calvin himself, but offering salvation to a wider selection than had the old-timers. Rather than seek compromise or accommodation, Edwards— referred to as "Dr.," "Jr.," or "the Younger," to distinguish him from his famous father—took what he deemed the most logically consistent position. Dr. Edwards maintained that anyone could be saved who received God's grace. God could give grace to everyone if he chose because Christ did not die for the sins of any individual person, but rather for mankind in general. So each man could, in effect, make his own atonement, and salvation was open to all. Baptism, however, could be administered only after a personal profession of faith and a convincing statement of personal regeneration. Indeed, Edwards went so far as to hold that moral behavior prior to regeneration was mere hypocrisy, for all men were naturally sinners. Since few late nineteenth-century Yankees were willing to claim a regenerative experience, the upshot was that Edwards' society, which had lost a third of its members to begin with, became very exclusive.[22]

Edwards' salary had been reduced during the hard times of the early eighties, a few months after his wife had drowned when her horse and chaise plunged into a mill pond. But it was not for a year or two after these two catastrophes that his doctrines became so strict as to alienate large numbers of his parish. In 1782 he had about eight hundred people to minister to, but by 1789 the number had shrunk to nineteen men and their families. Ezra Stiles, no friend to the New Divinity, didn't believe that there was a single member of Edwards' congregation who was as strict as the minister. Indeed, he wrote that Edwards' "incessant Preachg of New Divy & Rigidity in Chh. administration have disgusted them." But the final straw was laid on in 1788, when Edwards publicly attacked for his universalist beliefs the much respected member of the New Haven Common Council, Dr. Ebenezer Beardsley.[23]

Efforts were made by the society's two leading deacons, Roger Sherman and his close friend, father-in-law to his son John, David Austin, to heal the breach. Sherman got Edwards to write a conciliatory note, which the deacon took to Beardsley. But the doctor pointed out that Edwards still gave no indication that he felt him secure in his faith, and so refused to reply.[24] The controversy continued, and even Austin began to move away from Edwards' support. Indeed, by 1790 only Sherman remained the unbending theologian's champion; but he was off at Congress.

Sherman's church history goes back to his fight against the New Light separatists in New Milford in the 1750's, through his easy conversion to New Light membership on his removal to New Haven in 1761, to a position in 1789, unusual for a man of his compromising nature. He published in that year a sermon dealing with the qualifications for communion, one's readiness to share in the Lord's Supper. Mankind, he said, is in "a state of depravity, guilt and misery, exposed to the eternal curses of the law;—dead in tresspass and sins;—by nature prone to evil and averse to good, and entirely unable to deliver ourselves." But Jesus through atonement had opened man to deliverance, which could come about through utter faith in Him. We must be convinced that we hate all sin and have made every effort to purge it from our behavior; that we have faith in Jesus; that we feel a "supreme love" of God and a "hearty generous charity for our fellow man, especially for those of the household of faith. . . ."; and that we obey the commands of God as the "rule of our whole behavior." Only when we have full self-assurance of these matters are we ready for communion. But it is in man's interest to see these things, for an absolute faith is the first prerequisite of regeneracy—a condition desired by every rational man.[25]

This last view put Sherman athwart Edwards' cousin Samuel Hopkins, to whom Sherman wrote a pair of long letters in the spring of 1790. Samuel Hopkins, the leading follower of Jonathan Edwards, Sr., exactly Sherman's age, had graduated from Yale the same year that the semi-educated cobbler had come to Connecticut. He was now in the forty-seventh year of a ministry that would continue for thirteen years, and at the height of his prominence and influence among the New England divinity. In 1773 he had published "An Inquiry into the Nature of true Holiness," which Sherman read in the spring of 1790.[26]

Hopkins had defined all sin as emanating from self-love. Self-love was the opposite of holiness, which consists of universal love, and one should love oneself only to the degree that one is part of the universe; since an individual person was only an infinitesimal part, then one was due only infinitesimal self-love. Further, Hopkins maintained that this thrusting off of self-love should go so far as to "be willing to be damned, if this be necessary for the glory of God."

Sherman had long subscribed to, and a generation earlier had written, the fundamental assumption of not only his morality, but his politics as well, that "Reason and passion answer one great Aim, / And true self-love and social are the same." His empirical common sense was, then, affronted by this pair of dogmatic innovations. Indeed, the second he believed downright crazy. "It still appears to me," he wrote, "that no moral agent ever was or can be willing to be damned, and that no such thing is required by divine law or the gospel. If a person could be willing to be forever abandoned to sin and misery, he must be lost to any sense of good or happiness, as not to be capable of any regard to the glory of God, or the good and happiness of the moral system. . . . " The other point also seemed irrational to the pragmatic puritan. None of God's "rational creatures are miserable but for their own fault. He inflicts punishment, not in a way of mere sovereignty, but as a righteous Judge or Governor; and for the general good." Since man's chief end is the glorification of God and to "enjoy him forever . . ." therefore when a person seeks his own highest good and happiness in the enjoyment of God, and in connection with his glory, he answers the end of his creation. "Our temporal as well as spiritual good may be lawfully sought and enjoyed and our sensitive appetites gratified, so that it be not done in a manner or degree prohibited by law. . . . Moral good and evil," after all, "consists in exercises and not in dormant principles."

Sherman's view was rational and pragmatic, and informed by as many years in business, law, and politics as Hopkins had spent in the pulpit. The old divine was not moved one jot, but neither was he anything but respectful. Hopkins signed off "with high esteem, and much affection," wishing that each man "be led into all important in truth."

Actually, Sherman doesn't seem to have known which way to turn. Reasonable and pragmatic when writing Hopkins, he became dogmatic and inflexible when entering the lists for his own pastor. He admitted to having held the view "that if a brother should be of the opinion that all would finally be saved, it would not be sufficient ground to debar him from the communion if his life & conduct was morrale. . . ." but he changed his mind after finding an earlier statement of the church on the matter. Edwards was right, he wrote David Austin from New York, in opposing the idea of universal salvation. Such views are "very erroneous & if believed will tend to relax the restraints on vice arising from the threatenings of the divine law against impenitent sinners. . . . I think we are as much bound to believe the threatenings as the promises of the gospel." Punishment threatened is the best way to accomplish the divine will, "And any principles that tend to diminish the influence of those sentiments must be of dangerous tendency."[27]

But Austin, who less than a year earlier had agreed with Edwards that the regenerate of White Haven should not take communion with the unregenerate of the First Church, was on the spot in New Haven, where Edwards had virtually no support. It wasn't only theology that split the people from the parson. He just wasn't doing his job; he spent time transcribing some of his father's sermons for publication and sale—a project that could bring him £75 or more; he was speculating in Genesee lands; he wasn't visiting his parishioners; he spent his time writing answers to the pamphlets of the late liberal Charles Chauncy. Austin thought that he and Sherman could agree if they could just spend a day discussing the matter. "I impute our difference in the state of affairs in our Church & Society to your partial acquaintance with Dr. Edwards' conduct, & Preaching, you having been abroad a great part of your time for several years." There was no hope, said Austin, unless Edwards changed his opinions. About the only thing sustaining him in New Haven was Sherman's support. "I have heard it observed," wrote Austin, "by a number of brothern, that they believe Dr. Edwards would never have carried matters so far as he has done, had he not leaned on you for support, and I have frequently heard that he has made use of this argument with some persons . . . that Esqr Sherman thinks so, or is of the opinion in matters of controversy. . . ." Sherman's reply must have disappointed Austin, for he supported most of Edwards' activities, and declared that though he had been to many services in his years of traveling, Edwards was the best preacher he had ever heard. And he wrote to Baldwin the same, adding that he thought Edwards "sound in Faith, & pious and diligent in his studies and attention to the duties of his office." It would be "highly criminal to insist upon" joint lectures with Dr. Dana of the First Church, because some of "our people" would object. But always the practicing politician, he could not refrain from suggesting a compromise: "Let each preach his own lecture, & every one may attend either, or both, at pleasure."[28]

Though Sherman received reports from his son-in-law Simeon Baldwin from April 1790 through 1791 that affairs in the society went well, it was in fact a tenuous truce. He had written at the height of the crisis in early 1790 that it would be wise to "avoid calling society meetings unnecessarily, as I think it would only promote dissention. Our Savior says 'Wo to the world because of offences; but Wo to that man by whom the offence cometh.' " Despite the temporary truce, however, the society found difficulty in raising Edwards' salary, either from inability or unwillingness. Sherman suspected the latter, and wrote that there were some members who could afford to pay more than their share—whom he listed; the money was raised forthwith. Sherman knew that if Edwards was forced out the White Haven society would cease to exist; he said so several times. Indeed, the anti-Edwards forces, who by 1790 had won over David Austin, were in fact really conniving at a reunion with the First Church, which was also squabbling with its minister David Austin, Jr., son of White Haven's deacon, another New Divinity man. The young Reverend Austin left in early 1790 to take a pulpit in Elizabethtown, New Jersey, so the push was made to get Edwards out then, also. It failed, with Sherman's aid, for the time being, but only awaited a new incident or a change of heart in Sherman to succeed.[29]

Edwards did not forget his friend at court. When Sherman died in 1793 he preached the eulogy:

> His abilities were remarkable, not brilliant, but solid, penetrating and capable of deep and long investigation. In such investigation he was greatly assisted by his patient and unremitting application and perseverance. While others weary of a short attention or dissipation, he was employed in prosecuting the same business, either by revolving it in his mind and ripening his own thoughts upon it, or conferring with others.

But this prime beneficiary of that perseverance also paid compliment to his protector's theological knowledge.

> He could with reputation to himself and improvement to others converse on the most important subjects of theology. I confess myself to have been often entertained, and in the general course of my long and intimate acquaintance with him to have been much improved by his observations on the principal subjects of doctrinal and practical divinity.[30]

But Edwards' troubles were not over.

This was a temporary respite, and the minister was deceived into thinking it permanent. "On the death of my good and able friend Mr. Senator

Sherman," he wrote in the fall of 1794, "I expected my troubles would break out with greater fury than ever. But God's ways are not as our ways, nor are his thoughts as our thoughts. Ever since his death we have been more quiet than before. Yet it seemed that he, while alive, was the great means of keeping us so quiet. . . ." But by the next summer Edwards was in hot water again, and was dismissed late that year. He moved on to a call from Colebrook, and then in 1799 to the presidency of Union College for the last two years of his life. White Haven and its old mother society, the First Church, were then rejoined and formed the present United Church.[31]

Another religious concern that interested Sherman during the last years of his life was the question of divorce. He was involved with the divorces of his sons, William in 1781, John in 1792, and the estrangement of his own sister, Rebecca, who was over sixty in 1792.* In this last case it was apparently Rebecca's husband who wished to bring about a reconciliation, and Sherman urged his sister to rejoin her husband, who was living a lonely life in New Milford. In the case of his son John, Sherman wrote to the president at Princeton, Dr. John Witherspoon, to get agreement that simple desertion is as good ground for divorce as incontinency. He said he had found substantiation for his view in I Corinthians vii:15, and Witherspoon agreed.[32]

Sherman's Finances

In addition to the Sherman family's domestic trials there was the question of money. Like most of the Revolutionary figures who had given their time to the public, Roger Sherman had been forced to neglect his personal business affairs. The parsimonious General Assembly never paid on time, and in the fall of 1789 Sherman had to petition for the remaining £775 of the £2172 due him for services done between 1775 and 1780. He needed as much of the money as he could get then, but asked for £150 immediately because he had "lately been at considerable expense by advancement by way of settlement to several of my children." He added somewhat desperately that he would take £100 if £150 were not available. Now he had to wait until the Federal Congress passed appropriations before he could pay his bills, though as early as 1786 he had been unable to pay his New Milford land taxes, and his real estate there was threatened by a forced sale.[33]

---

*Sherman's Rebeccas can be confusing. His father's first wife, his own sister, his second wife, a daughter, and a daughter-in-law all bore the name Rebecca Sherman. At one time there were four women of that name living in New Haven—and one of them was no relation at all.

Sherman's daughters were making pairs of gloves by the dozens to be sold by "a wholesale merchant that I deal with who may sell them at the same price as imported ones—If Marten Skins can be procured as cheap as you mention it might be well to manufacture Muffs and Tippets for sale," wrote the Yankee merchant. Sherman was also selling and giving presents of coffee, "though none of the family [with whom he was staying in New York] knew that it wasn't imported Coffee, nor should I wish to have anything said about what you send here...." And he could pick up a little cash by selling sermons he had printed. Clothes to be laundered he sent home to New Haven by boat, for it cost him three-quarters of a dollar in New York for the job. But the picture would soon brighten, he continued, "assumption will probably be passed and debt paid with hard cash." By 1791 Sherman's older son of his second marriage, Roger, Jr., was able to take charge of the family business, and his father sent him explicit and detailed instructions from Congress. Despite his frequent complaints of lack of funds, in 1791 Sherman was able to instruct Roger to go to Hartford and take out some of the new funded securities, and two years later he bought six hundred dollars' worth himself.[34]

Indeed, Sherman's poverty was more apparent than real. Actually it was largely a result of the shortage of good circulating medium that he had been so busy trying to maintain during his long service in the old and new Congresses. A will drawn in August, 1792, showed distributable liquid estate of about £1430, probably mostly in government bonds, a library worth at least £20, various furniture and other items worth well over £330. In addition to this he owned land valued at over £1830. So his net worth was well over £3000, probably much closer to £4000. Sherman's hints of poverty can only be interpreted to refer to a lack of cash. He did not live in ostentation, perhaps, but neither did he live the simple and spare existence supposed to be characteristic of the old Puritan tradition. He owned three each of hats, coats, suits, and gowns, four vests, five pairs of breeches, fifteen pairs of socks and twenty pairs of stockings, and twenty shirts. He had a good deal of silver, brass, tin, and pewter as well as five looking glasses. The portrait of himself and a Sherman Coat of Arms hardly give the impression of total modesty. He had two desks, six feather beds and nineteen coverlets, which is understandable, but what he did with fifteen tables and fifty chairs is hard to imagine. He had a fine library on a wide variety of subjects from tables of logarithms and maps to John Milton and Barlow's *Vision of Columbus*. Principally, however, the library consisted of political and religious works.[35]

Whether in financial straits or not, Sherman still wanted to provide his family with some of the luxuries of life. He promised his wife a new carpet on one occasion, to be bought on his next trip to New York, and a piece of "India Taffity" for his daughters Becca and Betsey, which he could not find in New York. His two youngest sons, Roger and Oliver, were both sent to Yale and then to Tapping Reeve's law school in Litchfield, although Roger, Jr., was afraid at one time that "Par" might be forced to withdraw him for financial reasons. Oliver had expected to start at Yale in 1790 when he was thirteen years old, but his father preferred that he wait until he was a year or two older.[36]

The First Citizen of New Haven

Besides church, business and family duties, Roger Sherman also had to perform his functions as Mayor of New Haven. He had to sign a "Diploma," for instance, giving Vice-President Adams the freedom of the city. Sherman was absent at Congress on the occasion of presentation, and Adams wrote, "I suppose myself chiefly indebted to your Friendship for the favorable Representation of my character among your neighbors which has produced this obliging result. I hope it will not be long before we can renew our former acquaintance and intimacy."[37]

He had to dedicate bridges, and preside at the meetings of the City Council, and he was pressing for adoption of city fire protection measures. He had an interest in the crazy inventions of a New Haven resident, one Doctor Jedediah Strong, who had invented some sort of a vehicle run by machinery which "will be small and enclosed in a cage." When Sherman saw it, his only comment is reported to have been, "The machine will be a success if it will go." The machine did not go, and therefore was not a success, bearing out Sherman's remarkable prophecy. Strong wrote Sherman begging forgiveness for all his youthful follies, promising never to indulge in mechanical experiments again, berating himself for using up all of his friends' money, and asking for an appointment as Surgeon's Mate.[38]

Failing Health

Roger Sherman was a big man, and robust, but during his Congressional years he had not been well. His troubles began in May 1790, when for two weeks he was laid low with influenza. Though he recovered by the end of the month, his health remained a cause for concern to his family and friends.[39] During the First Congress he made frequent trips back and forth between New York and New Haven, usually by boat, but sometimes by chaise. In his absence Rebecca, his wife, could take care of affairs at home. In the only letter to her husband known to exist, she reported that the heifer had calved, and that Roger was due home from college soon. His wife and two young sons accompanied him to New York on occasion, but more often he went alone and returned home by boat for a long weekend. In the spring of 1793 Sherman did not go to Philadelphia for the opening of the Third Congress, in which he was to have resumed his Senate seat. He was forced to keep up with Senate business by sending for the journals, and on April 15 he performed what is thought to be his last public act.[40] This was the laying of the cornerstone for South College at Yale, a college for which he had served as treasurer for years, and from which he held an honorary M. A.

Sherman became seriously ill about the middle of May 1793, and was forced to remain in bed, bilious, drowsy, and too weak to turn himself. He died in the early evening of July 23, 1793, at the age of seventy-two. Two days later his funeral was held in great pomp. "The Students and Tutors of the University formed the Head of the Procession," wrote President Stiles,

> then the 2 City Sheriffs preceded the City Officers, the Common Council, 4 Aldermen, 2 Justices, 2 Members of Congress & a Judge of the Supr Court, the Clergy, Eight Ministers, the Bearers & Corps [sic] (no Pallbearers) Mourners & Citizens Male & Female, a large Concourse. Sermons were preached by Edwards at the Meeting House and by Dr. Dana at the Grave. Every part was conducted with respectful Decency & Solemnity.[41]

At the White Haven church Jonathan Edwards pronounced eulogia on his dead friend. But in summary he was perhaps most accurate when he said:

> His proper line was politics. For usefulness and excelence in this line, he was qualified not only by his acute discernment and sound judgement, but especially by his knowledge of human nature. He had a happy talent of judging what was feasible and what was not feasible, or what men would bear, and what they would not bear in government. And he had a rare talent of prudence, or of timing and adapting his measures to the attainment of his end. . . .[42]

He had "that Dignity which arises from doing every Thing perfectly right," wrote Ezra Stiles. "He was an extraordy Man—a venerable uncorrupted Patriot."[43]

List of Abbreviations

AAS	American Antiquarian Society
AHA	American Historical Association
AHR	*American Historical Review*
CHS	Connecticut Historical Society
CR	*Public Records of the Colony of Connecticut*
CSL	Connecticut State Library
DAB	*Dictionary of American Biography*
HSP	Historical Society of Pennsylvania
JCC	*Journals of the Continental Congress*
LC	Library of Congress
MHS	Massachusetts Historical Society
NHCHS	New Haven Colony Historical Society
NLCHS	New London Colonial Historical Society
NYHS	New York Historical Society
NYPL	New York Public Library
SR	*Public Records of the State of Connecticut*

Citations

CHAPTER I:

The Making of a Solid Citizen

1. Election sermon by Richard Salter, May, 1768, quoted in Bushman, *From Puritan*, p. 277. Bushman deals excellently with the question of social and theological concepts of self-love in the changing intellectual life of eighteenth-century Connecticut, Ch. XVI.

2. Kingman, "Sherman"; New Milford "Town List" for 1759; Kingman, "Technical America."

3. "Earliest Town Records Including Summons For First Town Meeting," Town Records, Stoughton Town Hall.

4. Huntoon, *Canton*, p. 236.

5. Sherman, *Genealogy*, pp. 135–38; Huntoon, *Canton*, p. 236.

6. New Milford "Town Records Manuscript," V:136. There is a notation stuck in among the transfers for 1742/3, "New Milford January 28:1728 William Sherman's Record of Land," being a layout of three acres "on East side of Great River & west side of Long Mountain." It is witnessed by Roger Brownson, registrar, and Roger Sherman, and dated January 27, 1742/3; New Milford "Town Records Manuscript," V:41.

7. Sherman, *Genealogy*, pp. 135–38; Huntoon, *Canton*, p. 236; Suffolk County Land Registration Office, Book 67, p. 212 (sold December 23, 1742, and registered February 7, 1743); Yale, Hist. Ms. Room, "Sherman Collection," receipt from James Buck; Suffolk Land Records, 35:337, 456, 36:149, 182, 183–84, 43:360, New Series, 21:300–301.

8. Main, *Structure*, pp. 14–15. CSL, "Towns and Lands," Ser. 1. VIII:1–25, 32, 33ab; CSL, "Ecclesiastical Affairs," IX:292–99; *The Sherman Sentinel*, November 13, 1968.

9. New Milford "Minutes of the Town Meeting." April 13, 1743.

10. *CR* IX:173, X:416; CSL, "Civil Officers," Ser. 1. III:96. Apparently there was no contest for the office.

11. For the controversy over the surveyorship see CSL, "Civil Officers," Ser. 1. III:359, 394–95, 405, 410, 443, Ser. 2. XXIII:20, 23, 26. Sherman was replaced by David Ferris, also from New Milford. CSL, "Civil Officers," Ser. 1. XXIII:33, 34.

12. Boardman, *Sherman*, p. 25; Sherman's *Norwood* was in the Framingham, Massachusetts, Historical Society Library in 1960, but has since been reported missing.

13. Kingman, "Colonial Surveyor."

14. *CR*, III:132e, 117; New Milford "Land Records," VI:203; New Milford "Town Records Manuscript," 1746-1800, *passim*; list of land transactions compiled by the New Milford Registrar in 1800. Yale, Beinecke Library, "Sherman Papers"; Grant, *Kent*, p. 74; Kingman, "Sherman."

15. New Milford Land Records, VI:107; Boardman, *Sherman*, p. 40.

16. Grant, *Kent*, pp. 112-14.

17. See New Milford "Town Records Manuscript" volumes V-IX for total purchases (1746-1792) of 1148 acres and sales (1749-1783) of 547½ acres.

18. See Ralph Earl portrait at Yale; Boutell, *Sherman*, p. 304; Mason, *Memoir*, ps. 123, 192; "Memoir of Roger Sherman," *New Haven Morning Courier*, July 29, 1843; Jonathan Edwards, Jr., *Works*, p. 182; other physical descriptions are found in Adams' and Pierce's notes on the debates of the Constitutional Convention.

19. Endicott, *Record*, ps. 60, 63.

20. Corner, ed., *Benjamin Rush*, p. 145.

21. Bates, "Connecticut Almanacs," pp. 408-16; Paltsits, "Almanacs," ps. 225, 216; Boardman, *Sherman*, p. 43.

22. For other examples see Paltsits, "Almanacs," pf. 244 and Boardman, *Sherman*, pp. 45-51. For a full discussion of eighteenth-century ideas of virtue see Wood, *Creation*, ps. 53, 61, 69, 96-97, 117-118.

23. The notebook is in the Roger Sherman Papers, LC.

24. Advertisement in the *Connecticut Gazette*, July 12, 1760; NYHS *Collections*, XIX:86-88.

25. New Milford "Minutes of the Town Meeting," February 6, 1743/4.

26. Grant, *Kent*, pp. 107-10.

27. New Milford "Minutes of the Town Meeting," May 10, 1749, December 10, 1750, December 9, 1751, November 13, 1752, December 11, 1752.

28. New Milford "Minutes of the Town Meeting," December 10, 1753, January 7, 1754; *CR*, X:353, 358.

29. *CR*, X, XI, *passim*.

30. Farrell, "Administration of Justice," p. 210; CSL, Records of the Litchfield County Court; LC, "Sherman Papers," Sherman notebook; Stiles, *Lit. Diary*, III:500; LC, "Sherman Papers," RS to Theophailact Bache (August 15, 1763).

31. CHS, "Johnson Papers," RS to W. S. Johnson (December 5, 1766). Yale, Hist. Ms. Room, "Sherman Collection," RS to Simeon Baldwin (January 21, 1791).

32. Orcutt, *New Milford*, p. 447; Yale, Hist. Ms. Room, "Sherman Collection," Daybook of Sherman and Carpenter.

33. Probate Records at Woodbury Town Hall, III:143-44.

34. Gipson, "Connecticut Taxation," p. 5n; Bronson, "Connecticut Currency," NHCHS *Papers*, I:65. Stoughton Town Records, "Earliest Town Records," pp. 67–69 (May 19, 1740).

35. CSL, "Litchfield County Court Records," vault 15, file box 17, 1754–1755, A–Z.

36. There is a copy of the pamphlet at Yale.

37. Quoted in Bushman, *From Puritan*, pp. 131–32. See Chapters VII and VIII of Bushman for a full discussion of the rise of commercialism in the first half of the eighteenth century.

38. Bushman, *From Puritan*, p. 132; Zeichner, *Controversy*, p. 259 n119; *CR*, X: 105; CSL, "Finance and Currency," Ser. 1. IV:69.

39. CLS, "Colonial Wars," Ser. 1. VII:197ab; VIII:101, 246, 232–33 tell Law's side of the story.

40. New Milford "Town Records Manuscript," IX:562; Sherman account book at NHCHS; New Haven "Records," XXIII:97.

41. The inventory and the account book are in the Beinecke Library at Yale. See also the *Connecticut Gazette* for February 6, 1762 and July 19, 1765 for examples.

42. RS to Simeon Baldwin (February 4, 1792), Samuel Safford to RS (June 11, 1777), act of Assembly (May 27, 1782) appointing RS executor of William's bankrupt estate, petition and resolve of Assembly making James Hillhouse and David Austin executors of William's estate, list of thirty-four creditors, all in Yale Hist. Ms. Room, "Sherman Collection"; LC, "Sherman Papers," plea of William's New York creditors.

CHAPTER II:
The Connecticut Scene

1. Stamps, "Political Parties," p. 2; Labaree, *Conservatism*, p. 22.

2. Bushman, *From Puritan* is especially helpful in demonstrating the causes and nature of this dynamism.

3. Bushman, *From Puritan*, pp. 9–10.

4. Andrews, *Earliest Settlements*, p. 132; Labaree, *Conservatism*, pp. 21–24.

5. For the Spanish Ship case see Hooker, *Spanish Ship*; for the election of 1766 see Zeichner, *Controversy*, Ch. III or Nutting, "Governor Thomas Fitch."

6. McKinley, *Suffrage*, pp. 419–20.

7. Robinson, *Jeffersonian Democracy*, ps. 7, 3-4.

8. Purcell, *Transition*, p. 91; *SR*, XI:introduction *passim.*

9. See below, pp. 283.

10. Silas Deane to John Trumbull (October 20, 1775) in NYHS *Collections*, XIX:86; John Adams' Diary (September 15, 1775), *Adams Papers*, I:173.

11. See for instance Welling, "Connecticut Federalism," p. 266.

12. Stiles, *Lit. Diary*, I:443.

13. Boyd, *Susquehannah Papers*, I:li–lii.

14. Olson, *Agricalatural Economy*, pp. 11-13; NHCHS *Collections*, IX:446; Rosenberry, *Migrations, passim;* Morrow, *Connecticut Influences, passim.*

15. The economic revolution in eighteenth-century Connecticut is suggested by Bushman, *From Puritan*, and thoroughly documented in Saladino, "Economic Revolution," from which much of this section is taken. But see also Van Dusen, "Trade of Revolutionary Connecticut"; Olson, *Agricultural Economy*; Hooker, *Colonial Trade*.

16. Saladino, "Economic Revolution," ps. 1-4, 22, 12.

17. Saladino, "Economic Revolution," ps. 4, 12, 17; Van Dusen, "Trade of Revolutionary Connecticut," pp. 141-47.

18. Saladino, "Economic Revolution," ps. 4, 12, 17; *CR*, XI:505; Levermore, *Republic of New Haven*, pp. 199-202; Saladino, "Economic Revolution," p. 17. Stiles gives the edge to New London, *Extracts*, p. 28, as does Hooker in *Colonial Trade*, p. 38; but Schlesinger agrees with Saladino. *Colonial Merchants*, p. 26.

19. Stiles, *Extracts*, p. 49; Osterweis, *Three Centuries*, p. 83; Levermore, *Republic of New Haven*, p. 229.

20. An excellent discussion of this movement is found in Bushman, *From Puritan*, Chs. XII, XIII, XIV.

21. Stiles, *Extracts*, p. 414.

22. *CR*, VII:107.

23. *CR*, IX:516-17.

24. Trumbull, *Connecticut*, II:89,157; Stiles, *Extracts*, ps. 269, 299.

25. Boardman, *Sherman*, pp. 24-25; Orcutt, *New Milford*, pp. 145-50; Stiles, *Extracts*, p. 79; Giddings, *Two Centuries*, p. 10.

26. This story can be traced in the New Milford Congregational Church Records, "Meetings 1716-1779," in manuscript at the Church. The split within the church seems to have no economic basis. In New Milford rich and middling are found on both sides, and studies for other towns provide the same conclusion. See for instance Bushman, *From Puritan*, p. 185.

27. Bushman, *From Puritan*, p. 238; Stiles, *Extracts*, 182; New Milford Cong. Ch. Records, "Meetings 1716-1779," p. 14.

28. New Milford Cong. Ch. Records, "Meetings 1753-1836," ps. 1, 9, 23; *Ibid*, "Meetings 1717-1779," ps. 56, 77, 79.

29. Benjamin Gale to Jared Ingersoll (January 13, 1766), quoted in Bailey, "Radicalism," p. 242n.

30. Stiles, *Extracts*, p. 335-37; Bushman, *From Puritan*, pp. 260-61; Bacon, *Thirteen Discourses*, p. 232; New Milford Cong. Ch. Records, "Meetings 1716-1779," pp. 10-13; Stiles, *Lit. Diaries*, I:118; Stiles, *Extracts*, p. 50; Levermore, *Republic of New Haven*, pp. 228-30; Tucker, *Protagnist*, pp. 213-25.

31. Zeichner, *Controversy*, pp. 25-26; CHS, "Johnson Papers," WSJ to John Beach (January 4, 1763).

32. For a full discussion of this intellectual shift generally, and for considerable support see Bushman, *From Puritan*, pp. 275-78.

33. Boyd and Taylor, eds., *Susquehannah Papers*, and Boyd, *The Susquehannah Company* provide excellent accounts.

34. Bushman *From Puritan*, Ch. VIII. The following account is taken from Boyd, *Susquehannah Papers*, I:Introduction.

35. Boyd, *Susquehannah Papers*, II:231 n34, 230.

36. Sanderson, *Signers*, III:240; Boyd, *The Susquehannah Company*, p. 3.

37. Boyd, *Susquehannah Papers*, III:55, 199, I:13, 172, 106.

38. Boyd, *Susquehannah Papers*, I:lxv; Zeichner, *Controversy*, p. 152; *Connecticut Courant*, March 15, 1774; CSL, "Trumbull Papers," XXI:32a; see also Osterweis, *Three Centuries*, p. 117.

39. Groce, "Gale," p. 701. The following material on Gale is from the same source.

40. Stiles, *Extracts*, ps. 63–64, 470, 28. See also Peck, *Loyalists*, p. 3.

CHAPTER III:
The Politician Comes of Age

1. Tucker, *Protagonist*, p. 121; McAnear, "Selection of Alma Mater," ps. 431, 435.

2. Boardman, *Sherman*, pp. 75–76; Bennett, "American Mothers," p. 51. The following paragraph is mostly from Bennett also.

3. Gipson, "Parliamentary Aid," pp. 722–25. In the Bancroft Papers at NYPL there is a statement of Governor Fitch on the colony's willingness to bear imperial burdens.

4. Gipson, "Parliamentary Aid," p. 726; Stuart, *Trumbull*, p. 171; Gipson, *Connecticut Taxation*, pp. 9–10.

5. Boyd, *The Susquehannah Company*, p. 25; Bailey, "Radicalism," Chs. IV and V.

6. Stiles, *Extracts*, pp. 581–82.

7. Stiles, *Extracts*, p. 582.

8. *CR*, XII:*passim*.

9. *CR*, XI:574, XII:78, 226, 294, 415, 454.

10. CSL, "Revolutionary War," Ser. 1. I:11, 15.

11. Zeichner, *Controversy*, p. 52.

12. *Connecticut Gazette*, August 9, 16, 1765.

13. *Connecticut Gazette*, July 19, 1765, November 1, 1765; Jensen, *Founding*, p. 151; Yale, Beinecke, "Sherman Papers," Day Book; Saladino, "Economic Revolution," p. 12; *Connecticut Gazette*, August 9, 1766.

14. *Connecticut Gazette*, September 20, 1765.

15. CHS, "Johnson Papers," Instructions to delegates dated only 1765, in RS's handwriting.

16. Zeichner, *Controversy*, p. 266 n71; Beardsley, *Johnson*, ps. 193–94, 32; Stiles, *Extracts*, p. 221.

17. *Connecticut Gazette*, October 18, 1765. The deputies are listed by name with asterisks indicating new members; CSL, "Revolutionary War," Ser. 1. I:11.

18. *CR*, XII:120-21.

19. CSL, "Revolutionary War," Ser. 1. I:29; *CR*, XII:420; New Haven Town Meeting, "Minutes," September 17, 1765; Boutell, *Sherman*, p. 51; *Connecticut Gazette*, September 20, 1765.

20. Zeichner, *Controversy*, p. 60; Jensen, *Founding*, p. 150; Boardman, *Sherman*, p. 90; *Connecticut Gazette*, May 10, 1766.

21. Trumbull, "Sons of Liberty," p. 312. See Zeichner's appraisal of the real leadership of the radicals where he names Jonathan Trumbull. *Controversy*, pp. 271-72.

22. Zeichner, *Controversy*, pp. 61-62; Dexter, ed., "Ingersoll Papers," p. 372; NHCHS, Ezra Stiles to Leverett Hubbard, (September 21, 1766); *Connecticut Gazette*, April 5, 1765; Zeichner, *Controversy*, pp. 63-64.

23. The letter is printed in Boardman, *Sherman*, pp. 91-92.

24. *Connecticut Gazette*, April 15, February 21, 1766.

25. Records of the Town of New Haven, "A True Copy," Ms. in City Clerk's office, p. 563; CSL, "New Haven County Court Records," vol. I in vault 18; Morgan, *Stiles*, p. 201.

26. Zeichner, *Controversy*, p. 66; *Connecticut Gazette*, February 7, 14, 21, 1766. Arnold's statement of the case in February 14, 1766.

27. *Connecticut Gazette*, February 6, 1766; Records of the Town of New Haven, "A True Copy," pp. 565-66 (p. 489 of original); *Connecticut Gazette*, February 14, 21, 1766.

28. *Connecticut Gazette*, February 21, 28, 1766; Stiles, *Extracts*, p. 462; *Connecticut Gazette*, February 28, 1766.

29. *Connecticut Gazette*, January 17, 1766; Beardsley, *Johnson*, p. 194.

30. See PHILALETHES in *Connecticut Gazette*, May 17, 1766; *Connecticut Gazette*, February 28, May 24, 1766.

31. Fitch, "An Explanation of Say-Brook Platform," p. 38. There is a copy in the Beinecke Library at Yale.

32. Hobart, "An Attempt." There is a copy at Beinecke; Stiles, *Extracts*, p. 511.

33. *Connecticut Courant*, March 31, 1766; Stiles, *Extracts*, p. 64. Nutting, "Fitch," Ch. VII. The campaign can be followed in the *Connecticut Gazette* and *Connecticut Courant* for April and May 1766 and April 1767. See also Bushman, *From Puritan*, Ch. XV.

34. *Connecticut Courant*, supplement to April 6, 1767; Stiles, *Extracts*, ps. 582, 463.

35. For comparison see Main, *Upper House*, pp. 82-83.

36. CHS, "Johnson Papers," RS to W. S. Johnson (December 5, 1766); Wood, *Creation*, quotes Dickinson, p. 5.

37. Wood, *Creation*, pp. 350-51.

38. Fitch, "Reasons Why," p. 7. There is a copy at Beinecke.

39. *Connecticut Gazette*, February 28, March 7, 14, 21, April 11, 1767.

40. *Connecticut Gazette*, April 11, 1767; Stiles, *Extracts*, p. 463.

41. Stiles, *Extracts*, pp. 492–93; NHCHS, Leverett Hubbard to Ezra Stiles (September 21, 1766); Stiles, *Extracts*, pp. 465–66; Records of the Town of New Haven, "A True Copy," ps. 570, 575, V:3.

42. *Connecticut Gazette*, July 25, 1767; see parody of Sherman's honesty in letter of John Trumbull to Silas Deane, NYHS, *Collections*, "Deane Papers," pp. 86–87; Stiles, *Extracts*, p. 463.

43. Bailey, *Radicalism*, p. 190; Groce, "Dyer," p. 293; Bailey, *Radicalism*, p. 238.

44. *CR*, XI:574, XII:78, 226, 294, 415; Stiles, *Extracts*, pp. 63–64.

45. Zeichner, *Controversy*, ps. 60–61, 65.

46. *Connecticut Gazette*, February 14, 1766.

47. *Connecticut Gazette*, January 31, 1766; Zeichner, *Controversy*, pp. 60–61.

48. Quoted in Boutell, *Sherman*, p. 294.

CHAPTER IV:
The Politics of Leadership

1. LC, "Sherman Papers"; Tucker, *Protagonist*, p. 255; quoted in Baldwin, "Memoir," *Connecticut Gazette*, June 18, August 6, 1763; Dexter, *Sketches*, II:699–701.

2. Tucker, *Protagonist*, pp. 237–38.

3. LC, "Sherman Papers," RS to Theophailact Bache (August 15, 1764); Yale, Beinecke, "Sherman Papers," (Papers Relating to the Estate of Roger Sherman); Stiles, *Extracts*, ps. 51, 188; account books at Beinecke and at NHCHS; *Connecticut Gazette*, July 19, 1765, August 9, 1766, July 23, 1768, for typical advertisements; *Connecticut Gazette*, June 13, 20, 1767 carries the article on paper money; Day Book at NHCHS entry for November 3, 1768 is an example of such dunning.

4. Saladino, "Economic Revolution," pp. 8–11.

5. Stiles, *Lit. Diary*, II:331; Gipson, *Taxation*, pp. 15–16; *Connecticut Gazette*, February 21, 1766.

6. Zeichner, *Controversy*, p. 59; Stiles, *Extracts*, p. 463; Zeichner, *Controversy*, p. 59.

7. Beardsley, *Johnson*, p. 60; Saladino, "Economic Revolution," ps. 5, 12–15, 64.

8. See Sherman's account books at Yale and NHCHS; Yale, Beinecke, "Sherman Papers."

9. Saladino, "Economic Revolution," p. 167; Yale, Beinecke, "Sherman Papers," (RS Day Book); *Connecticut Gazette*, August 3, 1765.

10. I have told this story in detail in NHCHS, *Journal*, September, 1968; Stiles, *Extracts*, pp. 460, 460n.

11. *CR*, XIII:87–88.

12. Zeichner, *Controversy*, p. 84; CHS, "Johnson Papers," RS to Johnson (June 25, 1768); NYPL, Bancroft Transcriptions, Johnson to RS (September 28, 1768).

13. New Haven Town Records in City Clerk's Office under February 28 and March 4, 1768 in volume IV; Gipson, *Ingersoll*, p. 276.

14. Zeichner, *Controversy*, p. 85; *CR*, XIII:72-74.

15. Schlesinger, *Colonial Merchants*, p. 151; CHS, *Collections*, "Pitkin Papers," XIX:189-90, 193.

16. Boutell, *Sherman*, p. 57; Zeichner, *Controversy*, p. 86.

17. The letter, printed in full in Boutell, *Sherman*, pp. 58-59, is at NYPL, "Emmet Collection" #357.

18. Zeichner, *Controversy*, p. 88; New Haven Town Records at City Clerk's Office, volume IV under September 18, 1770; Boardman, *Sherman*, p. 109.

19. Schlesinger, *Colonial Merchants*, p. 196; Zeichner, *Controversy*, p. 88; Stiles, *Extracts*, p. 494.

20. Ashbel Woodbridge quoted in Heimert, *Religion*, p. 363; Stiles, *Lit. Diary*, I:393; Stiles, *Extracts*, p. 269.

21. Heimert, *Religion*, ps. 372, 365.

22. Boutell, *Sherman*, p. 271; CHS, "Johnson Papers," RS to W. S. Johnson (June 25, 1768). It is printed in full in Boardman, *Sherman*, pp. 104-05 and Boutell, *Sherman*, pp. 65-68.

23. Sherman, ed., "A Vindication."

24. *Warren-Adams Letters*, I:73.

25. These two letters are printed in full in Boutell, *Sherman*, pp. 61-63.

26. Miller, *Origins*, p. 325.

27. Clinton Rossiter traces Franklin's path through these woods, and deals with this development in particular. *Seedtime*, ps. 308, 333.

28. Adams, ed., *Works*, II:347.

29. Quoted in Bailyn, *Pamphlets*, p. 448.

30. Adams, ed., *Works*, II:371.

31. See Rossiter, *Seedtime*, p. 340, to locate Sherman's relative position on the political spectrum.

32. Zeichner, *Controversy*, pp. 135-41.

33. Boyd, *The Susquehannah Company*, pp. 26-38.

34. Osterweis, *Three Centuries*, p. 117.

35. LC, "Ingersoll Papers," (December 29, 1769); Boyd, *Susquehannah Papers*, III:55, 191.

36. Boyd, *The Susquehannah Company*, p. 36; Boyd, *Susquehannah Papers*, III:224; Taylor, *Susquehannah Papers*, V:xxxii.

37. Boyd, *The Susquehannah Company*, p. 3; Boyd, *Susquehannah Papers*, IV:49. Boyd says that Sherman was at Wyoming in March 1770, but he was at Windham attending the county court then. William Sherman, Roger's son, was, however, in the west doing some surveying at this time. IV:80 mentions a Sherman and p. 389 incorrectly identifies him as Roger.

38. CSL, Colonial Office, "Trumbull Papers," XX:7ab.

39. *CR*, XIII:421; CSL, "Trumbull Papers," XXI:32a; CSL, "Susque-hannah Settlers," Ser. 1. I:31; CSL, "Trumbull Papers," III:172a, 175a.

40. Boyd, *Susquehannah Papers*, III:55, 191; CSL, "Susquehannah Settlers," I:50.

41. The full text is printed in Boutell, *Sherman*, pp. 70–72.

42. Zeichner, *Controversy*, p. 146.

43. CSL, "Trumbull Papers," III:186ab (March 21, 1774), 192ab (April 11, 1774).

44. CHS,"Joseph Trumbull Papers," (April 11, 1774). The town was Windsor; CHS, "Joseph Trumbull Papers," ED to Joseph Trumbull (April 19, 1774).

45. Taylor, *Susquehannah Papers*, VI:155–56.

46. Levermore, *Republic*, p. 209; *Connecticut Courant*, February 22, 1774; *Connecticut Journal*, April 29, 1774.

47. *Connecticut Courant*, March 15, 1774; Sherman's paper is also printed in Boutell, *Sherman*, pp. 72–79. See also Taylor, *Susquehannah Papers*, VI:179–83, 179n. My account is from the *Connecticut Journal*, April 8, 1774.

48. Boyd, *The Susquehannah Company*, p. 42.

49. Bailey, *Radicalism*, p. 224.

50. New Haven Town Records, V:34-35; *Connecticut Journal*, April 15, 1774; Levermore, *Republic*, p. 109.

51. CSL, "Trumbull Papers," III:191a.

CHAPTER V:
The First Continental Congress

1. Trumbull, "Sons of Liberty," pp. 299–313; NHCHS *Papers*, "Ingersoll Papers," IX:276 (August 9, 1762); Ingersoll was married twice: in 1743 to Hannah Whiting and in 1780 to Hannah Miles, widow of Enos Alling. Ingersoll died in 1781.

2. Zeichner, *Controversy*, ps. 62–63, 72–73, 116, 119, 300 n36; *Connecticut Gazette*, February 14, 1766.

3. See for instance Osborn, "Colonial Period," p. 271.

4. *Connecticut Courant*, March 29, 1774; Zeichner, *Controversy*, p. 177.

5. See above, p. 54.

6. *CR*, XII:156; CHS, "Joseph Trumbull Papers," SD to Joseph Trumbull (July 23, 1773).

7. NYPL, "Emmet Collection," #641 (June 16, 1773), signed by Erastus Wolcott, Nathan Wales, Jr., Samuel H. Parsons, and Joseph Trumbull.

8. Zeichner, *Controversy*, p. 164.

9. New Haven Town Records, "Minutes," ps. 34, 41, 42.

10. Corner, *Rush*, p. 145.

11. *CR*, XIV:324; CSL, "Revolutionary War," Ser. 1. I:56ab.

12. NYPL, Bancroft Collection, II:399 (August 20, 1774); CSL, "Trumbull Papers," II:38a.

13. CHS,"Joseph Trumbull Papers," S. H. Parsons to Joseph Trumbull (July 28, 1774); CHS, "Johnson Papers" (August 2, 1774).

14. CHS, "Johnson Papers" (August 1, 1774); NYPL, Bancroft Collection, "Samuel and William Johnson Papers," p. 405 (September 8, 1774); Butterfield, *Adams Papers*, III:340.

15. CHS, "Joseph Trumbull Papers," Deane to Joseph Trumbull (August 9, 1774); CHS, *Collections*, "Dean Papers," II:138; NYPL, Bancroft Collection, "Samuel and William Johnson Papers," pp. 400, 401, WSJ to Richard Jackson (August 30, 1774).

16. Groce, "Dyer," p. 293.

17. Groce, "Dyer," p. 303; Hutchinson, *Madison Papers*, VI:371n3; Adams, *Works*, I:67, 195; Burnett, *Letters*, VI:514.

18. See Charles Isham's Introduction to the Deane Papers in NYHS *Collections*, vol. XIX; CHS, *Collections*, vols. I and II; Ferguson, *Power of the Purse*, ps. 81-93, 197.

19. Alexander, *Duane*, p. 99; Burnett, *Letters*, I:6, 10, 67, 70, 123.

20. Stiles, *Lit. Diary*, III:9; See Wood, *Creation*, pp. 475-83 for concepts of class stratification and mobility during the Revolution. The Goddard quotation is Wood, p. 477.

21. NYHS, *Collections*, XIX:6-8; CHS, *Collections*, II:164.

22. Boardman, *Sherman*, p. 124; CSL, "Revolutionary War," Ser. 1. I:56, 57ab; AAS, RS to Major [Andrew] Adams (September 1, 1778).

23. Adams, *Works*, II:343; Boutell, *Sherman*, p. 291, quotes Adams to John Sanderson (November 19, 1822).

24. Corner, *Rush*, p. 145.

25. Burnett, *Congress*, pp. 36-38.

26. Jensen, *Articles*, pp. 58-59.

27. Burnett, *Letters*, I:69.

28. *JCC*, I:27; Burnett, *Congress*, pp. 41-42.

29. Quoted in Jensen, *Articles*, p. 59.

30. *CR*, XV:18-21.

31. Boutell, *Sherman*, pp. 61-62; Adams, *Works*, II:371; Jensen, *Founding*, p. 493; CHS, "Deane Diary," ps. 3, 6.

32. Burnett, *Congress*, p. 54.

33. Burnett, *Letters*, I:69; Boutell, *Sherman*, pp. 59-61; *JCC*, I:121.

34. Burnett, *Congress*, ps. 55-56, 46; CHS, "Deane Diary," pp. 7-8; Burnett, *Congress*, p. 55; *JCC*, I:80.

35. CHS, *Collections*, II:148; Adams, *Works*, II:343; *JCC*, III:484.

36. CHS,"Joseph Trumbull Papers," Theop. Morgan to Joseph Trumbull (September 3, 1774); CHS, "Wyllys Papers," V:6 (September 8, 1774). See also Zeichner, *Controversy*, pp. 168-69.

37. New Haven Town Records, "Minutes," vol. I (November 14, 1774); *Connecticut Journal*, November 18, 1774.

38. *Connecticut Journal*, March 1, 1775; Zeichner, *Controversy*, p. 189; *Connecticut Journal*, March 1, April 20, 1775.

39. *Connecticut Journal*, December 9, 28, 1774, February 2, 8, March 1, 8, June 14, 1775.

40. Schlesinger, *Colonial Merchants*, p. 444; Jordan, "*Connecticut Politics*," pp. 86–87.

41. Saladino, "Economic Revolution," p. 12; LC, "Sherman Papers," Isaac Sears to William Sherman (March 23, 1775).

42. *Connecticut Journal*, August 6, 1775.

43. CSL, "Revolutionary War," Ser. 1. III:603-05, 640; *CR*, XIV:387; HSP, RS to William Nelson (January 16, 1775); NLCHS, *Collections*, II:270.

44. *CR*, XV:4–5, 174; Burnett, *Letters*, I:xlii; Butterfield, *Adams*, I:159.

45. CHS, "Deane Fragment," pp. 86–87; Zeichner, *Controversy*, p. 109.

46. Zeichner, *Controversy*, p. 190; Boardman, *Sherman*, p. 127; New Haven Town Records, "Minutes," vol. I (April 21, 1775); quoted in Zeichner, *Controversy*, p. 184.

47. Quoted in Gipson, *Ingersoll*, pp. 331–32.

48. Gipson, *Ingersoll*, pp. 328–36, Ch. XII, *passim*.

49. Gipson, *Ingersoll*, p. 332n; Zeichner, *Controversy*, pp. 184–85.

50. CSL, "Trumbull Papers," IV:24 (September 14, 1774); Loucks, "Connecticut in the Revolution," p. 63.

51. Zeichner, *Controversy*, p. 178; CHS, "Johnson Papers." Benjamin Gale to W. S. Johnson (April 12, 1775); Groce, *Johnson*, pp. 102–03; CHS, "Joseph Trumbull Papers," Samuel H. Parsons to Joseph Trumbull (June 2, 1775).

52. NYPL, "Emmet Collection," E. Wolcott and others to the Massachusetts Committee of Correspondence (June 16, 1773); Huntington, *Letters*. p. 29 (Benjamin Huntington to wife, May 20, 1776).

53. LC, "Sherman Papers"; Boardman, *Sherman*, p. 142; *Connecticut Courant*, September 25, 1775.

54. Huntington, *Letters*, ps. 17, 21–22 (Benjamin Huntington to wife, April 29, May 24, 1775); *CR*, XV:192–93, 486, 411; *SR*, I:4.

55. CSL, "Trumbull Papers," V:425ad, 433ab.

56. Stiles, *Lit. Diary*, I:540; Boardman, *Sherman*, pp. 127–28; Zeichner, *Controversy,* p. 190.

57. Zeichner, *Controversy*, ps. 191, 332 n13. See note 43 above.

CHAPTER VI:
The Second Continental Congress

1. NYHS, *Collections*, XIX:42. For Dyer's account of the trip see CHS, "Joseph Trumbull Papers," ED to Joseph Trumbull (May 18, 1775).

2. CHS, *Collections*, "Deane Papers," II:22; NYHS, *Collections*, XIX:47-48.

3. The statement is in *CR*, XV:18–21; Stuart, *Trumbull*, pp. 166–67.

4. Stuart, *Trumbull*, pp. 170–72.

5. Burnett, *Congress*, pp. 66-67; Marsh, "2nd Continental Congress," p. 131.

6. *JCC*, II:106.

7. Adams, *Works*, II:418; CSL, "Gov. Joseph Trumbull Collection," I:40a, ED to Joseph Trumbull (June 17, 1775), ED to Joseph Trumbull (June 20, 1775).

8. CHS, *Collections*, II:289n, RS to David Wooster (June 23, 1775); Burnett, *Letters*, I:178-79, RS to William Williams (July 28, 1775); Burnett, *Letters*, I:164, Deane to his wife (July 15, 1775); CHS, *Collections*, II:289n.

9. Lee, *Letters*, I:312n-13n; *DAB*; *CR*, XV:107; Loucks, "Connecticut in the Revolution," p. 97.

10. NYHS, *Collections*, XIX:73-74.

11. CSL, "Gov. Joseph Trumbull Collection," I:30a (June 18, 1775). Other parts of this letter, but not that included here, are in Burnett, *Letters*, I:133.

12. HSP, Wooster to RS (July 7, 1775); Burnett, *Letters*, I:200.

13. HSP, Wooster to RS (July 7, 1775); Burnett, *Letters*, II:288.

14. Burnett, *Letters*, I:154; Dwight, *Travels*, I:160.

15. Burnett, *Letters*, I:144, 179, 181.

16. *JCC*, II:236; Burnett, *Letters*, I:xliii says they left on August 1, but they signed a letter to Zebulon Butler dated Philadelphia, August 2. Yale, Beinecke, "Sherman Papers."

17. CHS, *Collections*, II:293; CHS, "Deane Fragment," pp. 93-94.

18. CHS, "Joseph Trumbull Papers," ED to Joseph Trumbull (September 2, 1775).

19. Burnett, *Congress*, p. 94.

20. Burnett, *Congress*, p. 273; Boardman, *Sherman*, pp. 134-135, quotes RS to Joseph Trumbull (July 6, 1775); Adams, *Works*, II:445-46; *JCC*, III:472-73 (Adams' notes).

21. *JCC*, III:473; Washington, *Writings*, XVII:3ll, XX:339.

22. *JCC*, III:479; HSP, John Alsop to RS (December 14, 1775); *JCC*, III:484, 308, 314.

23. Burnett, *Congress*, p. 141.

24. LC, "Sherman Papers," Notebook, undated, untitled.

25. LC, "Sherman Papers," Notebook, undated, untitled.

26. *JCC*, IV:57; Adams' quote is from Becker, *Declaration of Independence*, p. 129; Burnett, *Congress*, p. 140; Adams, *Works*, II:506, 485-86.

27. Burnett, *Letters*, I:154; *JCC*, III:307; Butterfield, *Adams Papers*, III:355.

28. Adams, *Works*, I:188.

29. CHS, "Trumbull Papers," RS to Jonathan Trumbull (November 6, 1775 enclosed in letter of November 17).

30. LC, "Sherman Papers," Notebook, undated, untitled.

31. Burnett, *Letters*, I:460.

32. Burnett, *Letters*, I:427; CHS, "Wolcott Papers," OW to wife (March 19, and March undated, 1776); LC, "Sherman Papers," Notebook, undated, untitled.

33. NHCHS, *Collections*, IX:453, 465.

34. Adams, *Works*, II:511; Burnett, *Congress*, p. 174.

35. Adams, *Works*, II:512, III:221.

36. CSL, Ms "Journal of a Member of the General Assembly" (May and October, 1773); *CR*, XV:173-74; CHS, "Jonathan Trumbull, Sr., Papers," Memo Book 1776; CSL, "Gov. Joseph Trumbull Collection," IV:457.

37. Zeichner, *Controversy*, ps. 220, 228, 227.

38. Zeichner, *Controversy*, p. 231; *CR*, XV:54; *Connecticut Journal*, May 24, 1775. Captain Amos Brownson and an Ensign Scovil of Waterbury, for instance, were cashiered.

39. *SR*, I:409; *CR*, XV:54.

40. *CR*, XV:185, 192-95; Zeichner, *Controversy*, p. 209; New Haven Town Records, Vol. I, December 1, 1777.

41. Burnett, *Letters*, I:449 (both letters May 16, 1776).

42. CSL, "Jonathan Trumbull Papers," IV:409; *CR*, XV:281; *SR*, I:5.

43. *CR*, XV:319, 399, 269.

44. *CR*, XV:414-16.

45. *SR*, I:3, 367.

46. *CR*, XV:252-59, 265.

47. *JCC*, III, IV: *passim*. Sherman's work in supply is dealt with in detail in Ch. X below.

48. Washington, *Writings*, V:128n; Burnett, *Congress*, p. 121; Butterfield, *Adams Papers*, III:342. By far the best treatment of this important body is Ward, *The War Office*.

49. Syrett, *Hamilton Papers*, I:306. For a discussion of Sherman's military talents see Ch. X below.

50. Dartmouth College, RS to Wheelock (March 22, 1775); Burnett, *Letters*, I:144.

51. *JCC*, VI:1078, III:350; Burnett, *Letters*, I:385.

52. Burnett, *Letters*, I:195; Boutell, *Sherman*, p. 292.

53. *JCC*, IV:159.

54. Burnett, *Congress*, p. 144; NYHS, *Collections*, XX:475.

55. Burnett, *Letters*, I:230; Alexander, *Duane*, p. 150.

56. Burnett, *Letters*, I:232; NYHS, *Collections*, XIX:83-84.

57. *CR*, XV:136; Stiles, *Lit. Diary*, I:654.

58. Burnett, *Letters*, I:229; Zeichner, *Controversy*, p. 344 n81.

59. Stiles, *Extracts*, p. 395.

60. Burnett, *Letters*, I:324, 293, 313; LC, *Force Transcripts*, "Trumbull Papers," II:127.

61. NYHS, *Collections*, XIX:86-88.

62. LC, "Sherman Papers."

63. *Connecticut Courant*, June 10, 17, 1766; Jordan, "Connecticut Politics," pp. 67-69; *SR*, II:264.

64. Butterfield, *Adams Papers*, III:340.

65. Burnett, *Congress*, pp. 360-61.

66. Burnett, *Letters*, II:406; LC, "Sherman Papers."

67. NYHS, *Collections*, XXIII:336, XX:482-83.

68. LC, *Force Transcripts*, "Trumbull Papers," II:127; Burnett, *Letters*, III:167.

69. CSL, "Gov. Joseph Trumbull Collection," III:243ac. It is printed in Burnett, *Letters*, I:154, but these passages are omitted.

70. This faction-building can be traced through Burnett, *Letters*, Vols. I-III:*passim* and has been described in Loucks, "Connecticut in the Revolution," pp. 96-101. Also see below, Ch. X.

71. Burnett, *Letters*, IV:254; Burnett, *Congress*, p. 363.

72. Burnett, *Congress*, p. 364.

73. NYHS, *Collections*, XIX:x.

CHAPTER VII:
The Articles of Confederation

1. *JCC*, V:433.

2. Burnett, *Congress*, p. 217.

3. Yale, Beinecke, "Yale Letters." It is printed in Taylor, *Susquehannah Papers*, VI:337-38.

4. Luden, "History of 2nd Session," p. 170; Burnett, *Letters*, I:230.

5. Jensen, *Articles*, pp. 152-53. Other detail is found in Gerlach, "Firmness and Prudence."

6. *JCC*, VI:1078; Jensen, *Articles*, pp. 153-54.

7. See below, Ch. X.

8. *JCC*, VI:1082.

9. Jensen, *Articles*, pp. 159-60.

10. Burnett, *Letters*, III:90.

11. Boutell, *Sherman*, pp. 107-108.

12. Burnett, *Letters*, IV:232, 507-508.

13. *SR*, III:177-78.

14. Burnett, *Letters*, V:461.

15. Burnett, *Letters*, V:502-503.

16. Jensen, *Articles*, p. 138; *SR*, II:463; Burnett, *Letters*, VI:368.

17. Burnett, *Letters*, VI:439; Boyd, *Jefferson Papers*, VI:474-76, 480n.

18. AAS, "Sherman Papers"; Boyd, *Jefferson Papers*, VI:481; the commission is Yale, Beinecke, "Sherman Papers."

19. The petition is printed in full in Boyd, *Jefferson Papers*, VI:498. Hand's letter is VI:500.

20. Boyd, *Jefferson Papers*, VI:482n; Burnett, *Letters*, VII:453-54, 480.

21. Jordan, "Connecticut Politics," pp. 241, 241 n36; Burnett, *Letters*, VII:453-54; Taylor's ms. of introduction to Vol. VIII of *Susquehannah Papers* in author's file. Sherman's letter to Griswold is Yale, Hist. Ms. Room, "Lane Family Collection" (May 8, 1784).

22. Yale, Hist. Ms. Room, "Lane Family Collection," S. Huntington to Griswold (August 4, 1784); Jordan, "Connecticut Politics," p. 244.

23. Boyd, *Jefferson Papers*, VI:485.

24. *SR*, V:277; Taylor, *Susquehannah Papers*, Ms. copy of introduction to Vol. VIII:22.

25. Boyd, *Jefferson Papers*, VI:574.

26. *JCC*, XXVI:111–12, 143.

27. Burnett, *Letters*, VIII:373.

28. Taylor, *Susquehannah Papers*, Ms. copy of introduction to Vol. VIII:21–28.

29. *JCC*, XVIII:915, XXVI:249; Treat, *National Land System*, ps. 68, 319–25.

30. Boardman, *Sherman*, pp. 160–61.

31. Burnett, *Letters*, VI:340–41 prints Madison's whole paper, "Observations Relating to the Influence of Vermont and the Territorial Claims on the Politics of Congress" (May 1, 1782).

32. Morrow, "Connecticut Influence," p. 1; Rosenberry, "Migrations," p. 11.

33. Burnett, *Letters*, II:321.

34. Smith, *Memoirs*, I:89.

35. Burnett, *Letters*, VI:327n, Arthur Lee to James Warren (April 8, 1782); *State Papers of Vermont*, V:64–65; Saladino, "Economic Revolution," p. 100; *JCC*, VIII:497; Burnett, *Congress*, p. 157.

36. Smith, *Adams*, I:164; Burnett, *Letters*, II:395.

37. Burnett, *Letters*, II:397.

38. Burnett, *Letters*, II:410.

39. Dartmouth College, Payne to RS (October 28, 1778).

40. Dartmouth College, RS to Payne (October 31, 1778). Printed in part in Boutell, *Sherman*, pp. 109–10.

41. *JCC*, XIV:675–76.

42. Burnett, *Congress*, p. 541.

43. Ward, *Revolution*, p. 731; *JCC*, XX:770–72.

44. MHS, "Messech Ware Papers." Printed in part in Boutell, *Sherman*, pp. 332–34.

45. See above, p. 143.

46. *JCC*, XXI:837–38, 842; Burnett, *Congress*, p. 543; AAS, "Sherman Papers," RS to S. Huntington (August 20, 1781).

47. Burnett, *Letters*, VI:220; Gerlach, "Vermont," pp. 192–93.

48. Collier, "New Hampshire Grants," pp. 211–19 contains additional detail; Farrand, *Records*, II:463.

49. Mason, *Memoir*, pp. 15–16.

50. *JCC*, VI:1081.

51. Burnett, *Letters*, II:540–41, RS to R. H. Lee (November 3, 1777).

52. CHS, "Williams Papers" (September 22, 1777).

53. *JCC*, III:489; Burnett, *Letters*, I:360; CHS, "Wolcott Papers," RS to Oliver Wolcott (May 13, 1777).

54. Levermore, *Republic*, p. 216; CSL, "Revolutionary War," Ser. 1. XVIII:243.

55. Jensen, *Articles*, p. 253; *SR*, I:467.

56. Jordan, "Connecticut Politics," pp. 63–65; Levermore, *Republic*, p. 217; *SR*, I:521n; Jordan, "Connecticut Politics," p. 71.

57. *SR*, I:532–33.

58. *SR*, I:533; *JCC*, XI:677.

CHAPTER VIII:

Financial Problems

1. Stuart, *Trumbull*, ps. 181n, 204n.; *SR*, I:253–54.

2. Boyd, *Jefferson Papers*, III:34; CHS, William Sherman to Benedict Arnold (September 3, 1780); CSL, "Trumbull Papers," X:271c.

3. Boardman, *Sherman*, p. 195; CSL, "Revolutionary War," Ser. 1. XV:269a, 235, VII:463, 465; *SR*, II:374; Burnett, *Letters*, IV:xlix.

4. Adams, *Familiar Letters*, pp. 250–51.

5. Burnett, *Congress*, pp. 101–02; Ferguson, *Power of the Purse*, pf. 28.

6. *JCC*, IV:294, 382, 321, 330; Boardman, *Sherman*, p. 185.

7. Ferguson, *Power of the Purse*, p. 46.

8. LC, "Sherman Papers," RS to William Williams (August 18, 1777). Jordan, "Connecticut Politics," p. 103.

9. *SR*, I:139, 242, 377, 425.

10. *SR*, I:530–31.

11. MHS, "Paine Papers"; CSL, "Trumbull Papers," XII:117ac; HSP, "Sherman Papers," RS to Oliver Ellsworth (September 5, 1780).

12. Boutell, *Sherman*, p. 112; CSL, "Trumbull Papers," XII:117ad.

13. Burnett, *Congress*, pp. 249–50.

14. Burnett, *Congress*, p. 404; Burnett, *Letters*, II:540–41; Burnett, *Congress*, p. 102.

15. *JCC*, VII:107, 136–38, 143, VIII:161; Boutell, *Sherman*, p. 104.

16. CSL, "Revolutionary War," Ser. 1. VIII:43c; CHS, "Williams Papers" (September 22, 1777). Taylor, ed., *Susquehannah Papers*, VIII:222 (WSJ to RS, April 20, 1785).

17. Burnett, *Letters*, II:540; Burnett, *Congress*, p. 510; Jensen, *New Nation*, p. 39.

18. Ferguson, *Power of the Purse*, p. 32; CSL, "Trumbull Papers," XII:ll7ac.

19. Burnett, *Letters*, III:378, 442.

20. Burnett, *Congress*, p. 381.

21. Burnett, *Letters*, III:443.

22. Burnett, *Congress*, p. 382.

23. Burnett, *Letters*, III:467–68.

24. *JCC*, VIII:143, XII:1075.

25. MHS, "Samuel A. Green Papers" (December 8, 1778); *JCC*, XIII:17.

26. Burnett, *Congress*, p. 406; Bullock, "Finances," p. 130; Burnett, *Congress*, pp. 407–409; *JCC*, XIV:728–30, 730n.

27. *JCC*, XV:1128, 1149, XVI:41; Burnett, *Letters*, IV:542, V:84.

28. Bullock, "Finances," p. 130; Stiles, *Lit. Diary*, II:243.

29. *JCC*, XVI:205. See Sherman's long report of February 26, 1780; Bronson, "Connecticut Currency," I:129.

30. Ferguson, *Power of the Purse*, pp. 46–47; *JCC*, XVI:265–67.

31. Ferguson, *Power of the Purse*, p. 66.

32. MHS, "Miscellaneous Bound," notes for a speech, apparently the one given April 12, 1790; *Annuls*, II:1366.

33. Boutell, *Sherman*, p. 119, RS to Lyman Hall (January 20, 1784); Boutell, *Sherman*, p. 121 (May 4, 1784).

34. CHS, "W. S. Johnson Papers," RS to WSJ (April 12, 1785), draft reply on the back of that letter; Burnett, *Letters*, II:305; CHS, "W. S. Johnson Papers," RS to WSJ (May 13, 1786). See also Main, *Antifederalists*, ps. 74, 74 n5, 90–99.

35. CHS, "Wolcott Papers," Oliver Wolcott to wife (October 8, November 24, 1776); Burnett, *Letters*, II:305; Boutell, *Sherman*, p. 100; CSL, "Revolutionary War," Ser. 1. V:107a, 108a; *JCC*, VIII:508.

36. Yale, Hist. Ms. Room, "Knollenberg Collection" (March 11, 1777—photostat).

37. CSL, "Revolutionary War," Ser. 1. VI:84a; Yale, Beinecke, printed table in RS Papers; LC, "Sherman Papers," RS account book; MHS, "R. T. Paine Papers," Vol. III, RS to Cushing (September 9, 1777); CSL, "Revolutionary War," Ser. 1. XX:249.

38. Burnett, *Letters*, VI:137, 200.

39. CSL, "Revolutionary War," Ser. 1. XXII:140, 141.

40. CSL, "Revolutionary War," Ser. 1. XXXII:387a, 92ab, XXXVII: 104, XI:440a; *SR*, III:341, 388, 498.

41. Boutell, *Sherman*, ps. 186, 189; Yale, Beinecke, *Gaines Pocket Almanac* in Sherman Papers.

42. AAS, "Sherman Papers"; Ferguson, *Power of the Purse*, pp. 186–88; *SR*, VIII:194–95; LC, "Sherman Papers," John Sherman to RS (July 23, 1790).

43. Burnett, *Letters*, II:260.

44. Burnett, *Congress*, pp. 234–36; Dorfman, *Economic Mind*, I:213.

45. *SR*, I:62–63; Jordan, "Connecticut Politics," pp. 101, 111; *Connecticut Courant*, December 30, 1777, quoted in Jordan, p. 98; Jordan, "Connecticut Politics," pp. 94–100; Huntington, *Letters*, pp. 35–37 (Benjamin Huntington to wife, May 29, 1777).

46. Burnett, *Congress*, pp. 234; Burnett, *Letters*, V:14.

47. *JCC*, IV:321, VII, 94, 94n, 121; Burnett, *Congress*, pp. 236–38; *JCC*, VII:124.

48. *SR*, I:599–607.

49. LC, "Roger Sherman Papers"; MHS, "R. T. Paine Papers," RS to Thomas Cushing (September 9, 1777); *SR*, I:413–14.

50. CSL, "Revolutionary War," Ser. 1. X:124; *SR*, I:612.

51. Baldwin, "New Haven Convention," pp. 47–48. The report is printed in *SR*, I:607–20.

52. *SR*, I:614; MHS, "R. T. Paine Papers" (February 27, 1778).

53. Burnett, *Letters*, III:177-78; Scott, "Price Control," p. 463.

54. CHS, "Jonathan Trumbull, Sr. Papers" (February 26, 1777); *JCC*, X:235, 244; Scott, "Price Control," *passim*.

55. CSL, "Revolutionary War," Ser. 1. XIII:325.

56. CSL, "Trumbull Papers," X:288ad, XI:18a.

57. LC, *Force Transcripts*, "Trumbull Papers," XI:42, 64; *SR*, II:572, 579; Burnett, *Congress*, p. 424.

58. Scott, "Price Control," p. 472.

59. Jordan, "Connecticut Politics," p. 105; *S.R.*, II:172-73; 256-63; *Connecticut Courant*, May 4, 1779, quoted in Jordan, p. 107.

60. Jordan, "Connecticut Politics," pp. 109-18.

CHAPTER IX:
The Last Days of Congress

1. *JCC*, III:472, 367, 475.

2. *JCC*, VIII:433-48; Burnett, *Letters*, II:506, 572; CSL, "Governor Joseph Trumbull Collection," V:521; Wadsworth to Joseph Trumbull (February 29, 1776).

3. Burnett, *Letters*, V:113, VIII:59n, 74n; Yale, Hist. Ms. Room, "Knollenberg Collection," Greene to Wadsworth (March 17, 1780).

4. Burnett, *Letters*, II:315, 563; CHS, "Jonathan Trumbell, Sr. Papers," Vol. IV (June 29, 1778).

5. Burnett, *Letters*, III:77; *JCC*, XII:1024-25.

6. CHS, "Jeremiah Wadsworth Papers," Letterbook I, JW to Henry Champion (January 7, 1780); NYHS, "Jeremiah Wadsworth Papers," JW to John Chaloner (February 13, 1780); CHS, "Jeremiah Wadsworth Papers," JW to Oliver Ellsworth (April 25, 1780).

7. Burnett, *Congress*, p. 401.

8. Burnett, *Letters*, V:71; Yale, Hist. Ms. Room, "Knollenberg Collection," N. Greene to JW (July 15, 1780).

9. Burnett, "Committee of the States," p. 152; *JCC*, XX:658; Burnett, *Letters*, VI:133.

10. CHS, "Trumbull Papers," RS to Jonathan Trumbull (May 26, 1777); Yale, Hist. Ms. Room, "Knollenberg Collection" (August 14, 1780).

11. Yale, Hist. Ms. Room, "Knollenberg Collection" (August 29, 1780).

12. CHS, "Jonathan Trumbull, Jr. Papers," Correspondence with Congressmen, I:1 (August 21, 1780); CHS, "Jeremiah Wadsworth Papers," Trumbull to JW (August 31, 1780).

13. Yale, Hist. Ms. Room, "Knollenberg Collection," NG to JW (February 12, 1780).

14. Yale, Hist. Ms. Room, "Knollenberg Collection," NG to JW (February 12, 1780).

15. Yale, Hist. Ms. Room, "Knollenberg Collection," NG to JW (March 2, and 17, 1780).

16. Yale, Hist. Ms. Room, "Knollenberg Collection," NG to JW (May 8, and March 17, 1780).

17. Yale, Hist. Ms. Room, "Knollenberg Collection," NG to JW (May 8 and March 17, 1780).

18. Yale, Hist. Ms. Room, "Knollenberg Collection," NG to JW (May 8, 1780). For a discussion of nationalist sentiment in Congress, 1781-83, see Ferguson, "Nationalists."

19. *SR*, II:264, 462, III:388, IV:61, V:207; Burnett, *Letters*, V:lv, VI:xliii.

20. "House Journal 1783-1785," pp. 73-74 (October 31, 1783); Wood, "Congressional Control," p. 38.

21. *SR*, II:264; Stiles, *Lit. Diary*, I:654.

22. *JCC*, XXVI:15.

23. Yale, Hist. Ms. Room," Gibbs Family Collection," RS to Henry Gibbs (April 9, 1784); CHS, "Williams Papers," RS to William Williams (December 25, 1783); New Haven Town Records, minutes for meeting of January 5, 1784, at which Sherman was moderator.

24. Burnett, *Congress*, p. 595.

25. Burnett, *Congress*, pp. 593-96; Burnett, *Letters*, VII:451.

26. See above, Ch. VII, *JCC*, XXVI:*passim Jefferson Papers*, VI:550-506.

27. *JCC*, XXVI:121; Burnett, *Congress*, p. 605.

28. *JCC*, XXVI:140, 397; Yale, "Franklin Collection," Connecticut Delegates to Governor Griswold (May 21, 1784); *JCC*, XXVII:386, 409, 415-16.

29. Burnett, *Letters*, VII:534.

30. *JCC*, XXVI:430-31, 450, *passim*; Yale, "Franklin Collection," Connecticut Delegates to Governor Griswold (May 21, 1784).

31. Burnett, "Committee of States," *passim*.

32. Burnett, *Letters*, VII:539.

33. CHS, "Williams Papers," Connecticut Delegates to William Williams (n.d., April, 1784).

34. *JCC*, XXVII:561; Burnett, *Letters*, VI:lxiv; Burnett, *Congress*, p. 609.

35. Hoar, *Autobiography*, p. 701; Boutell, *Sherman*, pp. 292-93.

36. "House Journal 1783-1785," pp. 48-50, 78-82, 90-96, 101.

37. Draft Code, p. 1.

38. Draft Code, ps. 33, pf. 177.

39. Draft Code, ps. 45-55, 100; "House Journal 1783-1785," ps. 75, 103.

40. Draft Code, ps. 50, pf. 177; *SR*, V:323-24.

41. Boutell, *Sherman*, p. 190; *SR*, V:323-24.

42. Draft Code, ps. 56, 5-6, 2.

43. The Act officially adopting the code and authorizing the printing of 500 bound copies is in *SR*, V:281; CSL, "Revolutionary War," Ser. 1. XXVII:342.

44. Saladino, "Economic Revolution," p. 64; Levermore, *Republic of New Haven*, p. 218. See note 3, ch. VIII.

45. Saladino, "Economic Revolution," ps. 97, 104-106.

46. Saladino, "Economic Revolution," p. 166; Stiles, *Lit. Diary*. III:128.

47. Dexter, "New Haven in 1784," p. 131; Levermore, *Republic of New Haven*, p. 222.

48. CSL, "Towns and Lands," X:1ad: *Connecticut Courant*, May 25, 1784. The copy at the NYPL Rare Book Room has a marginal comment by Webster; *SR*, V:324-26.

49. Levermore, *Republic of New Haven*, p. 223; "House Journal 1783-1785," ps. 72-74, 83 (January 19, 1784, the date on which the incorporation bill passed); *SR*, V:257-67.

50. Saladino, "Economic Revolution," pp. 132-33; CSL, "Revolutionary War," Ser. 1. XV:269a, 235, VII:463, 465; Stiles, *Lit. Diary*, III:111-12.

51. Stiles, *Lit. Diary*, III:69-70.

52. CSL, "Revolutionary War," Ser. 1. XXVI:247a; Zeichner, "Loyalists," pp. 316-17.

53. Jordan, "Connecticut Politics," p. 131; *SR*, V:115-16.

54. CSL, "Revolutionary War," Ser. 1. XXIV:259ad; Jordan, "Connecticut Politics," p. 169; CSL, "Revolutionary War," Ser. 1. XXVI:247ab.

55. Stiles, *Lit. Diary*, III:70.

56. Stiles, *Lit. Diary*, III:107-11; Dexter, "New Haven in 1784," pp. 134-35.

57. Stiles, *Extracts*, p. 5n; Levermore, *Republic of New Haven*, p. 216; Stiles, *Lit Diary*, III:111-12.

58. Boardman, *Sherman*, pp. 211-12; Levermore, *Republic of New Haven*, p. 213.

59. Saladino, "Economic Revolution," p. 170.

CHAPTER X:
Who Should Rule at Home?

1. Saladino, "Economic Revolution," ps. 96-97, 196.

2. Saladino, "Economic Revolution," ps. 94-95, 151-52; CSL, "Trumbull Papers," IV:2ab, 8ab.

3. *Connecticut Courant*, June 5, October 30, November 6, October 2, 1786.

4. Saladino, "Economic Revolution," ps. 153, 158.

5. Saladino, "Economic Revolution," p. 159.

6. *SR*, V:325-26; Saladino, "Economic Revolution," pp. 205-206.

7. CSL, "Revolutionary War," Ser. 1. XVIII:243; Burnett, *Letters*, VII:284.

8. Main, *Antifederalists*, pp. 90-91; Burnett, *Letters*, VII:496, 450; VIII:13.

9. For example *SR*, V:328-38, 432.

10. Burnett, *Letters*, VII:626, 618, VIII:16, 189n, 318.

11. Saladino, "Economic Revolution," ps. 162, 168; Yale, Hist. Ms. Room, "Baldwin Family Collection," Baldwin to James Kent (March 8, 1788); *SR*, VI:122, 122n.

12. Saladino, "Economic Revolution," p. 175; *SR*, V:438. See table of taxes levied and types of money acceptable for them in *Connecticut Journal*, June 27, 1787.

13. *SR*, VI:19, 22, 96; *Middlesex Gazette*, June 18, 1786; *SR*, VI:19, 95–96; *SR*, V and VI, *passim.*

14. *SR*, I:365, II:172, 256–63; *Connecticut Courant*, April 18, 1780. See also Loucks, "Connecticut in the Revolution," pp. 216–21.

15. *SR*, V:375–76.

16. Hamilton's remark was made during the Philadelphia Convention, June 26, 1787; Burnett, *Letters*, VIII:581.

17. *Connecticut Courant*, February 5, 12, 19, 1787.

18. Saladino, "Economic Revolution," pp. 205–206; *Connecticut Courant*, January 1, 1787.

19. Burnett, *Letters*, VIII:568; *Connecticut Courant*, April 3, 1786, March 26, 1787, June 5, 1786; *Connecticut Gazette*, February 10, April 7, 1786.

20. Jordan, "Connecticut Politics," pp. 288–90; *Middlesex Gazette*, April 10, 1786.

21. *Connecticut Courant*, June 11, 1787; "House Journal 1787–1788," p. 31; *Connecticut Journal*, June 27, 1787; "House Journal 1787–1788," p. 1.

22. Burnett, *Congress*, p. 313.

23. MHS, *Collections*, seventh series, II:232; Jordan, "Connecticut Politics," p. 135; *JCC*, X:392–96.

24. Burnett, *Congress*, p. 315; *JCC*, XI:639–40.

25. Jordan, "Connecticut Politics," p. 139; *SR*, IV:154; CSL, "Revolutionary War," Ser. 1. XXII:258, 277.

26. Burnett, *Letters*, VI:372, 397.

27. Burnett, *Letters*, VI:406–408, VII:72n, 73; Hutchinson, *Madison Papers*, VI:301, 301n2, 370, 371n4, 377n3.

28. *JCC*, XVIII:958–969; *SR*, II:532–533, IV:154; Jordan, "Connecticut Politics," p. 153; Stiles, *Lit. Diary*, III:120; *SR*, V:253, 317.

29. Saladino, "Economic Revolution," ps. 104, 106; e.g., R. H. Lee in Burnett, *Letters*, VIII:66.

30. Webster, *A Collection*, pp. 319–22. The best account of the commutation issue and the Cincinnati versus Middletown Convention battle is Miner, *Our Rude Forefathers*, Ch. VI, based largely on the Webster Papers, NYPL. For Judd's visit to Congress see Hutchinson, *Madison Papers*, VI:51–52, 52n6, 190n10.

31. Miner, *Our Rude Forefathers*, p. 94; *Connecticut Courant*, August 19, September 2, 1783 quoted in Jordan, "Connecticut Politics," pp. 175, 176.

32. Miner, *Our Rude Forefathers*, p. 88. The poem on p. 92 of Miner is from the *Connecticut Courant*, January 13, 1784; Webster, *A Collection*, p. 319.

33. *Middlesex Gazette*, September 12, 1783; *Connecticut Courant*, September 9, 1783; Jordan, "Connecticut Politics," pp. 156-59.

34. Jordan, "Connecticut Politics," p. 178; "House Journal 1783-1785," ps. 64, 67.

35. Stuart, *Trumbull*, pp. 600-608; Zeichner, "Loyalists," *passim*, Loucks, "Connecticut in the Revolution," pp. 131-35.

36. *SR*, V:207; "House Journal 1783-1785," pp. 73-74.

37. Burnett, *Letters*, VII:259, 288, 291. See also Kaplan, "Veteran Officers," p. 37.

38. *JCC*, XXVI:15; "House Journal 1786-1787," p. 8; *JCC*, XXVI:21; Burnett, *Letters*, VII:418.

39. AAS, "Sherman Papers." The document is printed in Boutell, *Sherman*, pp. 329-33.

40. Boutell, *Sherman*, pp. 122-23. It is the same letter that is incorrectly cited as Boutell, p. 12 in Burnett, *Letters*, VIII:513.

41. *SR*, V:317, 318, 323; Stiles, *Lit Diary*, III:120; *Connecticut Courant*, April 20, 1784.

42. Jordan, "Connecticut Politics," p. 222; "House Journal 1783-1785," pp. 33-34; Saladino, "Economic Revolution," p. 197; *SR*, V:326-27.

43. *Connecticut Courant*, March 5, 1787; Burnett, *Letters*, VIII:363; CHS, "Johnson Papers," RS to William S. Johnson (May 13, 1786).

44. *SR*, VI:171-72; *JCC*, XXXI:654-55.

45. Jordan, "Connecticut Politics," p. 251; "House Journal 1785-1786," ps. 146, 152.

46. Saladino, "Economic Revolution," ps. 174, 140.

47. Burnett, *Letters*, VIII:353-54, 356-57, 365-66, 368-69.

48. Burnett, *Letters*, VIII:467.

49. Jordan, "Connecticut Politics," pp. 256-259; *SR*, VI:5.

50. *SR*, VI:237-38; "House Journal 1787-1788," ps. 24, 49, 33, 84. See also Treat, *National Land System*, pp. 319-325.

CHAPTER XI:
E Pluribus Unum?

1. CHS, Benjamin Gale to Erastus Wolcott, bound letter (February 10, 1787).

2. Jordan, "Connecticut Anti-Federalism," *passim*; "House Journal 1783-1785," p. 90.

3. *Connecticut Courant*, January 29, March 20, April 10, and *passim* throughout the first six months, 1787.

4. Webster, *A Collection*, p. 321.

5. *Connecticut Courant*, November 20, 1786. Groce, *Johnson*, p. 135n, identifies the author as Webster.

6. *Connecticut Courant*, March 19, 1787.

7. *Connecticut Courant*, September 28, 1786. The copy of the *Connecticut Courant* at Yale's Beinecke Library is autographed by Webster with the notation "written at Providence when I was reading lectures." See also Bromberger, "Noah Webster."

8. *Middlesex Gazette*, November 13, 1786; "House Journal 1785-1786," p. 151.

9. *American Mercury*, May 21, 1787 prints Huntington's speech; Humphrey, *Humphrey*, I:405-06.

10. *Connecticut Courant*, March 5, 1787.

11. For instance see the *Middlesex Gazette*, March 17, June 9, 1786; *Connecticut Courant*, December 22, 29, 1786, January 22, 1787.

12. Jordan, "Connecticut Politics," pp. 286-90; "House Journal 1787-1788," p. 7; *Middlesex Gazette*, June 4, 1787.

13. "House Journal 1787-1788," p. 1. See the debates in the *American Mercury*, May 21 to June 2, 1787.

14. Steiner, "Connecticut's Ratification," pp. 76-77; *Middlesex Gazette*, May 28, 1787; *Connecticut Journal*, May 23, 1787.

15. CHS, "Johnson Papers," SMM to W. S. Johnson (August 9, 1786).

16. AAS, "Sherman Papers," Johnson and Mitchell to Governor Griswold (April 12, 1786); Burnett, *Letters*, VIII:645-46; Burnett, *Congress*, pp. 676-78.

17. Stiles, *Lit. Diary*, III:296; King, *King*, I:221.

18. Boyd, *Jefferson Papers*, XI:155; Burnett, *Letters*, VIII:645.

19. See Saladino, "Economic Revolution," pp. 182-83, whence much of this summary is borrowed.

20. "House Journal 1787-1788," pp. 10-11; Jordan, "Connecticut Politics," p. 298.

21. CSL, "Revolutionary War," Ser. 1. XXXVII:278a, 274a, 276a; *SR*, VI:292, 293. Election figures for 1787 are in *Gaines Almanac for 1787* in Yale, Beinecke Library, "Sherman Papers."

22. Groce, *Johnson*, p. 130; Brown, *Ellsworth*, p. 116.

23. King, *King*, I:221; MHS, "Henry Knox Collection" (June 3, 1787).

24. Main, *Antifederalists*, pp. 184-86.

25. *SR*, I:223, 417; Burnett, *Letters*, III:li, *SR*, II:249.

26. CSL, "Finance and Currency," Ser. 2. III:40, 41; Yale, Beinecke, "Sherman Papers" (Papers Relating to the Estate of RS); CSL, "Revolutionary War," Ser. 2. XXXII:387a; Yale, Beinecke, "Sherman Papers" (Papers Relating to the Estate).

27. *SR*, VI:292-93.

28. Yale, Beinecke, "Sherman Papers," *Gaines Pocket Almanac for 1787*; Tansill, *Documents*, p. 85.

29. Brown, *Ellsworth*, pp. 37-38.

30. Farrand, *Records*, III:88-89.

31. Farrand, *The Framing*, p. 35; Farrand, *Records*, III:233-34. My translation.

32. Corner, *Rush*, p. 145.

CHAPTER XII:
The Constitutional Convention

1. Yale, Beinecke, "Sherman Papers"; *Gaines Pocket Almanack for 1787*.

2. Citations to the Philadelphia debate are given by date so that any edition of Madison's Notes may be consulted with ease. Quotations here are taken from Tansil, *Documents Relating*.

3. Yale, Hist. Ms. Room, "Roger Sherman Collection," Samuel Huntington to RS, OE and WSJ (July 9, 1787).

4. *JCC*, XIV:624.

5. *JCC*, XIV:675, XXVI:169, 249; but see above, p. 195, for Sherman's attempt to get the Connecticut Assembly to accept foreign treaties made under the Articles as state law.

6. This paper is printed in full in Boutell, *Sherman*, pp. 132-34. It is of uncertain date and could have been written any time between 1784 and 1787. Boutell believes it to have been written in "the last days of the Confederation." J. Franklin Jameson thought that it was Sherman's summary of the resolutions of the Committee of the Whole modified by changes up to July 2. AAS, "Sherman Papers." Jameson to G. F. Hoar (May 6, 1903). Madison spoke on July 17 of a paper from which Sherman read, calling it "an enumeration." Sherman's proposed amendments as reported by Madison are nearly verbatim from Boutell's paper. Farrand quotes Bancroft as saying that the plan which Sherman presented "in importance stands next to that of Virginia." Farrand believes the paper to be Sherman's contribution to the New Jersey Plan. Farrand, *Records*, III:615-16. Since the plan is more nationalist than Sherman would wish, I would place its composition between July 2 and July 17, and call it a summary of adopted resolutions with some innovative compromises of Sherman's own.

7. *JCC*, III:489, XXXVII:431-36.

8. *JCC*, XVI:69-70.

9. *SR*, V:323-24.

10. *SR*, V:319.

11. See his July Paper discussed in note 6 above in Farrand, *Records*, III:615-16; Ferguson, *Power of the Purse*, p. 292; Elliot, *Debates*, I:491-92.

12. *JCC*, XVIII:915-16. See also Sherman's additions to Samuel Adams' report of August 12, 1780 in *JCC*, XVII: 726-27.

13. RS to William Williams (May 4, 1784) in Boutell, *Sherman*, p. 122. See also Boardman, *Sherman*, p. 257 and Farrand, *Records*, III:379.

14. CSL, "Revolutionary War," Ser. 1. XVIII:243.

15. See above Chapter X, note 21.

16. *JCC*, XVIII:915-16.

17. Burnett, *Letters*, VIII:124-25, 161; *SR*, VI:237-38.

CHAPTER XIII:
E Pluribus Unum!

1. Wright, *Fabric*, p. 168.

2. *JCC*, VI:1081. Madison, in a footnote to his journal for July 5, says this suggestion was made in 1777, but I find it on August 1, 1776.

3. Farrand, *Records*, III:188-90, 264-66, contains accounts of these committee discussions.

4. *Annals*, I:350; Yale, Hist. Ms. Room, "Sherman Collection," RS to Simeon Baldwin (January 2, 1792); Boutell, *Sherman*, pp. 250-53.

5. Burnett, *Letters*, VII:lXiii; *JCC*, XXIV:261; Hutchinson, *Madison Papers*, VI:406, 473 n7.

6. *Connecticut Journal*, September 26, October 3, June 20, 1787; *Connecticut Courant*, October 29, 1787.

7. *Connecticut Courant*, December 10, 1787; Baldwin, *Baldwin*, p. 395; Hugh Ledlie to John Lamb, quoted in Main, *Antifederalists*, p. 199; King, *King*, p. 264.

8. Ellsworth's, Sherman's and William Williams' letters are in Scott, *The Federalist*, pp. 566-614. Perkins' reports of the speeches in the ratifying convention are in Elliot, *Debates*, II:185-202. See also summary in Steiner, "Connecticut's Ratification."

9. CHS, "Johnson Papers," Ledlie to WSJ (December 3, 1787); Brown, *Ellsworth*, p. 171; CHS, "Johnson Papers," WSJ to his son, Samuel W. Johnson (November 29, 1787).

10. Yale, Hist. Ms. Room, "Baldwin Family Collection," Simeon Baldwin to James Kent (March 8, 1788); Yale, Hist. Ms. Room, "Sherman Collection," contains the originals together with several typescript copies. One is addressed "Dear Sir" and dated December 8, 1787, and the other is headed "Observations on the new federal constitution." They contain many identical and similar phrases.

11. Stiles, *Lit. Diary*, III:296.

12. CHS, "Johnson Papers," Gale to WSJ (November 13, 1787), WSJ to his son, Samuel W. Johnson (November 29, 1787).

13. Steiner, "Connecticut's Ratification," p. 125-26; *Connecticut Journal*, September 26, 1787.

14. Stiles, *Lit. Diary*, III:298; Steiner, "Connecticut's Ratification," p. 109; Beardsley, *Seabury*, p. 317.

15. Steiner, "Connecticut's Ratification," p. 109.

16. *Connecticut Courant*, February 4, March 3, 1788, prints letters between "Landholder" (Ellsworth) and Williams. The letters are printed in Scott, *The Federalist*, pp. 566-606.

17. Waln in Sanderson, *Signers*, III:278; *Connecticut Courant*, January 14, 1788.

18. Stiles, *Lit. Diary*. III:299-300; Jordan, "Connecticut Politics," pp. 341-42.

19. Jordan, "Connecticut Politics," pp. 355-57.

20. King, *King*, p. 264; *SR*, VI:565; Yale, Hist. Ms. Room, "Baldwin Family Collection," Enoch Perkins to Simeon Baldwin (January 15, 1788); New York Historical Society, "Lamb Collection," Hugh Ledlie to General John Lamb (January 15, 1788).

21. Jordan, "Connecticut Politics," pp. 356-66.

22. *SR*, VI:496-97; Jordan, "Connecticut Politics," pp. 372-73; "House Journal 1786-1787," ps. 54, 134, 144; CSL, "Revolutionary War," Ser. 1. XXXVII:297; "House Journal 1786-1787," ps. 129, 137; *SR*, VI:142-44.

23. Stiles, *Lit Diary*. III:300.

24. Waln in Sanderson, *Signers*, III:279.

CHAPTER XIV:
No Rest for the Weary and Aged

1. Boutell, *Sherman*, p. 291, JA to John Sanderson (November 19, 1822).

2. *Connecticut Journal*, October 22, 1788, January 7, 1789; *SR*, VI:496, 497; "House Journal 1788-1790," p. 6.

3. CSL, "Revolutionary War," Ser. 1. XXXVII:290, 291; Purcell, *Transition*, p. 69; *SR*, VI:497.

4. For appraisals of Sherman as a legalist and for some of his recorded opinions see Boutell, *Sherman*, pp. 182-90.

5. Boutell, *Sherman*, pp. 191-92; Stiles, *Lit. Diary*, III:341.

6. Miller, *Federalist Era*, pp. 4-5, 9; Brant, *Father of the Constitution*, p. 256.

7. See above, Chapter XII, and citations, 8-12 for that chapter.

8. Yale, Hist. Ms. Room, "Gibbs Family Collection," RS to Henry Gibbs (May 11, 1789); *Annals*, I:317.

9. Elliot, *Debates*, I:491-92.

10. *Annals*, I:317.

11. CHS, "Oliver Wolcott, Sr. Papers"; Elliot, *Debates*, I:491-92.

12. *Annals*, I:188, 256; Miller, *Federalist Era*, ps. 15-16, 19. See also Charles, *Party System*, pp. 98-99.

13. *Annals*, I:316.

14. For the unique character of the Treasury Office see Meyer, "A Note . . . on the Hamiltonian System."

15. *Annals*, II:1447, I:630, II:1454, 1456.

16. *Annals*, I:1197-98, II:1354; Ferguson, *Power of the Purse*, p. 294.

17. *Annals*, I:1472, 1108-1109, 1487; Brant, *Father of the Constitution*, pp. 302-305.

18. Schachner, *Hamilton*, pp. 255-56.

19. Miller, *Federalist Era*, p. 41; Ferguson, *Power of the Purse*, pp. 314-18.

20. Ferguson, *Power of the Purse*, pp. 307-308; *JCC*, XVII: 915-16.

21. Yale, Hist. Ms. Room, "Lane Collection," RS to Governor Huntington (September 17, 1789), printed in Boutell, *Sherman*, p. 219; *Annals*, II:1140–41, 1457.

22. *Annals*, II:1140–41.

23. Stamps, "Political Parties," pp. 7–9; Ferguson, *Power of the Purse*, pp. 275–82; Syrett, *Hamilton Papers*, VI:120.

24. Saladino, "Economic Revolution," pp. 179–80; *Connecticut Journal*, June 13, 1787.

25. *Connecticut Journal*, March 17, 1790, September 7, 1791, December 27, 1790, September 7, 1791, September 8, 1790.

26. AAS, "Sherman Papers," Nathaniel Sherman to RS (March 14, 1789); CSL, "Revolutionary War," Ser. 1. XXXVII:13; Collier, "Continental Bonds," *passim*.

27. *Connecticut Journal*, February 2, 1791; MHS, "Miscellaneous Bound," Eliphalet Dyer to RS and Benjamin Huntington (April 12, 1790).

28. Yale, Hist. Ms. Room, "Sherman Collection," RS to Simeon Baldwin (February 27, 1790, April ?, 1790); *JCC*, XVIII:915–16, XVII:726–27; The Constitutional Convention, August 18, 1787.

29. *Connecticut Journal*, October 13, 1790.

30. Yale, Hist. Ms. Room, "Sherman Collection," RS to Simeon Baldwin (January 23, 1790); MHS, "Miscellaneous Bound," Sherman's Receipt for notes on Connecticut's assumed debt (July 3, 1792).

31. Beard, *An Economic Interpretation*, p. 142; Corner, *Rush*, p. 200.

32. *Annals*, II:1366, 1365, 1341.

33. *Annals*, II:1376; Ferguson, *Power of the Purse*, pp. 314–15. Yale, Hist. Ms. Room, "Sherman Collection," RS to wife (March 6, 1790).

34. Maclay, *Journal*, pp. 236.

35. *Annals*, II:1576; *JCC*, XVII:726–27, XVIII:915–16; *Annals*, 1577; Maclay, *Journal*, p. 237.

36. Schachner, *Hamilton*, pp. 258–59; Yale, Hist. Ms. Room, "Sherman Collection, " RS to Simeon Baldwin (April ?, 1790).

37. Miller, *Federalist Era*, p. 48; *Annals*, II:1585.

38. *Annals*, II:1585.

39. Ames, *Works of Ames*, I:116–118.

40. *Connecticut Journal*, September 8, 1790; MHS, "Miscellaneous Bound," Dyer to RS and Benjamin Huntington (April 12, 1790); Gibbs, *Washington and Adams*, p. 34.

41. Yale, Hist. Ms. Room, "Sherman Collection," RS to Simeon Baldwin (May 15, 1790); Yale, Hist. Ms. Room, "Gibbs Family Collection," RS to Henry Gibbs (June 10, 1790); Brant, *Father of the Constitution*, p. 312.

42. *New Haven Morning Courier*, (July 29, 1843), "Memoir of Roger Sherman," probably written by Simeon E. Baldwin; Ames, *Works of Ames*, I:78.

43. Boutell, *Sherman*, pp. 242–44. Notes for this speech are in a Sherman notebook in "Miscellaneous Bound" at MHS. See also George Hoar's letter in AAS *Proceedings*, XII (new series) October, 1897–98.

44. *JCC*, XXVI:223; *Annals*, I:816, 817, 908, 919, 920, 960. The vote on the Germantown location shows he might have won. *Annals*, I:962, II:1728.

45. Schachner, *Hamilton*, p. 261; Miller, *Federalist Era*, p. 48; Ferguson, *Power of the Purse*, p. 321 gives generally the same view, citing Sherman's figures without mentioning him.

46. Rutland, *Bill of Rights*, p. 194; Burnett, *Letters*, VIII:829.

47. Brant, *Father of the Constitution*, pp. 236–38; Rutland, *Bill of Rights*, pp. 196–98.

48. Yale, Hist. Ms. Room, "Sherman Collection," RS to Dear Sir (December 8, 1788).

49. The letter was not printed in Connecticut newspapers. It is in the *Salem Mercury*, June 20, July 7, 1789; Yale, Hist. Ms. Room, "Gibbs Family Collection," RS to Henry Gibbs (June 1, July 16, 1789); National Archives, "Sherman Papers," RS to David Howell (May 6, 1789). Typescript in the office of the Archivist of an original at Brown University.

50. Hunt, *Madison*, V:346n.

51. *Annals*, I:445.

52. Rutland, *Bill of Rights*, p. 207; *Annals*, I:465–66.

53. *Annals*, I:686–87; Yale, Hist. Ms. Room, "Gibbs Family Collection," RS to Henry Gibbs (August 4, 1789).

54. *Annals*, I:740 (Benson's speech), 735.

55. *Annals*, I:739, 744.

56. *Annals*, I:790, 782, 800, 781, 789.

57. Ballagh, *Lee*, II:496.

58. *Annals*, I:742.

59. *Annals*, I:795.

60. *Annals*, I:808; Rutland, *Bill of Rights*, p. 212; *Annals*, I:808; Yale, Hist. Ms. Room, "W. G. Lane Collection," RS to Governor Huntington (September 17, 1789).

61. CSL, "Civil Officers," Ser. 2. XXII:3a, 4ad, 5a; "House Journal 1788–1790," n. p. May 18, 1790; "House Journal 1790–1791." n. p. May 24, 25, October 16, 25, 1790.

CHAPTER XV:

The Wheel Turns and the Cog Wears Down

1. Miller, *Federalist Era*, p. 57; Brant, *Father of the Constitution*, pp. 328–31.

2. *Annals*, I:790.

3. *Annals*, II:1364.

4. Boutell, *Sherman*, p. 261 prints a facsimile of the note, the original of which is in AAS, "Sherman Papers." See also Hoar, *Autobiography*, I:136.

5. *Annals*, I:753–54, 763; MHS, "Miscellaneous Bound," RS to Governor Huntington (March 21, 1791); Yale, Hist. Ms. Room, "Sherman Collection," RS to Simeon Baldwin (March 14, 1791).

6. *Annals*, I:329.

7. *Annals*, I:735–36.

8. *Annals*, II:1646 lists a speech which is printed in Boutell, *Sherman*, pp. 219–20.

9. *Annals*, I:510–11, 514–16, 558, 598, 603.

10. Boutell, *Sherman*, pp. 311–28 prints the correspondence in full.

11. *Annals*, I:1122.

12. *Annals*, II:1365.

13. Boutell, *Sherman*, p. 212.

14. Stiles, *Lit. Diary*, III:111; HSP, "Sherman Papers," RS to Pierpont Edwards (December 25, 1774).

15. *Connecticut Journal*, September 16, 1789.

16. *Connecticut Journal*, May 5, 1790; Yale, Hist. Ms. Room, "Sherman Collection," RS to Simeon Baldwin (August 22, September 22, 1789); *Connecticut Journal*, September 23, 1789.

17. *Connecticut Journal*, May 26, June 30, September 1, 8, 1790; *American Mercury*, September 6, 1790.

18. *Connecticut Journal*, September 15, 1790.

19. Yale, Hist. Ms. Room, "Sherman Collection," RS to Simeon Baldwin (July 21, 23, 27, 1789, January 21, 1791, January 30, 1792); NYPL, Emmett Collection, James Wadsworth to Pierpont Edwards (July 26, 1789); CSL, "Miscellaneous Unbound Manuscripts," RS to Richard Law (October 30, 1789).

20. *Connecticut Journal*, September 22, 1790.

21. Yale, Hist. Ms. Room, "Sherman Collection," RS to Simeon Baldwin (January 21, 1790); *Connecticut Journal*, September 29, 1790; CSL, "Governor Joseph Trumbull Collection," I:53ad, Pierpont Edwards to Jeremiah Wadsworth (July 18, 1790).

22. *Connecticut Journal*, September 29, October 13, 1790.

23. *Connecticut Journal*, September 22, 29, 1790.

24. *Connecticut Journal*, November 10, 1790.

25. "House Journal 1788–1790," n.p. October 15, 1790.

26. Jacobus, *Hale, House*, pp. 530–31. See also *New York Genealogical and Biographical Record*, vols. 72–73.

27. *Connecticut Courant* and *Connecticut Journal*, December, 1790, *passim* both print a series of letters by and about Edwards; *SR*, VII:221, 247.

28. *Connecticut Journal*, December 1, 29, 1790; Stiles, *Lit. Diary*, III:451n; *Connecticut Courant*, December 13, 1790; *Connecticut Journal*, January 12, 1791.

29. HSP, "Sherman Papers," RS to Governor Huntington (November 2, 1790); Baldwin, *Baldwin*, p. 279; CHS, "Williams Papers," Vol. II. RS to Williams (February 1, 1791).

30. MHS, "Miscellaneous Bound," RS to Governor Huntington (November 21, 1790), quoted in full in Boutell, *Sherman*, pp. 263–65; AAS, *Brotherhead's Book of Signers*, RS to Governor Huntington (December 10,

1790); Yale, Hist. Ms. Room, "Sherman Collection," RS to Simeon Baldwin (January 2, 1790).

31. Yale, Hist. Ms. Room, "Sherman Collection," RS to Simeon Baldwin (July 21, September 21, 1789); Boutell, *Sherman*, pp. 225-26.

32. Yale, Hist. Ms. Room, "Sherman Collection," Samuel A. Otis to RS (April 10, 1793).

33. Hoar, *Autobiography*, I:9; Boutell, *Sherman*, pp. 291-92.

34. *New Haven Morning Courier*, July 29, 1843, "Memoir of Roger Sherman"; Sherman, *Genealogy*, p. 179.

CHAPTER XVI:
A Venerable Uncorrupted Patriot

1. Mason, *Autobiography*, pp. 15-16.

2. Yale, Hist. Ms. Room, "Sherman Collection," RS to Simeon Baldwin (December 29, 1791); Yale, Beinecke, "Sherman Papers," RS, Jr. to Comptroller of the Treasury (July 26, 1798); CSL, "Jonathan Trumbull Papers," VI:7a (January 6, 1777).

3. LC, "Sherman Papers," John Sherman to RS (December 8, 1788).

4. LC, "Sherman Papers," John Sherman to RS (July 23, 1790). See above, p. 174.

5. Yale, Hist. Ms. Room, "Sherman Collection," RS to Simeon Baldwin (December 22, 1790).

6. Yale, Hist. Ms. Room, "Sherman Collection," RS to Simeon Baldwin (December 22, 1792, January 7, 1793).

7. Yale, Hist. Ms. Room, "Sherman Collection," John's children to RS (January 21, 1793); Yale, Hist. Ms. Room, Simeon Baldwin to Isaac Sherman (October 24, 1794).

8. Boardman, *Sherman*, p. 71; LC, "Sherman Papers," Petition of William's creditors.

9. *JCC*, V:523; Yale, Hist. Ms. Room, "Sherman Collection," Samuel Safford to RS (June 11, 1777); Washington, *Writings*, XVII:311; *JCC*, XVI:843; Washington, *Writings*, XX:339.

10. CHS, William Sherman to Benedict Arnold (September 3, 1780); CSL, "Revolutionary War," Ser. 1. XV:234, 269a.

11. Sherman, *Genealogy*, RS' will on p. 194; CHS, William Sherman to Benedict Arnold (September 3, 1780); Yale, Hist. Ms. Room, "Sherman Collection," Draft of petition and resolve appointing David Austin and James Hillhouse executors of William's estate.

12. Boardman, *Sherman*, p. 182n, 183n; AAS, "Sherman Papers," William Sherman to RS (June 10, 1782).

13. Yale, Hist. Ms. Room, "Gibbs Family Collection," RS to Henry Gibbs (August 4, 1789); Yale, Hist. Ms. Room, "Sherman Collection," RS to RS, Jr. (January 23, 1792), RS to Simeon Baldwin (February 9, 1792), RS to wife (June 29, 1789).

14. Boardman, *Sherman*, p. 333n; Sherman, *Genealogy*, p. 20; Washington, *Writings*, VI:190, 190n.

15. *JCC*, XXIX:542, 574n, XXXI:660, 687, XXXII, 123n, XXXIV:61, 335; Sherman, *Genealogy*, p. 203.

16. Yale, Hist. Ms. Room, "Sherman Collection," RS to Simeon Baldwin (May 1, 1790); Boardman, *Sherman*, p. 279n.

17. MHS, "Baldwin Collection," Simeon Baldwin to Isaac Sherman (June 11, 1797, February 1, 1795), Isaac Sherman to Simeon Baldwin (June 2, 1797); Sherman, *Genealogy*, pp. 203-205.

18. Yale, Hist. Ms. Room, "Sherman Collection," Account book; Yale, Hist. Ms. Room, "Baldwin Family Collection," Bethiah Baldwin to Simeon Baldwin (November 18, 1781). See also Baldwin, *Baldwin*, Ch. VI for this courtship and marriage; Boardman, *Sherman*, p. 324n.

19. Boardman, *Sherman*, p. 298.

20. Boardman, *Sherman*, p. 216, 310; Boutell, *Sherman*, p. 348; Baldwin, *Baldwin, passim.*

21. Stiles, *Extracts*, ps. 472, 592; NHCHS, Samuel Whittelsey to Ezra Stiles (December 27, 1768); Stiles, *Lit. Diary*, III:317-18, 384-85, 273-74.

22. Foster, *Genetic History*, Ch. VIII.

23. Yale, Hist. Ms. Room, "Connecticut Miscellaneous Ms., United Church Papers," box 2. RS' report of December 23, 1782; Stiles, *Lit. Diary*, III:28, 14, 344.

24. Yale, Hist. Ms. Room, "Connecticut Miscellaneous Ms., United Church Papers," box 2. Ebenezer Bearsdley to RS (November 1, 1788).

25. Sherman, "A Short Sermon."

26. Peabody, *Correspondence, passim*; Foster, *Genetic History*, pp. 129-61. The material in the following paragraphs is from Peabody, *Correspondence.*

27. Yale, Hist. Ms. Room, "Sherman Collection," RS to David Austin (March 1, 1790), David Austin to RS (February 20, 1790).

28. Yale, Hist. Ms. Room, "Sherman Collection," RS to David Austin (March 1, 1790), David Austin to RS (February 20, 1790), RS to Simeon Baldwin (February 4, 1790).

29. Yale, Hist. Ms. Room, "Sherman Collection," RS to Simeon Baldwin (February 4, 1790, January 4, 1791, February 24, 1791); Stiles, *Lit. Diary*, III:343.

30. Edwards, *Works*, "God A Refuge And Help," a funeral sermon, pp. 182-83.

31. AAS, "Sherman Papers." Copy of a letter from Jonathan Edwards to ? (September 12, 1794); Stiles, *Lit. Diary*, III:562; Heimert, *Religion*, p. 558.

32. MHS, "Miscellaneous Bound," RS to John Witherspoon (July 10, 1788).

33. CSL, "Revolutionary War," Ser. 1. XXXIII:92ab, XXXVII:104; Yale, Hist. Ms. Room, "Sherman Collection," RS to Simeon Baldwin (December 22, 1791); *Connecticut Courant*, January 23, 1786.

34. Yale, Hist. Ms. Room, "Sherman Collection," RS to wife (March 6, 1790); Sherman, *Genealogy*, p. 198; Yale, Hist. Ms. Room, "Sherman Collection," RS to Simeon Baldwin (January 13, 1793).

35. Yale, Beinecke, "Sherman Papers." Roger Sherman, Jr., Day Book; Yale, Hist. Ms. Room, "Sherman Collection," Inventory at time of death.

36. Yale, Hist. Ms. Room, "Sherman Collection," RS to wife (March 6, 1790, January 29, 1789); Yale, Hist. Ms. Room, "Baldwin Family Collection," Roger Sherman, Jr. to Elizabeth Sherman (August 23, 1792); Yale, Hist. Ms. Room, "Sherman Collection," RS to Simeon Baldwin (July 15, 1790).

37. Yale, Hist. Ms. Room, "Sherman Collection," John Adams to RS (May 14, 1789).

38. Boardman, *Sherman*, p. 217; Yale, Hist. Ms. Room, "Sherman Collection," RS to Simeon Baldwin (February 27, 1790, December 22, 1791); Yale, Hist. Ms. Room, "Sherman Collection," Jedediah Strong to RS (April 2, April 18, 1792).

39. Yale, Hist. Ms. Room, "Gibbs Family Collection," RS to Henry Gibbs (June 10, 1790); Yale, Hist. Ms. Room, "Sherman Collection," RS to wife (May 31, 1790); Yale, Beinecke, "Sherman Papers," RS to Roger Sherman, Jr. (January 23, 1792); Yale, Hist. Ms. Room, "Gibbs Family Collection," Roger Sherman, Jr. to Henry Gibbs (May 14, 1792).

40. Yale, Hist. Ms. Room, "Sherman Collection," RS to wife (July 7, 1790); LC, "Sherman Papers," Rebecca Sherman to RS (December 12, 1792); Yale, Hist. Ms. Room, "Sherman Collection," Samuel A. Otis to RS (April 10, 1793).

41. Sherman, *Genealogy*, p. 181; Boutell, *Sherman*, p. 282; Stiles, *Lit. Diary*, III:499.

42. Edwards, *Works*, p. 184.

43. Stiles, *Lit. Diary*, III:500.

A Note on the Sources

Sherman Papers

There is no corpus of Roger Sherman papers. Yale University has the largest collection: one box in Beinecke Library consisting of a few letters, a couple of account books, and some miscellaneous papers; and about two hundred items in a single box in the Historical Manuscripts Room at Stirling Library, the largest group consisting of letters taken from the Baldwin Family Collection covering only the last five years of Sherman's life. Forty-one papers and a notebook are located at the Library of Congress. A number of letters and papers are at the American Antiquarian Society in Worcester, where there is also a child's bib said to have been worn by Sherman (presumably as a very young man). Groups of up to a dozen or so letters can be found at the Massachusetts Historical Society, the New Haven Colony Historical Society (where the collection includes an account book), the Historical Society of Pennsylvania, and the Connecticut Historical Society. Dartmouth, Harvard, and Brown Universities also have about a half-dozen letters each. The Litchfield Historical Society has a few writs and orders of Sherman's as a justice of the peace, and the New-York Historical Society has three letters of little significance.

Copies of Sherman letters are found in the Joseph Trumbull papers in the Force Transcripts at the Library of Congress, and in the Bancroft Collection at the New York Public Library. There are no original Roger Sherman papers at the National Archives, but Marion Tinling has transcribed a number of unpublished speeches of Sherman's during the First Federal Congress. These transcriptions do not materially alter the sense of the published reports of the speeches.

Other Manuscript Sources

The unpublished papers of the Colony and State of Connecticut housed in the Archives at the State Library are an unending source of information. Sherman's 1784 draft revision of the state statutes is preserved there, as are drafts of many of his bills and committee reports. The unpublished minutes of the town meeting and the records of the town clerk of New Milford located at the Town Hall provided information on Sherman's early career. The minutes of the New Haven town meetings, kept in the office of the City Clerk, were less revealing, but useful. The records of the Fairfield and Litchfield County courts at the State Library were not used extensively, but some of Sherman's decisions are recorded, and there are frequent references to him as an attorney. The probate records of the Town of Woodbury yielded the will of Roger's brother William. The history of New Milford's ecclesiastical squabbles can be traced through the records of the First Congregational Society at the church.

The State Library is the single richest repository of materials on colonial and early national Connecticut. Not only are the legislative, executive, and judicial records kept there, but so are the tax records for many towns, most of the county court records, society records for numerous churches, and private papers of many public people. A full description of the General Assembly Papers, the elaborately indexed archivial series, can be found in Sylvie Turner's "The Connecticut Archives."* The collection of Jonathan Trumbull, Sr. papers being put together by Albert Van Dusen and Glenn Weaver, now in carefully arranged photostats at the office of the Trumbull Papers project at the Connecticut State Library, is of inestimable assistance even during the early stages of the editors' work.

The Connecticut Historical Society has good collections of Ellsworths, Johnsons, Wadsworths, Williamses, Wolcotts, and several other major families of late eighteenth-century Connecticut. Most of the Deane papers at the New York and Connecticut historical societies have been published, but a few have not. The Bancroft and Emmet collections at the New York Public Library yielded a number of useful items, though the most significant documents from those groups have been published. Yale University has a number of relevant collections such as the Yale Papers, the Gibbs, Baldwin, and Lane Family Collections, and the Knollenberg Collection.

Newspapers

Connecticut newspapers were used extensively. The earliest of these is the *Connecticut Gazette* (1755-1768), which was published in New Haven. *The New London Summary* (1758-1763) became *The New London Gazette* (1763-1773) and then *The Connecticut Gazette and Universal Intelligencer* (1773-1787), after which it became *The Connecticut Gazette* again. *The Connecticut Journal*, established in 1767 and published until well into the nineteenth century, emanated from New Haven, and is the most often cited newspaper in this work. Second to it in importance to this study is Hartford's *Connecticut Courant* (1764-1820+). For the significant period of the Confederation new papers were established. I have used the *New Haven*

---

*Full bibliographic information for all works mentioned in this essay will be found in the list of "Works Cited" which follows.

Gazette (1784–1786), which became the *New Haven Gazette and Connecticut Magazine* (1786–1789), and for the anti-federal position, the *Middlesex Gazette* (1785–1787), published at Middletown. The *American Mercury* (1784–1833) of Hartford was useful for the years of Sherman's congressional service. Full data for these papers, including the information that only a few men were responsible for the publication of all of them, can be found in Clarence Brigham's newspaper bibliography.

Typed Manuscripts

Three doctoral dissertations and a masters' thesis have been of great help in specific sections of this work. Philip Jordan's study of Connecticut politics, 1783–1789, pointed me to certain materials and strengthened my own interpretation of the period. Gaspare Saladino's encyclopedic study of Connecticut's economy during the second half of the eighteenth century makes clear much of the tension underlying the political divisions during Sherman's career. Richard Bushman's interpretive and at times rather impressionistic study (later published) articulates very convincingly the changing nature of colonial attitudes toward the objectives and structure of society.

Charles Loucks' Master's thesis of some 360 pages brings together published materials relevant to the coming of the Revolution to Connecticut. Though drawn from newspapers, published records, and secondary accounts, the study is a compendium of undisputed value. Loucks' careful analysis of tax policy is especially helpful. A final typescript document is the essay written by Edward D. Kingman on Sherman's career as a surveyor and land speculator. Kingman, a professor of civil engineering, brings to this study a technical expertise rarely found in the field of historical scholarship.

Published Records

Published public records are well known. The obligation this study owes to the *Public Records* of the Colony and State of Connecticut, variously edited by Trumbull, Hoadly, Labaree, Fennelley, Van Dusen, and myself, is obvious. Hoadly's *Acts and Laws of His Majesty's Colony of Connecticut* and the official *Acts and Laws of the State of Connecticut* published by Timothy Green were useful. W. C. Ford's *Journals of the Continental Congress* provided much of the material for Chapters VI–IX. Both Farrand's and Tansill's editions of the records and Madison's notes of the Federal Convention were consulted in writing Chapters X–XII. They were checked against more recently published Hamilton, Madison, Adams, and Lansing material. *The Annals of the Congress* for the years 1789–1793 were used for Chapters XIII–XV. The Newton, Massachusetts *Vital Records to 1850* were also consulted.

Published Works by Sherman

In addition to the almanacs, published once or twice a year from 1750 to 1761, Sherman also published a number of pamphlets, sermons, and letters. The letters appeared in various Connecticut and other newspapers throughout his public career and are cited where relevant. The almanacs are discussed in Victor Paltsits, "The Almanacs of Roger Sherman." The other published pamphlets are:

"A caveat Against Injustice by Philoeunomes." New York, Henry Deforeest, 1752.

"A Short Sermon on the duty of Self Examination preparatory to receiving the Lord's Supper. showing the necessity of a personal profession of true Christianity to entitle persons of Adult age to the privileges of Communion with the visible Church whether Baptized in Infancy or not." New Haven, Able Morse, 1789.

"A Vindication of the validity and Divine Right of Presbyterian Ordination as set forth in Dr. Chauncy's Sermon at the Dudleian Lectures; and Mr. Welles Discourse upon the same subject in Answer to the exceptions of Mr. Jeremiah Leaming contained in his late Defense of the Episcopal gov't of the church by Noah Welles A.M. (edited by and published for Roger Sherman) New Haven, Samuel Green, 1768.

Secondary Accounts

There are two previous biographies of Sherman. The first was written by Lewis Henry Boutell, a professional historian, but writing from the canons of the 1890's. His work is narrative-descriptive, without analysis except of Sherman's participation in the Convention of 1787 and the first two federal congresses, and even here it is superficial. Boutell had access to various collections of papers, principally those of Sherman's grandson, George Frisbie Hoar, the remains of which now reside at the American Antiquarian Society. These collections are now apparently scattered, but I have located nearly every significant paper Boutell used, though he wrote without citations.

A second biography was published in 1938 by Roger Sherman Boardman, who appears to have had access to little material that Boutell did not. Boardman's work is a charmingly written account, but lacks sophistication and indicates no awareness of historiographic dimensions. This book, too, provides only occasional citations to documents used.

A number of well-known special studies have been used extensively in providing background for the running narrative of Connecticut and national history during the second half of the eighteenth century. Oscar Zeichner's account of the Revolution in Connecticut is still a good starting point for a study of the period. E. C. Burnett's *The Continental Congress* is indispensable, but must be supplemented by Merrill Jensen's *The Articles of Confederation* and *The New Nation*. Edmund Morgan's biography of Ezra

Stiles and Lawrence Gipson's of Jared Ingersoll are full of interesting and in many cases significant detail. E. James Ferguson's work on the fiscal history of the war and the Confederation is a tremendous aid to anyone working in the field; he makes clear much that I formerly thought incomprehensible. The series of pamphlets published for the Tercentenary Commission of the State of Connecticut by Yale University Press in the mid-thirties is still very useful. My great debt to E. C. Burnett's *Letters of Members of the Continental Congress* is obvious, as a glance at the citations at the end of the text will show. Gordon Wood's *The Creation of the American Republic, 1776–1789* and Merrill Jensen's *The Founding of a Nation: A History of the American Revolution, 1763–1776* were published after the manuscript was completed. For the most part, contributions from these two valuable works are therefore unfortunately confined to footnotes. Many other accounts have been used to one degree or another; some perhaps should be singled out, as have these, and my debt is great to all those found in the following list of "Works Cited."

List of Works Cited

Abernethy, Thomas Perkins, *Western Lands and the American Revolution*. New York, D. Appleton-Century Company, 1937.

*Adams, John, *The Adams Papers* (L.H. Butterfield, ed.), Series 1, *The Diaries*. Cambridge, The Belknap Press of the Harvard University Press, 1961. 4 vols.

Adams, John, *The Works of John Adams* (Charles Francis Adams, ed.). Boston, Little, Brown and Company, 1856. 10 vols.

Adams, John and Abigail, *The Familiar Letters of John Adams and his wife Abigail Adams During the Revolution* (Charles Francis Adams, ed.). Boston, Houghton, Mifflin and Company, 1875. 2 vols.

Alexander, Edward P., *A Revolutionary Conservative: James Duane of New York*. New York, Columbia University Press, 1938.

Ames, Fisher, *The Works of Fisher Ames* (Seth Ames, ed.). Boston, Little, Brown and Company, 1854. 2 vols.

Andrews, Charles M., *Our Earliest Colonial Settlements*. Ithaca, Cornell University Press (Great Seal Books), 1959.

Anonymous, *A History of Congress: 1789-1793*. Philadelphia, Lee and Blanchard, 1843.

Atwater, Edward E., *History of the Colony of New Haven to its Absorption into Connecticut*. New Haven, The Author, 1881.

Bailey, Edith A., "Influences Toward Radicalism in Connecticut, 1754-1775," *Smith College Studies in History*, V (July, 1920), 4:179-252.

Bailyn, Bernard ed., *Pamphlets of the American Revolution, 1750-1776*, Volume I, 1750-1765. Cambridge, The Belknap Press of the Harvard University Press, 1965.

Baldwin, Simeon, "Memoir of Hon. Roger Sherman," *New Haven Morning Courier*, July 22, 25, 29, 31, 1843.

Baldwin, Simeon E., *The Life and Letters of Simeon Baldwin*. New Haven, The Tuttle, Morehouse & Taylor Company, 1919.

---

*Letters and papers have been listed under the author rather than the editor.

————, "The New Haven Convention of 1778," *Three Historical Papers*. New Haven, Tuttle, Morehouse & Taylor Company, 1882.

Barry, Richard Hayes, *Mr. Rutledge of South Carolina*. New York, Duell, Sloan and Pearce, 1942.

Bates, Albert C., "Connecticut Almanacs of the Last Century," *The Connecticut Quarterly*, IV (October-November-December, 1898), 4:408–16.

Beard, Charles A., *An Economic Interpretation of the Constitution of the United States*. New York, The Macmillan Company, 1935.

————, ————, *Economic Origins of Jeffersonian Democracy*, New York, Macmillan (Free Press Paperback), 1965.

Beardsley, E. Edwards, *Life and Times of William Samuel Johnson, LL.D.* Boston, Houghton, Mifflin and Company, 1886.

————, ————, *Life and Correspondence of Samuel Seabury, D. D.* Boston, Houghton, Mifflin and Company, 1881.

Becker, Carl L., *The Declaration of Independence: A Study in the History of Political Ideas*. New York, Random House (Vintage Books), 1958.

————, *The History of Political Parties in the Province of New York, 1760–1776*. Madison, University of Wisconsin Press, 1960.

Bennett, Katherine P., "American Mothers of Strong Men," *Journal of American History*, III (1909), 3:49–52.

Boardman, Roger S., *Roger Sherman: Signer and Statesman*. Philadelphia, University of Pennsylvania Press, 1938.

Bond, Henry, *Genealogies of the Families and Descendents of the Early Settlers of Watertown, Mass.* 2nd ed. Boston, New England Historical-Genealogical Society, 1860.

Boutell, Lewis Henry, *The Life of Roger Sherman*. Chicago, A. C. McClurg and Company, 1896.

————, "Roger Sherman and the Constitutional Convention." *Annual Report* of the A.H.A., 1893.

Boyd, Julian P., "The Susquehannah Company: Connecticut's Experiment in Expansion," *Tercentenary Pamphlets*. New Haven, Yale University Press, 1935.

————, ed., *The Susquehannah Company Papers*. Wilkes-Barre, Wyoming Historical and Geological Society, 1933. 8 vols.

Brant, Irving, *James Madison: Father of the Constitution*. New York, Bobbs-Merrill Company, 1950.

Brigham, Clarence S., *History and Bibliography of American Newspapers, 1690–1820*. Hamden, Conn., Archon Books, 1962. 2 vols.

Bromberger, Bonnie, "Noah Webster's Notes on His Early Political Essays in the *Connecticut Courant*" *Bulletin* of the New York Public Library, vol. 74 (May, 1970) 5:338–342.

Bronson, Henry, "An Historical Account of Connecticut Currency," *Papers* of NHCHS, I (1865), 1–192.

Brown, William Garrott, *The Life of Oliver Ellsworth*. New York, The Macmillan Company, 1905.

Bullock, C. J., "Finances of the United States, 1775-1789," *Bulletin* of the University of Wisconsin, I (June, 1895), 2:117-273.

Burnett, Edmund C., "Committee of States," *Annual Report* of the A.H.A., I (1913), 141-158.

———, *The Continental Congress.* New York, The Macmillan Company, 1941.

———, ed., *Letters of Members of the Continental Congress.* Washington, Carnegie Institute, 1921-1938.8 vols.

Bushman, Richard, *From Puritan to Yankee: Character and the Social Order in Connecticut, 1690-1765.* Cambridge, Harvard University Press, 1967.

Charles, Joseph, *The Origins of the American Party System.* New York, Harpers (Torchbook), 1961.

Collier, Christopher, "Continental Bonds in Connecticut on the Eve of Assumption," *William and Mary Quarterly*, Third Series, XXII (October, 1965), 4:647-56.

———, "Roger Sherman and the New Hampshire Grants," *Vermont History*, XXX (July, 1962), 3:211-19.

———, "When the Hessians Came to New Haven, 1767," *Journal* of the NHCHS, XVII (September, 1968), 3:79-81.

Commager, H. S. and Morris, R. B., eds., *The Spirit of 'Seventy-Six.* New York, Bobbs-Merrill Company, 1958. 2 vols.

Connecticut, *Acts and Laws of the State of Connecticut.* New London, Timothy Green, 1784.

———, *Public Records of the Colony of Connecticut.* J. H. Trumbull and C. J. Hoadly, eds., Hartford, Case, Lockwood and Brainard Company, 1850-1890. 15 vols.

———, *Public Records of the State of Connecticut .* C. J. Hoadly, L. Labaree, K. Fennelley, A. E. Van Dusen, C. Collier, eds., Hartford, Case, Lockwood and Brainard (later the Connecticut Printers), 1894-1967. 11 vols.

Deane, Silas, "Inside the American Revolution: A Silas Deane Diary Fragment" (C. Collier, ed.), *Bulletin* of the CHS, XXIX (July, 1964), 3:86-96.

———, "Silas Deane Reports on the Continental Congress: A Diary Fragment" (C. Collier, ed.). *Bulletin* of the CHS, XXIX (January, 1964), 1:1-8.

———, "The Papers of Silas Deane," *Collections* of the CHS. Hartford, CHS, 1930. 2 vols.

———, "The Deane Papers," *Collections* of the NYHS. New York, NYHS, 1887-1890.

Dexter, Franklin Bowditch, "A Selection from the Correspondence and Miscellaneous Papers of Jared Ingersoll," *Papers* of the NHCHS., vol. IX. New Haven, NHCHS, 1918.

———, *Biographical Sketches of the Graduates of Yale College.* New York, Henry Holt and Company, 1885-1912. 6 vols.

————, "New Haven in 1784," *Papers* of the NHCHS., vol. IV. New Haven, NHCHS, 1888.

Dorfman, Joseph, *The Economic Mind in American Civilization*. New York, The Viking Press, 1946–55. 4 vols.

Dwight, Timothy, *Travels in New England and New York*. New Haven, Timothy Dwight, 1821. 4 vols.

Edwards, Jonathan Jr., *The Works of Jonathan Edwards Jr*. (Tyron Edwards, ed.). Andover, Allen, Morrill and Wardwell, 1842. 2 vols.

Elliot, Jonathan, ed., *The Debates in the Several State Conventions on the Federal Constitution*. New York, Burt Franklin, 1966. 5 vols.

Endicott, Frederick, ed., *The Record of Births, Marriages and Deaths and Intentions of Marriage in the Town of Stoughton*. Canton, Mass., Bense, 1896.

Farrand, Max, ed., *The Records of the Federal Convention of 1787*. New Haven, Yale University Press, 1911. 4 vols.

Farrell, John T., "The Administration of Justice in Connecticut About the Middle of the Eighteenth Century." Unpublished Doctoral dissertation, Yale, 1937.

Ferguson, E. James, *The Power of the Purse*. Chapel Hill, University of North Carolina Press, 1961.

————, "The Nationalists of 1781-1783 and the Economic Interpretation of the Constitution," *Journal of American History*. LVI (September 1969) 2:241–61.

Fitch, Thomas, *An Explanation of Say-Brook Platform; The principles of the consociated churches in the Colony of Connecticut: collected from their Plan of Union. By one that heartily desires the Order, Peace and Purity of these Churches*. Hartford, Thomas Green, 1765.

————, *Reasons Why The British Colonies In America Should Not Be Charged with Internal Taxes*. New Haven, B. Mecom, 1764.

Ford, W. C., ed., *The Journals of the Continental Congress, 1774–1789*. Washington, U.S.G.P.O., 1904–1937. 34 vols.

Foster, Frank Hugh, *A Genetic History of the New England Theology*. New York, Russell & Russell, 1963.

Foster, Hannah Webster (A Lady of Massachusetts), *The Coquette; or the History of Eliza Whorton. A Novel Founded on Fact*. Boston, Samuel G. Drake, 1855 (first published in 1796).

Gerlach, Larry, "Connecticut Delegates and the Continental Congress: From Confederation to Constitution, 1774–1789." Unpublished Masters' thesis, University of Nebraska, 1965.

————, "Connecticut, the Continental Congress and the Independence of Vermont, 1777-1782," *Vermont History*, XXIV (July, 1966), 3:188–93.

————, "Firmness and Prudence: Connecticut, the Continental Congress and the National Domain, 1776-1786," *Bulletin* of CHS, XXXI (July, 1966), 3:65–75.

Gibbs, George, *Memoirs of the Administrations of Washington and John Adams*. New York, William Van Norden, 1846.

Giddings, Minot S., ed., *Two Centuries of New Milford, Conn.* New York, The Grafton Press, 1907.

Gipson, Lawrence H., "Connecticut Taxation, 1750-1775," *Tercentenary Pamphlets.* New Haven, Yale University Press, 1933.

_____, "Connecticut Taxation and Parliamentary Aid," *AHR*, XXXVI (July, 1931), 3:721-39.

_____, *Jared Ingersoll: A Study of American Loyalism in Relation to British Colonial Government.* New Haven, Yale University Press, 1920.

Goodrich, Rev. Chauncey, "Invasion of New Haven By The British Troops, July 5, 1779," *Papers* of the NHCHS, II (1877), 31-92.

Grant, Charles S., *Democracy in the Frontier Town of Kent.* New York, Columbia University Press, 1961.

Groce, George C., "Benjamin Gale," *New England Quarterly*, X (December, 1937), 4:697-716.

_____, "Eliphalet Dyer: Connecticut Revolutionist," *The Era of the American Revolution*, R. B. Morris, ed. New York, Columbia University Press, 1939.

_____, *William Samuel Johnson, A Maker of the Constitution.* New York, Columbia University Press, 1937.

Hamilton, Alexander, *The Papers of Alexander Hamilton* (H. C. Syrett and J. E. Cooke, eds.). New York, Columbia University Press, 1961- . 6 vols. to date.

Heimert, Alan, *Religion and the American Mind From the Great Awakening To The Revolution.* Cambridge, Harvard University Press, 1966.

Hinman, Royal R., *An Historical Collection of the Part Sustained in the Revolution.* Hartford, E. Gleason, 1842.

Hoar, George F., *Autobiography of 70 Years.* New York, Charles Scribner's Sons, 1905. 2 vols.

Hobart, Noah, *An Attempt to illustrate and confirm the ecclesiastical Constitution of the Consociated churches in the Colony of Connecticut occasioned by a late "Explanation of the Saybrook Platform."* New Haven, B. Mecom, 1765.

Hooker, Roland M., "The Colonial Trade of Connecticut," *Tercentenary Pamphlets.* New Haven, Yale University Press, 1936.

Huntington, Benjamin, *The Huntington Letters* (W. D. McCrackan, ed.). New York, *The Appleton Press.* 1897.

Huntoon, Daniel T. V., *The History of Canton, Mass..* Cambridge, John Wilson and Son, 1893.

Jacobus, D. L., and Waterman, E. F., *Hale, House and Related Families.* Hartford, CHS, 1952.

Jefferson, Thomas, *The Papers of Thomas Jefferson* (J. P. Boyd, ed.). Princeton, Princeton University Press, 1950- . 18 vols. to date.

Jensen, Merrill, *The Articles of Confederation.* Madison, University of Wisconsin Press, 1959.

_____, *The Founding of A Nation: A History of the American Revolution, 1763-1776.* New York, Oxford University Press, 1968.

————, *The New Nation.* New York, Alfred A. Knopf, 1950.

Johnson, George H., "Historical Address," in *Two Hundred Years In An Old New England Parish.* New Milford, First Congregational Church, 1916.

Jordan, Philip, ed., "Connecticut Anti-Federalism on the Eve of the Constitutional Convention," *Bulletin* of CHS, XXVIII (January, 1963), 1:14-21.

————, "Connecticut Politics During the Revolution and Confederation, 1776-1789," Unpublished Doctoral dissertation, Yale, 1962.

Kaplan, Sidney, "Veteran Officers and Politics in Massachusetts, 1783-1787," *William and Mary Quarterly.* IX (January, 1952) 1:29-57.

King, Rufus, *Life and Correspondence of Rufus King* (C. L. King, ed.). New York, G. P. Putnam's Sons, 1894-1900. 6 vols.

Kingman, Edward Dyer, "Early Technical Americana." Typed manuscript n.d., n.p. formerly in Roger Sherman Papers, Historical Manuscripts Room, Yale University.

————, "Roger Sherman, Colonial Surveyor," *Civil Engineering,* X (August, 1940), 8:514-15.

Labaree, Leonard Woods, *Conservatism in Early American History.* Ithaca, Cornell University Press (Great Seal Books), 1959.

Lansing, John Jr., *Proceedings of the Federal Convention* (J. R. Strayer, ed.). Princeton, Princeton University Press, 1939.

Lee, Richard Henry, *Letters of Richard Henry Lee* (J. C. Ballagh, ed.). New York, The Macmillan Company, 1912. 2 vols.

Levermore, Charles H., *The Republic of New Haven.* Baltimore, Johns Hopkins University Press, 1886.

————, *Town and City Government of New Haven: A History of Municipal Evolution.* Baltimore, Johns Hopkins University Press, 1886.

Logan, Gwendolyn Evans, "The Slave in Connecticut During the American Revolution," *Bulletin* of CHS, XXX (July, 1965), 3:73-80.

Loucks, Rupert Charles, "Connecticut In The American Revolution." Unpublished master's thesis, University of Wisconsin, 1959.

Lossing, Benson J., *The Pictorial Field-Book of the Revolution.* New York, Harper & Brothers, 1851.

Ludin, Robert A., "A History of the Second Session of the Second Continental Congress." Unpublished Doctoral dissertation, University of Southern California, 1942.

Maclay, William, *Journal of William Maclay* (E. S. Maclay, ed.). New York, D. Appleton and Company, 1890.

McAnear, Beverly, "The Selection of an Alma Mater by Pre-Revolutionary Students," *Pennsylvania Magazine of History and Biography,* LXXIII (October, 1944), 3:429-40.

McDonald, Forrest, *E Pluribus Unum: The Formation of the American Republic, 1776-1790.* Baltimore, Penguin Books, Inc., 1965.

————, *We the People: The Economic Origins of the Constitution.* Chicago, University of Chicago Press (Phoenix Editions), 1958.

McKinley, Albert E., *The Suffrage Franchise in the Thirteen Colonies.* Philadelphia, University of Pennsylvania Press, 1905.

Madison, James, *The Writings of James Madison* (Gillard Hunt, ed.). New York, G. P. Putnam's Sons, 1900–1910. 10 vols.

———, *The Papers of James Madison* (Hutchinson and Rachal, eds.). Chicago, The University of Chicago Press, 1962–   . 6 vols. to date.

Main, Jackson Turner, *The Antifederalists: Critics of the Constitution, 1781–1788.* Chicago, Quadrangle Books, 1964.

———, *The Social Structure of Revolutionary America.* Princeton, Princeton University Press, 1965.

———, *The Upper House in Revolutionary America, 1763–1788.* Madison, University of Wisconsin Press, 1967.

Marsh, Esbyon R., "A History of theFirst Session of the Second Continental Congress." Unpublished Doctoral dissertation, University of Southern California, 1939.

Mason, Jeremiah, *Memoir, Autobiography and Correspondence of Jeremiah Mason.* Cambridge, Riverside Press, 1917 (1873).

Meyer, Freeman, "A note on the Origins of the Hamiltonian System," *William and Mary Quarterly*, Third Series, XXI (October, 1964), 4:579–88.

Miller, John C., *The Federalist Era, 1789–1801.* New York, Harper and Brothers, 1960.

———, *Origins of the American Revolution.* Boston, Little, Brown and Company, 1943.

Miner, Louie M., *Our Rude Forefathers: American Political Verse, 1783–1788.* Cedar Rapids, Iowa, The Torch Press, 1937.

Morgan, Edmund S., *The Gentle Puritan: A Life of Ezra Stiles, 1725–1795.* New Haven, Yale University Press, 1962.

———, and Helen M., *The Stamp Act Crisis: Prologue to Revolution.* Chapel Hill, University of North Carolina Press, 1953.

Morrow, Rising Lake, "Connecticut Influences in Western Massachusetts and Vermont," *Tercentenary Pamphlets.* New Haven, Yale University Press, 1936.

New England Historical Genealogical Register, IX (1855), 191 has a review of Foster's *The Coquette,* identifying the characters.

New Haven, "Town Records," in manuscript at the City Clerk's office. Vol. IV (February 22–March 4, 1768); Vol. V (September 18, 1770–November 17, 1774).

New Milford First Congregational Church, "Records: Meetings, 1716–1779." Manuscript at the church.

Nutting, P. Bradly, "Thomas Fitch: Charter Governor." Unpublished master's thesis, University of North Carolina, 1968.

Olson, Albert Laverne, "Agricultural Economy and the Population in Eighteenth-Century Connecticut," *Tercentenary Pamphlets.* New Haven, Yale University Press, 1935.

Orcutt, Samuel, *A History of New Milford and Bridgewater, 1703-1882.* Hartford, Case, Lockwood and Brainard Company, 1882.

Osterweis, Rollin G., *Three Centuries of New Haven, 1638-1938.* New Haven, Yale University Press, 1953.

Paltsits, Victor Hugo, "The Almanacs of Roger Sherman," *Proceedings* of AAS, XVIII (1907), 213-58.

Peabody, Andrew P., ed., *Correspondence between Roger Sherman and Samuel Hopkins.* Worcester, Charles Hamilton Press, 1889.

Peck, Epaphroditus, "The Loyalists of Connecticut," *Tercentenary Pamphlets.* New Haven, Yale University Press, 1934.

Peckham, Howard H., *The War for Independence: A Military History.* Chicago, The University of Chicago Press, 1958.

Purcell, Richard J., *Connecticut in Transition.* Middletown, Connecticut, Wesleyan University Press, 1918.

Robinson, William A., *Jeffersonian Democracy in New England.* New Haven, Yale University Press, 1916.

Rogers, Ernest E., "Connecticut's Naval Office at New London," *Collections* of NLCHS, Vol. II. New London, the Society, 1933.

Roll, Charles W. Jr., "We, Some of the People: Apportionment in the Thirteen State Conventions Ratifying the Constitution," *Journal of American History*, LVI (June, 1969), 1:21-40.

Rosenberry, Lois K., "Migrations From Connecticut Prior to 1800," *Tercentenary Pamphlets.* New Haven, Yale University Press, 1934.

Rossiter, Clinton, *1787: The Grand Convention.* New York, The Macmillan Company, 1966.

————, *Seedtime of the Republic.* New York, Harcourt, Brace and Company, 1953.

Rush, Benjamin, *The Autobiography of Benjamin Rush; His "Travels Through Life" Together with His Commonplace Book for 1789-1813* (G. W. Corner, ed.). Princeton, Princeton University Press, 1948.

Rutland, Robert A., *The Birth of the Bill of Rights.* New York, Crowell-Collier (Collier Books), 1962.

Saladino, Gaspare John, "The Economic Revolution in Late Eighteenth-Century Connecticut." Unpublished Doctoral dissertation, University of Wisconsin, 1962.

Schachner, Nathan, *Alexander Hamilton.* New York, Appleton,* 1946.

Schlesinger, Arthur M., *Colonial Merchants and the American Revolution, 1763-1776.* New York, Columbia University Press, 1917.

Scott, E. H., ed., *The Federalist and Other Constitutional Papers.* Chicago, Albert, Scott and Company, 1894.

Scott, Kenneth, "Price Control in New England During the Revolution," *New England Quarterly*, XIX (December, 1946), 4:453-73.

Sedgwick, Charles F., *General History of the Town of Sharon* (3rd ed.). Amenia, N. Y., Charles Walsh, 1898.

Shepard, James, "The Tories of Connecticut," *Connecticut Quarterly*, IV (January, July, 1898) 146-51, 257-63.

Sherman, Roger, *A Caveat Against Injustice by Philoeunomos.* New York, Henry DeForeest, 1752.

———, *A Short Sermon on the duty of "Self Examination preparatory to receiving the Lord's Supper. showing the necessity of a personal profession of true Christianity to entitle persons of Adult age to the privileges of Communion with the visible Church whether Baptized in Infancy or not.* New Haven, Able Morse, 1789.

Sherman, Thomas T., *Sherman Genealogy.* New York; Tobias A. Wright, 1920.

Simpson, Alan, *Puritanism in Old and New England.* Chicago, University of Chicago Press, 1961.

Smith, Page, *John Adams.* New York, Doubleday and Company, 1962. 2 vols.

Smith, William, *Historical Memoirs from 16 March 1763 to 9 July 1776* (W. H. Sabine, ed.). New York, Colburn and Tegg, 1956. 2 vols.

Stamps, Norman L., "Political Parties in Connecticut, 1789–1819." Unpublished Doctoral dissertation, Yale University, 1950.

Steiner, Bernard C., "Connecticut's Ratification of the Federal Constitution," *Proceedings* of AAS, XXV, new series (April, 1915), 70–127.

Steiner, Bruce, "New England Anglicanism: A Genteel Faith?," *The William and Mary Quarterly.* XXVII (January, 1970) 1:122–35.

Stiles, Ezra, *Extracts from the Itineraries and Other Miscellanies of Ezra Stiles, D.D., LL.D., 1755–1794 with a selection from his correspondence* (F. B. Dexter, ed.). New Haven, Yale University Press, 1916.

———, *The Literary Diary of Ezra Stiles* (F. B. Dexter, ed.). New York, Scribner's Sons, 1901. 3 vols.

Stuart, Isaac William, *Life of Jonathan Trumbull, Sen., Governor of Connecticut.* Boston, Crocker and Brewster, 1859.

Sutherland, Stella H., *Population Distribution in Colonial America.* New York, Columbia University Press, 1936.

Tansill, Charles C. ed., *Documents Illustrative of the Formation of the Union of the American States.* Washington, U.S.G.P.O., 1927.

Taylor, Robert J., ed., *The Susquehannah Company Papers.* Wilkes-Barre, Wyoming Historical and Geological Society, 1933–1969. 8 vols.

———, "Trial at Trenton," *William and Mary Quarterly.* XXVI (October 1969) 4:502–47.

Treat, Payson Jackson, *The National Land System.* New York, E. B. Treat and Company, 1910.

Trumbull, Benjamin, *A Complete History of Connecticut Civil and Ecclesiastical, 1630–1764.* New London, H. D. Utley, 1898. 2 vols.

Tucker, Louis Leonard, *Puritan Protagonist: President Thomas Clap of Yale College.* Chapel Hill, University of North Carolina Press, 1962.

Turner, Sylvie, "The Connecticut Archives," *Bulletin* of CHS, XXXIII (July, 1968), 3:81–89.

U.S. Congress, *Debates and Proceedings in the Congress of the United States,* 1789–1824 (Annals). Washington, U.S.G.P.O., 1834–1856. 42 vols.

Numbered by columns. There are two printings of this series which differ only in pagination. I have used the second printing. For a description of the two editions see Laurence F. Schmeickebier, *Government Publications and Their Use* (2nd ed.).Washington, Brookings Institution, 1939, pp. 119-20.

Van Dusen, Albert E., "The Trade of Revolutionary Connecticut." Unpublished Doctoral dissertation, University of Pennsylvania, 1948.

Vermont, "Petitions for Grants of Land, 1778-1811," *State Papers of Vermont*. Brattleboro, the Secretary of State, 1939. Vol. V of 10 vols.

Waln, Robert, Jr., "Roger Sherman," *Biography of the Signers to the Declaration of Independence* (J. Sanderson, ed.). Philadelphia, R. W. Pomeroy, 1823. 9 vols.

Ward, Christopher, *The War of the Revolution*. New York, The Macmillan Company, 1952. 2 vols.

Ward, Harry M., *The Department of War, 1781-1795*. Pittsburgh, University of Pittsburgh Press, 1962.

Warren, James, "The Warren-Adams Letters; Being Chiefly a Correspondence among John Adams, Samuel Adams, and James Warren," *Collections* of MHS, LXXII (1917) and LXXIII (1925).

Washington, George, *The Writings of George Washington from the Original Manuscript Sources, 1745-1799* (J. C. Fitzpatrick, ed.). Washington, U.S.G.P.O., 1931-1944. 39 vols.

Watertown Historical Society, *The Watertown Records*. Watertown, Mass., the Society, 1894. 7 vols.

Webster, Noah, *A Collection of Papers on Political, Literary and Moral Subjects*. New York, Webster and Clark, 1843.

Welles, Noah, *A Vindication of the Validity and Divine Right of Presbyterian Ordination as set forth in Dr. Chauncy's Sermon upon the same subject in Answer to the exceptions of Mr. Jeremiah Leaming contained in his late Defense of the Episcopal Government of the Church*. New Haven, Samuel Green, 1767.

Welling, James Clarke, *Addresses, Lectures and Other Papers*. Cambridge, Riverside Press, 1904.

Williams, William, "Rough Sketch of the Proceedings of the Lower House of the General Assembly in May, 1757." CHS, typescript of Sylvie Turner.

Wood, George C., *Congressional Control of Foreign Relations During the American Revolution, 1774-1789*. New York, H. Ray Haas and Company, 1919.

Wood, Gordon S., *The Creation of the American Republic, 1776-1787*. Chapel Hill, University of North Carolina Press, 1969.

Wright, Esmond, *The Fabric of Freedom*. New York, Hill and Wang, 1961.

Zeichner, Oscar, *Connecticut's Years of Controversy, 1750-1776*. Chapel Hill, University of North Carolina Press, 1949.

————, "Rehabilitation of the Loyalists in Connecticut," *New England Quarterly*, XI (June, 1938), 2:308-330.

Other Sources Consulted

A full bibliography of general works and articles on eighteenth-century American history and historiography would be superfluous. I have listed below only those works of a special nature bearing directly on Roger Sherman and the political milieu in which he moved.

Roger Sherman materials

Baldwin, Simeon E., "The Authorship of the Quatre Lettres D'Un Bourgeois De New-Haven Sur L' Unité De La Legislation," *Papers* of NHCHS, VI (1900), 262-81.

Boyd, Julian P., "Roger Sherman: Portrait of a Cordwainer Statesman," *New England Quarterly*, V (April, 1932), 2:221-36.

Dickerson, Oliver, "Review" of R. S. Boardman's *Roger Sherman. Mississippi Valley Historical Review*, XXV (December, 1938), 3:402-03.

Farrand, Max, "Review" of R. S. Boardman's *Roger Sherman*, *AHR*, XLIV (July, 1939), 4:926-27.

Phyfe, R. Eaton, "Roger Sherman, A Maker of the Constitution," *The Connecticut Magazine*, VII (1902), 3:234-48.

Wing, Donald G., "A Roger Sherman Notebook," *Papers in Honor of Andrew Keogh*. New Haven, printed privately, 1938.

Local Histories

Ames, Ellis, *The Redman Farm* [Early Canton, Mass. School]. Boston, William Bense, 1870.

Atwater, Edward E., ed., *The History of the City of New Haven* by an Association of Writers. New York, W. W. Munsell and Co., 1887.

Bacon, Leonard, *Thirteen Historical Discourses on the completion of the First Church in New Haven*. New Haven, Durrie and Peck, 1839.

Baldwin, Ernest H., *Stories of Old New Haven*. New York, The Abbey Press, 1902.

Barber, John W., *History and Antiquities of New Haven*. New Haven, J. W. Barber, 1831.

Brown, Lloyd A., *Loyalist Operations at New Haven*. Meriden, Conn., Timothy Press, 1938.

Daggett, David, "An Oration Pronounced in the Brick meeting-house in the City of New Haven, on July 4, 1787." New Haven, T. and S. Green, 1787.

Davis, Andrew Mcf., "A Connecticut Land Bank of the Eighteenth Century," *Quarterly Journal of Economics*, XIII (October 1898), 3:70-84.

Dexter, Franklin P., "Notes On Some of The New Haven Loyalists Including Those Graduated at Yale," *Papers* of NHCHS, IX (1918), 29-45.

Dwight, Timothy, *A Statistical Account of the City of New-Haven*. New Haven, Walter and Steele, 1811.

Farrell, John T., "The Superior Court Diary of William Samuel Johnson, 1772-1773." [Typescript at Columbia University Library.] Washington, AHA, 1942.

Larned, Ellen D., *The History of Windham County, Connecticut*. Worcester, C. Hamilton (for the author), 1874-80. 2 vols.

Newton, Mass., *Vital Records to 1850*. Boston, New-England Historical and Genealogical Society, 1905.

Osterweis, Rollin G., *Three Centuries of New Haven, 1638-1938*. New Haven, Yale University Press, 1953.

Trowbridge, Thomas R., *History of the Ancient Maritime Interests of New Haven*. New Haven, Tuttle, Morehouse & Taylor, 1882.

Watertown (Mass.) Historical Society, *The Watertown Records*. Watertown, The Society, 1894. 7 vols.

Connecticut Histories

Anonymous, "Colony Rights and States Rights in Connecticut," *Knickerbocker Magazine*, LXIII (1864), 265-82.

Baldwin, Simeon E., *The Colonial Period of Connecticut* (Vol. 1 in Norris G. Osborn, ed., *The History of Connecticut in Monographs*). New York, States History Co., 1925.

————, "The Early History of the Ballot in Connecticut," *Papers* of AHA, IV (October, 1890) 4:81-96.

Beers, W. P., *An Address to the Legislature and People of Connecticut . . . on dividing the state into districts. . . .* [By a Citizen of Connecticut, sometimes attributed to Roger Sherman, but not expressive of his views]. New Haven, T. & S. Green, 1791.

Clark, George Larkin, *Silas Deane: A Connecticut Leader in the American Revolution*. New York, G. P. Putnam's (The Knickerbocker Press), 1913.

Connecticut, State of, *Acts and Laws of the State of Connecticut*. New London, Timothy Green, 1784.

Fowler, W. C., "Local Laws of Connecticut," *New-England Historical and Genealogical Record*, XXIV (January-April, 1870), 1:33-42, 2:137-46.

Gale, Benjamin, *Remarks on a Pamphlet Entitled 'A Dissertation on the Political Union. . . .* [Pelatiah Webster] ' *By A Connecticut Farmer* [Attributed by some to Roger Sherman, but not expressive of his views] . No place, no pub., 1784. See Edmund Morgan below.

————, *The Present State of Connecticut Considered*. New London, no pub., 1755.

Gilbert, G. A., "Connecticut Loyalists," *AHR*, IV (January, 1899) 2:273-91.

Gilmore, Robert C., "Connecticut and the Foundation of Vermont." Unpublished Doctoral dissertation, Yale, 1953.

Hobart, Noah, *On the Ecclesiastical Constitution of the Consociation of Churches of Connecticut*. New Haven, no pub., 1765.

Hollister, G. H., *The History of Connecticut, from the First Settlement of the Colony to the Adoption of the Present Constitution*. New Haven, Durrie and Peck, 1855. 2 vols.

Jones, Frederick Robertson, "History of Taxation in Connecticut: 1636-1776," Johns Hopkins University *Studies*, XIV (August, 1896), 8:339-409.

Katz, Judith Maxen. "Connecticut Newspapers and the Constitution, 1786-1788," *Bulletin* of CHS, XXX (April, 1965), 2:33-44.

Kinloch, Herbert G., "Anglican Clergy in Connecticut, 1701-1785." Unpublished doctoral dissertion, Yale, 1959.

Lines, Edwin S., "Jared Ingersoll, Stamp Master, And The Stamp Act," *Papers* of NHCHS, IX (1918), 174-200.

Loomis, Dwight and Calhoun, J. Gilbert, *The Judicial and Civil History of Connecticut*. Boston, The Boston History Company, 1895.

Mead, Nelson P., *Connecticut as a Corporate Colony*. Lancaster, Pa., The New Era Printing Company, 1906.

————, "Land System of Connecticut Towns," *Political Science Quarterly*, XXI (March, 1906), 1:59-76.

————, "Report on the Public Archives of Connecticut," *Report* of the AHA, II(1906) 53-127.

Middlebrook, Louis F., *History of Maritime Connecticut during the American Revolution*. Salem, The Essex Institute, 1924. 2 vols.

Morgan, Edmund, ed., "The Political Establishments of the United States, 1784," *William and Mary Quarterly*, 3rd Ser., XXIII (April, 1966), 2:286-308.

O'Neil, Maud, "Samuel Peters: Connecticut Loyalist." Unpublished Doctoral dissertation, University of California at Los Angeles, 1947.

Osborn, Norris G., ed., *History of Connecticut in Monographs*. New York, The States History Company, 1924. 5 vols.

Pickering, Octavius, *The Life of Timothy Pickering*. Boston, Little, Brown and Co., 1868. 2 vols.

Trumbull, James H., "Sons of Liberty in Connecticut in 1775," *The New Englander*, XXXV (April, 1876), 299-313.

Walradt, Henry F., "The Financial History of Connecticut, 1786-1861" *Transactions* of the Connecticut Society of Arts and Sciences, XVII (March, 1912).

Weaver, Glenn, *Jonathan Trumbull: Merchant*. Hartford, CHS, 1956.

Weld, Ralph Foster, *Slavery in Connecticut*. New Haven, Yale University Press (Tercentenary Pamphlet), 1935.

Collected Papers, Letters, Journals

Adams, Samuel, *Writings of Samuel Adams* (Harry A. Cushing, ed.). New York, G. P. Putnam's Sons, 1907. 4 vols.

Deane, Silas, *Paris Papers: Mr. Silas Deane's late intercepted Letters*. New York, James Rivington, 1781.

Farrand, Max, *The Papers of the Johnson Family of Connecticut*. Worcester, AAS, 1913.

Fitch, Thomas, "The Fitch Papers," *Collections* of the CHS (Albert C. Bates, ed.), XVII–XVIII (1918, 1920).

Ford, Worthington C., "Some Letters of Aaron Burr," *Proceedings* of the AAS (April, 1919), 1:43–128. Includes some Sherman letters.

Hancock, John, *et al.*, "Six Letters of Signers," *Pennsylvania Magazine of History and Biography*, XL (October, 1916), 4:484–92. Includes one by Sherman.

Payne, Elisha, "Letter to Roger Sherman on the dissolution of New Hampshire Townships, October 28, 1778," *Proceedings* of the Vermont Historical Society, I (1930), 4:183–85.

Pitkin, William, "The Pitkin Papers," *Collections* of CHS (Albert C. Bates, ed.), XIX (1921).

Sparks, Jared, *The Diplomatic Correspondence of the American Revolution*. Boston, N. Hale and Gray & Bowen, 1829–30. 12 vols.

Webb, Samuel B., *Correspondence and Journals of Samuel B. Webb* (W. C. Ford, ed.). Lancanster, Pa., Wickersham Press, 1893–94, 3 vols.

Wharton, Francis, ed., *Revolutionary Diplomatic Correspondence*. Washington, U.S.G.P.O. 1889. 6 vols.

Other Special Studies

Boyd, Julian P., "Attempts to Form New States in New York and Pennsylvania, 1786–96." Proceedings, vol. XXIX, of the New York State Historical Association, bound into *Quarterly Journal*, XII (July, 1931), 3:257–70.

Coleman, Edward M., "A History of the 3rd Session of the 2nd Continental Congress, December 20, 1776–February 27, 1777." Unpublished Doctoral dissertation, University of Southern California, 1940.

Corwin, Edwin S., "The Progress of Constitutional Theory between the Declaration and the Convention," *AHR*, XXX (April, 1924), 3:511–36.

Dickerson, Oliver M., "Writs of Assistance as a Cause of the Revolution" in R. B. Morris ed., *The Era of the American Revolution*. New York, Columbia University Press, 1939.

Dunbar, Louise B., "Study of Monarchial Tendencies in the United States, 1776–1801" in University of Illinois *Studies in the Social Sciences*, X (n. d.), 1:1–150.

Farrand, Max, "Compromises of the Constitution," *Annual Report* of the AHA, I (1903), 73-84.

Greenough, Chester N., "New England Almanacs, 1766-75," *Proceedings* of the AAS, XLV (October, 1936), 2:288-315.

Harlow, R. V., "Aspects of Revolutionary Finance," *AHR*, XXXV (October, 1929), 1:46-68.

Hoar, George F., "The Connecticut Compromise," *Proceedings* of the AAS. XV n.s. (October, 1902), 2:233-58.

Jensen, Merrill,"The Cession of the Old Northwest," *MVHR*, XXIII (1936), 1:27-48.

Sachs, William S., "The Business Outlook in the Northern Colonies; 1750-75." Unpublished Doctoral dissertation, Columbia University, 1957.

Sanders, Jennings B., *Evolution of Executive Departments of the Continental Congress, 1774-89.* Chapel Hill, University of North Carolina Press, 1935.

Index